Oxford Studies in European Law

General Editors: Paul Craig and Gráinne de Búrca

REGULATING CARTELS IN EUROPE

Regulating Cartels in Europe

A Study of Legal Control of Corporate Delinquency

CHRISTOPHER HARDING
and
JULIAN JOSHUA

OXFORD
UNIVERSITY PRESS

OXFORD

UNIVERSITY PRESS

Great Clarendon Street, Oxford OX2 6DP

Oxford University Press is a department of the University of Oxford.
It furthers the University's objective of excellence in research, scholarship,
and education by publishing worldwide in

Oxford New York

Auckland Bangkok Buenos Aires Cape Town Chennai
Dar es Salaam Delhi Hong Kong Istanbul Karachi Kolkata
Kuala Lumpur Madrid Melbourne Mexico City Mumbai Nairobi
São Paulo Shanghai Taipei Tokyo Toronto

Oxford is a registered trade mark of Oxford University Press
in the UK and in certain other countries

Published in the United States
by Oxford University Press Inc., New York

British Library Cataloguing in Publication Data
Data available

Library of Congress Cataloging in Publication Data
Data available

ISBN 0-19-924244-5

1 3 5 7 9 10 8 6 4 2

Typeset by Newgen Imaging Systems (P) Ltd., Chennai, India
Printed in Great Britain
on acid-free paper by
T.J. International Ltd, Padstow, Cornwall

GENERAL EDITORS' PREFACE

The control of cartels is central to any effective competition policy and this is especially true of competition policy within the European Union. This volume is, therefore, a most welcome addition to the Studies in European Law. It combines the insights of Julian Joshua who has played such a central role in the enforcement of cartel policy within the European Union, with the more general academic perspective of Christopher Harding. The result is a book that will be of interest to all those who are concerned with the enforcement and regulation of cartel policy. This is especially so given the broad geographic and conceptual focus of the book. It deals with the nature of cartels from both a macro- and a micro-economic perspective, and considers modes of legal control and regulation in North America and Europe. The temporal discussion of the legal regulation of cartels in Europe enables the reader to perceive the changing nature of policy in this area, from the late nineteenth century until the present day. The temporal perspective is complemented by discussion of central issues such as the proof of cartel delinquency, which is so important in cases of tacit collusion and concerted practice, and the way in which the Court of First Instance has assessed the cogency of the evidence in judicial review actions. This is followed by analysis of the various sanctions than can be used, and the way in which offers of leniency can assist in breaking the code of silence that often surrounds cartel arrangements. The book concludes with stimulating thoughts and observations about how cartel law is likely to develop in the twenty-first century. It is written in a lively and engaging style and many of the more particular themes discussed, such as the relationship between the CFI and Commission in judicial review cases, will be of more general interest to EU lawyers and public lawyers alike.

Paul Craig
Gráinne de Búrca

PREFACE

Working on this book has been an encouraging experience in that our sense of the significance of the subject has grown rather than diminished since the inception of the project. As we moved into the twenty-first century, the regulation of business cartels certainly gained more attention as a legal topic, as the dynamic of international enforcement efforts became more evident and perceptions altered noticeably, producing the two trends singled out for discussion towards the end of the book: global enforcement and criminalization. Indeed, the recent British criminalization of involvement in cartels has coincided neatly with the completion of the book, conveniently signalling the topicality and significance of the subject but also some of its complexity and continuing uncertainty. But also we should stress that this is far from being the end or closing stages of the story—we are at present in the midst of some striking legal developments which have yet to unravel fully. Thus what we have to present here is far from being a final word, but rather signifies the coming of age of our subject matter.

Our intention was also to combine in a complementary fashion some different experience and expertise, that of enforcement practice on the one hand and that of academic reflection on the other—or, to put the combination in somewhat different terms, the view from within and the view from outside. The inside view (that of JJ) is based on a wide experience of enforcement activity: working for over 20 years on most of the largest cartel investigations carried out by DG IV of the Commission, and eventually as Deputy Head of the Anti-Cartel Unit (established in 1998), liaising also in that role with the US Department of Justice, before moving more recently into private practice, advising on the risks and legal consequences of cartel involvement. During that time, that insider experience of legal enforcement had been converging with a certain external perception of the subject. CH had published in the early 1990s *European Community Investigations and Sanctions* (sub-titled 'the supranational control of business delinquency') which identified and analysed the emergence of the phenomenon of the serious violation of EC competition law, largely by reference to the cases which JJ had handled. The book attracted the attention of JJ, contact was established, and not so long afterwards, the idea of a joint work on the subject of cartels in Europe was enthusiastically agreed. The resulting collaboration has sought then to link theory with practice, and engagement with reflection. In this way we feel that we have been able confidently to pursue, for example, both discussion of epistemology and the strategic niceties of leniency programmes. Thus it is hoped that the reader will thereby reap the benefit of this joint venture and gain both insight and information in relation to a subject which hitherto has rarely (in legal literature) been given a distinctive and separate place on the bookshelf. It is our plan also that what follows here should engage the interest not just of those in the legal field, but also those working in other disciplines, such as economics, sociology, international relations, and history, to name just the more obvious related fields of study.

Much of the argument and ideas set out in the book has had the benefit of being tested in discussion with a number of individuals and at a number of academic venues and we would like to thank collectively all those who have at different times over the last three years commented on our ideas and explanations, not infrequently pointing us in further useful directions. We should also like to thank our publishers, Oxford University Press, for their ready response to our idea for the project and their enthusiastic support during our work on the book.

We have taken our account of the subject up to January 2003. It is not unlikely that on some specific points the discussion may soon be overtaken by events, but we have endeavoured also to anticipate some of the more important developments in the near future.

CH, JJ
Aberystwyth/Brussels, February 2003

ACKNOWLEDGEMENTS

The authors would like to express their thanks to the Editors of the *Maastricht Journal of European and Comparative Law* for their permission to draw, in Chapter II, upon some of the argument used in the article by Christopher Harding, 'Business Cartels as a Criminal Activity: Reconciling North American and European Models of Regulation', which was published in (2002) 9(4) *Maastricht Journal*.

CONTENTS

TABLES OF CASES

Commission Decisions (alphabetical)

European Court of Justice (chronological)

Court of First Instance (chronological)

European Commission and Court of
Human Rights (chronological)

Germany (chronological)

UK (chronological)

US (chronological)

TABLES OF TREATIES, LEGISLATION, AND NOTICES

Treaties

EC Regulations

EC Competition Notices

Legislation

Germany

Norway

UK

US

GLOSSARY OF KEY TERMS

Antitrust (law): An American term, broadly connoting what Europeans now generally refer to as 'competition law'. The two terms are sometimes used interchangeably but the term 'antitrust' does have a connotation of strongly prohibitive regulation, literally 'against trusts' (the anti-competitive corporate combinations which emerged in the second half of the nineteenth century in the United States). American antitrust law comprises a significant element of criminal law and 'penal' (i.e. triple damages) tort law, both of which have been hitherto largely absent from European systems of regulating or protecting competition. The European terminology of 'competition law and policy' historically has implied a more consensual and administrative system of legal control, as does the more specifically British vocabulary of 'restrictive trade practices' and 'unfair trading'.

Cartel: From the French *cartel*, Italian *cartello*, and German *Kartell*: originally a challenge, the terms of a challenge, and then a suspensive arrangement between belligerents for the exchange of prisoners. Hence its meaning as a suspension of hostilities, a truce between combatants, analogous to the American term 'trust'. It is helpful to understand the modern pejorative meaning of 'cartel' as an arrangement of truce, whereby natural rivals come together in uneasy alliance. The term remains subtle and complex, combining elements of cessation of rivalry, unnatural and therefore uncertain collaboration, and, also now, damage to another (broader public) interest.

Chicago School: From the dominating philosophy of relevant departments in the University of Chicago from the 1950s onwards: a label often used to denote economic and legal theory which favours a non-interventionist approach in economic policy, giving free rein to the invisible forces of market competition, and an economic cost-efficiency analysis in the legal arena, down-playing elements of moral and social judgement. In the context of antitrust and competition policy, a 'Chicago School approach' would emphasize economic outcomes and market structures rather than a moral or social evaluation of the motives and attitudes of market actors.

Dawn raid: An unannounced or 'surprise' inspection of a company's premises by competition regulators intended to exploit the unpreparedness of the company so as to collect incriminating evidence.

Game theory: A method of predicting the strategies likely to be adopted by independent actors making apparently rational and interest-maximizing choices: an application of mathematical reasoning to situations of conflict and collaboration. The application of game theory to cartel activity occurs, for instance, in relation to the behaviour of suppliers in an oligopolistic market, or the situation of companies deciding whether to blow the whistle and gain the benefits of **leniency**. The latter situation presents a classic example of the 'Prisoner's Dilemma' game: whether to confess first and gain immunity, or to stay silent in the hope that fellow defendants will do the same but risk that another will confess.

Horizontal restriction: An anti-competitive arrangement between market actors at the same level of activity (e.g. as between producers; or between distributors at certain levels, such as wholesalers, retailers). Generally viewed in competition theory as more damaging to competition and the public interest than vertical restrictions (e.g. distribution or licensing arrangements) between market actors at different levels. Typical cartel arrangements (e.g. price fixing, market sharing, quotas, bid rigging) are horizontal restrictions.

Leniency: In the context of cartel regulation, not so much forbearance in the imposition of sanctions as a shorthand term for an enforcement device to gain crucial evidence. 'Leniency', in the form of 'immunity' from sanctions (or an 'amnesty') is offered in return for being the first member of a cartel to provide hitherto undisclosed significant evidence of illegal activity. It presents members of a cartel with a tempting but difficult calculation of the relative risks of 'blowing the whistle' (providing evidence) or maintaining the code of silence, and in the terms of **game theory**, raises the 'prisoner's dilemma'. In an American context the term 'leniency' has a fairly precise meaning: full immunity from prosecution in return for being the first to provide evidence. In the EC context, the term is used more loosely to cover a range of situations, including what under American law would be termed 'plea bargaining'.

Oligopoly: A market structure compromising a relatively small number of large producers, whose individually powerful position may, according to some economic theory, naturally lead to an interdependence in market behaviour, manifesting itself in phenomena such as parallel pricing of commodities and other parallel market strategies relating to the supply of goods and services. In the context of cartel control, the problem is to distinguish such 'spontaneous' parallel behaviour from anti-competitive collusion.

Ordoliberalism: A fusion of economic and politic theory, associated with the Freiburg School in Germany in the middle years of the twentieth century, which emphasized the need for the operation of markets to be contained within a constitutional framework, so that a competitive economic system could be used to achieve a prosperous, free, and fair society.

Plus factors: American terminology for categories of evidence which have a strong probative value over and above a deduction of collusion from just market circumstances, such as parallel pricing. Most obviously such 'conduct plus' would include direct documentary evidence or oral testimony of communications relating to planned anti-competitive conduct. While each plus factor may not in itself prove collusion beyond reasonable doubt, taken together and in their proper context they may lead inevitably to that conclusion.

Regulators: Public officials charged with the task of implementing and enforcing competition policy, through legal processes such as the examination of registered agreements and the investigation of prohibited activities: as such, key players in the field of cartel and antitrust regulation, e.g. the US Department of Justice (DOJ), the EC Commission, the UK Office of Fair Trading (OFT), the German Bundeskartellamt (BKA). National agencies of this kind are now referred to in European parlance as National Competition Authorities (NCAs).

Introduction: Talking about Cartels: The Main Elements of Analysis and Discussion

1. Epistemology: the control of cartels as a subject

One of the most contentious and high profile aspects of EC competition law and policy in recent years has been the regulation of what are now usually described as cartel violations, typically involving large and powerful corporate producers and traders operating across Europe, if not also in a wider international context. Such infringements are usually based on deliberate, highly organized and covert collaborative efforts to achieve goals such as price fixing, market sharing and production quotas, designed to maximize profits or at least preserve profit margins in declining markets. There is now little disagreement in terms of competition theory and policy at both international and national levels about the damaging effect of such arrangements on public and consumer interests, and such cartels have become strongly and consistently condemned in the legal process of regulating and protecting competition. This therefore can be seen as the 'hard end' of the enforcement of competition policy, calling up more confrontational and repressive methods of regulation yet also presenting considerable challenges to effective enforcement on account of the economic power, sophistication and determination of the typical participants in such cartels.

Hitherto, the subject of European cartel control has received little in the way of distinct treatment in the legal literature on competition matters. Although the topic naturally figures prominently in the major works on competition law, this is usually only as part of a much wider picture of the whole field of competition regulation, much of which comprises a lower profile and a more bureaucratic and consensual structure of enforcement. Legal commentators (apart from a few forays in periodical literature) have tended not to probe too far beneath the surface of the legal process of control to enquire into the origins and underlying structure of 'antitrust delinquency'.[1]

Moreover, the emphasis in European competition law on the need for market analysis has distracted attention from this core of serious violations, which is less problematical in terms of economic analysis, but raises significant questions of a legal and moral character, which indeed go to the heart of the jurisprudence of attempts at legal regulation of economic activity.

This study will therefore present a distinctive account and analysis of a central issue in the now very important field of competition or antitrust law. The focus of the discussion will be a critical evaluation of the way in which European-level regulation has evolved to deal with the problem of anti-competitive cartels, although it is also necessary to include some consideration of policy and law at the national level, and especially that of the United States. The study will also be distinctive in encouraging a shift from the prevailing perspective in legal literature on competition law. Much of the legal writing on competition law in a European context has tended to assume a readership mainly comprising those who are or may be subject to the rules—almost, it might be said, having a mission to advise those whom the rules seek to control. A major object of this work is to provide a different perspective on cartel enforcement, combining an analysis of enforcement practice with a legal theory of corporate behaviour and corporate strategy.

2. Political economy: the phenomenon and concept of the anti-competitive cartel

It is necessary both to define more exactly and describe more fully the essential subject matter of this discussion. Anti-competitive cartels may be defined and analysed in economic, legal and sociological terms. This part of the study will introduce the subject in presenting the main types of

---

[1] The American term 'antitrust' carries a pejorative meaning, and so applies very differently from the neutral European vocabulary of 'competition regulation'. See the Glossary of Key Terms.

cartel, their scope and objectives, how they typically operate, providing some examples of notable cartel-type arrangements. There will therefore be some exposition of the commercial and industrial context of some notorious American, European and global cartels. There will also be some broader, introductory discussion of the main approaches to economic analysis and legal definition of such activities, with the broad intention of supplying at this stage a profile of the main features and problems presented by such corporate collaboration, especially in a European context.

3. Legal control: competition law as a model of regulation

A key aspect of the argument being presented here concerns the methodology of regulation and enforcement in relation to anti-competitive activities. In broad terms, European competition law encompasses two main approaches to regulation: first, a consensual and bureaucratic model dealing with quantitatively the larger part of anti-competitive trading activity; and secondly a more aggressive, confrontational and repressive model of enforcement in relation to deliberate and highly anti-competitive violations. However, the basic principles relating to competition as enunciated in the main provisions of the EC Treaty, Articles 81 and 82, do not explicitly provide for this significant bifurcation of enforcement but rather suggest a market analysis oriented approach which is then also reflected in much of the commentary and legal literature. In effect, therefore, a more adversarial and combative system of enforcement (in some senses a quasi-criminal law model) has been grafted onto a 'softer' more administrative culture of regulation, giving rise in turn to legal issues that are not addressed in the original Treaty provision. Thus, the issue of the legal character of the Commission's powers of investigation and use of sanctions in relation to major cartels has given rise to a great deal of litigation and debate, linking the subject to that of basic rights protection, intellectually some way removed from the traditional province of the competition lawyer.

The result is a challenging situation for both legal theory and legal practice. Substantive competition law is redolent of economics (market analysis) and private law (activities arising from a variety of contractual arrangements). The procedural aspects and enforcement of competition law is largely a matter of regulatory intervention—an aspect of public law. The outcome is effectively an uneasy co-existence of two very different legal cultures and also some ambivalence in the judicial control of such enforcement activities.

An important aim of the present study is to provide a more explicit focus on *cartel control* as a distinctive and significant element within the broader field of competition law, and in turn raise fundamental questions concerning the purposes and role of competition law itself, or at least this part of competition law.

4. Drama: cartel control—the main actors

Who are the main 'players' on this stage of cartel control? Four main types of actor may be identified:

- the 'offenders' (large corporate actors);
- the 'regulators' (competition authorities);
- the 'referees' (courts of law);
- the 'observers', or the view from outside (commentators, media and public).

It is also part of the argument in this work that an understanding of this 'sharp end' of European competition regulation requires an appreciation of the position, interests and interrelation of certain key players in 'antitrust drama'. As stated above, the regulation of cartels has assumed an adversarial and litigious character, so pitting regulators against large corporate actors. Both of these players—regulatory authorities and large international trading companies—operate within particular legal cultures and clearly represent different interests. But, alongside these opponent parties, an important refereeing role is also carried out (with very important results in terms of legal development) by courts and other personnel (for instance, in an EC context, the Court of Justice and Court of First Instance). Within this more confrontational domain of EC competition law, the appellate role of the European courts has been crucial, and so in turn the composition, background and self-perception of the members of these tribunals is a relevant issue. Finally, the legal arena is then subject to comment, debate and analysis by inter-ested observers—whether academic (critical legal literature), official (at both national and EC levels), or within the media. This 'external' per-ception of the subject may also eventually contribute to and influence legal development.

It will therefore be part of the method of the study to analyse legal developments by reference to the relationships between these participants in the legal drama of competition regulation. In this way, some insight will be provided into the evolution of a regulatory system: for instance, by examining the way in which the European courts have tested their own 'refereeing' role; and by considering the impact of procedural arguments (the outcome of adversarial tactics) on questions of legal substance.

5. History: a twentieth-century overview of European cartel control

This in one sense is the core area of legal discussion of the subject: the body of rules which govern the activities of cartels, both in substan-tive terms (what is prohibited as anti-competitive) and procedural terms (the legal structure of investigation and decision-making on the part of the regulatory authority). In the EC context the legal basis provided by Article 81 (ex Article 85) of the EC Treaty and Council Regulation 17 has now been supplemented by both secondary legislation and case law, developed over a period of more than 30 years, so that there is now a sub-stantial body of EC 'cartel law'. This centres upon the legal analysis of a number of strongly condemned and well-defined anti-competitive prac-tices typically engaged in by major cartels, and the body of rules relating to evidentiary and enforcement issues arising from their prosecution. A detailed study of the development of this area of EC competition law, from the late 1960s to the present, is in itself instructive legal narrative. But an effective account of the subject also requires some comparative reference to the approach to cartel regulation at the national level, par-ticularly the experience and methodology of American law and the more well-developed European national systems.

It is characteristic of this area of competition law that many of the more enduring and challenging problems arise from procedure rather than sub-stance. By the close of the twentieth century, the seriously anti-competitive nature of cartel activity (for instance, price fixing or market sharing) was beyond argument. Typically, the problem had become one of proving the case and so in the instances of major EC litigation the legal argument has concerned such matters as powers of investigation and sufficiency of evidence. Consequently, economic argument relating to market analysis has been used in relation to inferences which may be drawn from market circumstances rather than the substantive assessment of actual anti-competitive practices. Cartel law as a legal category is therefore characterized by a relatively small number of big cases centred upon procedural and evidential issues.

After some 30 years of EC case law on the subject, there is now a line of historical development which may be traced: 'exploratory' cases during the 1970s; more full-blooded investigations during the early 1980s; significant legal challenges to and testing of the Commission's competence and powers during the later 1980s and early 1990s; and a more recent judicial 'recovery' of the Commission's position as a cartel regulator. The control of cartels at a European level has in effect become a significant legal laboratory for testing the limits of regulation of commercial activity. As a former Director-General of DG IV (Ehlermann) commented, 'in no other field of law are the limits of judicial protection and due process so frequently tested as in competition cases'.[2] Thus while the general textbook discussion of competition law continues to emphasize the 'market analysis' approach, the more specific area of cartel law has become increasingly dominated by formal and procedural legal argument, to the extent of taking on board the language of human rights violation. It provides an instructive study of the way in which powerful commercial interests can promote a line of legal development.

6. International relations: the global dimension

Although the European system of regulation is concerned with the impact of cartels on conditions of competition within the geographical territory of the EU, the membership of major international cartels frequently includes companies based in North America, Japan or elsewhere in

---

[2] Claus-Dieter Ehlermann and Berend Drijber, 'Legal Protection of Enterprises: Administrative Procedure, in particular Access to Files and Confidentiality' (1996) 17 *European Competition Law Review* 375.

Europe. This fact gives rise most obviously to problems of jurisdiction, but also in a more practical sense has promoted some measures of co-operation and co-ordination with other regulatory authorities and courts. Taking on board the global dimension reveals a range of problems, on the one hand relating to questions of jurisdiction and different legal process, but also on the other hand issues arising from different policies of enforcement and differences in legal culture (for instance, the fact that corporate executives may face prison sentences in North American jurisdictions, while companies face fines in Europe).[3] Moreover, this international context of enforcement is one within which an increasingly complex array of legal tactics may have to be employed by corporate actors and defence lawyers. There is also an important prospective aspect to this part of the discussion: will the locus of regulation shift from the present main centres, North America and Europe, to some kind of global authority, for instance the WTO, as a kind of world cartel police? If so, how quickly, in what way and with what consequences for existing national and supranational systems of control?

7. Pathology: antitrust delinquency as the target of legal action

The central argument of this study is concerned with a more explicit identification and expression of the objections to the kind of anti-competitive behaviour underlying cartel arrangements at the European level. Unlike many other types of anti-competitive practice, the deliberate and covert character of many cartel arrangements take the subject into a domain of unambiguous condemnation and resort to repressive sanctions. Motive and instrument are important objects of regulation: deliberate and secretive manoeuvres intended to maximize profit, carried into effect by means of sophisticated and obfuscating measures. Analysis and proof of *collusion or conspiracy* is the real meat of the subject, rather than administrative assessments of the relativities within a market.

The core of the thesis is therefore based on a perception of serious anti-competitive behaviour as a largely distinct *genus*, most appropriately characterized as a form of delinquency on account of the degree of 'antitrust

---

[3] Prison terms for individuals now constitute a possibility in some European national systems, as discussed in Chapter IX below, but so far none have been imposed.

awareness', deliberate and furtive collusion, and power and sophistication of the typical participants in European-wide cartels. A resulting question is one of appropriate legal process: whether a fully fledged criminal proceeding (with its attendant level of legal safeguards) is the most appropriate model of regulation, or something juridically different, such as the model of administrative penality used already in a number of European national systems and also, at least in formal terms, in the field of EC competition law at present. But there are further more specific issues which should also be addressed as part of this wider enquiry. First, the question arises whether in dealing with cartel activity the most appropriate organizing concept is that of conspiracy rather than market circumstances. Secondly, it may be asked how an appropriate balance may be attained between requirements of due process and the risk of strategic manipulation of increasingly complex procedures. Finally, there is the assessment of the effectiveness of sanctions, in particular, comparing the efficacy of 'carrots' (for instance, rewards for breaking ranks and becoming a witness for the prosecution, as laid down in the successful leniency strategies of the 1990s, discussed in Chapter VIII below) with that of 'sticks' (for instance, fines, which may be appealed and are of uncertain deterrent impact; or the American (and now perhaps European) option of prison sentences).

I

Business Cartels: Sleeping with the Enemy

1. A history of ambivalence: is it a criminal law rap?

Business cartels have been an established, significant, and well-known feature of commercial life in industrialized countries for over a hundred years. Their activities are important in both an economic and political sense in that they affect the operation of markets and the position and interests of a range of actors, both traders and consumers. The subject also has an intellectual significance, in that it has generated some very different legal and regulatory responses, although this differing reaction has not attracted so much attention in legal literature. It is important at the outset of this discussion to emphasize and indicate clearly the nature of this diverse reading of the behaviour of trading cartels since this underpins and informs the whole history of this area of regulation. A study of this subject is necessarily a comparative study of legal cultures and legal construction, whether the context is national or supranational law and policy. Discussion of the subject thus contains an instructive narrative of competing perceptions and methodologies. What in one part of the world has for a long time been regarded as delinquent behaviour and the subject of rigorous legal control, has elsewhere been a subject of condonation or consensual regulation. That the former model appears at the turn of the twentieth and twenty-first century to be gaining the upper hand in what may be a process of legal globalization,[1] in no way lessens the interest in this story of competing perceptions.

It is perhaps characteristic of the subject that, while it possesses a strong and full identity in economic terms, legal discussion and definition of cartels

---

[1] See the discussion in Chapters II and X below.

and their typical behaviour has been much more sketchy. There is a rich but for the most part non-legal vocabulary within the subject area.[2] This is well illustrated by the recent appearance of the term 'hard core cartel', used generally to indicate a business cartel, the behaviour of which is unacceptable and therefore a fit subject for legal control, but possessing little specific legal content beyond a listing of typically objectionable practices. A starting point for discussion, then, is the recognition that in non-legal terms it is not difficult to supply a fairly well agreed description of cartel activity in an economic and business context. But specific legal definition, and indeed the point and function of such definition, remains underdeveloped. More specifically, the enduring question has been and remains whether this a matter of bad conduct, deserving villification and normative control, or a matter of responding pragmatically to problematic outcomes? More generally, an underlying question concerns the very nature and role of 'cartel law'.

From a reader's point of view, there are two important perspectives on this subject as a whole. First, there is a more practical and immediate view of the question, concerned with an enquiry into how business cartels behave, the consequences of their behaviour and the role of law (if any) in regulating this behaviour. This is most obviously the view of the business person, the competition regulator, the lawyer and perhaps the consumer. But secondly, there is a view which may be described as more theoretical and philosophical. Here the focus shifts to a wider type of enquiry, relating to the way in which society reacts to competitive and collusive behaviour, the values which are accorded to these two different kinds of conduct, and consequently different models of regulation which may be employed. This study seeks not only to clarify the behaviour of legal and other reactions to business cartels, but also to set such a discussion in the context of a theory of control or regulation.

This theme may perhaps be indicated briefly at this early stage of discussion by posing a basic question about the nature of competition and collusion in an economic and trading context. At first sight, this question may appear somewhat puzzling, but it may help to illuminate the ambivalence of attitude that appears to pervade this subject. Taking the issue in its broadest terms, as the phenomenon of business competitors deciding to co-operate rather than compete, it may be asked: should this be viewed as a human activity or a business activity? Or, to put the question a little

---

[2] English language legal textbooks, for instance, tend not to use the term 'cartel' as a major category of exposition.

more fully—is this a matter of individual human beings, working within a corporate and business context, but taking decisions as individuals which then affect the lives of other individuals, even if collectively? Or is it a matter of corporate actors, behaving as businesses and taking action which affects markets? Such a question takes us to the very identity of the subject matter, as either human activity or the operation of markets, and hence its comprehension and evaluation. It may be objected that it is not possible to disentangle these two possible dimensions of the subject—that it is at one and the same time both human and market activity and the two are inextricably linked. In an empirical sense this is clearly true. But a main part of the argument being presented here is that, in an analytical sense—for moral, legal and political purposes—much may depend on how such behaviour is interpreted and deconstructed in order to answer questions concerning agency, personality and responsibility.

For legal purposes, in particular, much depends on this kind of question and analysis. It will be argued that this approach, asking this kind of question, helps to provide an understanding of the evolution of legal control in this area and also to construct possible solutions. In crude terms, then, there is a significant choice of paradigm for discussion and regulation. On the one hand, there is the argument that this is a juridical matter: human conduct, affecting other human beings and therefore susceptible to normative control. On the other hand, the opposing argument emphasizes the primacy of the economic 'behaviour' of markets as determining human activity in such a context. This is a clash of both philosophy and perception and it colours the narrative of legal development in a very significant fashion. Ultimately, it helps to explain the competition between two very different models: criminalization and administrative regulation.

2. Defining cartel arrangements

At the outset it should be noted that discussion of the subject is complicated by some revealing vagaries of vocabulary. As Stocking and Watkins noted in 1946:

The term cartel was virtually unknown to the American language a generation ago. Like most borrowed words, when first taken over it meant different things to different persons. Time was required to crystallize its meaning.[3]

---

[3] George W Stocking and Myron W Watkins, *Cartels in Action: Case Studies in International Business Diplomacy* (Twentieth Century Fund, 1946) 3.

Indeed, it may be argued that the process of refining and further defining the meaning of the term continues today. The word has now a broadly agreed general usage (ranging at present through contexts such as legitimate business and organized crime), but its more precise definition remains elusive.

Before considering the problems of definition in more detail, it would clearly be useful to begin with a concise working description. For purposes of the present stage of discussion, a business cartel may be described in generic terms as:

an organization of independent enterprises from the same or similar area of economic activity, formed for the purpose of promoting common economic interests by controlling competition between themselves.

The classic illustration is provided by price fixing collusion. Producers of the same commodity would normally compete with each other by charging lower and therefore more attractive prices to gain a larger share of the market. But in certain economic conditions, it may be in their mutual interest to agree not to do so and so maintain prices at a particular level in order to ensure for each a certain level of profit. This is 'playing safe', but it may well mean that prices are then artificially high (that there is a 'supra-competitive profit'), to the detriment in particular of the consumers of the commodity, who pay 'over the odds'. The orthodox view, certainly now, is that such price fixing is an unjustifiably selfish practice which is both unfair on the consumer and bad for the market (the distinction between these two outcomes will be explored further in the discussion). For present purposes, price fixing between competing suppliers serves as a clear example of a classic business cartel activity. The 'cartel' comprises the anti-competitive collusive organization.

The word 'cartel' has a complex etymology. The basis of its modern usage is in the idea of a suspension of hostilities (or, by analogy, rivalry). The linguistic origins of the term are explained concisely in *The Dictionary of Political Economy*, in its 1919 edition:

Cartel means, in international law, the terms of agreement between belligerents for the exchange or ransom of prisoners. The 'cartel' of chivalry meant first of all the terms of a combat, and then simply the challenge; and the second is still its ordinary meaning on the Continent. By analogy, the word Kartell is now often used by German economists to denote a trust, i.e. an agreement between rival merchants to limit production or otherwise temper the extremity of competition;

so in 1889 it was used of the suspension of hostilities between conservatives and liberal parties in view of the common defence of the empire.[4]

This account conveys usefully the idea of natural rivals agreeing a truce in recognition of particular common interests. This is a useful sense, since it emphasizes the underlying—what may be termed 'natural'—condition of competition and rivalry, which may therefore reassert itself, so indicating the potentially temporary and precarious nature of the cartel alliance— really a truce. It also points to a possible clash of interests arising from such 'unnatural' co-operation. The interests promoted by competition and rivalry ('good' interests in the economic sphere) are compromised by the quest for shorter-term gain on the part of the competitors. But this explanation is also suggestive of the influence of external factors of economic and political exigency, which may have induced the co-operation of otherwise natural rivals (for instance, economic recession, or 'defence of the realm').

Etymologically, *Kartell* became the German term for what Americans, the other great pioneers of competition regulation, referred to as 'trusts' or 'combinations'. The word 'trust' is also very suggestive in this context: the idea that a person or organization is 'entrusted' with the protection of a common economic cause (typically, the common interests of producers within the same industry). The underlying sense, therefore, is of a situation of co-operation where normally one would expect rivalry. What remains ambiguous in this account, however—and this will be a major theme of this discussion—is the extent to which such co-operation may be autonomous and voluntary or driven by overriding external forces. Such an analysis is crucial, in particular, for legal purposes, but requires some understanding of the dynamics of anti-competitive collusion.

At this point, pejorative and non-pejorative shades invade the attempts at definition, reflecting different explanation and appreciation of the co-operative impulse. On the one hand, for instance, Debora Spar's social scientific account suggests a sinister and delinquent mode of activity:

[cartels] arise because the competitors realize that they can advance their own self-interest by working with each other. Together, they can dominate the market and dictate the price that consumers must pay. By refraining from competition, cartel members reap the rewards of greater stability and higher long-term profits.[5]

---

[4] *Dictionary of Political Economy* (London, 1919) vol 1, 229.

[5] Debora Spar, *The Cooperative Edge: the Internal Politics of International Cartels* (Cornell University Press, 1994) 2.

This description may be contrasted with the more benign view arising from the perception of the business cartel as a reasonable defensive arrangement, promoting economic stability and responding to economic disruption and crisis. Writing in the 1920s, Robert Liefmann commented:

For it is one of the chief purposes of cartels generally, and thus of international cartels also, to stabilise and equalise conditions in their particular industry. In their most usual form, the *regional*, they are, above all, designed to prevent or equalise the disturbance in industry caused by commercial or political measures and their frequent oscillations: even at times, to ward them off altogether.[6]

These differing descriptions and analyses no doubt help to explain the ambivalence and generality of legal language relating to cartels, especially at the legislative level. Such legal vocabulary tends to identify the instrument used by a cartel rather than its substantive behaviour as a subject of regulation. Thus the Sherman Act in the United States (at one extreme of the spectrum of legal response in its criminalization of cartels) refers to 'every contract, combination in the form of trust or otherwise, or conspiracy, in restraint of trade or commerce'. Article 81 of the EC Treaty prohibits 'agreements, decisions of associations, or concerted practices' which prevent, restrict or distort competition. Chapter 1 of the UK Competition Act 1998 uses the same formula as Article 81. The earlier British legislation, the Restrictive Trade Practices Act 1976, referred to agreements between two or more persons containing listed prohibited kinds of restriction. Rarely, then, can there be found in legal language reference to the concept of a cartel as an *organization* of anti-competitive collusion, matching the fuller exposition of the phenomenon of business cartels found in economic and sociological literature, although the Sherman Act's use of the general term 'conspiracy' goes further in suggesting elements of delinquent planning.

More recently, however, the concept of a cartel, and in particular, that of a 'hard core cartel' has been used with greater precision and with fuller content, especially in regulatory language and the implications of this shift in and development of legal vocabulary will be considered further below. For the present, some examples should suffice to indicate this sharper delineation and tone in relation to the idea of the business cartel.

---

[6] Robert Liefmann, 'Report on International Cartels', in *Weltwirtschaftsliches Archiv* (English translation, 1927) 82.

Thus, the Office of the UK Director General of Fair Trading, in its guidance notes on the Competition Act 1998 states that:

Generally speaking, a cartel is an agreement between undertakings to fix prices or other trading condition or to share out markets. A distinctive form of cartel is known as collusive tendering or bid rigging... The aim of a cartel is to increase prices by restricting or removing competition between the participants. Cartels are operated secretly and can be hard to detect.[7]

What is of particular interest in this description is the reference to an impliedly delinquent objective and also a furtive mode of operation. At the EC level, the Commissioner for Competition, Mario Monti in an address given in 2000, explained the idea of the cartel as a delinquent organization:

Cartels differ from most other forms of restrictive agreements and practices by being 'naked'. They serve to restrict competition without producing any object-ive countervailing benefits... Cartels, therefore, by their very nature eliminate or restrict competition. Companies participating in a cartel produce less and earn higher profits. Society and consumers pay the bill. Resources are misallocated and consumer welfare is reduced. It is therefore for good reasons that cartels are almost universally condemned.[8]

While focusing on the outcome of market damage, this exposition does also imply an element of design and unfair treatment, and employs the more graphic language of 'naked' conduct. This last term has a similar impact to the now widely used label of 'hard core cartel'. A notable, and fully worked out, example of this term is provided by the OECD Council Recommendation of March 1998, specifically entitled *Effective Action Against Hard Core Cartels*. The Recommendation couples an explicit recognition of the objectionable character of such cartels:

Considering that hard core cartels are the most egregious violations of competi-tion law and that they injure consumers in many countries by raising prices and restricting supply, thus making goods and services completely unavailable to some purchasers and unnecessarily expensive for others

with an explicit definition of the substantive role of hard core cartel activ-ity as anti-competitive agreements, concerted practices, or arrangements by competitors 'to fix prices, make rigged bids (collusive tenders), estab-lish output restrictions or quotas, or share or divide markets by allocating customers, suppliers, territories, or lines of commerce'.[9]

---

[7] (www.oft.gov.uk/html/comp-act/help/questions.html).

[8] Mario Monti, 'Fighting Cartels—Why and How?', opening speech at Third Nordic Competition Policy Conference, Stockholm, 11 September 2000.

[9] OECD, Paris, 27–28 April 1998 (C(98)35/Final).

More recently, then, legal language has been evolving more specifically, to employ the concept of the cartel to indicate more serious, objectionable, and indeed delinquent, types of anti-competitive behaviour, and has moved towards a vocabulary of delinquency ('naked', 'brazen', 'egregious' and 'hard core'). Yet, as some of the above examples demonstrate, and as will be explored further, the relative emphasis to be placed on elements of conduct and elements of market outcome remains obscure. Lawyers and regulators are still some way distant from a clear formulation of the 'cartel offence'.

3. The co-operative instinct: 'the customer is our enemy'

The concept of the cartel embodies a paradox at the heart of economic relations: the desire of competitors not to compete. Clearly any exercise seeking to assess the activity and impact of business cartels should be based on an appreciation and understanding of this apparent irony of power relationships—the attractions of a truce between major rivals. This basic question raises complex issues of both economic and sociological theory, for it suggests an assumption that economic competition is in some sense a natural condition, so that the cessation of rivalry is then an unexpected, unnatural and problematical market phenomenon. In short, if there is to be any judgement of 'cartel-like' behaviour, its origins in a natural disposition towards either collaboration or rivalry should be considered.

It is clearly an enduring problem of both political science and economic analysis to determine the extent to which human society naturally and effectively follows routes of peaceful co-existence or hostile engagement. Taking for the moment the widest perspective—embracing biology, social anthropology and international relations as well as economic argument— and following broadly Darwinian precepts, one key argument asserts that a certain level of aggressive and competitive behaviour is necessary for human advance and even survival. Following this line of argument, from a modern standpoint (whether the subject be interpersonal, international or commercial relations) the crucial question is probably that of determining the appropriate limits on aggressive behaviour so as to optimize the role of such aggression in human development. In this respect, the suggested limits appear to depend on context. For instance, in terms of both interpersonal and international relations, twentieth-century thinking has moved progressively towards a restriction on the use of open force and violence and the preferred employment of peaceful and consensual modes of interaction. On the other hand, in such fields as commercial activity and education and learning, conditions of rivalry and competition have to a large extent[10] continued to be seen as necessary components of achievement. There remains in these latter domains an underlying logic which argues that innovation and quality of performance are stimulated by human desire to prove oneself in comparison with others: to win or lead in the 'game', the 'contest' or 'competition'.[11]

However, desirable levels of rivalry and competition remain open to argument, whatever the context, and the issue is complicated by an inevitable lack of agreement regarding the base-point for calculating such matters. In terms of economic relations this last problem was identified for example by J S Mill in a suggestive remark about the assumptions of economists:

In political economy for instance, empirical laws of human nature are tacitly assumed by English thinkers, which are calculated only for Great Britain and the United States. Among other things an intensity of competition is constantly supposed, which, as a general mercantile fact, exists in no country in the world except these two.[12]

Such a statement also provokes reflections on the role of ideology (e.g. Marxism), geography, natural environment and historical forces on the 'natural' (and relative?) starting-point for competitive impulses.[13]

---

[10] But the issue has always been contested: for some earlier discussions of the perceived ill within competitive attitudes see e.g. Frédéric Bastiat, *Harmonies Economiques* (Paris, 1851) 293; F N Taylor, *Principles of Economics* (New York, 1921) 28; Alfred Marshall, *Principles of Economics* (London, 1920) 6. Taylor identifies some of the nuance in this kind of argument: 'Certain types of men talk and write with much eloquence about the wicked and unchristian character of competition, and roundly affirm that cooperation would be so much more human and Christian, meaning by cooperation this time, cooperation among *like* units' (Taylor, *Principles of Economics*)

[11] In an academic and research context, the late twentieth-century emergence of competitive 'research assessment' is just one recent example of this ideology.

[12] J S Mill, *A System of Logic* (Longman, London, 1936), vol 6, 591. As to whether such a distinction is tenable on the basis of twentieth-century evidence, note the point made by Ervin Hexner, in *The International Steel Cartel* (University of North Carolina Press, 1943) xiii.

[13] As Professor Kreps observed in response to questioning during the US Temporary National Economic Committee (TNEC) hearings: what is understood by the term 'cartel system' 'depends in part on one's economic predilections, in part to one's political convictions' (TNEC, *Hearings*, pt 25, 13039–40).

Despite these underlying theoretical difficulties, the second half of the twentieth century has witnessed an impressive development and consolidation of policy and legal regulation in relation to conditions of *economic* competition, at both national and supranational levels. All developed countries and relevant international organizations now assume the necessity for some kind of regulation of market behaviour in a 'public' interest requiring some kind of economic competition. The argument is no longer 'if', but 'how' and 'at which point'. The essential dilemma of such regulation was concisely identified by Wolfgang Friedmann writing some 40 years ago:

The basic problem of anti-trust is the definition of the public policy criteria which balance the value of cooperation against the benefits of competition. This is as perennial a problem as it is elusive. Nor can it be answered in absolute terms.[14]

Friedmann goes on to illustrate the balancing act necessarily performed by anti-trust law by referring to the need to evaluate cartel activity carefully according to its economic and political context, and cites the dissenting judgment of Brandeis J in the US Supreme Court to that effect:

The refusal to permit a multitude of small rivals to cooperate, as they have done here, in order to protect themselves and the public from the chaos and havoc wrought in their trade by ignorance, may result in suppressing competition.[15]

The underlying point to be emphasized therefore at this stage of discussion is the need to judge and appreciate collaborative trading behaviour in its appropriate historical, economic and political context. Clearly, competition or antitrust law as it relates to cartels is concerned to evaluate such activities in a public interest, but more specifically that task is one of locating this kind of behaviour along a continuum which embraces beneficial co-operation at one extreme and delinquent conspiracy at the other end of the spectrum. Moreover, such a task may be carried out by employing different criteria, the choice of which may not easily be agreed. This problem has been succinctly identified by Gerber:

It is important, therefore, to ask who is evaluating competition, in what contexts and for what reasons, and to uncover the values which are being applied. The political ideologies, social visions and even religious sensibilities of legislators,

---

[14] Wolfgang Friedmann, *Law in a Changing Society* (2nd edn, Penguin, 1972) 308.
[15] Brandeis J, in *American Column and Lumber Co v United States*, 257 US 418, at 418–19 (1921).

bureaucrats and judges have played important roles in the development and operation of competition law regimes.[16]

It is also clear that such variable influences will change over time, spatially as well as between cultures and political and legal orders. Understanding this shifting economic, political, and cultural context is a necessary condition for any appreciation of legal change and the choice of different legal strategies.

(a) Collusion: the main defences

In terms of their potential economic (or social or political) damage, how bad are anti-competitive business cartels? This is a crucial question, underpinning policy and law in this area, but (for the reasons suggested immediately above) is a difficult one to answer. In practice, much is likely to depend upon the context of markets and levels of economic activity, and the subject also remains muddied by continuing theoretical disagreement. Despite the overall shift of opinion against certain types of cartel, defences and justifications have been and continue to be put forward. Many of these arguments question the value of economic competition itself, and some have a more specific relevance to the kind anti-competitive conduct typically engaged in by cartels.

(i) Special markets or sectors of economic activity

It may be argued that competition is not appropriate in some economic sectors, often for particular social or political reasons—agriculture, transport, labour, certain 'professional' activities, defence and education come to mind, for instance. Indeed, public interest or sectoral policy considerations may lead to the adoption of a separate regulatory regime in some economic sectors, a prime example being agriculture, which has been specially regulated at both the national and European levels (the notorious Common Agricultural Policy). At the international level, governments may support or become directly involved in collaborative anti-competitive and cartel-like arrangements, such as international commodity agreements and intergovernmental cartels such as OPEC (see further discussion below). Indeed, it is interesting to note that historically efforts at legal control of cartels have tended to focus on particular areas of trade

---

[16] David J Gerber, *Law and Competition in Twentieth Century Europe* (Oxford University Press, 1998, reprinted 2001) 11–12.

and commerce, typically the supply of raw materials and manufacturing industry. For these reasons, policy towards cartels and measures of legal enforcement are both likely to appear selective in their scope.

(ii) Industrial policy

A related argument arises from economic and political objectives in other areas of industrial policy. Anti-competitive practices, while for example injuring consumer interests, may at the same time serve other acknowledged interests or longer-term goals, such as the protection of employment or regional prosperity, or securing investment in innovation and development. In this way, competition policy may conflict with policies relating to such matters as employment and intellectual property. Of more particular relevance to the issue of cartels is the 'structural' problem of market decline. To avoid the economic dislocation which may result from either cyclical depressions or long-term decline in particular markets or industries, defensive or 'crisis' cartels may be formed spontaneously or with governmental encouragement, in order to manage such disruption and ensure 'stability'. Historically, this is a significant context of cartelization and represents a significant challenge—in economic, political, and social terms—to the perception of delinquency in cartel behaviour. This is a classic 'determinist' kind of argument, which sees the cause of cartelization as market-driven and structural, so that appropriate responses are then also seen as structural.

(iii) Non-economic values

A more general argument against competition as such relates to the promotion of non-economic values which may be jeopardized by a highly competitive pursuit of market share. Thus it may be argued that the safety of products and other standards of quality may be compromised in this way. It may be thought that the cost of ensuring such standards can be more effectively achieved by anti-competitive collaboration and in this way some categories of both horizontal and vertical restrictive trading practices may be distinguished from the more objectionable species of cartel and co-operation.

(iv) Economic efficiency

Another general line of argument may be deployed to assert that competition does not necessarily result in allocative and productive efficiency, but may in some respects prove economically wasteful. For example, suppliers may engage competitively in energetic and costly advertising campaigns which divert money into the advertising sector rather than stimulate the market for the original product. Or again, consumers may 'waste' resources on costly shopping around when there appears to be a substantial choice in a market. In this sense, consumers may be said to benefit from the 'easier' choice within a more restricted and tied up market. This, however, is an economic argument, which tends to disregard the 'cultural gain' arising from diversity and greater freedom to chose and innovate as a consumer (for instance, to satisfy a preference for organic or non-genetically modified foodstuff).

(v) 'Apparent cartelization': the problem of oligopoly

This species of economic argument presents one of the main challenges to regulators seeking to control cartels, since it undermines the very notion of the cartel: what appears to be collusive price fixing or market sharing is not so in reality, but simply parallel behaviour arising from the nature of the market. If the market is characteristically one dominated by a small number of relatively large suppliers, parallel behaviour on their part may be a structural feature of the market—another instance of economic determinism. This argument is summarized concisely by Whish in the following terms:

> Thus the theory runs that in an oligopolistic market rivals are interdependent: they have a heightened awareness of each other's presence and are bound to match one another's marketing strategy. The result is that price competition between them will inevitably be minimal or even non-existent. Oligopoly produces non-competitive stability.[17]

However, arguments relating to oligopoly are contestable, and empirical research which claims to support such argument has been challenged. In particular, there is the conundrum that some oligopolistic markets are demonstrably competitive, characterized, for instance, by periodic price wars (as in the case of petrol suppliers) or active non-price competition such as intensive advertising (as in the case of the lager market). Moreover, the whole issue of parallel pricing is beset with theoretical and empirical difficulties, especially concerning the phenomenon of interdependent price rises. Various theories of 'price leadership' have been developed to explain how this may occur.[18] In short, the subject of cartels

---

[17] Richard Whish, *Competition Law* (4th edn, Butterworths, 2001) 461.
[18] Markham, 'The Nature and Significance of Price Leadership' (1951) 41 *American Economic Review* 891 remains the classic text. See the discussion in Chapter VI below.

and oligopolistic markets is like a theoretical and policy minefield, and contributes in itself to the history of conflicting perceptions of cartel activity.

4. The macro-economic context: typical markets?

Is it true to say, then, that business cartels are likely to appear under certain economic conditions in certain markets, and employ typical strategies, engaging in particular types of practice? Orthodox economic argument tends to assume that cartels do operate in such a typical fashion, in particular kinds of market and using common anti-competitive devices: hence the 'classic' image of the price fixing, market sharing producer cartel in a concentrated or oligopolistic market. This typology of cartels (largely derived from economics literature) may be considered under two main headings: the market context (a macro-economic perspective); and types of restrictive practice (a micro-economic perspective).

(a) Markets: areas of trade and production

Many economists perceive a strong relationship between market structure and cartelization, and this is repeated in official statements. For example, a recent statement from the UK Office of Fair Trading observes:

Some sectors are more susceptible to cartels than others because of the structure or the way in which they operate. For example, where: there are few competitors; the products have similar characteristics, leaving little scope for competition on quality or service; communication channels between competitors are already established; the industry is suffering from excess capacity or there is general recession.[19]

This approach to explaining the phenomenon of cartelization may be described as *structural*. The line of argument is analysed by Spar in the following terms:

Beginning with the premise that market structure determines market behavior, economists have examined the cartel problem from the outside in, looking to identify the precise structural characteristics that make markets particularly susceptible to cartelization. Their central focus has been the environment in which the individual firm finds itself and their central concern has been to specify how this external environment shapes the prospects for cooperation. To explain cartels, they have looked to the structure of oligopolistic markets.[20]

[19] (www.oft.gov.uk/html/comp-act/cartels).   [20] Spar, n 5 above, 4.

The importance of this kind of argument for purposes of understanding the evolution of legal control in this area should be noted. The idea of a market being *susceptible* to cartelization has, of course, implications for any discussion of responsibility. This economic structural model will therefore provide an important theme for the whole discussion.

According to structural analysis there are thus significant market conditions and characteristics which favour competitor co-operation. Three main elements may perhaps be identified. First, the *nature of the commodity* is such that it makes competition difficult. Basic and homogeneous products which do not have distinguishing features and cannot easily be substituted are likely to be supplied in a stable, uniform manner. How, it may be asked, may suppliers of rubber, basic chemicals, steel tubes, thermoplastics, sugar, cardboard, or wood pulp compete when they are all supplying broadly the same, undifferentiated commodity, produced in a similar way? Secondly, *concentration* makes a non-competitive environment more likely and more feasible. This is where the theory of oligopoly comes into play, coupled with the fact of small numbers which, at the least, heightens mutual awareness, or more actively, facilitates collusive links. Thirdly, if a market is *over-supplied or in recession*, instincts of self-protection will tempt market participants mutually to seek the easy life rather than engage in costly and uncertain redeployment of their resources. Taken together, such structural factors combined sometimes with the historical contingency of market decline make cartelization a predictable and understandable economic process.

This market-led analysis therefore has both explanatory and justificatory features. It produces a list of 'usual suspects', who in turn will put forward usual defences. Historically, there appear to be a number of high profile cartelized economic sectors, predominantly in markets for raw materials and basic manufactured commodities. This is typified by the thriving cartel culture in the chemical and pharmaceutical industries. Leiden University's *Interwar Cartel Database*[21] provides a detailed list of some 50 chemical and pharmaceutical products dominated by cartel activity between the two World Wars and a number of these markets feature prominently in major American and EC investigations in the later years of the century (for instance, citric acid, dyestuffs, plastics, quinine, white lead, and vitamins). Consequently, some corporate names recur in the history of cartels and their legal control (such as ICI, Du Pont, and Hoechst).

---

[21] Leiden University Historical Institute (www.let.leidenuniv.nl/history).

However, a market-based mapping of cartels may have to be handled with some caution, since the conditions on which it is based may be relevant but not sufficient in explaining cartel formation. As Spar has noted:

Cartels have formed in markets that bear few of the suggested structural criteria and have floundered in some of the supposedly ideal markets...structural theories define the conditions that are conducive to a co-operative outcome, but they tell us little about the means by which this outcome is achieved...although these theories may be perfectly adequate for an economist interested in linking inputs to outcomes, they are less satisfying when one is trying to understand the process by which a cartel is formed and sustained.[22]

Thus, for example, cartels might have been expected to have flourished in the markets for tin, silver and uranium, but cartels in those markets (as Spar put it) floundered. The structural, market-led analysis of cartel formation takes us some, but not the whole way to an understanding of the phenomenon. In turn, then, depending on one's understanding of the process of cartel formation, the repetition of names and products may appear very differently, as either a predictable fact of economic life, or as delinquent recidivism.

(b) Markets: private or public management

In drawing up any typology of markets for purposes of discussing cartel formation a further aspect of market character ought to be considered— the degree to which there is governmental or public intervention in market activity which may favour or encourage cartelization, or remove possible legal controls. From a present-day standpoint cartel activity is frequently viewed very much as a private or independent entrepreneurial activity. Indeed, it is the private character of cartels (and 'private' may be applied in two senses: commercially independent *and* hidden from view) which is often seen as offensive to the public interest. In other words, what is regarded as particularly delinquent on the part of many contemporary cartels is their determined and selfish pursuit of economic gain, to the cost of consumers and often employing secretive methods.

In the earlier part of the twentieth century, however, the activities of business cartels were not so clearly divorced from the realm of public authority. Partly, this was due the more ambivalent attitude towards trading cartels, especially in continental Europe, so that in some contexts there was governmental encouragement, participation in or even establishment of

---

[22] Spar, n 5 above, 5–6.

cartels. But partly also, it was a reflection of a much lesser degree of inter-governmental 'public' regulation of international trade which resulted in a certain amount of governmental 'steering' of commercial actors into collaborative arrangements, in particular in order to stabilize a market. While there is no simple and clear-cut distinction between 'private' and 'public' cartels, it may nonetheless be possible to identify a number of significant categories along a sliding scale of private and public participation:

- the cartel as a private treaty;
- governmental encouragement;
- 'compulsory' cartels;
- commodity agreements.

(i) Cartels as 'institutions of private economy'

This may perhaps be regarded as the 'classic' type of cartel—independent business entities working together to restrict competition for their own ('private') gain. Undoubtedly this is the main sense in which the term has been used during the later part of the twentieth century, with the implication that there is no public interest justification for such cartels' restrictive behaviour and indeed that such behaviour is clearly contrary to the wider public and community interest.

In an international context, the operation of major cartels may be seen as private systems of transnational regulation of trade and thus as private treaty regimes. While lacking the formality and status of intergovernmental systems of regulation, international cartels may nonetheless possess an economic significance which may match or even exceed instruments of public international law. Again, it may be objected that cartels are characterized by impermanence and some lack of regularity in terms of internal structure and functioning. Nonetheless, in practice many cartels operate with effectiveness as normative orders with an international dimension. This view of the cartel as a significant but private form of normative organization will be discussed further below.

(ii) Governmental encouragement

In the earlier part of the twentieth century some European governments fostered the formation of cartels in certain markets as a means of stabilizing such markets. It may be useful to distinguish, on the one hand, a toleration or encouragement of private cartel organization without any real dictation of their specific aspects, and, on the other hand, a degree of compulsion and direction of policy on the part of governments or public agencies. Hexner, for instance, writing in the early 1940s, sought to make this distinction:

The cartel relationship must be voluntary. Traditionally, the cartel concept is limited to marketing controls in which no compulsion to join is exercised by public authorities and in which policies are not decidedly influenced by general or particular regulations of the respective governments...A marketing scheme to which the entrepreneur must adhere and the policies of which are subject to determination by public agencies approaches a public agency. It is not, therefore, an institution of private economy.[23]

But Hexner conceded that there were 'many transitional forms between free and compulsory institutions' and referred elsewhere to the fact that publicly owned enterprises could be members of cartels and—further along the scale of private to public character—that intergovernmental ('diplomatic') agreements could be the basis for establishing private cartels. The latter was evident in relation to such commodities as tin, rubber and tea. In fact, neat classifications are not possible, as is evident from the example of governmentally sponsored cartels. The tin cartel survived until the 1980s, under the direction of the International Tin Council, an intergovernmental organization set up under successive International Tin Agreements. The whole arrangement (before it was disbanded in October 1985) was described as a cartel, administered by 23 states party to the agreement, with the objective of ensuring an orderly and stable world supply of and market for tin.[24] For Hexner, the important point of distinction lay with the degree of commercial autonomy in the hands of the cartel members and he uses for this purpose the concept of the 'entrepreneur', which:

implies a business unit in which decisions as to establishing and abolishing his enterprise and as to setting up and changing marketing policies rests with the entrepreneur. He has to bear the risks of uncertainties resulting from his free (or voluntarily restricted) marketing policies. In a 'compulsory cartel' the activities of the entrepreneur are determined by an external authority and it is questionable whether he may be still looked upon as an entrepreneur in the traditional sense.[25]

---

[23] Ervin Hexner, *International Cartels* (Pitman, 1946) 27.

[24] See C Warbrick and I Cheyne, 'The International Tin Council' (1987) 36 *International and Comparative Law Quarterly* 931.

[25] Hexner, *International Cartels*, n 23 above, 30. The complexity of such classification is evident in the case of ICI, which Lord McGowan appeared to regard virtually as an arm of British diplomacy (as the use of 'Imperial' in the name might imply): see Stocking and Watkins, n 3 above, 406 *et seq*.

Nonetheless, in practical terms the dividing line between governmental encouragement and compulsion may not have been very clear, when for instance (as Hexner himself reported) in the later 1930s, groups of companies within international cartels responded more and more to the wishes of their governments. In the final analysis, it is difficult to escape the impression that so much was a matter of degree.

(iii) Compulsory cartels

The term 'compulsory cartel' is probably best reserved to describe a phenomenon mainly evident in the 1930s, involving a degree of governmental direction and control of cartel activity which in practical terms amounted to a governmental take-over of 'private industry'. In effect, such cartels, as they existed for instance in Nazi Germany and also Italy and Japan, were groups of notionally private and independent enterprises organized for purposes of carrying out state trading policies. Nazi economists referred to such organizations as 'total cartels':

It is the organization of producers of a commodity. By safeguarding the rules of rationalization and the interest of public welfare this organization is charged with regulation of the production and marketing of that commodity and with the organic co-ordination of these functions with the national economic structure as a whole.[26]

Such 'total' cartels may appear now as being largely of historical interest but may also remain instructive in so far as they demonstrate a potential convergence of private and governmental interests. As Schweitzer comments in his study of business in the Third Reich:

big business and the oligarchic clique saw the role of cartels in the same light. Party leaders favoured a more effective supervision of cartel policies, whereas big business desired governmental support primarily for the benefit of influential cartel members.[27]

The lessons to be drawn from such material for contemporary purposes may be relevant therefore to the potential contacts and relations between business persons engaged in restrictive trading activities and corrupt regimes or government officials.

---

[26] Arno Sölter, *Das Grossraumkartell* (Dresden, 1941) 87–8.

[27] Arthur Schweitzer, *Big Business in the Third Reich* (Eyre & Spottiswoode, 1964) 271. See generally Schweitzer's discussion at 269 *et seq* for a fuller discussion of the Nazi 'complulsory cartels'. See also Joseph Borkin, *The Crime and Punishment of I.G. Farben* (Andre Deutsch, 1979).

(iv) Intergovernmental commodity agreements

Again, it may not be easy in practice to draw a clear boundary between governmental encouragement of cartel activity, governmental requirement and control of such arrangements and, thirdly, the kind of structure often referred to as an international commodity agreement (ICA), except that the latter is a visible creature of international law. All three categories entail some degree of public intervention in the market-place, ostensibly at least to promote a more general or 'public' economic interest, and often use techniques of regulation which require some 'discipline' of competition between producers and suppliers. But commodity agreements are at one end of the spectrum in terms of their highly visible intergovernmental and formal status. Indeed, they would now qualify as part of that sector of international law more colloquially referred to as the 'world trading system'. Jackson, for instance, lists ICAs as part of the 'landscape' of international economic institutions which supply the structure for the late-twentieth-century world trading system.[28] It is worth noting the existence of such agreements for their promotion of a certain kind of cartel—a category of collaboration which is officially approved—since it again illustrates some of the economic and political ambivalence of attitude on the whole subject of cartels. In short, ICAs represent an attempt to deal with market problems in particular economic sectors by methods which, if they were employed in a private entrepreneurial context, might well be regarded as illegitimate, yet which gain respectability through their 'public' character. ICAs are often, in one sense, price-fixing arrangements, but acquire acceptability as measures designed 'to stabilize international market prices'. This should serve to remind the student of cartel regulation of the fact that the delinquency inherent in cartel behaviour resides in motive and context as much as restrictive method.

The general point to bear in mind is that sovereign states and, more recently, intergovernmental organizations are no strangers themselves to cartel activity. Admittedly, such 'public international' cartels now require justification in a broad public interest and it is unlikely that the early example of an international cartel treaty comprising the agreement of 1470 between the Papacy and the Kingdom of Naples, with the objective of maintaining as high as possible the prices for alum, would now attract widespread approval.[29]

---

[28] John Jackson, *The World Trading System* (MIT Press, 1989) 28–9.
[29] See Hexner, *International Cartels*, n 23 above, 26–7, and the sources referred to there.

On the other hand, more recent UNCTAD-sponsored agreements, such as the International Natural Rubber Agreement of 1979, would appear as desirable international measures of market stabilization.[30]

The underlying issue is therefore one concerning definition and terminology. In a present-day context in which 'hard core cartels' are being increasingly characterized as delinquent arrangements, the term 'cartel' as part of a vocabulary of censure is very much linked to a context of private, selfishly motivated and furtive activity. If there are 'good' and 'bad' cartels, they occur in very different kinds of legal and economic environments. The key distinction is not so much one of restrictive technique as one of private and public interest.

5. The micro-economic context: the quest for supracompetitive profit

Having considered the context in which business cartels are likely to appear (the questions: why, when, and where?), a cartel typology needs also to consider the characteristic behaviour of such cartels at the more specific level of trading practices—what kind of anti-competitive activity is typically engaged in (the questions: what and how?)

There is a well-established textbook list of horizontal restrictive trading practices, which are now usually considered to typify the most objectionable aspects of cartel behaviour, as economically unjustifiable and especially injurious to consumer interests: in particular, price fixing, market sharing, quotas and bid rigging (a useful checklist of such practices is contained in the OECD definition of a 'hard core cartel', referred to above). In short, when competing suppliers agree not to compete in the most obvious ways in which they would be expected to compete, as regards conditions of sale and supply and securing customers, they are now commonly regarded as engaging in some of the most 'naked', 'hard core', and 'egregious' forms of anti-competitive behaviour. The prevailing legal view of this conduct is summarized by Whish:

Horizontal agreements between independent undertakings may be entered into in order to limit output and increase price and be devoid of any beneficial consequences which can offset this harm to consumer welfare. Cartel agreements of this

---

[30] See Richard Stubbs, 'The International Natural Rubber Agreement: Its Negotiation and Operation' (1984) 18 *Journal of World Trade Law* 16.

type are perhaps the most obvious target for any system of competition law...so too are horizontal restraints which are designed to foreclose potential competition from other firms in order to protect the privileged position of the cartel members.[31]

Regulatory statements and documentation are increasingly explicit in their exposition of the objectionable character of such practices. There are now a number of references to 'overcharges' to consumers and business purchasers as the result of price collusion and attempts to quantify the level of such unlawful gain. An example is provided by the Irish Competition Authority's *Guideline on Cartels*:

The total cost to consumers and the economy of cartels cannot be measured with any certainty but almost certainly amounts to hundreds of millions of pounds. A cartel which adds a few pence to the price of a product purchased by the vast majority of consumers would earn substantial profits at their customers' expense. In addition, cartels impose losses on society in terms of reduced efficiency, and lower output (known as dead-weight losses). Estimates suggest that such dead-weight losses can amount to 1–2% of total GDP which is a substantial cost.[32]

This kind of statement is based upon a formula which identifies the price increase resulting from the fix, multiplied by the quantity of the product sold, added to the dead-weight loss. A conservative estimate would be considered to be an average price increase of 10 per cent, plus dead-weight loss at 10 per cent of the volume of trade, plus interest over the duration of the fix.[33] When the gains from price alignment, market sharing and quotas are identified in this way, it is not surprising to find such horizontal restrictions at the sharp end of censure and enforcement in competition law regimes.

The thrust of the objection is therefore that supracompetitive profits are generated by practices such as the alignment of prices, collusion on bids, and conservation of customer bases through market sharing. Production quotas, market sharing, and other restrictions are invariably used to reinforce such measures as price fixing. It is important to identify the essential objection to these anti-competitive devices, since their lack of economic justification coupled with particular reasons for employing them translates into censure, a sense of delinquency and then, perhaps, criminalization. In this respect, the concept of *supracompetitive profit* is

---

[31] Richard Whish, *Competition Law* (3rd edn 1993) 390.

[32] *Guideline on Cartels*, ch 1 (www.irlgov.ie/compauth/CARTEL.htm).

[33] See e.g. Gregory J Werden and Marilyn J Simon, 'Why Price Fixers Should Go to Prison' (1988) *The Antitrust Bulletin* 924.

useful, since it provides the idea of economic gain over and above what might be expected in the normal operation of a market—a gain which is therefore unfair, causes loss to others and hence an appropriate subject of regulation and sanctions. The 'naked' categories of restrictive practice listed above are likely (in the absence of particular and rare economic justifications) to be used for purposes of achieving such illicit profit and therefore acquire a kind of presumptive evidential value. Thus the now common legal assertion that price alignment, if arising from collusive contacts between competitors rather than a result of oligopolistic interdependence, is *prima facie* illegal. This listing of anti-competitive strategies, located within a framework of seeking supracompetitive profit, therefore, provides some basis for defining the elements of an 'antitrust' or 'cartel offence'.

Table I.1 contains what may be regarded as the main categories of restrictive trading practice which may be used by cartels when their goal is to attain supracompetitive profits. Such a list is drawn from textbook accounts and regulatory case law, and most of these practices will appear in the later discussion. In some cases, some economic justification may be accepted by regulators and courts, for instance some limitations on production as part of a justifiable specialization or joint research and development programme. But for the most part, these restrictions are now closely associated with a delinquent quest for supracompetitive profit.

Table I.1: Principal methods of achieving supracompetitive profit

- Direct price fixing
- Limiting production (quotas)
- Geographical allocation of markets (market sharing)
- Agreement on other conditions of supply:
  - discounts
  - credit
  - delivery
  - after-sales
  - guarantees
- Collusive tendering (e.g. a rota of winning bids)
- Advertising restrictions
- Creating barriers to entry:
  - collective reciprocal exclusive dealing
  - aggregrated rebates
  - collective boycotts
- Information exchanges (as a means of facilitating the above)

6. Cartel dynamics: the cartel as a private treaty regime

(a) Inside looking out

The above discussion of the subject of cartels has been largely from an external perspective, in the sense of the view taken by outsiders, whether the latter comprises other parties in a market, regulators, and policy-makers, or more detached observers. Such a perspective has naturally been predominant among both economists and lawyers. The former have been interested in locating cartel *activity* within the context of markets and their operation, while lawyers not surprisingly would be concerned to place the issue of cartel *behaviour* within a normative context of particular systems of rules. Both contexts are clearly of major importance. Business cartels have an economic function and necessarily operate in a market context. Equally, once the operation of cartels has become a subject of regulatory attention, their operation will acquire a normative dimension. But there is a further dimension which is arguably of equal importance, although by its nature it will have attracted the attention of sociologists rather than economists and lawyers. This is the view from the inside, and is concerned with the internal dynamics of the cartel as an organization. While the cartel, as an organization, may be seen as having economic objectives and be subject to some kind of external regulation, this role and the range of responses to external forces will necessarily forge an internal dynamic, which requires understanding by both economists and regulators. The important questions which arise in this regard concern the relations between members of the cartel, its internal constitution and politics and the cartel-contingent forces which shape its establishment and demise.

As is true of any other organization (states, families, corporate entities, gangs, or whatever), it may well be misleading to read their actions in a purely generic way and to ignore their internal working. None of these are monolithic entities, and it is sometimes a crucial failing of both academic commentary and legal regulation to treat them as such. Generic classifications are necessary and convenient for purposes of exposition and, in particular, legal organization, but they frequently obscure the less clear-cut and more impenetrable actuality of the matter. Thus cartels, like states or companies, often differ from each other in their specific character and objectives, and the nature of their membership and consequently internal politics may vary. Indeed, such individual characteristics may be important in explaining outcomes, as Spar has suggested, for instance, in understanding the appearance and 'success' of cartels in some markets but not others.[34]

At the same time it is important to appreciate that individuals who work for companies which participate in cartels have their own perspective on what is happening which is necessarily different from that of an economist, a consumer, or a competition regulator. Marketing managers and the like inhabit first of all a specific corporate environment, and then a particular business environment, both of which fashion individual and collective behaviour and outlook. Such people see themselves, for instance, as an executive of Hoffmann-La Roche, working in the pharmaceuticals industry and market, before they see themselves as a subject of textbook discussion or a character in litigation. If it is asked why some companies repeatedly engage in illegal price fixing following successful prosecution and the imposition of sanctions, part of the answer at least should be sought in the disjunction between the 'external' viewpoint of the regulator and the 'internal' viewpoint of the company executive: different goals, different interests, different values and therefore different behaviour (see the discussion in Chapter IX below). Some appreciation of, and insight into, this 'internal' perspective should therefore both aid and inform the conventional 'external' view of the subject.

Looking at cartels from such a standpoint also indicates another dimension of their activity which has not hitherto received so much attention or analysis: the fact that, as a purposive organization, a cartel establishes a normative regime of its own, with internal mechanisms for controlling and enforcing certain modes of conduct. Moreover, cartels which function in a transnational context, may then be seen as establishing, across national boundaries, a kind of international 'private' treaty regime which, at a low level of visibility, governs some important aspects of international business life. Thus the internal dynamic may be analysed not only in sociological and political terms, but also as an example of a discrete normative order. In turn, this kind of enquiry can lead usefully to an examination of the tensions which then naturally arise between the distinct cultures of the business community and individual cartels on the one hand and of the 'public interest' (whether national or supranational) operation of economic policy and legal control on the other hand.

---

[34] Spar, n 5 above.

This kind of general analysis can for convenience be undertaken in two stages, looking respectively at the broader context of the business community and the more specific context of the individual cartel.

(b) The business community: 'I wanna be closer to you than I am to any customer'

Individual cartels are located within a wider 'business' environment, which comprises not only an economic element of markets, as discussed above, but also a more elusive element of 'culture'—an historical amalgam of experience, custom, practices, attitudes, and expectations. It is such a cultural element which helps to explain the economically 'unnatural' bonding of business rivals, captured so well in the legendary 'you are my friend, the customer is our enemy' aphorism:

> The only thing we need to talk here because we are gonna get manipulated by these God damn buyers...They can be smarter than us if we let them be smarter... They are not your friend. They are not my friend. And we gotta have them. Thank God, we gotta have 'em, but they are not my friends. You're my friend. I wanna be closer to you than I am to any customer.[35]

Business entities are established with the aim of succeeding in a particular area of business activity, and suppliers will have different specific interests and goals as compared to buyers and consumers. For the supplier, in economic terms, consumer welfare will be a major goal only in so far as it contributes to the supplier's own profitability. Thus, for example, larger retailers became interested in the non-genetically modified food market upon the realization that they were in a stronger position to exploit that part of the market compared to smaller retailers; in that way, consumer welfare and potential profit coincided. But generally, it may be expected that suppliers, even though competing with each other, have shared goals and values, understand well each other's position and so have a common culture which may facilitate a dynamic of co-operation. More prosaically, 'rival' marketing managers meeting together are likely to have more to say to each other than they would talking to consumers. On reflection, this may seem like stating the obvious, yet it is worth emphasizing as an important aspect of business culture which explains the existence of a co-operative instinct. Historically, institutional arrangements such as

---

[35] US Department of Justice, Vitamin Cartel investigation, transcript from recording of a cartel meeting in Maui, Hawaii, 10 March 1994.

guilds and trading associations reflect a more systematic exploitation of this dynamic in business culture. Put in that context, the cartel is then just one further example of a common interest grouping, and a predictable phenomenon. Moreover, it is possible that such a co-operative culture may be more precisely located within larger corporate structures. Marketing managers are more specifically concerned with prices and profit margins, whereas other executives may be more accountable for purposes of consumer and competition regulation and so there may be a divergence of interest within a single corporate structure, with some employees interested in furtive cartel negotiation, while others are nervous about antitrust compliance.[36] The culture of collusion is thus significant but complex.

At the same time it should be understood that the sense of alliance which underpins the formation of cartels is also potentially fragile and unpredictable. Since it is ultimately dictated by business self-interest, this is also something which may change over time and vary as between partners. Also, as certain kinds of anti-competitive collusion have become subject to stronger legal prohibition and so driven underground, the secretive nature of the arrangement produces an additional sense of stress and nervousness in the relations between the cartel partners. This edginess and uncertainty has now been famously exploited by regulators offering 'leniency' as a reward for breaking ranks, as will be discussed later, in Chapter VIII below. The general point is that most cartels, although founded upon a shared instinct for co-operation, are nonetheless uneven and potentially unstable. The individual gain for participants may vary according to their particular market position and circumstances.[37] Typically, there are 'leaders' within the cartel membership, who take the initiative, and undertake an important motivating and organizing role. In legal and moral terms, such actors may now be cast as the major delinquents, the 'leaders of the gang', who should be subject to more severe sanctions. The actual operation of a cartel has its own costs: the business of negotiation, followed by policing and enforcement of the agreed strategies. In short, activating and implementing the co-operative instinct is

[36] See for instance the account of the Swedish company Stora, a member of the *Cartonboard Cartel*, discussed in Chapter IX below: Case T-354/94, *Stora v Commission* [1998] ECR II-2140–1.

[37] Even to the extent of a 'maverick' or 'outsider' being 'recruited' into the cartel to end determined competition—consider for instance the attempts to recruit the awkward rival Powerpipe into the *Pre-Insulated Pipes Cartel* (OJ 1999, L 24/1). See generally, Scherer and Ross, *Industrial Market Structure and Economic Performance* (3rd edn, 1990), chs 5, 7, and 8.

not necessarily an easy business and, given the increasingly informal and furtive character of cartel arrangements, is fraught with a sense of uncertainty. Returning to the example quoted above from the transcript of a cartel meeting, it is interesting to note the wheedling tone of the negotiation: 'it is important for us to stick together, because our interests really are the closest.' Nonetheless, the sense of trust may be uncertain, and that of economic contingency all too real.

(c) Internal organization: the leader and the pack

At an individual level, cartels have a rich internal dynamic. Once established, each cartel has its own internal constitution, arrangement of power, politics and interplay of economic interest. An understanding of the power and success of a particular cartel depends to an important extent on an appreciation of the internal working and interrelationship of its membership and the kind of political and normative structure it has established for itself: not only what has been agreed, but how that agreement came about and the regime of implementation. As a potential subject of revealing sociological enquiry, the cartel could rank alongside such entities as the family, the gang, the company, or the political organization.

For present purposes an important point to note is the way in which analysis of the internal dynamic of cartel operations can usefully be taken together with more well established external, 'structural' and market-centred enquiries. The work of Deborah Spar, in particular, has contributed an interesting insight into the subject, by supplementing earlier more narrative studies of particular cartels and 'structural' explanations offered by economists. Spar's comparative analysis of cartelization, or the lack of it, in four economically comparable international markets (diamonds, uranium, silver, and gold) led her to identify certain 'internal' elements of viability of cartelization (that 'to understand cooperation more broadly, we need to consider the internal characteristics of the competitors as well as the structure in which they are arrayed'):

Cartels form, I argue, not only because a market is predisposed to joint action but also because at least two major producers have certain internal characteristics that enable them to initiate and maintain a cooperative relationship. Specifically, I present three levels of explanation. First, I suggest that autonomous competitors— those with the power to discipline and command their own factions—will be best able to make the commitments that enable them to participate in and perpetuate cooperative endeavors. Second, I argue that autonomy is determined primarily by internal factors. And, third, I indicate that insofar as the initiation and maintenance of cartels entails a continuous process of bargaining, it will be best managed by those producers who are able to keep the circle of negotiators small, the rules flexible, and the power to retaliate as strong as possible.[38]

She further explains this argument in the following terms:

the problem of cooperation is really a problem of commitment and credibility. If we presume that cooperation is indeed possible under competition, then we must also recognise that it rests on a delicate balance of perception, promises and threats. If cooperation is ever to emerge, each competitor must convince the other that it is serious, that it will match cooperation with cooperation and defection with defection.[39]

This analysis usefully emphasizes the key role of leading players in a cartel arrangement, in particular as regards their ability to construct, manage, and exercise discipline over an alliance. The individually commanding and authoritative position of such leaders is thus a crucial element in the establishment of an effective order (or, it might even be said, normative system) as a *sine qua non* of any cartel. Typically, in Spar's account, such leaders are companies with an authoritarian and centralized corporate structure, which itself acts as a guarantee of commitment and determination to maintain and enforce such commitment.[40]

Take away this sense of authority, discipline, and commitment and the viability of the cartel is at risk. In legal terms, there are two significant consequential points which will be explored in detail later (in Chapter VIII below). First, there is the issue of the moral and legal responsibility of the cartel leader as a delinquent actor (for instance, for purposes of any legal immunity within a leniency programme, or the calculation of sanctions). Secondly, the issue of the cohesion of the cartel is an important element in the regulatory strategy of offering leniency, since this turns in a large part on the ability to tempt nervous cartel members to break ranks and defy the internal authority of the cartel.

7. Mapping the discussion

In this chapter a number of themes and issues have been identified which will inform the subsequent discussion of the development of legal control of business cartels. In particular, it is important to recognize an ambivalence

[38] Spar, n 5 above, 218–19.   [39] Ibid., 15.

[40] Ibid., 15–20. Cf. Conley and O'Barr's analysis of the role of Archer Daniels Midland in the *Lysine Cartel*: J M Conley and W M O'Barr, 'Crime and Custom in Corporate Society: A Cultural Perspective on Corporate Misconduct' (1997) 60 *Law and Contemporary Problems* 5.

of attitude on the matter, associated with complexities of both economic and legal argument. In summary, at this stage a number of key issues of argument and enquiry may be listed as points which will provide some shape and direction in the more detailed examination of the subject to come:

- different perceptions of the operation of business cartels: historically, American condemnation versus European agnosticism;
- economic argument relating to the anti-competitive character of cartel activity;
- the market context of cartel activity;
- consequent difficulties of legal definition;
- the culture of participation in cartels and contrasting views of cartel behaviour from within and from the outside;
- the perception of the cartel as a form of business delinquency and the respective roles of corporate and individual actors in a system of legal control.

II

Models of Legal Control:
North America and Europe[1]

1. Atlantic crossing: the usual suspects, but differing perceptions and models of legal control

A comparative study of the evolving legal control of business cartels will quickly reveal a significant and intriguing difference in approach and policy as between the two historically important sites of legal activity, North America and Europe. This is a difference which is important for purposes of appreciating the present 'global' legal position, since any regulation now of cartels which have an international scope will necessarily engage with the historical tension between these two main legal models. Moreover, if there was at the close of the twentieth century some sense of a convergence between these two approaches, an understanding of any such process of *rapprochement* will require some insight into the earlier emergence of different policies and modes of control. Also, this aspect of the subject gains further significance from the empirical observation that the subject matter of this legal control—the cartels themselves—have not differed so markedly in their character or operation in different countries and jurisdictions. This perception has become more marked as major cartels have acquired an increasingly international dimension and participation, and evidently shared characteristics across national boundaries. In this way, the relative homogeneity of the subject matter but dichotomy of legal response becomes all the more striking. The point is made forcefully

---

[1] The argument and presentation of material in this chapter draws to some extent on Christopher Harding, 'Business Cartels as a Criminal Activity: Reconciling North American and European Models of Regulation' (2002) 9 *Maastricht Journal of European and Comparative Law* 393.

in the following recent observation by a US Department of Justice (DOJ) official that:

we are often asked by defense counsel to treat a certain member of a cartel more favorably because he/she resides in a country where cartel activity is treated differently than it is in the United States. The fundamental problem with this argument is that it is our experience, without exception, that the conspirators are fully aware that they are violating the law in the United States and elsewhere, and their only concern is avoiding detection. The international cartels that we have cracked have *not* involved international business persons who for cultural, linguistic or some other innocent reason find themselves mistakenly engrossed in a violation of US antitrust laws.[2]

Thus it has (historically at least) been a case of the usual suspects engaging in the usual business,[3] but the latter has been viewed differently by law-makers, lawyers, and regulators on different sides of the Atlantic.

From the legal standpoint, these different approaches to regulation are crucial, and indeed supply a major theme of discussion in this work as a whole. On the one hand, the North American approach has been, since the end of the nineteenth century, one of categorical censure, embodied then in a clear recourse to criminalization of antitrust violations as a central plank of legal control. Moreover, the significant use of civil liability as well in the American system, allowing for the award of treble damages in respect of anti-competitive injury, has also thereby embodied a clear penal element. On the other hand, the general European approach, tellingly employing the vocabulary of 'competition regulation' rather than 'antitrust', has been altogether more tentative, more agnostic and more empirical, giving more weight to economic argument and analysis, and only in recent years moving towards an uncompromising condemnation of cartel activity and testing the possibilities of criminal law regulation. This difference of attitude lies at the heart of the subject, since it informs argument concerning the objectionable nature of the conduct in question. It would thus be helpful at this stage in the discussion to explore and attempt to explain these two principal modes of regulation, and bear this in mind as a frame for the subsequent and more detailed enquiry into the development of the European system of legal control.

[2] Griffin, US Department of Justice, 2000.
[3] See the discussion of the history of the *Dyestuffs Cartel* in Ervin Hexner's work, *International Cartels* (Pitman, 1946), 308–12, which gives some idea of the continuity and common membership of major international cartels.

This comparative treatment also has a significance in a wider and more theoretical context, concerning the epistemology of the subject, which has naturally had a bearing on its classification for purposes of debate and exposition. Much follows from the initial identification of business cartels as criminal or non-criminal phenomena. Viewed as the latter, and consequently lacking a sense of strong moral opprobrium and delinquency, cartels have fallen, in the European context, into the domain of economists and lawyers (though not criminal lawyers), but hardly that of criminologists or sociologists. This may well change in the wake of stronger legal control, embodying a definite vilification of cartels and some moves towards criminalization in *fin-de-siècle* (twentieth/twenty-first century) Europe. But there are in any case some points of particular interest for experts on crime and criminal law in this discussion of dichotomy in legal control. Most importantly, it provides a revealing case study of the construction of delinquent and criminal behaviour in relation to a significant area of economic activity. It is therefore relevant to the general theory of criminal sanctions and their appropriate field of deployment. But it is also in other ways an illuminating aspect of the interdisciplinary relationship between legal and economic or business processes. In particular, the comparison of regulatory models provides a useful springboard for exploration of the ethical (and hence legal) objection to business collusion, from which much of the legal debate naturally arises.

2. Surveying perceptions of the subject: the debate on cartels

One way of gaining an appreciation of the differing North American and European approaches to the regulation of business cartels is to compare statements over a period of time, on the part of both those 'inside' commerce and industry and of informed 'external' commentators. Such illustrative statements may be mapped on a grid which is both temporal (early to late twentieth century) and spatial (different jurisdictions and legal cultures). Necessarily, such a mapping of stated perceptions of the subject will contrast defensive and critical comments on cartel activity, though also should include attempts at achieving a more balanced, middle position. What emerges from such an exercise is a consistent cartel 'apologia' in terms of the benefits of economic stability, and, on the other hand, an equally consistent critical concern in relation to abusive exploitation of economic power.

The benefits arising from cartels as a strategy for market regulation and minimizing the risks of uncertain markets appear as a clear theme in early twentieth-century European argument. Robert Liefmann, writing in the 1920s, commented that 'even if the first incentive towards them is mainly on the side of the business men who have been injured or mulcted through the Peace Treaties or other political events, they are currently accepted by the politicians as one of the best means of overcoming these economic damages and distresses'.[4] Similarly, responding to concerns about the concentration of economic power in cartels, Carl Duisburg, the Chairman of the Board of Directors of I G Farbenindustrie, thus presenting the view from 'inside' German industry, argued that 'these industrial combinations are the consequence of necessity. Doubtless, the underlying idea of their establishment is thoroughly economic, the need to economize'.[5] There were similar arguments presented by British 'industrial' spokesmen. Sir William Larke, representing the steel industry, deplored in 1927 the element of public opinion in the United States which 'lagged behind' the view held in Europe in asserting that industrial combinations worked against the public interest.[6] Lord McGowan of Imperial Chemical Industries (ICI) described cartels as a way of assuring orderly marketing, planned expansion of international trade, elimination of cut-throat prices, and 'all that is admirable and reasonable'.[7] Even in the United States, the philosophy underlying the Sherman Act was not uncontested, such leading legal opinion as that of Oliver Wendel Holmes declaring that that legislation was 'a humbug based on economic ignorance and incompetence'.[8]

On the other side of the debate, as will be seen in the following chapter, even in early twentieth-century European discourse there had been a certain degree of suspicion relating to the exercise of market power through private cartels. The essential economic argument against cartels

---

[4] Robert Liefmann, *International Cartels, Combines and Trusts* (Europa Publishing and George Routledge, 1927; introduction by Charles T Hallinan) 91.

[5] 'Die Verbundenheit der Wirtschaft', *Kölnische Zeitung*, 28 September 1929; English translation in Ervin Hexner, *International Cartels*, n 3 above, 8.

[6] See Hexner, n 3 above, 156.

[7] See Edward S Mason, 'International Commodity Controls; Cartels and Commodity Agreements', in Seymour E Harris (ed), *Economic Reconstruction* (McGraw-Hill, 1945); George W Stocking and Myron W Watkins, *Cartels in Action* (Twentieth Century Fund, 1946), 407–11.

[8] Oliver Wendel Holmes, 'Privilege, Malice and Intent' (1894) 8 *Harvard Law Review* 1.

was summarized in the succinct statement provided by *The Economist* in 1941 that they 'had a bias in favour of easy life, of high profits on low turnover'.[9] But much of the critical argument had a political as well as economic thrust, especially after the experience of fascist convergence of government and industry and state exploitation of cartels in Germany, Italy, and Japan in the 1930s and 1940s. For instance, Feller argued in 1940 that:

it may be naïve to speak of cartelization as a cause of fascism; yet experience has shown it to be a ready instrument of those forces which seek to establish a fascist state... cartelization involves such danger to democratic processes that we may well exclude it as a possible technique.[10]

Certainly a great deal of the American objection to cartels and trusts comprised political principle as much as economic argument, as will be discussed more fully below. In the American context this political objection evolved into a *per se* legal prohibition which put to one side any possibly extenuating economic analysis. By 1940 the US Supreme Court had arrived at a categorical condemnation of cartels in the following terms:

Any combination which tampers with price structures is engaged in an unlawful activity... they would be directly interfering with the free play of market forces. The [Sherman] Act places all such schemes beyond the pale and protects that vital part of our economy against any degree of interference. Congress has not left us with the determination of whether or not particular price fixing schemes are wise or unwise, healthy or destructive.[11]

This view was then reinforced by observation of the political manipulation of the economic power of cartels by fascist regimes in the 1930s and 1940s, as is evident from the 'Roosevelt letter'.[12]

Such divergence of opinion inevitably produced vigorous debate in the European context, leading by the late 1940s to the emergence of what was to become the dominant European approach, one of balancing the pro- and anti-competitive features of cartels by means of a process of examination and market analysis. Writing in 1945 Mason had regretted the

---

[9] *The Economist*, 8 March 1941, 298.

[10] A H Feller, 'Public Policy of Industrial Control', quoted in C J Friedrich and E S Mason (eds), *Public Policy* (Cambridge, 1940).

[11] Douglas J in *United States v Socony-Vacuum Oil Co*, 310 US 150, 221 (1940).

[12] Letter of the President of the United States to the Secretary of State concerning cartel policies, 6 September 1944. *See Appendix 1 to this chapter below.*

apparent polarization of attitude, stating that 'people are either for or against cartels, and very little of the recent literature is devoted to careful description or cool appraisal of cartel activities'.[13] In fact, such a policy of 'cool appraisal' had been announced by the British Government in a White Paper of 1944:

> Such agreements and combines do not necessarily operate against the public interest; but the power to do so is there. The government will therefore seek power to inform themselves of the extent and effect of restrictive agreements, and of the activities of combines; and to take appropriate action to check practices which may bring advantages to sectional producing interests but work to the detriment of the country as a whole.[14]

While this kind of regulatory approach was destined to become the European norm in relation to the general field of anti-competitive activities, highly anti-competitive cartels engaged in such practices as price fixing and market sharing (what would eventually be termed 'hard core cartels') would eventually be castigated as being for practical purposes, though not exactly prohibited *per se*, certainly beyond the pale. Thus by the end of the century, EC Commissioner for Competition, Mario Monti was moved to describe international cartels as 'cancers on the open-market economy'[15] and a leading British commentator on competition law opined that 'if competition policy is about one thing, it is surely about the condemnation of horizontal price-fixing, market-sharing and analogous practices: on both a moral and practical level, there is not a great deal of difference between price-fixing and theft'.[16] By the 1990s there had been established at the European Community level a strong and categorical legal control of 'classic' cartel activity. The cartels themselves had been driven legally underground but were still operating vigorously and were taking every opportunity to challenge the means used to control their activities (see the discussion in Chapters V, VI, and VII below). But by that time, the main activities of business cartels were no longer easily defensible in the European context and the focus of argument had shifted to the means of legal control: *how* rather than *if*.

But if the terms of the public debate have demonstrated something of a transatlantic convergence in the later years of the twentieth century, there probably continues some divergence between the public rhetoric of

---

[13] Mason, n 7 above.   [14] UK Government White Paper, *Employment Policy* (1944) 19.

[15] Opening speech at the Third Nordic Competition Policy Conference, Stockholm, September 2000.

[16] Richard Whish, 'Recent Developments in Community Competition Law, 1998–99' (2000) 25 *European Law Review* 219.

law and policy and a resilient motivation and self-justification within at least some sections of commerce. This is a perception conveyed as long ago as the 1940s by Stocking and Watkins, from their detailed study of the operation of international cartels, but one which supplied a prescient view for the remainder of the century:

A strikingly wide divergence is shown in these case studies between business philosophy and business practice, between business rhetoric and business behavior. In surveying the actual conduct of business, one encounters with less and less frequency evidences of those economic principles and habits of thought which supposedly animate a free private enterprise system. The assumptions of unhindered initiation of productive enterprise, of unobstructed flow of investment into whatever channels promise a differential return so that profit margins are equalized all along the line, of single-minded pre-occupation by enterprisers with cost reduction and sales expansion, and of unmitigated rivalry for patronage—with the humble consumer in the enviable position of the biblical meek—these assumptions are the gist of the folklore by which businessmen keep alive their faith in the current economic system. And their advertising managers, like the king's jesters, do not let them—or us—forget these heart-warming anachronisms...What was once a way of life in the business world is fast becoming a way of rumination—or oratory. If competition is to survive, it must be more than a shibboleth or a slogan. The discrepancy between the truths which men live by—in business—and the truths which they profess but do not live by, is one of the most significant, and disturbing, revelations of this survey.[17]

What is referred to there as the gap between 'philosophy' and 'practice' provides, in the European context, the main theme of the discussion in this work. As will be seen, powerful corporate actors participating in cartels continue to exploit legal procedures and complex economic argument in their resistance to legal surveillance. Moreover, there still appears to be a significant 'cartel culture' in Europe. A press report in 2000, for example, stated that:

Robert Koehler returned to his position as chairman and chief executive of SGL Carbon AG in Germany after the company was fined $135 million in May 1999 for fixing the price of graphite electrodes used in the steel industry. Mr Koehler was personally fined $10 million. But SGL shareholders made no complaints about such enormous losses. They presumably had benefited handsomely from the $1.7 billion in graphite electrode sales in the United States during the five years in which manufacturers conspired.[18]

---

[17] George W Stocking and Myron W Watkins, *Cartels in Action: Case Studies in International Business Diplomacy* (Twentieth Century Fund, 1946) 12–13.

[18] *International Herald Tribune*, 24 October 2000. In contrast, Koehler's American counterpart, Krass, received a 17-month prison term and lost his position.

Despite, therefore, something of a convergence in the global public debates, there is in the European context a continuing ambivalence of attitude which affects the processes of legal control and it will be useful to probe further the origins of such ambivalence.

3. The North American tradition: the delinquency of the business cartel

(a) Part of the American way of life

A key to understanding the underlying philosophy of American antitrust law is an appreciation of the fact that the American objection to concentration of economic power and anti-competitive practice is as much political as economic. While some contemporary opinion, such as that of Oliver Wendel Holmes, castigated the Sherman Act as 'humbug based on economic ignorance',[19] others at that time could more comfortably accept the political imperative which gave rise to the legislation. As Senator Platt of Connecticut observed, it was felt to be necessary 'to get some bill headed: "A Bill to Punish Trusts" with which to go to the Country'.[20] By the later 1880s both major political parties in the United States were committed to a programme of strong legal control of 'trusts' (what would now for practical purposes be termed producer cartels), responding to an evident public distrust and fear of the power of manufacturing corporations. In the words of another contemporary observer: 'the social atmosphere seems to be surcharged with an indefinite, but almost inexpressible fear of trusts.'[21] As Hofstadter commented about the policy of President Theodore Roosevelt:

He saw the trust problem as something which must be dealt with on the political level; public concern about it was too urgent to be ignored. He understood how important it was to assure the public that the government of the United States had the will and the power to assert its authority over large corporations. Accordingly, his antitrust prosecutions, although few, were in some cases appropriately spectacular.[22]

---

[19] See n 8 above.

[20] Quoted in Hans B Thorelli, *Federal Antitrust Policy* (John Hopkins Press, 1955) 198.

[21] George Gunton, 'The Economic and Social Aspects of Trusts' (1888) 3 *Political Science Quarterly* 385.

[22] Richard Hofstadter, 'What Happened to the Antitrust Movement?' in E Thomas Sullivan (ed), *The Political Economy of the Sherman Act* (Oxford University Press, 1991), 20 at 26.

Thus, in stark contrast to the European experience, antitrust in the United States should be seen as a matter of political principle. Timberg, for instance, has commented that 'the Sherman Act is more than a theorem in law and economics; it is also a proposition in social psychology and constitutional law', arising from 'a strong and continuing current of opposition to all forms of concentrated power—political as well as economic'.[23] The origins of such a doctrinal stance should be sought in the popular experience of North American social and economic development, containing a potent amalgam of frontier exploration, individual initiative, economic opportunity, and democracy. Thus Hofstadter has argued:

The antitrust movement and its legislation are characteristically American...In America competition was more than a theory: it was a way of life and a creed. From its colonial beginnings through most of the nineteenth century, ours was overwhelmingly a nation of farmers and small-town entrepreneurs—ambitious, mobile, optimistic, speculative, anti-authoritarian, egalitarian, and competitive. As time went on, Americans came to take it for granted that property would be widely diffused, that economic and political power would be decentralized.[24]

Such nineteenth-century political battle-lines, formed around the resistance to centralizing political and economic tendencies during the later years of the century, were evident on the Western frontier. Brown, for instance, has spoken of 'antagonistic social forces aligned against each other' in a 'Western Civil War of Incorporation':

On one side of that war—whose venues were the gun battles, riots and lynchings of the cattle ranges, mining camps, mill towns, logging shows, wheat fields and urban metropolises of the West—was the conservative consolidating authority of capital spearheaded by the corporate forces of industry, finance, business and land enclosure. On the other side were the dissident—often outlaw—forces of violent resistance to the trend that was...incorporating all of America, not just the West, into a society dominated by the conservative forces of property.[25]

---

[23] Sigmund Timberg, Report on the United States, 403 *et seq* in W Friedmann (ed), *Anti-Trust Laws: A Comparative Symposium* (Stevens, 1956) 404.

[24] Richard Hofstadter, 'What Happened to the Antitrust Movement?', in Sullivan (ed), n 22 above, 20. Similarly, David Millon and Rudolph J Peritz in contributions to the same collection stress the 'political' value of individual liberty in the genesis of policy underlying the Sherman Act. Thorelli argues that Sherman and many of his colleagues in Congress saw the Sherman Act as 'an important means for achieving freedom from corruption and maintaining freedom of independent thinking in political life': *Federal Antitrust Policy*, n 20 above, 227.

[25] Richard Maxwell Brown, 'Desperadoes and Lawmen: The Folk Hero', ch 15 in Craig L LaMay and Everette E Dennis (eds), *The Culture of Crime* (Transaction Publishers, 1995).

(In fact, that political confrontation informs a good deal of 'revisonist' cinema depicting that period: see in particular Robert Altman's *McCabe and Mrs Miller* (1971), Sam Pekinpah's *Pat Garrett and Billy the Kid* (1973), and Michael Cimino's *Heaven's Gate* (1980).) All of this is important context for an understanding of the emergence of American antitrust philosophy: in its most dramatic terms, a battleground of political interests, with farmers and small businessmen on one side and 'trusts' in the consumer goods industries, encouraged by 'Eastern' financiers, on the other side. But all of this was representative of a deeply embedded attitude. As Letwin has commented: 'Hatred of monopoly is one of the oldest American political habits and like most profound traditions, it consisted of an essentially permanent idea expressed at different times.'[26]

The immediate and more precise antecedents of the Sherman Act have provoked debate, as to whether the objectives were purely political or a mix of political and economic goals.[27] But the longer-term outcome is not open to doubt: an enduring political, then legal resolve to keep in check the exercise of overweening corporate power. In more precise legal terms, from the end of the nineteenth century there was both strict legal control and correspondingly the disappearance of cartel activity as a visible and legitimate commercial enterprise. Price-fixing cartels and the like were strictly outlawed and so, in so far as they continued to operate, were driven underground by the threat of prosecution and sanctions.[28] It seems to have been the clear legislative intention in 1890 to ban all price fixing and market-sharing cartels, since proposed amendments to allow cartels which were set up to deal with overproduction and market depression, or to allow price fixing which was 'just and reasonable and fair', were not adopted.[29]

---

[26] William L Letwin, 'Congress and the Sherman Act: 1887–1890' (1956) 23 *University of Chicago Law Review* 221.

[27] See, for instance, Sullivan, Preface to *Political Economy of the Sherman Act*, n 22 above; H Thorelli, *The Federal Antitrust Policy: Origination of an American Tradition* (John Hopkins Press, 1955); George J Stigler, 'The Origins of the Sherman Act', in Sullivan (ed), n 22 above, 32; Robert H Bork, 'Legislative Intent and the Policy of the Sherman Act', in Sullivan (ed), n 22 above, 39; Robert H Lande, 'Wealth Transfers as the Original and Primary Concern of Antitrust: The Efficiency Interpretation Challenged', in Sullivan (ed), n 22 above, 71. See also Rudolph J R Peritz, *Competition Policy in America 1888–1992: History, Rhetoric, Law* (Oxford University Press, 1992).

[28] See Hexner, n 3 above, 308 et seq to this chapter below, relating to the *Dysetuffs Cartel*: possible American participation in the European cartel was subject to Congressional investigation, and for their part the cartel members expressly excluded the American market from their agreements.

[29] See Robert H Bork, 'Legislative Intent and the Policy of the Sherman Act', in Sullivan (ed), n 22 above, 52–5.

Subsequent enforcement of the Sherman Act then identified collusive, cartel-like behaviour as the 'classic' antitrust offence. This evolution of legal enforcement is conveniently conveyed by Posner in the following terms:

by 1898 the Supreme Court had firmly established the principle, immensely important to the development of a sound antitrust policy, that cartels and other price fixing agreements were illegal regardless of the 'reasonableness' of the price fixed...the Court decided that collusive pricing was inefficient and should be forbidden; the reasonable price was the competitive price...by 1940, when the Supreme Court uttered its definitive statement of the rule against price fixing in the *Madison Oil* case, the requirement of demonstrating a probable impact on the market price had disappeared. The offense was no longer the charging of a monopoly price—it was the *attempt* to charge a monopoly price; and no evidence that the defendants were likely to succeed in their attempt was required. The rule against price fixing had become a part of the law of conspiracy instead of a part of the law of monopoly.[30]

This emphasizes a fundamental difference in European and American approaches to the legal and economic regulation which should help in understanding later twentieth-century attitudes to the subject. In 1945 there would have been, on the one hand, a collective European memory of open, significant, and frequently encouraged cartelization. For an American at that date, however, it would not have been possible to take such a retrospective view, embodying for instance a sanguine profile and statistical analysis of cartel activity. Rather, the subject would have been material for a crime survey.

(b) The crime model

American antitrust law thus represents a strong mindset of political culture: a distrust of concentration of power (in an economic context, of powerful corporate actors) and an instinctive, individualistic protection of the 'small guy' (typically the farmer and the small retailer). Such a cultural production of heroes and villains can help to explain the emergence of a system of regulation which cast economic behaviour in *morally unambiguous terms* and favoured therefore a *judicial scheme* of implementation. An important point to take on board is that the *political* condemnation of collusive anti-competitive

---

[30] Richard A Posner, *Antitrust Law: An Economic Perspective* (University of Chicago Press, 1976) 24–5. For the judgments referred to, see *United States v Trans-Missouri Freight Association*, 166 U.S. 290 (1897); *United States v Socony-Vacuum Oil Co.*, 310 U.S. 150 (1940).

behaviour pushed aside more ambiguous and complicated economic assessments and allowed for a relatively straightforward process of using evidence and imposing sanctions. In short, it led to the deployment of criminal law and a strong sense of antitrust offending.

From a comparative perspective, the method of legal control of anti-competitive collusion embodied in the Sherman Act has a number of key characteristics. In the first place, as the term 'antitrust' itself might suggest, it is *proscriptive* and *negative*. Certain behaviour is identified as illegal in principle and thus subject to a prohibition, supported by criminal sanctions. Unlike the European approach, this is a strategy unhindered by tentative argument or complex evidentiary issues. This sense of moral certainty underlying the prohibition has been reinforced in the subsequent jurisprudence of the US Supreme Court, working towards a presumption of collusion from certain market behaviour, and showing an unwillingness to allow economic justification (e.g. market recession) in defence. In shorthand, there is a *per se* condemnation.[31]

Secondly, this is an approach inspired by political sentiments of individualism and egalitarianism. Considerations of economic rationality or efficiency (despite the later efforts of the Chicago School) do not drive such a programme. Economists have continued to question the *economic logic* of the Sherman Act, even granted a need to protect small business or prevent abuses of political power.[32] But the working of the American antitrust system remains the province of lawyers.

Thirdly, despite the categorical nature of its prohibition, the American legislation is actually selective in its application, exempting some sectors of commercial activity, in particular agriculture, public utilities, the production of strategic material, the retail trade, and professional activities. In fact, the commercial target of American antitrust law has been predominantly manufacturing industry and wholesale trading. But this is in accordance with the original political impulses, as Allen observed:

The price support schemes for agriculture and the legal defence accorded to RPM accord ill with the deference paid by the law to competition in manufacturing and wholesale trade. An explanation of the paradox is not hard to find. The policies just mentioned as exceptional rest primarily on a desire to support the 'little man', especially the farmer and the small retailer. Thus, American opinion is not concerned simply with sustaining competition because it is believed to provide a

---

[31] See A D Neale, *The Antitrust Laws of the USA* (2nd edn, Cambridge University Press, 1970); Sullivan (ed), n 22 above.   [32] See, e.g., Posner, n 30 above.

necessary stimulus to efficiency and progress. It also insists that efforts should be made to preserve a large number of independent business units, because these are believed to be socially and politically desirable.[33]

As noted already in Chapter I above, context is important and much may depend on considerations of public interest and other aspects of policy. In the international arena, for example, the producer cartel that evolved into OPEC has not been the subject of such legal control, and the same is true of a number of international cartels based on so-called 'commodity agreements'.

Finally, the application of American antitrust law has been both presumptive and legalistic. The Sherman Act identifies anti-competitive collusion in clear terms as an illegal and criminal activity. As a consequence of this 'dogmatic' approach, companies engaged in determined and conscious collusion, aware of its own manifest illegality, have been driven 'underground', and this additional element of furtive behaviour has in effect increased the element of criminality, by adding a dimension of contumacious 'antitrust awareness'. This produces a 'spiral' of delinquency, since it is not simply the anti-competitive behaviour in itself but also the determination to defy the prohibition and take steps to avoid detection which contributes to a heightened perception of delinquent behaviour. The important point underlying this observation relates to *the legalistic emphasis on the way power is being used rather than a concern with measuring economic performance* (often seen as a primary objective of competition law in the European sense of the term). Under such a system, what is being mainly prosecuted is a 'bad attitude'. As Allen has commented, in relation to the well-known *Alcoa* judgment,[34] what was being addressed in particular was the aggressive nature of the company's behaviour. But this may raise problems from the perspective of economic analysis:

These are nice questions for lawyers, but to the layman it does not seem easy to distinguish between aggressive behaviour (when unaccompanied by restrictive practices) and ordinary successful competition. Both leave diminished opportunities for other firms or new-comers.[35]

This once more serves to emphasize the different outcomes associated with a politically inspired legalistic analysis on the one hand and, on the other hand, an evaluation in economic terms.

[33] G C Allen, *Monopoly and Restrictive Practices* (George Allen and Unwin, 1968) 135.
[34] *US v Aluminium Company of America (ALCOA)*, 148 F. 2d 416 92d Cir. (1945).
[35] Allen, n 33 above, 140.

4. The European experience: a culture of toleration

In contrast to the American position, the European regulation of business cartels has been achieved only gradually and to the accompaniment of a good deal of debate during the course of the twentieth century. From a European perspective the Sherman Act appeared for a long time both a precipitate and controversial event. The European approach has been, and to an extent remains, agnostic, involving both a greater moral toleration and a greater willingness to consider economic argument in favour of cartel activity. The energy of EC-led 'prosecution' of cartels during the last 30 years has tended to obscure this underlying ambivalence of attitude, which still tends to inform some legal and commercial opinion.[36]

The evolution of European regulation of cartels may be traced through three main phases of legal development.

During the later part of the nineteenth century and the first half of the twentieth century manufacturing cartels were a common feature of commercial life in a number of European countries (in central Europe in particular, less so in Britain).[37] As a matter of economic and legal policy, they were for the most part tolerated or even sometimes encouraged in most European countries. Admittedly, there was always a certain amount of debate regarding their economic consequences[38] and, especially in Germany in the 1920s, some moves towards legal regulation.[39] But there was little support, before the 1930s, for the view that they were so harmful in either their economic or political aspects, that they should be outlawed. However, the encouragement, and then direction of cartels by totalitarian governments in Germany[40] and elsewhere in Europe during the later 1930s and the early 1940s inevitably led to a greater polarization of argument.

In the aftermath of the Second World War, the economic and political context had changed radically. In economic terms, the fact that so much had to be rebuilt meant that many of the earlier assumptions underlying the international trading system were now open to question. In political

---

[36] See in particular the discussion in Chapters VI and VII below.

[37] See the more detailed discussion in Chapter III below.

[38] See e.g. Hexner, n 3 above; Edward S Mason, *Economic Concentration and the Monopoly Problem* (Harvard University Press, 1957); David Gerber, *Law and Competition in Twentieth Century Europe: Protecting Prometheus* (Clarendon Press, 1998), chs 4 and 5.

[39] Gerber, n 38 above, ch 5.

[40] See Albert Schweitzer, *Big Business in the Third Reich* (Eyre and Spottiswoode, 1964).

terms, cartel activity—especially that based in Germany—had become discredited through Nazi connections. Overall, opinion shifted sufficiently to favour a degree of legal scrutiny, by means of an administrative procedure comprising a case-by-case evaluation. This approach, which evolved into the characteristic European model of legal control of cartel and other anti-competitive behaviour, was well exemplified in the policy laid down in the British Government White Paper of 1944 referred to above. This triggered the development of public interest criteria for weighing sectional industrial interests against broader consumer interests: the beginnings of what is now described in most legal systems as 'competition law'. The important observation for purposes of the present discussion, however, relates to the method of control: *regulatory rather than confrontational, administrative rather than judicial, employing economic rather than moral evaluation.*

The third main phase coincided with the establishment of the European Economic Community in the late 1950s and the consequent need to protect legally the setting up and operation of a common or single European market. At that level, there was a further dimension to the regulation of competition: the complementary role of ensuring that the single market was not jeopardized by 'private' division resulting from market sharing arrangements and other strategies commonly employed by commercial cartels. Thus the threat posed to the newly established common market by strong European business cartels brought the latter within the regulatory firing line at the European level and served to turn economic argument against such collaborative arrangements. Market sharing, export bans, and like devices were anathema to the single market and as such transformed cartel activity into a 'classic' infringement of Article 85 (now Article 81) of the EC Treaty, subject to increasingly rigorous enforcement. This was not strictly speaking a criminalization, since the EC had no competence to employ such sanctions, but the regulation of cartels by the EC Commission evolved into a tough system of enforcement, in some respects suggestive of a criminal proceeding.

But there remains a qualitatitive difference between this European framework of legal control and that established under the Sherman Act in the United States. This is perhaps best expressed as a difference in moral perception since, despite a now widespread recognition of an illicit profit motive in activities such as price fixing and market sharing, cartel participants have been rarely (at least until very recently) cast as criminal conspirators. But while the American commitment to protection of the 'small guy' and suspicion of concentrated power is a well-accepted cultural phenomenon, this contrasting European toleration of collusive activity appears to have received less attention.

An understanding of the difference should be sought in the longer-term history of political and economic practice. What may be of significance in this regard is the prominence in European history, over several centuries, of trading combinations and a perception of their value for economic and political development. In short, there has been a powerful European tradition of both trading co-operation and economic monopoly. As Braudel has commented, in his historical overview of the emergence of capitalism in Europe, 'peaceful co-existence would have to be the rule... capitalist rivalries always admit a degree of complicity, even between determined adversaries'.[41] Brief reference may be made, for instance, to the medieval guilds and especially the emergence of the Hanseatic League, which dominated trade in Northern Europe from the thirteenth to the fifteenth centuries. The *Hanse* grew out of the co-operation between groups of Rhenish merchants and comprised an organization of cities and groups of traders, bound together for purposes of defending their mutual trading interests. Subsequently, during the earlier phase of European colonial exploitation, individual traders began to pool their resources in the exploitation of overseas trade through the establishment of powerful trading monopolies, notably the various East India Companies: the English East India Company (1600), the Dutch *Vereenigde Oost-Indische Compagnie* (1602), the French *Compagnie des Indes Orientales* (1664), and the Hudson's Bay Company (1670). Moreover, it may be possible to regard the whole European venture of colonial expansion, involving the acquisition of territory in the Americas, Africa, and parts of Asia and the Pacific, as a huge market sharing operation between a number of sovereign states.

In short, while on the one hand there has been historically a vigorous trading tradition in Europe, and individual traders, cities, and states have competed with each other commercially, they have also co-operated for purposes of conserving market shares and protecting similar interests. Collusion of a certain kind has therefore been well embedded in European culture. Thus, one American observer, commenting on the enforcement of newly established competition law in some European countries in the

---

[41] Fernand Braudel, *Le Temps du Monde / Civilization and Capitalism*, vol III, *The Perspective of the World* (Librairie Armand Colin, 1979; transl. Sian Reynolds, Collins, 1984). See also Philip D Curtin, *Cross-Cultural Trade in World History* (Cambridge University Press, 1984).

1950s, observed that:

price cartels, illegal per se in the United States, have often been disregarded by legislators and enforcements agencies in Europe, despite—or perhaps because of—their being quite common in that part of the world.[42]

Attitudes have changed somewhat over the last 40 years, but within such a perspective the moral censure of collusive business behaviour, certainly as a prerequisite for criminalization,[43] may present a difficult cultural leap.

5. The quest for *mens rea*: differing perceptions of antitrust delinquency

This discussion of the contrasting North American and European legal cultures of regulation of anti-competitive activity may then elucidate the development of models of enforcement of rules against cartels respectively in American and European jurisdictions. On the one hand, a predominantly *political* objection has inspired the deployment of *criminal law and judicial process*, while on the other hand, a primarily *economic* objection has favoured a more careful and *empirical method of regulation*, using *administrative process*. The former approach, based on a clearly conceived moral condemnation, has focused on *conduct*, while the latter approach, derived from a concern with certain market conditions, has focused on *outcome*. This dichotomy may also be related to the difference between 'structural' and 'internal behavioural' or 'process' theories of co-operative phenomena. In this way two alternative lines of explanatory argument may be delineated, as shown in Figure II.1.

A. market structure > regulation of outcomes > empirical
   methodology > administrative control

B. internal characteristics of actors > regulation of conduct or
   behaviour > moral condemnation > offence-based judicial control

---

Figure II.1: Alternative theories of co-operative behaviour

---

[42] Hans B Thorelli, 'Antitrust in Europe: National Policies after 1945' (1959) 26 *University of Chicago Law Rev* 222, at 236.   [43] See the discussion in Chapter IX below.

Reference has already been made in Chapter I above to Deborah Spar's investigation of the 'internal' dynamics of cartel formation, and her argument that co-operation between rivals is not only explicable in terms of market or political structures but also by reference to the internal characteristics of the competing/co-operating actors. Spar refers to structural theories of co-operation, typified by much economic argument or that of 'realist' international relations theory:

Many of the most common and powerful theories of cooperation are grounded squarely in a structural, or systemic, approach. In both economics and international relations, these structural theories treat cooperation as a phenomenon of the broader system in which it occurs. They take the system itself as a unit of analysis and the structure of this system as its ordering or defining characteristic.[44]

But for Spar, on the evidence of her research into the formation of cartels, such an approach does not offer a sufficient explanation: there is an explanatory gap that needs to be addressed, since certain structural features have not always corresponded with collusive behaviour. Spar argues that a deficiency of the structural theories is that they:

are concerned mainly with explaining cooperative *outcomes*. I look, by contrast, for evidence of cooperative *behavior* and paint a picture of cooperation that is intimately connected to the internal characteristics of the competitors involved. Specifically, I argue that particular types of competitors are better equipped to create and maintain cooperation than are others. This is not to suggest that the nature of competitors is the sole or even the most important determinant of cooperation. Rather, it is to argue that internal characteristics help bridge the gap that separates the conditions *conducive* to cooperation from the actual *formation* of a successful cooperative agreement.[45]

If, therefore, the causes of anti-competitive collusion may be sought in both structural aspects of markets *and* the character of market actors, this may help in understanding the emergence of significantly different models of legal control, since such models may focus on one rather than another explanation of collusion. Political and legal culture in the United States steered a perception of collusion that emphasized the autonomous role and conduct of corporate actors within markets. The historically different political and legal culture across Europe favoured a more determinist understanding of collusion as a product of market circumstances. The final result of these two processes has been respectively a preference for criminal law and a penal civil liability in the American context and for

---

[44] Deborah Spar, *The Cooperative Edge: The Internal Politics of International Cartels* (Cornell University Press, 1994) 3–4.   [45] Ibid., 11.

administrative regulation in the European context. This may be put another way in saying that the former model of legal control is concerned with the regulation of delinquency (that is, a form of conduct), whereas the latter is concerned with the regulation of undesirable harm (a form of outcome).[46]

A major theme to be pursued in subsequent chapters of this work is the tracing of the shift in Europe towards a more delinquency-oriented approach to the regulation of business cartels. As will be seen, by the closing years of the twentieth century it had certainly become possible to talk in terms of an EC competition or cartel 'offence' (though in legal terms an 'administrative' rather than 'criminal law' offence) and in this way European law was searching for a sense of delinquency in the activity in question. This quest for *mens rea* is an important part of this study and it explains for instance something of the difference between the still administrative EC 'offence' of violating Article 81 of the EC Treaty and the newly emergent national criminal offences of engaging in cartel conduct (compare the discussion in Chapter VI and Chapter IX below). Arguably, these different kinds of offence may also be seen as reflecting different senses of delinquency, perhaps best summed up in the idea of a 'conduct-oriented delinquency' on the one hand, and an 'outcome-oriented delinquency' on the other hand.

(a) 'Conduct-oriented' antitrust: the cartel as a conspiracy

A reading of the Sherman Act and its judicial interpretation will reveal that the focus of the American regulation of cartels has been their *collusive* character. The element of conspiracy has provided the ground for censure, so leading to an emphasis on conduct and attitude—or more exactly, bad attitude. This point is illustrated by Sullivan:

The statutory phrase 'contract, combination or conspiracy', conjures up the classic image of robber barons gathering clandestinely to carve up a market. The statute, classically conceived, aims at bad conduct, at conspirators who deliberately decide on evil, who eschew competition, who plan and execute action to strike market forces and who, conscious of their own wrongdoing, take precautions to hide their own conduct or disguise it.[47]

---

[46] It is tempting of course to draw some analogy with earlier criminological argument concerning the causes of criminal behaviour and the determinist challenge to the idea of the responsible autonomous criminal actor: see in particular Barbara Wootton, *Crime and the Criminal Law: Reflections of a Magistrate and Social Scientist* (Stevens, 1963), and H L A Hart, *Punishment and Responsibility: Essays in the Philosophy of Law* (Clarendon Press, 1968), ch 7.

[47] Sullivan, n 22 above, 311.

Former Attorney-General Robert Kennedy argued in a similar way:

We are talking about clear-cut questions of right and wrong. I view the business-man who engages in such conspiracies in the same light as I regard the racketeer who siphons off money from the public in crooked gambling...A conspiracy to fix prices or rig bids is simply economic racketeering and the persons involved should be subject to as severe punishment as the courts deem appropriate.[48]

The legal outcome of applying the 'bad actor' theory are further spelt out by Sullivan in discussing the approach taken by American antitrust law:

It is also manageable; courts and juries are used to conduct standards, to deciding whether arrangements are consensual or not, to deciding whether or not defend-ants, having a range of choices open to them, have elected for their own gain to strike out on a forbidden course which adversely affects the public. This approach integrates nicely with the criminal character of the statute.[49]

This last statement conveys very well the core sense of the *mens rea* of the criminal antitrust offence, by capturing the idea of deliberate, planned, and conspiratorial discussion, carried out with a clear awareness of its illegal nature. In terms of models of legal control, there may be seen to be some clear advantages in this approach. In the first place, it is squarely founded on a process of moral censure, clarifying the justifica-tion for legal liability. Then, secondly, proof of the prohibited conduct is largely a matter of establishing collusion, which in legal terms is a cleaner process than argument concerning economic justification, and becomes complicated only when it is sought to rely on circumstantial evidence of non-competitive behaviour (see the discussion in Chapter VI below). In this way, the primary process of legal control[50] (apart perhaps from some aspects of the decision about sanctions) avoids more intractable issues of anti-competitive injury by assuming that the subject matter of the collu-sion amounts in itself to an unacceptable injury. The target of regulation for purposes of criminal law is the anti-competitive will. Anti-competitive results then fall to be dealt with by other legal processes, such as claims for compensation or injunctive relief.

---

[48] Quoted in Gordon B Spivack, 'The System of Enforcement' in BIICL, *Comparative Aspects of Anti-Trust Law in the US, the UK and the EEC* (BIICL, 1963) 45.

[49] Sullivan, n 22 above, 320.

[50] This argument is of course based on an assumption that the *primary* process of legal control is an enforcement of the prohibition of anti-competitive conduct, either by means of criminal law or administrative regulation.

(b) 'Outcome-oriented' antitrust: the cartel as an instrument of damage

One of the most striking comparisons between American 'antitrust' law and European 'competition' law is the prevailing method of the latter to analyse matters in terms of market impact rather than the attitude of the actors. As long ago as 1958, Thorelli, writing from an American perspective, observed that it was:

characteristic of European laws that they look to the effect rather than to the intent of restrictive business practices in delineating the grounds for public action.[51]

What is then observable in this approach is the tendency, when the search for some sense of delinquency began, to work backwards from an identified impact on the market in order to delineate the lines of an 'offence'. In other words, the sanctioning process, and more specifically discussion of the amount of penalties, by seeking to reflect the extent of market damage, supplied the main substance of offence-definition. Thus the shape of what has emerged as the EC anti-competitive offence may be most readily identified from the statements of the Commission and EC courts regarding the amount of fines as a reflection of the seriousness of the offending activity. A summary of this approach may be found in the EC Commission's *Guidelines on the Method of Setting Fines Imposed Pursuant to Article 15(2) of Regulation 17*,[52] which provides a ranking of the seriousness of 'serious' competition infringements (the 'offences'), indicating the main elements of different levels of seriousness. Three such levels are listed: *minor infringements*: 'vertical' restrictions, with limited market impact, affecting a relatively limited part of the EC market; *serious infringements*: 'horizontal' and 'vertical' restrictions, more rigorously applied, with wider market impact and affecting extensive areas of the EC market; and *very serious infringements*: 'horizontal' restrictions, particularly cartels, jeopardizing the operation of the single market, especially those resulting in the partitioning of national markets.

Two points in particular may be noted in this process of ranking. First, there is the clear preoccupation with damage to the market and, in the

---

[51] Thorelli, n 42 above, 234.

[52] Commission of the EC, *Guidelines on the Method of Setting Fines Imposed Pursuant to Article 15(2) of Regulation 17*, OJ 1998, C 9/3.

case of more serious offending, the way in which the integrity of the single European market may be jeopardized. There is little explicit reference to 'bad attitude' elements which appear so prominently in the American rules. Secondly, combining a reading of these guidelines with the Commission's ('sentencing') practice in fixing the amount of fines, suggests that market impact considerations are used to establish what may be termed the *cardinal* or 'base' points on a 'sentencing tariff'. At this first stage of determining offence gravity the factors commonly taken into account are duration of the infringement, the extent of the market affected, the market turnover of the parties and their share of the market, and the nature of the restrictive practice. What may be termed attitudinal factors—in particular, organized collusion, furtiveness and secrecy, 'antitrust awareness' and recidivism—tend to make their appearance as aggravating factors, or *ordinal* points, which may be moved up and down the tariff, within a range determined by the 'base gravity' worked out from market impact. (Moreover, in the appellate judgments of the Court of Justice and Court of First Instance, it is difficult to detect any *tone* of censure in relation to clearly illegal and even recidivist cartel activity.) There is a more detailed account and further discussion in Chapter IX below of this 'sentencing' activity.

Thus in the EC context, in so far as there has been some discussion of the seriousness of cartel offending, it tends to read like an exercise in quantification, with an emphasis on recovering competitive damage. As an 'outcome-oriented offence' it tends to be based on a backward-looking economic calculation, rather than moving forward, as a process of moral assessment, from a bad intention.

6. The dilemma for European cartel regulation: which model?

It is clear that, purely as a matter of legal technique, a number of models for the regulation of business cartels may be available. The list on the menu conveys a spectrum of options, ranging from criminalization, through the use of civil liability, to various administrative processes, the latter including for instance more repressive penal strategies but also more benign systems of registration and examination. But by the close of the twentieth century there had emerged a broad international consensus regarding 'hard core' cartels: that these should be outlawed and their prohibition be reinforced by strong sanctions. In this way the American preference for criminalization had now dominated the agenda and it seemed that the American model had been successfully exported. The EC approach was clearly penal, though not 'criminal law', and national jurisdictions in Europe and elsewhere were actively considering the use of criminal sanctions.

Yet at the same time, the conclusion of this chapter, and also a theme of discussion which should inform much of what follows, is that the successful deployment of a particular legal model may require more than simple legislative choice. The historically different preferences of American antitrust law and European competition law are rooted in the experience of political and legal culture. *Effective criminalization* in the European context may also therefore be a matter of public and official attitude, conditioning a willingness and resolve to employ new methods. Most importantly, European policy-makers and lawyers may need to shake themselves free from the mantle of an economics-based and market-oriented approach and acquire some sense of autonomous delinquent behaviour on the part of corporate and individual actors, all of which is encapsulated, in legal terms, in the search for *mens rea* in cartel activity.

Appendix 1

Letter from the President of the United States to the Secretary of State concerning cartel policies, 6 September 1944: Kilgore Committee, *Mobilization Hearings*, Part 16, 2038:

September 6, 1944

To the Secretary of State:

Dear Mr. Secretary: During the past half century the United States has developed a tradition in opposition to private monopolies. The Sherman and Clayton Acts have become as much a part of the American way of life as the due-process clause of the Constitution. By protecting the consumer against monopoly these statutes guarantee him the benefits of competition.

This policy goes hand in glove with the liberal principles of international trade for which you have stood through many years of public service. The trading agreement program has as its objective the elimination of barriers to the free flow of trade in international commerce; the antitrust statutes aim at the elimination of monopolistic restraints of trade in interstate and foreign commerce.

Unfortunately, a number of foreign countries, particularly in continental Europe, do not possess such a tradition against cartels. On the contrary, cartels have received encouragement from some of these governments. Especially is this true with respect to Germany. Moreover, cartels were utilized by the Nazis as governmental instrumentalities to achieve political ends. The history of the use of the I. G. Farben trust by the Nazis reads like a detective story. Defeat of the Nazi armies will have to be followed by the eradication of these weapons of economic warfare. But more than elimination of the political activities of German cartels will be required. Cartel practices which restrict the free flow of goods in foreign commerce will have to be curbed. With international trade involved, this end can be achieved only through collaborative action by the United Nations.

I hope that you will keep your eyes on this whole subject of international cartels, because we are approaching the time when discussions will almost certainly arise between us and other nations.

Very sincerely yours,
FRANKLIN D. ROOSEVELT.

III

Cartels in Europe, 1870–1945:
Das Kartellproblem

1. The centrality of the German experience: the 'land of cartels'

Any discussion of the emergence of business cartels in Europe during the modern period—or more exactly in the second part of the nineteenth and the earlier twentieth centuries—requires an appreciation of the central role of German experience in this respect. Certainly up to the time of the First World War, cartelization within Europe was a special feature of German economy and society. Both economic and political circumstances (rapid industrialization, a concentration of heavy industry, unification of the German state, and a determined and energetic sense of nationhood) combined to render the appearance of cartels a pre-eminently German phenomenon. In turn, this led to a distinctively German preoccupation with and discussion of the subject which was later to transform into a kind of intellectual leadership in responding to cartelization in a European context.[1] At the same time that opinion and law in the United States was turning decisively against business trusts in major industries, the newly unified German state was confronted with an analogous process of industrial combination and collusion, but the reaction was significantly different in many respects: a positive perception that was only gradually qualified by a sense of disquiet regarding the impact of concentrated economic power. Although business cartels were by no means confined to

---

[1] This crucial role of German experience, policy, and regulation is a central theme of David Gerber's work, *Law and Competition in Twentieth Century Europe: Protecting Prometheus* (Oxford University Press, 1998, reprint 2001), the main source for this area of the discussion.

Germany in the period before the Second World War, the focus for economic and subsequently legal policy was very much the German market.

The theme of this discussion is well encapsulated in the observation offered some 30 years ago by Landes, who commented that:

Cartels for the control of prices and output—an institution that went back to the seventeenth century and beyond...—began to multiply, especially after periods of prolonged or severe depression. Characteristically they were found in industries like coal, iron, or chemicals, where homogeneity of product facilitated the specification of quotas and prices, and where lumpy capital requirements yielded important economies of scale, the number of competing units was consequently small, and entry was difficult. They were most numerous and effective in Germany, where entrepreneurial psychology, the structure of industry, legal institutions... and tariff protection against interlopers all combined to promote agreements in restraint of trade.[2]

In addressing the question 'why Germany in particular?' a number of illuminating factors may thus be listed for the structuring of a more general discussion:

- broad economic trends (for instance, industrialization, economic downturn, and over-production);
- types of market;
- political contexts (for instance, nation-building, national ambition, and protectionism);
- business and regulatory culture.

It should be noted that such elements of economic development and change, political organization and culture are interrelated for purposes of understanding cartelization, and that it may be misleading to ascribe the emergence or vitality of cartels to sole or predominant causes, such as economic downturn or overproduction.[3] A study of the significant cartelization of the German economy during the Wilhelmine period reveals the significant interaction of such factors in the evolution of a 'cartel culture'.

---

[2] David S Landes, *The Unbound Prometheus: Technological Change and Industrial Development in Western Europe from 1750 to the Present* (University of Cambridge Press, 1969) 245.

[3] As Henderson has argued, for example: 'Some economists have argued that cartels are always the offspring of trade depressions. This is not so. Many different factors influenced the formation of cartels and a considerable number were established when trade was booming': W O Henderson, *The Industrial Revolution on the Continent 1800–1914* (Frank Cass, 1967) 59. See also the discussion by Debora Spar, referred to in Chapters I and II above: Debora L Spar, *The Cooperative Edge: The Internal Politics of International Cartels* (Cornell University Press, 1992).

2. Cartels in economic longitude: industrialization and economic downturn

Undoubtedly the particular character of industrialization in Germany during the nineteenth century contributed in significant ways to the appearance of cartels as a distinctive aspect of German business organization in the later years of the century. Although by the end of the century Germany and Britain were perhaps the two leading economic and industrial rivals in Europe, the process of industrial transformation had occurred later in Germany, in the middle years of the century, following German unification and its resulting provision of economic infrastructure for a large new state. But once started, industrialization in Germany was rapid and this had its own consequences. As Gerber has argued: 'the speed and intensity of industrialization in Germany made its concomitant social transformations particularly abrupt' and (relevantly for purposes of the present discussion) 'caused competition to appear particularly menacing'.[4] In economic terms the transformation of Germany into a major industrialized economic power by the earlier years of the twentieth century was impressive. As a simple measure of economic growth, the average annual national income increased from 15,100 million marks in 1871–5 (or 364 marks per head of population) to 47,300 million (716 marks per head) in 1911–13.[5]

But this economic transformation possessed particular market, industrial, and organizational features. It was characterized by the development of heavy industry and related manufacturing and processing industries. In the financial context, German banks were closely involved with the development and emerging form of these industries. In the broader political context, a resurgent sense of national identity and imperial expansion affected industrial opportunities and directions. Finally, the pace of these developments affected perceptions, whether popular or those of the business and political elites. In particular, it should be appreciated that, although the period as a whole was one of remarkable economic growth, there was not necessarily a consistent confidence. Industrialization resulted in some social dislocation and at the same time shorter-term economic downturns undermined earlier expectations and bred a certain feeling of insecurity. An important outcome, in short, was a strong conviction from the 1870s onwards, that the German economy was volatile and potentially

[4] Gerber, n 1 above, 69.   [5] Henderson, n 3 above, 74.

uncontrollable and thus required determined efforts of management and ordering to maintain stability. A number of options presented themselves, ranging through governmental intervention (tariffs providing a classical example) and 'private' industrial self-regulation. Business cartels emerged as a preferred tool of industrial ordering in the face of such uncertainties.

The appearance of the cartel as a means of market ordering and regulation derived from a number of the features of German industrialization described above. The preponderance of homogenous 'heavy industry' and basic manufacturing products in the German markets made the cartel a feasible technique of regulation. Banks favoured cartels as vehicles for their own participation in the expansion of the economy and cartels made sense from the producers' viewpoint in markets which were capital intensive and dependent on new technologies. The Imperial Government also viewed cartels as useful and reliable partners in the furtherance of national industrial and trading policies. Consequently, cartels were not only significant as a matter of economic fact; they were perceived by many to be a natural and sensible arrangement in the context of German industry and markets at that time.[6]

Cartels were not unknown before the economic take-off of the mid-nineteenth century, but their significance from that point was undeniable. Earlier examples of cartelization were the Neckar Salt Union, established in 1828 in Württemberg and Baden, the Prussian alum purchasing syndicate (1836–44), and the Oberlahnstein Association set up in the 1840s to control the sale of pig-iron in Nassau. However, economic downturn in the 1870s, leading to overproduction, triggered the appearance of cartels in a number of heavy and basic manufacturing industries: the Gas-Coal Association (1879), the Potash Syndicate (1881), the Rhenish-Westphalian Coal Syndicate (1893), and the Steelworks Association and two major chemicals cartels (1904).[7] The increasing domination of German industry by cartels is revealed in a few statistics: the number of German cartels rose from four in 1865, to eight in 1875, to 90 in 1885, to 210 in 1890 and nearly 400 in 1905.[8] Moreover, during the 1880s and 1890s, German firms were participating increasingly in international cartel arrangements.

[6] See Gerber, n 1 above, 75–6.

[7] For a good overview of German cartelization in the Wilhelmine period, see Erich Maschke, 'Outline of the History of German Cartels from 1873 to 1914', in F Crouzet et al. (eds), *Essays in European Economic History 1789–1914* (London, 1969) 227.

[8] *Source*: Henderson, n 3 above, 60. A detailed narrative of a major German cartel of the Wilhelmine period is supplied by Henderson in his description of the Rhenish-Westphalian Coal Syndicate.

The process of cartelization in Wilhelmine Germany is summarized by Gerber in the following terms:

The size, power and number of German cartels impressed many observers... Although many of them originally were alliances of smaller firms against industry leaders, by the end of the century they frequently included industry leaders. As a result, they ceased to be primarily 'defensive' institutions designed to protect groups of relatively weak competitors and became powerful economic institutions that often controlled entire industries. They also became more permanent... in the 1890s a second wave of cartelization swept German industry, and by the turn of the century Germany had become known as the 'Land of the Cartels'.[9]

3. Wilhelmine cartels as vehicles for order and stability

While cartelization of the German economy was in itself a significant phenomenon of business life, the contemporary perception within Germany of the emergence of cartels was of equal importance. Broadly speaking, this perception was positive and should be contrasted with the political and moral censure which the American 'trusts' had attracted during much the same period. In the context of Wilhelmine Germany there was a strong conviction that the cartel was an approvable mechanism for assuring market stability and economic order.

As Gerber notes, this benign view of the matter was inextricably linked with an ambivalent and nervous reading of the forces of market competition in late-nineteenth-century Germany:

The intensity and character of German industrialization made competition seem not only an unreliable means of organizing economic life, but a menacing one as well. The exceptionally rapid growth of industry entailed abrupt economic and social disruptions, giving capitalism, competition and the entire process of economic modernization a somewhat demonic air. By the last decades of the century industrialization was seldom perceived as a 'friendly' process, even by those who supported it, and this tarnished images of 'capitalism' and 'competition', which were seen as its progenitors.[10]

Thus despite the clear evidence of economic development (especially from present hindsight), the Wilhelmine business and political community

---

[9] Gerber, n 1 above, 74–5.   [10] Ibid., 71.

reacted very unfavourably to any economic downturn punctuating this period of growth and the perception was dominated by the producers' concerns about overproduction and low profitability.[11] This particular psychological state had important consequences for both economic policy and the evolution of legal regulation, since it elevated market stability and order to the status of an imperative (see Figure III.1). Cartels were for

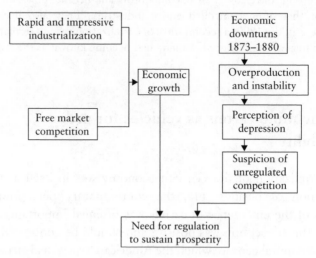

Figure III.1: Success of cartels in the German context

the most part understood as a means to that end, so that the regulatory question was never one of prohibition, but rather one of watching out for any incidental disadvantages. But it is also important to note that cartels, as a technique of regulation, represent a 'private' form of economic self-management and so naturally the preferred approach of a particular sector of the community: producers of primary commodities and the financial institutions to which they were closely linked. The competitive success of the cartel *as a means of regulation* in the German context requires some further consideration.

The popularity in Germany of the cartel as a solution to the problem of market management owes as much to contingent political and cultural factors as to contemporary features of economic development. While the dominance of heavy and manufacturing industry was an important component, this combined with less tangible elements of the German

[11] For a more detailed discussion of the reactions to the 'crash' of 1873, see Henderson, n 3 above, 46 *et seq.*

national psychology. In general terms, this was a matter of emergent German nationhood. More specifically, it resolved itself into aspects of imperial and industrial policy. Two main features may be noted: first, the political usefulness of business cartels from the perspective of the Wilhelmine Imperial Government (inherited later and more significantly by the Nazi regime); secondly, the resonance struck by cartels with a strong corporatist ethos in German society.

German economic policy from the time of unification onwards was characterized by an increasing degree of state involvement. This was associated with a number of factors, most importantly an ambitious nationalism which fed both colonial expansion and the development of military power, but also a range of economic and social policies (such as protective tariffs and welfare provision for workers) which required governmental intervention.[12] There occurred therefore a congruence of imperial and national ambition with concern for social policy which opposed the earlier prevailing 'Manchester' school of economics asserting a reduction of the role of government in economic life.[13] From the point of view of Bismarck's Government, cartels—particularly in the sector of heavy industry—were a conduit for the implementation of both external imperial and internal social welfare policies. An alliance between government and cartels was mutually beneficial in furthering the influence and power of both and served to rehearse the more ominous alliance of government and big business later under the Nazi regime.

A more elusive point concerns the culture of co-operation which was also dominant in late-nineteenth-century Germany. Both emergent nationhood and a need to address social dislocation as an accident of industrialization produced an ethos of community and an imperative of cohesion: in the broader interests of German society, co-operation was preferable to the divisions induced by a very competitive environment. The corporatist features of cartels thus found favour in such a political and moral climate. As Gerber, again, indicates, the philosophical arguments of German historicism could be used to present the (German) business cartel in an ethically favourable light:

The 'ethical' advantages of cartels were often contrasted with American trusts. According to the historical school, cartels encouraged positive ethical attributes such as restraint and honesty in economic conduct and concern for weaker

---

[12] See generally, Henderson, n 3 above, ch 3.
[13] See the sources referred to by Gerber, n 1 above, 81 *et seq*.

competitors. Trusts, on the other hand, were portrayed as naturally rapacious, deceitful and willing to harm not only consumers and competitors but society as a whole.[14]

This favourable economic, political, and ethical vision of the business cartel not surprisingly translated then into legal approval when other doubts began to be expressed about the possible harm which could flow from cartel activity. The important legal test was provided in the *Saxon Wood Pulp Case* decided by the Reichsgericht in 1897.[15] Interestingly the legal challenge in that litigation came not from consumers, but from one of the cartel participants, so that the legal argument was cast very much in terms of horizontal business freedom. The cartel, dominating the regional Saxon wood-pulp market, included a joint selling arrangement which had been breached by one of its members. The latter then challenged the legality of attempts by the cartel to enforce penalties for this infringement, as a violation of the principle of business freedom, as laid down in paragraph 1(1) of the Gewerbeordnung of 1869.

The court's judgment[16] represents one of the first significant and authoritative European analyses of the legality of collusive business behaviour. It combines a use of economic argument with constitutional, public law debate and, although its immediate conclusions were favourable to the operation of cartels, in the longer term it supplied what was to prove an enduring model of regulation in the European context. In one sense, it was an early example of application of the 'rule of reason', weighing the advantages and disadvantages of a course of conduct by reference to its particular context. The court applied the legislation by identifying two major aims of paragraph 1(1): the protection of public welfare, and the protection of individual freedom of trading. Regarding the objective of public welfare, the cartel could be judged as an organizational form which was positive for the economy since it preserved suppliers from ruin and averted the 'catastrophes of overproduction'. This was not, however, a blank cheque since the Reichsgericht accepted that there may be rare occasions when some legal intervention would be justified, for instance to avoid the creation of a monopoly or unfair exploitation of consumers.[17] In relation to the second objective of securing the individual freedom of the traders participating in the cartel, the court considered that this would only be jeopardized if the outcome would be permanent elimination from the

---

[14] Gerber, n 1 above, 88.
[15] See discussion in Gerber, ibid., 91 *et seq*, and also the sources referred to there.
[16] Reichsgericht, Decl. of 4 February 1897, 38 RGZ 155.   [17] Ibid., 158.

market. Thus, while it was accepted that there might be (exceptionally) some risks to both other traders and consumers from the operation of cartels, on balance their impact on the market was seen as being definitely benign. The approach taken here, a largely economic cost–benefit analysis, firmly located in market context, but proceeding from the assumption that the collusion was well-intentioned and likely to be beneficial, was to serve as a template for competition regulation across Europe.[18]

Therefore, only a few years after the Sherman Act categorically outlawed cartel-like activities in the United States as prohibited restraints of trade, the significant legal test in a European context resulted in a 'letter of immunity'. It must be borne in mind, however, that this was an outcome fashioned very much in the context of the German economy and German legal culture at the close of the nineteenth century and substantively very much represented the producers' view of the world.

4. The arguments against cartels and the need for regulation: *das kartellproblem*

While there was a formidable community of pro-cartel interests and actors in Wilhelmine Germany (heavy industry, big agriculture, the government, and many economists), there was nonetheless and to an increasing extent some concern regarding the operation of these powerful business organizations. As noted already in the discussion of the *Saxon Wood Pulp* judgment, at this time the objections were more significantly from a horizontal rather than a vertical source—from other traders rather than consumer interests. In broad terms, the main complaint against cartels related to their desire and ability to maintain prices at a supracompetitive level, especially on the home market. Henderson summarizes the evidence:

In May 1879 Eugen Richter, speaking in the Reichstag, criticised the builders of locomotives and the manufacturers of rails for selling more cheaply abroad than at home. It has been stated that at one time Germans were actually being charged 17 marks a ton for coal that was being sold in Austria at 8 marks a ton. In 1900 the price of wire was 185 marks a ton in Germany but only 115 marks a ton

---

[18] The *Saxon Wood Pulp* judgment remained a key element in much later discussion, for instance in that preceding the enactment of the significant German competition legislation of the 1950s: Franz Böhm, 'Das Reichsgericht und die Kartelle' (1948) 1 *ORDO* 197.

abroad. When trade was slack between 1900 and 1902 the rail cartel sold its products at 250 marks a ton in the home market and at 140 marks a ton abroad.[19]

Clearly this was to the detriment of consumer interests but the objection was articulated through other traders rather than the ultimate consumer. As Gerber notes, in Wilhelmine Germany what would now be termed consumer interests 'had neither a voice nor significant institutional support', since such interests 'seldom acquire definition and force unless democratic institutions provide opportunities for their development'.[20] Gerber identifies the thrust of the complaint as coming from three main groups of traders: immediate purchasers from cartels, sellers to cartels whose own prices were forced down, and small and medium-sized companies who were coerced into cartel membership. Consumers at the end of the line were not commonly identified as such, but rather as 'workers'. As such their interests were mainly represented by the Social Democratic Party, which at that stage tended to adopt an eschatalogical and Marxist view of cartels. In an eschatalogical sense, the cartel was seen as a useful phase of corporatist development which would facilitate the eventual takeover of the economy by the state (as indeed happened during the Nazi period). From a socialist perspective, in so far as cartels promoted stability, this could operate in the workers' interests by ensuring employment, even if the workers paid more for goods as consumers.[21] In the context of German politics, therefore, the main critic of cartel behaviour was the more Catholic Centre party, which represented the interests of small business (*Mittelstand*) as well as workers.[22] Even with the emergence after the First World War of consumer co-operatives who had good reason to criticize cartel pricing policies, there remained a wariness about attacking cartels in the abstract or as a form of organization, since co-operatives themselves possessed a structural similarity to cartels. The longer-term outcome was therefore the idea that any control should be directed at the abuses or excesses resulting from business collusion rather than co-operation in itself.

From the earliest years of the twentieth century there was thus in Germany some agitation for the introduction of legislative control, but it was very slow to bear fruit. The Government agreed to an inquiry into

[19] Henderson, n 3 above, 59–60.   [20] Gerber, n 1 above, 105.   [21] Ibid. 106.

[22] See more generally David Blackbourn, 'The Problem of Democratization: German Catholics and the Role of the Centre Party', in Richard J Evans (ed), *Society and Politics in Wilhelmine Germany* (London, 1978) 160.

cartel activity in 1902, but dragged its heels in implementing the collection of evidence, and a proposal for the establishment of a cartel office in 1908 met with a similar reaction. It was not until the early 1920s, with the advent of severe inflation, that popular feeling and agitation in the Reichstag finally led to what in European terms would prove to be pioneering legislation. The 'Cartel Regulation' of 1923[23] was politically promoted by the new Chancellor, Gustav Stresemann, a representative of *Mittelstand* interests, and the principal draftsman of the legislation was Hans Schäffer, an Economics Ministry civil servant strongly committed to constructive co-operation between government and economy. The important points to note about this legislation concern its focus on the control of abusive exploitation of economic power, by means of administrative supervision—arguably the main template for subsequent European approaches to the control of business cartels. Section 4 of the Regulation enabled the Minister of Economics to take action against cartels which were considered to endanger the economy as a whole or the general welfare (formulated as an abuse of the economic power of the cartel). The Minister had power to require reporting of cartel agreements, authorize the withdrawal of cartel members or ask the newly established Cartel Court to invalidate the cartel agreement. An alternative mechanism for enabling members of the cartel to withdraw was provided in section 8, which gave the Cartel Court jurisdiction to decide if there was 'good cause' for such withdrawal. Section 9 prohibited the use of boycotts and similar devices directed at non-members of a cartel, unless such measures were approved by the President of the Cartel Court. In this scheme, the main initiative lay with the Ministry of Economics and the Cartel Court was a special jurisdiction within the administrative, not the regular judicial system.

This legislation had an active role until about 1929. From that latter date, the advent of severe economic depression led to modifications in the law which reduced the role of the Cartel Court. Subsequently, the emergence of the Nazi regime in 1933 brought about radical legal change through a policy of compulsory cartelization and the incorporation of cartels into the apparatus of the state. But for a period of about six years during the 1920s the Cartel Regulation provided the most significant experience yet of competition regulation in practice in a European context. As such it

---

[23] *Verordnung gegen Missbrauch wirtschaftlicher Machtstellungen* (1923). For an English translation, see Robert Liefmann, *Cartels, Concerns and Trusts* (transl. D H MacGregor, New York, 1932) 351.

attracted a great deal of interest within Germany on the part of both lawyers and academics, but drew less attention outside Germany, where there has been a tendency to regard the law as somewhat ineffective. For instance, Kronstein and Leighton, writing from an American perspective in 1945,[24] were very critical of the 'control' model of regulation typified by German law and so clearly different from the 'prohibition' approach under American law. In almost scathing tones, these authors refer to:

the disposition of 'control' proponents to point repeatedly to the exemplary success of European regulation...historical fact would seem to indicate clearly that the success is only exemplary in terms of a shifting, irresponsible concept of public welfare.[25]

They cite the example of the justification for I G Farben's nitrogen cartel arrangements as enabling sufficient profits to be earned so as to carry out research in oil and rubber. The latter was seen as being of greater 'public interest' to Germany than the position of farmers, the principal nitrogen consumers. Such a critique thus draws upon the concern that an administrative system of control (or a weak judicial system) enables a politicized and partisan view of competition to prevail. But Kronstein and Leighton's argument is also based on an epistemological perception: that the German and European approach to regulation proceeded from a basically favourable view of cartels, which was then reinforced by the dominant position of practising lawyers and economists in the control process. They argue that under the 'control' model, courts of law:

were forced to acquiesce to the able briefs of cartel lawyers, against which the less powerful and less well represented could scarcely prevail. Nor were the courts successful in preventing cartels and combines from applying to their own advantage legal devices originally designed for quite different purposes.[26]

Similarly, Gerber refers to the domination of the contemporary literature on cartels by practising lawyers (often representing the cartel interests), rather than full-time scholars.[27]

In many respects, therefore, it is unsurprising that the Weimar experiment in legal regulation of cartels appeared to be predominantly 'pro-cartel'.

---

[24] Heinrich Kronstein and Gertrude Leighton, 'Cartel Control: A Record of Failure' (1945–46) 55 *Yale Law Journal* 297.   [25] Ibid., 299.

[26] Such as patent and trade mark rights. Ibid., 303.

[27] Gerber, n 1 above, 130–1. This is a significant point about the debate and critical literature on the subject. Arguably, the domination of legal literature by practising lawyers located in the 'industry' rather than the 'regulatory' camp is also a feature of more recent discourse: see the discussion at the end of Chapter VII below.

The initiative lay for the most part with the Ministry of Economics, which preferred to negotiate solutions to any concerns about the exercise of cartel power. The Cartel Court's role was confined in practice to considering the issue of 'internal coercion' of cartel members, on which question it tended to adopt a narrow view of the phenomenon of coercion and to proceed from a benign idea of the cartel as a 'protective community' (*Schutzgemeinschaft*).[28] Critics also point to the fact that the number of cartels increased significantly during this period: although the law was not intended directly to curb the number of cartels, it does not seem either that their profitability and appeal to producers were very much affected by attempts to regulate extreme or abusive cartel conduct.

On the other hand, it has also been urged that the less visible impact of the 'negotiated' control exercised in particular by the Ministry of Economics should not be dismissed too quickly. In fact, a large number of cartel provisions were changed by agreement, leading Gerber to conclude that:

the informal component of the system is likely to have been more effective in modifying cartel conduct than the formal compliance mechanism... The ability of ministry officials to influence cartel conduct in specific cases depended on a wide variety of factors, including the political situation, the power of the cartel involved, its sensitivity to negative publicity, its interest in maintaining the integrity of the informal enforcement system, and the importance of the issues to the cartel members and the economics ministry.[29]

But, as Gerber's own argument admits, in essence this was a discretionary system of control, very much influenced by a basically positive view of the business cartel as an institution, and through its preference for low-visibility negotiated solutions, prone to non-legal considerations. As such, in terms of legal and regulatory culture, it was far removed from the American model.

5. The wider European picture: respectable and necessary or suspect and delinquent organizations?

During the period of 70 years or so preceding the Second World War, it would seem that cartelization as a phenomenon of economic organization

---

[28] Gerber, ibid., 131. See in particular the decisions of the Cartel Court of 15 December 1932 (30 Kartell-Rundschau 106, 114 (No 172), and 15 May 1925 (23 Kartell-Rundschau 348 (No 54).
[29] Gerber, ibid., 136.

and the growing perception of it as problematic was a predominantly central and northern European experience. Undoubtedly Germany was in the forefront regarding both the experience of business cartels and discourse relating to their activities and possible control[30] although, as Gerber stresses, Austria almost took the lead in the discussion of cartels and proposals for legislative control in the 1890s.[31] Historical contingencies relating to the nature of industrialization in central Europe (in particular, the significance of heavy industry in that region) combined with cultural factors (in particular a Germanic predilection for corporate structures) to render the cartel first a popular form, but then, in some respects, a matter of concern.

Before the 1920s, cartels were a much less significant issue for the other major European economic powers, Britain and France. This is not to say that they were absent as a form of business organization—indeed, Britain had a longer history of industrial combination which had been identified earlier by Adam Smith in his classic reference to the tendency of traders to conspire.[32] But in terms of both economics and culture, conditions in those two countries encouraged looser and less formal collusive forms. Landes, for instance, points to the significance in France of the family firm, with its 'attachment to entrepreneurial independence' and the fact that in Britain 'most firms, even nominally public companies, were private in character and independent in behaviour'.[33] The trend, therefore, was towards looser and less visible 'gentleman's agreements'. There were restraints on competition, but they were more subtly embedded in social and cultural attitude, such as the French disapproval of price warfare as something almost morally suspect. In short, for both Britain and France, business combination was a less obvious phenomenon, and as something less formal, not such an appropriate matter for legal control.

Matters changed after the First World War, however, as cartels in some industries became more international in character and at the same time

---

[30] German authors took an almost proprietorial pride in the subject. Arnold Wolfers asserted for instance that 'the cartel movement remained until the World War a specific German and Austrian affair...that is why German scientific research felt itself charged with the task to develop, and elaborate on, a cartel doctrine' (*Das Kartellproblem im Lichte der Deutschen Kartell-literatur*, vol 180, Part 2 (Munich, 1931) 1). The first periodical devoted to cartels, *Kartell-Rundschau*, appeared in Germany in 1903.

[31] Ibid., ch 3, containing an instructive analysis of the upsurge of debate in fin-de-siècle Austria, but 'consigned to virtual obscurity by the cataclysmic end to the Habsburg Empire'.

[32] Adam Smith, *The Wealth of Nations*, Bk I, ch X: 'People of the same trade seldom meet together, even for merriment and diversion, but the conversation ends in a conspiracy against the public, or in some contrivance to raise prices.'   [33] Landes, n 2 above, 245–6.

governments were more willing to intervene in the market and engage in economic regulation. This led to a wider, more international discourse and a dissemination of ideas and arguments regarding the regulation of cartels. By the 1920s there was a growing recognition of the development of transnational cartels. Surveying the subject in 1927, Liefmann traced the earlier origins of international cartelization in the closing years of the nineteenth century through to what he described as a phenomenal emergence of such transnational combinations after the First World War.[34] Interestingly, of the 40 international cartels identified by Liefmann as being in existence by the mid-1890s (predominantly in the chemical and metallurgical industries), virtually all included German partners, the other significant nationalities being Austria, France, Belgium, and Britain. But the international cartels which were constructed during the inter-War period were notable not only for their range and number but also for the extent of their membership and domination of world markets. The Incandescent Lamp Cartel is frequently cited as an example of major inter-War cartelization: originating in the amalgamation of leading Germany companies into Osram, the latter took the initiative in 1925 in constructing a world cartel embracing producers from Britain, France, the Netherlands, Italy, Scandinavia, Hungary, Japan, China, Mexico, Brazil, and Canada and including notable names such as Philips, Siemens, and General Electric (acting through its international subsidiary based in Paris).[35] The contemporary view of these major international cartels is presented for instance by Liefmann, when he commented that:

It was only after the World War that international cartels and trusts acquired *political* significance and their problem was viewed from an entirely new angle. Formerly, perhaps, they were more feared on *economic* grounds: to-day—still speaking generally—they are furthered and approved and for *political* reasons they are viewed as a means of reducing the economic inequalities caused or emphasized by the war, and of minimizing the unfavourable effects of post-war conditions, either on individual States or on the world as a whole... Various leaders of industry in different countries have often recommended international cartels as instruments for overcoming the difficulties of the present economic situation throughout the world.[36]

[34] Robert Liefmann, *International Cartels, Combines and Trusts* (Europa Publishing, 1927) 32 *et seq.*

[35] For a more detailed account, see Ervin Hexner, *International Cartels* (Pitman, 1946) 357–60.

[36] Liefmann, n 34 above, 35–6. See also the material in ch 9 of George W Stocking and Myron W Watkins, *Cartels in Action: Case Studies in International Business Diplomacy* (Twentieth Century Fund, 1946).

Such international cartels have therefore to be regarded in the particular inter-War context of economic and political exigency: coping with the economic aftermath of the First World War, the crisis years of the Great Depression, followed by spiralling political problems during the 1930s. In this context the cartel was often perceived as a device for both constructive international collaboration—the concept of economic rapprochement[37]— and, later, political control of the economy, especially under authoritarian political systems, with the Nazi regime leading the way. The important general point to note is that, as regards cartelization at both the national and international levels, any concerns about their more specific economic consequences were very much tempered by a complex political view of their role which was historically contingent but, during that period, of considerable significance in a European context. This mix of economic and political considerations is evident in both the fledgling instances of legislative control in a number of European countries and in the growing international debate on the subject.

During the 1920s and 1930s a swathe of central and northern European states introduced legislation relating to anti-competitive practices, much of it inspired by the German model (in Gerber's words, 'shaped by the discourse that had developed in Austria and Germany').[38] Swedish legislation of 1925 allowed governmental investigation of cartels regarding the impact of collusive practice on prices and other aspects of competition, but the course of the preceding debates and the success of industrial interests in modifying the strength of the legislative proposals recalls the history of the German legislation. In contrast, the Norwegian Trustlov (Law on Restraints of Competition and Price Abuse)[39] was significantly tougher in its approach, reflecting the power of left-of-centre political coalitions in Norway during that period. In the view of Bernitz, this law stands as the first 'real' competition law of Europe.[40] It established a system of registration of restrictive practices with a Control Office, a body which was independent of government ministries and headed by a senior

---

[37] See, e.g., Eugene Grossman, *Methods of Economic Rapprochement* (C.E.C.P. 24(I), League of Nations Pub. 1926.II.29, 1927).

[38] Gerber, n 1 above, 155. Gerber provides a useful summary of the Swedish and Norwegian law of this period (see 155–9).

[39] A leading authority is Ulf Bernitz, *Marknadsrätt* (Stockholm, 1969). See also Liefmann, n 34 above, 140–6.   [40] Ibid., 394.

judge. The role of the control office was to examine practices and negotiate an informal termination of those considered to be objectionable; but
cases could be sent on to a Control Council, another independent body
which had power to make orders regarding prices and the termination of
cartels. Until its practical demise after the start of the Second World War,
this was an active system of control dealing with some 800 cases and characterized by Gerber as more consistently juridical than the German or
Swedish legislation. It was significant as a less administrative model and
as such would have been known to German experts, though perhaps less
well elsewhere in Europe.

During the 1930s legislation was enacted in a number of other
European countries. The Dutch Law of 1935[41] was closely modelled on the
German Cartel Regulation and the Danish Law of 1937 drew upon the
Norwegian Trustlov. Subsequent memory and experience of the legislation
in Czechoslovakia (1933), Poland (1933), and Yugoslavia (1934) was largely
lost in the political reorientation of those countries and their legal systems
in the period following the Second World War. The Italian Law of 1932,
on the other hand, was an early example of state take-over of cartelization,
enabling the government to establish compulsory cartels when deemed
necessary for the regulation of production and competition. In summary,
then, there was by the later 1930s a growing experience of legislative control of cartels in a number of European national systems; but with the
exception of Norway, the predominant model was that of Germany,
embodying an essentially administrative, discretionary, and (from a later
perspective) cartel-friendly approach.

Equally significant as these legislative developments in the longer-term
evolution of policy were some international debates dealing specifically
with the issue of cartels. In 1927 the League of Nations organized a World
Economic Conference in Geneva. This was a significant policy-debating
and forming event, drawing upon a wide representation of governmental
and private experts and addressing a range of international trade issues.
The detailed study and discussion of cartels provides an important indication of contemporary theorizing and practice on the matter.[42] It is perhaps

---

[41] For a brief account, see P Verloren van Themaat, entry in W Friedmann (ed), *Anti-Trust Laws: A Comparative Symposium* (Stevens, 1955) 258–9.
[42] See Gerber, n 1 above, 159–61; Liefmann, n 34 above, Pt II.

worth quoting in full the outcome of these discussions as embodied in the Geneva Resolutions on Cartels of 24 May 1927:

Geneva Resolutions on Cartels

Adopted May 24, 1927, by the International Economic Conference, with Russia, Turkey, Canada and United States delegations abstaining, also M. Jouhaux (France) personally.

Conference has examined with the keenest interest the question of industrial agreements, which have recently developed and have attracted close attention from those sections of the community whose interests are affected by them, and from the public opinion of the various countries.

The discussion has revealed a certain conflict of views, and has occasioned reservations on the part of the representatives of different interests and countries. In these circumstances, the Conference has recognized that the phenomenon of such agreements, arising from economic necessities, does not constitute a matter upon which any conclusion of principle need be reached, but a development which has to be recognized, and which from this practical point of view must be considered as good or bad according to the spirit which rules the constitution and the operation of the agreements, and in particular according to the measure in which those directing them are actuated by a sense of the general interest.

The Conference considers that the field of operation for agreements, both national and international, is usually limited to branches of production which are already centralized, and to products supplied in bulk or in recognized grades, and that, consequently, they cannot be regarded as a form of organization which could by itself alone remove the causes of the troubles from which the economic life of the world, and particularly Europe, is suffering.

Nevertheless, in certain branches of production they can—subject to certain conditions and reservations—on the one hand, secure a more methodical organization of production and a reduction in costs by means of a better utilization of existing equipment, the development on more suitable lines of new plant, and a more rational grouping of undertakings; and, on the other hand, act as a check on uneconomic competition and reduce the evils resulting from fluctuations in industrial activity.

By this means they may assure to the workers greater stability of employment, and at the same time, by the reduction of production and distribution costs, and consequently selling prices, bring advantages to the consumer. It is generally recognized that in this way agreements may in some cases be useful not only to producers, but also to consumers and the community in general.

Nevertheless, the Conference considers, on the other hand, that such agreements, if they encourage monopolistic tendencies and the application of unsound business methods, may check technical progress in production and involve dangers to the legitimate interests of important sections of society and of particular countries.

It consequently appears to the Conference that it is entirely necessary that agreements should not lead to an artificial rise in prices, which would injure consumers, and that they should give due consideration to the interests of the workers. It is further necessary that they should not, either in intention or effect, restrict the supply to any particular country of raw materials or basic products, or without just cause create unequal conditions between the finishing industries of the consuming and producing countries or other countries situated in the same conditions. Nor must they have for their object or effect any reduction in the economic equipment which any nation considers indispensable, nor should they stereotype the present position of production, whether from the point of view of technical progress or of the distribution of industries among the various countries in accordance with the necessities imposed upon each by its economic development and the growth of its population.

The Conference considered the question whether there was ground for establishing a special juridical regime and a system of supervision over agreements.

The documentation resulting from the labours of the Preparatory Committee shows that specific legislative or administrative measures in this direction have been taken by a limited number of countries only, and that the measures adopted are widely divergent both in conception and form.

The Conference recognized that, so far as regards agreements limited to the producers of a single country, it is for each Government to adopt such measures in regard to their operation as it may think advisable. It agreed, however, that it is not desirable that national legislation should place an obstacle to the attainment of the benefits which agreements might secure by exhibiting a prejudice against them as such.

So far as regards international agreements, it is generally recognized that the establishment of an international juridical regime is impossible in view of the divergencies between the measures which various countries have considered it necessary to take in the matter, and on account of the objections of principle which a number of States would feel on national and constitutional grounds to any such system. It has, moreover, been pointed out that the laws and regulations and the tribunals of each country have jurisdiction not only over national agreements, but also over international agreements in so far as they involve operations within the national territory.

On the other hand, it is desirable that voluntary recourse by parties to agreements to arbitral bodies should become general, subject to guarantees of the high competence of the latter in economic matters and their sense of the general interest.

From a more general standpoint the Conference considers that the League of Nations should closely follow these forms of international industrial co-operation and their effects upon technical progress, the development of production, conditions of labour, the situation as regards supplies, and the movement of prices, seeking in this connection the collaboration of the various Governments. It should collect the relevant data with a view to publishing from time to time such information as may be of general interest. The Conference is of the opinion that the publicity given in regard to the nature and operations of agreements constitutes one of the most effective means, on the one hand, of securing the support of public opinion to agreements which conduce to the general interest, and, on the other hand, of preventing the growth of abuses.

In one sense, the language of the Resolutions broadly anticipates the method later to be adopted under Article 81(3) of the EC Treaty in its attempt to balance the advantages and disadvantages of horizontal trade restrictions. But at the same time, the abstentions are significant. The reservations of the French delegate Jouhaux (that it was impossible 'to approve of cartels without at the same time adopting measures of control and publicity to guard against those dangers which undoubtedly existed, as was proved by the increasing number of complaints to American courts of law')[43] should be set in the context of a feeling that the conference had been largely taken over by government policy-makers and economists. Socialists, for example, complained that the intention of the Council of the League and the Preparatory Committee regarding representation of workers' interest at the conference had been frustrated.[44] The overall outcome of the proceedings was thus tentative in terms of conclusions and recommendations.

In contrast, the conclusions of the 27th Conference of the Interparliamentary Union (IPU) in London in 1930 were more determined. The delegates at this meeting were members of national legislatures, and less obviously representative of governmental and business interests. The specific proposal of the Resolution from the London Conference resonated more with Socialist and Social Democratic positions on cartels and the approach of the Norwegian Trustlov: an independent body in each state (a Committee on Trusts and Cartels) with authority to determine the anti-competitive harm resulting from cartels. In essence, this occasion demonstrated the political origins and provided an international articulation of a more 'juridical' model of control. In so far as the two conferences illustrated divergent approaches to the issue of regulating cartels,[45] they also supplied some template for the discussion which would begin again in the period following the Second World War and the earlier days of formulating a EEC competition policy.

6. The mid-century watershed

Political events in Europe in the later 1930s, culminating in the Second World War, inevitably diverted attention from the question of regulating

---

[43] Liefmann, n 34 above, quoted at 112.   [44] Gerber, n 1 above, 160.
[45] That is certainly the view of Gerber, n 1 above, 159–62.

cartels in the shorter term, while in the longer term the incorporation of some cartels into totalitarian state structures[46] resulted in a significantly different perception of their role by the later 1940s. Historically, therefore, the mid-century years of political crisis in Europe provides a natural pause and dividing line in the process of tracing the emergence of legal control of cartels. When consideration of the matter was resumed after 1945, the landscape of international and European politics and business had altered fundamentally. Many of the reservations relating to the operation of business cartels had hardened and there was a much stronger momentum towards regulation at both the international and national levels. Moreover, the establishment of the European Communities in the decade or so following the end of the war was also to provide the framework for a new dimension of regulatory strategy.

[46] For a general account, see e.g. Arthur Schweitzer, *Big Business in the Third Reich* (Eyre & Spottiswoode, 1964).

IV

Cartels in Europe, 1945–70: From Registrable Agreement to Concerted Practice

1. Post-war debates: back to the drawing board

In the narrative of legal control of business cartels, 1945 appears as an inevitable temporal marker. The end of the Second World War was a natural point for re-assessment of the question, presenting a new context of both political and economic reconstruction and reflection drawn from the lessons of the 1930s and war-time experience. In short, by 1945 there was a significantly different perspective on cartelization.

Despite the movement towards some kind of regulation of cartels in the 1920s and 1930s, noted in the preceding chapter, during the three decades spanning the two World Wars cartelization had become more widespread and significant, not the reverse. In some senses the phenomenon had moved towards a historical climax with the Second World War. Such a perception is offered by Thorelli, for instance, writing from a late 1950s' perspective:

Stagnationists and pessimists alike preached the merits of holding on to what one already had: any change was probably for the worse. Nazis and fascists sponsored the corporate state, in which each sector of the economy was governed by cartels or similar groups. Other nations found themselves grasping after public and private regulatory schemes in self-defence against the economic warfare of totalitarian states. Cartelization reached a logical climax in World War II.[1]

---

[1] Hans B Thorelli, 'Antitrust in Europe: National Policies after 1945' (1959) 26 *University of Chicago Law Review* 222. On some of the historical background, see the discussion in Joseph Borkin, *The Crime and Punishment of I. G. Farben* (Andre Deutsch, 1979).

But immediately after the end of the war cartels were tainted by bad association and also fitted uncertainly into a transformed global economic environment.

2. The political perspective: the cartel as a tainted organization

The incorporation of the business cartel as a device of totalitarian governance in Germany, Italy, and Japan inevitably influenced perceptions of such arrangements in the immediate post-war period. The potential for political abuse of concentrated and collusive power brought home to Europeans the earlier American fears and perhaps for the first time gave rise to a significant political will in a European context for legal control of cartelization on ideological grounds. In occupied Germany, for example, policies of decartelization were applied alongside programmes of deNazification. This political backlash against cartels therefore deserves some comment.

While it is correct to emphasize the psychological impact of this development in the subject, it is also as well to bear in mind one or two caveats. In the first place, as with other aspects of the conclusion of war in 1945, there were elements of victors' justice in policies such as decartelization. It should be remembered that some Allied countries had moved down the road of compulsory cartelization, though not so far as the main Axis powers. As Edwards noted:

When the Second World War began, restrictive business programs sponsored by governments were pervasive in Germany, Italy, and Japan, were broadly authorized by law in Belgium, the Netherlands, Latvia and New Zealand, and were in effect in important industries in the United Kingdom and France.[2]

In fact, both economic difficulties and the war-time circumstances had led most governments to see the virtues of compulsory market regulation and even with the return to peace in 1945, there were to remain and to be developed measures of state intervention and control of market behaviour, significantly so in some economic sectors. Most importantly, it should be

---

[2] Corwin D Edwards, *Control of Cartels and Monopolies: an International Comparison* (Oceana Publications, 1967) 6.

noted that in some contexts such as agriculture, banking, insurance, and transport, public regulation, often involving measures of subsidy and support and organization through cartel-type arrangements, have become commonplace. As had been the case in the United States, it was not the cartel in itself as a device of collaboration but the circumstances of its engagement which gave rise to concern, and in particular its use as an exploitation of *private* power for *private* gain.

Secondly, it would seem true to say that the sting in the end-of-war backlash against cartels had a subliminal rather than overtly legal outcome. Attitudes shifted irreversibly to the extent that the need for legal regulation was widely accepted. But, when the dust settled, the model for Europe for the remainder of the twentieth century was not one resembling the American system of prohibition, court orders, and litigation, but rather an administrative process of scrutiny to check that the public interest was not jeopardized. This difference of emphasis is well conveyed for example in an analysis by the New Zealand Trade Practices and Prices Commission in 1959; referring to price fixing arrangements the Commission commented:

Though the good will and good sense of the participants may limit the bias inherent in such arrangements, the public interest cannot rely upon this . . . Where government authority does not control prices, competition in prices is almost always needed as a continuing safeguard for the interests of all.[3]

The tainting of cartels was thus significant in terms of psychological transition, but less so for purposes of specific legal models: criminalization was still a distant prospect.

However, decartelization was set in motion in occupied Germany.[4] Its implementation was affected by divergent policies on the part of the occupying powers. Not surprisingly, the American approach to cartels and deconcentration within particular industries was tougher than that preferred by the United Kingdom and France, although in the event the American and British zonal decrees were similar, and the French markedly less severe. The former two decrees prohibited closely defined arrangements described either as cartels or excessive concentrations of economic power, explicitly including practices such as price fixing and the

---

[3] Decision No 3 of the Trade Practices and Prices Commission in the Matter of an Inquiry into an Agreement or Arrangement Between the Members of the Wellington Fencing Materials Association in Respect of Wire Netting, 7 September 1959.

[4] For a convenient summary, see Corwin D Edwards, *Trade Regulations Overseas: the National Laws* (Oceana Publications, 1966) 159 *et seq.*

use of quotas, although there was a system of exemptions. On the other hand, the French decree did not prohibit cartels as such, but required an examination of their anti-competitive effect. These laws were applied successively by the three military governments, the Allied High Commission and the German Minister of Economics from 1955 until the enactment of the new West German legislation in 1957. Prior to 1947 the occupying powers were primarily concerned with deconcentration in particular sectors such as coal and steel production, banking, motion pictures, and chemicals. From 1947, decartelization was vigorously enforced in the American zone (resulting in the formal termination of over 1,000 cartel agreements in one year), and a more widespread programme of decartelization operated from 1950. The pattern of legal action is summarized by Edwards in the following passage:

In 1950–51, Allied enforcement of decartelization began. In criminal proceedings, members of the abrasives industry and poultry breeders in Bavaria were convicted and fined for price fixing. Cease and desist orders were issued in the abrasives case, in a price fixing case involving electrical installations and the manufacture of electric light bulbs, and in a case involving restrictions in shoe machine leases upon the use of competitors' machines. As a result of these cases, various cartels were voluntarily terminated, complaints against other cartels began to be filed, and private suits began in the German courts to obtain damages for cartel activity or to invalidate cartel agreements.[5]

The impact of these measures may be judged from a contemporary account by a German writer, Franz Boehm, writing in the early 1950s:

The Allied decartelization laws are thus the most radical and consistent laws in the world for the prohibition of monopolies and the protection of competition... The German State governments (*Länder*) have appealed for some relaxation of these monopoly laws but so far with no success...The effect of these actions was considerable. They created a sensation in industrial circles and reminded the public of the existence of the decartelization laws. Some industries and associations voluntarily repealed agreements and measures like those which had been declared illegal in the case of the grinding materials industry.[6]

---

[5] Ibid., 163–4.

[6] Franz Boehm, 'Monopoly and Competition in Western Germany', in Edward H Chamberlin (ed), *Monopoly and Competition and their Regulation* (Macmillan, 1954) 151–2. Rather perplexingly, Gerber remarks that the cartelization laws 'were not strictly enforced, and, therefore, few businessmen or lawyers knew much about them or had occasion to consult them': David J Gerber, *Law and Competition in Twentieth Century Europe, Protecting Prometheus* (Oxford University Press, 2001) 270.

The shorter-term impact of these laws was thus considerable, yet in the longer term they did not provide an enduring model, having within Germany, the 'odour of an imposed system'[7] and in much of Europe would have appeared draconian. As Gerber notes, their effectiveness owed much to the enforcement power, and willingness to use that power, on the part of the occupation officials.[8]

3. Cartels and international trade: early attempts at international regulation

The transformation in the global political and economic environment following the end of the Second World War led to some significant attempts to construct an international system for the regulation of competition and in particular the control of cartels. With the exception of the regional EC initiatives, to be discussed below, these various projects proved either abortive or dormant. Yet their history is instructive. On the one hand, it demonstrates a lesson of American initiative followed by (fatal) non-participation and a more general reluctance on the part of governments to commit themselves to genuine measures of supranational legal control. On the other hand, the proposals provide a significant rehearsal of the strategies, policy, and deployment of legal language which was later to find expression in the EC model of competition regulation and control of cartels. The period between the late 1940s and early 1960s was in this respect fertile if not immediately productive and this international activity was certainly important as a trigger for legal developments at the national level.

By 1945 there was a much clearer awareness of the significance of business cartels in the context of international trade as well as at the level of national economies. This is evident, for instance, in the emerging expert literature on the subject, typified by such magisterial works as Ervin Hexner's *International Cartels*[9] published in 1946 and Stocking and

---

[7] Volker Berghahn, *The Americanisation of West German Industry 1945–1973* (Cambridge University Press, 1976) 84.　　　　　　　　　　[8] Gerber, n 6 above, 269.

[9] Ervin Hexner, *International Cartels* (Pitman, 1946). This work combines an impressive legal and economic analysis of the subject with a detailed account of the history of major cartels in a range of industries: a major and indispensable source for the period in question.

Watkin's *Cartels in Action*[10] of the same year. The latter authors, in their opening statement, set the scene rather dramatically but nonetheless in a manner which now serves to capture the feeling at the time:

During the War it became clear that the problems of monopoly—both national and international—which had been temporarily submerged under the urgent necessities of armed conflict, would rise up to plague the world again after the fighting stopped. Newspaper accounts of the relation between certain cartels and Germany's economic preparation for war had sharpened the determination of the public eventually to come to grips with these problems as part of any sound program to keep the peace.[11]

This contemporary perception linked political and economic concerns—political rivalries which had helped the drift towards global war were a component of the situation requiring to be addressed as a post-war global economic settlement and reconstruction would require efforts of international management, including the regulation of cartels. The 10 years or so following the end of the war therefore witnessed a number of international efforts to construct regimes of economic management, often driven by American preoccupations. In the earlier stages of these debates there was a clear tendency to pick up on the idea of the damage done to both trade and democracy by the totalitarian manipulation of cartels during the war years. Corwin D Edwards, a leading participant in this post-war discourse argued for instance that 'various business enterprises in the democracies had failed to see the political implications of cartel arrangements or had acquiesced in them'[12] and this kind of statement was characteristic of the American perspective. In 1945 American policy-makers therefore found themselves in a strong position to assert their traditional distrust of business collusion in discussion with their European counterparts and exercise leverage on legal developments in Europe. In 1944 Roosevelt had already articulated this sentiment: 'cartel practices which restrict the free flow of goods in foreign commerce would have to be curbed' and this would need to be accomplished through the United Nations.[13]

---

[10] George W Stocking and Myron W Watkins, *Cartels in Action* (Twentieth Century Fund, 1946). This was another major and detailed enquiry into cartel activity across a broad economic spectrum.   [11] Ibid., vii.

[12] Corwin D Edwards, 'Regulation of Monopolistic Cartelization' (1953–4) 14 *Ohio State Law Journal* 252, at 254.

[13] State Department Release, 8 September 1944 (communication to the Secretary of State). See Chapter II, above, for the text.

The first American-sponsored attempt to achieve this end was the move later in 1945 to establish a treaty-based International Trading Organisation (ITO), through the Havana Charter.[14] With the benefit of hindsight, this was an ambitious project aimed at the formulation and application of internationally agreed policies on commercial matters, employment, commodity agreements, and competition. The original Charter draft on competition followed to a large extent the American model, in particular incorporating a presumption that such practices as price fixing, market sharing, and the imposition of quotas (characteristic cartel arrangements) should be controllable and sanctionable practices. This hard-hitting approach encountered, unsurprisingly enough, opposition from many other governments for whom such a policy would have been completely novel and after further negotiation a second draft of 1948 modified the criteria for legal control. Restrictive practices—in fact those which were of economic significance on international markets—would now be investigated to determine whether they resulted in harm to competition. Such a regime would still have represented a significant development of international legal control and a number of countries in Europe and elsewhere anticipated its arrival by beginning to enact their own competition laws which facilitate compliance with these expected international obligations.[15] However (and not for the first time in the context of multilateral treaty-making), the project foundered through an internal American reluctance on the part of the US Congress to commit itself internationally to such a regime. Although American policy was enthusiastic for the adoption of American methods elsewhere, there was a familiar reluctance to transfer the authority to employ such methods to an international body.[16]

However, international initiatives in this area continued during the early 1950s. Discussion of measures equivalent to the restrictive practices provisions of the Havana Charter continued within the UN Economic and Social Council between 1951 and 1955,[17] once again promoted by the US Government. An ECOSOC ad hoc committee produced a report in 1953 which was circulated for discussion and received a broadly favourable

---

[14] See Edwards, n 2 above, 230–2; William A Brown, *The United States and the Restoration of World Trade* (The Brookings Institution, 1950) 125 *et seq*; Claire Wilcox, *A Charter for World Trade* (1949) 103–13.   [15] For instance, France from 1948 and Belgium from 1947.

[16] See Edwards, n 2 above, at 231. The strength of Congressional resistance dissuaded the US Government from seeking ratification for the Havana Treaty.

[17] For a more detailed account and official sources, see Edwards, n 2 above, at 231.

reaction from a number of states and the Consultative Assembly of the Council of Europe, but opposition from the International Chamber of Commerce and the US Chamber of Commerce. Finally, history soon repeated itself as the United States again withdrew its support for the establishment of a supranational system of control. In a very telling comment, the US Government stated:

present emphasis should be given not to international organizational machinery but rather to the more fundamental need of further developing effective national programs to deal with restrictive business practices, and of achieving a greater degree of comparability in the policies and practices of all nations in their approach to the subject.[18]

The forum for discussion then shifted to the recently established GATT, under whose auspices proposals, originating with the substance of the ECOSOC ad hoc committee's report, were debated between 1954 and 1960.[19] In this context, however, the debate was promoted by European countries, especially the Scandinavian states and Germany, and the main proposal was for the setting up of intergovernmental consultative machinery. A resolution was eventually adopted in December 1960, based upon the recognition that 'in present circumstances it would not be practicable for the Contracting Parties to undertake any form of control of such practices nor to provide for investigations'. What was provided for in essence was a classic 'soft law' mechanism:

at the request of any contracting party a contracting party should enter into consultations on such practices on a bilateral or a multilateral basis as appropriate. The party addressed should afford sympathetic consideration to and should afford adequate opportunity for consultations with the requesting party, with a view to reaching mutually satisfactory conclusions, and if it agrees that such harmful effects are present it should take such measures as it deems appropriate to eliminate these effects.[20]

The consensual approach evident in this measure, its respect for sovereignty and its use of discretionary language speaks volumes. States and their governments were still too careful about their own economic interests and the protection of their own traders to commit themselves to any compulsory supranational regime of control. The Resolution was not

---

[18] Economic and Social Council, Restrictive Business Practices, Comments of Governments, E/2612, Add. 2, 4 April 1955, 4–5.

[19] Again, see Edwards, n 2 above, 235 *et seq* for a more detailed account.

[20] GATT, *Decisions of the Seventeenth Session*, L1397, 5 December 1960.

used and expert opinion did not expect any action to follow from its adoption.[21] As Edwards noted, the whole approach was rhetorical and in practical terms not appropriate:

consultation between governments is appropriate only for matters that are individually important enough to justify intergovernmental negotiation. Few restrictive practices are individually of this magnitude. The damage that restrictive arrangements do to international trade, to standards of living, and to technological progress is the cumulative effect of many restrictions, few of which are individually of major importance.[22]

On the other hand, European regional co-operation was to prove more forthcoming, through the activities of a number of European organizations which were established in the post-war period: the Council of Europe (established in 1949), the European Coal and Steel Community (from 1951; ECSC), the European Economic Community (from 1957; EEC), and the European Free Trade Association (from 1960; EFTA). The Council of Europe produced a draft convention for the control of cartels, which was not adopted but provided a significant model; EFTA established a consultative procedure, which like that under GATT, was not used; and the two Communities established very significant and actual regimes of supranational control.

Interestingly, a European Convention on the control of cartels was one of the earliest projects to be put forward by the Council of Europe's Consultative Assembly and approved by its Committee of Ministers in 1950, and a draft was prepared by March 1951.[23] This was an ambitious scheme, requiring the registration of restrictive agreements covering the jurisdiction of two or more member countries, establishing a commission which would receive complaints from individuals or from governments, conduct hearings, and negotiate settlements and a European level court which could hear cases referred by the commission and award compensation, impose fines or delegate such tasks to member states. This structure (which of course resembles that established under the European Convention for Human Rights) was not acceptable to a number of states and Sweden put forward a less far-reaching regime, limited to a system of registration and transmission of complaints to governments. However,

---

[21] Edwards, n 2 above, 238.   [22] Ibid., 239.

[23] Council of Europe, *Memorandum on the Recommendation of the Consultative Assembly for the Preparation of a European Convention for the Control of International Cartels and Draft Convention Prepared by the Secretariat General*, SG/R (51) 15, 28 November 1951, 10–42.

the proposal was overtaken by the UN ECOSOC initiative, which a number of countries preferred for its wider participation, and when that faltered the Council of Europe proposal also fell into abeyance, despite a proposal from the Committee of Ministers to consider its completion in 1956. Nonetheless, the project remains of great theoretical importance and its practical impact lay in its serious discussion of a genuinely supranational system of control.

The EFTA Convention also provided for a system of regulating anti-competitive practices adversely affecting trade within the EFTA area, comprising a system of state complaints to the EFTA Council, which could be examined and result in recommendations to the state or states concerned.[24] However, since the Council possessed no powers of investigation, it was difficult to obtain any real knowledge about any alleged injurious practices, so undermining the effectiveness of this provision, which was never used in any significant way.[25] The more recent Economic Area (EEA) provisions on competition have, since the early 1990s, extended the EC supranational method of competition regulation to three of the surviving EFTA states (Norway, Iceland, and Liechtenstein) in relation to practices affecting both the EC and EFTA markets.[26]

Of much more practical significance was the establishment of the European Coal and Steel Community, which provided the first genuinely supranational regime of competition regulation, including significant provisions on cartels.[27] The ECSC is also of interest as a structure which provides at the same time a normative scheme for the protection of competition (and hence the regulation of cartels) while also seeking to achieve market stability via public organized cartel-like arrangements. It illustrates therefore the frequently ambivalent attitude towards cartels and the practice of drawing a distinction between their private and public manifestations. The European level management of the coal and steel sectors which was set up in the ECSC had originally both political and

---

[24] Edwards, n 2 above, 240–2; Andrew Martin, 'Restrictive Trade Practices in the European Free Trade Association', in *International and Comparative Law Quarterly Supplement No 1: Legal Problems of the EEC and EFTA* (BIICL, 1961), 89.

[25] Thérèse Blanchet *et al.*, *The Agreement on the European Economic Area: A Guide to the Free Movement of Goods and Competition Rules* (Clarendon Press, 1994) 9.   [26] Ibid., ch 8.

[27] See in particular Edwards, n 2 above, ch 15 (the best account of the early experience of the ECSC); Gerhard Bebr, 'The European Coal and Steel Community: A Political and Legal Innovation' (1953) 63 *Yale Law Journal* 1; Gerber, n 6 above, 335 *et seq* (containing an instructive account of the drafting of the ECSC Treaty provisions).

economic justifications, being seen as a means of reducing potential political tension in the context of a then key area of heavy industry (in the words of Robert Schuman, if coal and steel were subject to a common authority, war would be 'not only unthinkable, but materially impossible'). As Edwards noted, in Western Europe the coal and steel industries had already been subject to 'pervasive public and private control';[28] the ECSC then substituted a supranational system of extensive public management. Part of the latter entailed the ability of the new supranational body, the High Authority, to require conformity with arrangements reminiscent of a conventional business cartel. Article 58 of the ECSC Treaty enabled the High Authority to impose production quotas in response to crisis conditions or decline in demand. Article 61 allowed the High Authority to fix maximum and minimum prices. Article 63 enabled the High Authority to specify conditions of sale. To that extent the ECSC organized coal and steel producers into a kind of public cartel. As Friedmann and Verloren van Themaat observed:

a large part of the regulatory function normally exercised by private international cartels (e.g. the fixing of the level of prices and the imposition of production quotas in emergency situations) is transferred to a public supranational authority, the composition and function of which offers a guarantee against the prevalence of any one interest, and a balanced consideration of all the interests in question.[29]

But at the same time here was a significant prohibition of anti-competitive practices between the latter for other purposes. The key provision of competition policy was Article 65 of the ECSC Treaty, which laid down a prohibition (in language anticipating that of Article 81(1) (ex Article 85(1)) of the EC Treaty) of classic anti-competitive cartel practices: price fixing, quotas, and market sharing. This legal prohibition was subject to a system of exemptions, decided by the High Authority (for instance, in relation to specialization, joint buying, and joint selling), but equally was reinforced by sanctions in the form of legal nullity and the possibility of fines being imposed by the High Authority. In the European context the scheme of Article 65 was a major departure in two main respects. First, it employed an American-style prohibition, reinforced by the possible use of penal sanctions. Secondly, it transferred legal power in this area to a supranational authority.

---

[28] Edwards, n 2 above, 243.

[29] W Friedmann and P Verloren van Themaat, 'International Cartels and Combines', in W Friedmann (ed), *Anti-Trust Laws: A Comparative Symposium* (Stevens, 1956) 512.

The competition law provisions of the ECSC Treaty have been described as a blend of 'several European approaches to cartel questions with elements drawn from American practice and experience'.[30] The process of drafting and negotiating this part of the Treaty text involved some discreet but definite American advising. An important contribution was made by Robert Bowie, a Harvard Law professor then seconded to the office of the US High Commissioner for Germany, but the text was reworked into 'European idiom' by Maurice Lagrange, then a member of the French Conseil d'État and subsequently one of the first Advocates General to the European Court of Justice.[31] There was a complex interplay of interests involved in the process. While Americans were keen to export their model of antitrust, they did not want to provoke an adverse European reaction. German representatives were prepared to concede ground, so as to substitute an ECSC regime for decartelization of the coal and steel sector in the American Occupied Zone. France was seeking German participation in the Community as a way of preventing a resurgence of German power in heavy industry. Moreover, as Gerber points out, German negotiators were primarily of an 'ordoliberal' viewpoint,[32] persuaded of the need for a determined legal regulation of cartels, rather than spokesmen for German economic or industrial interests. The outcome was a fertile cocktail of policy and theory: a clear prohibition, supported by significant sanctions and investigatory power, was combined with the use of an administrative rather than judicial process, but transferred to a supranational level. This approach was therefore different from both the established American model and the emerging orthodoxy within European national legal orders. Moreover, and very significantly, of course, it provided the blueprint for the EEC model of competition regulation which was to be established a decade later.

Gerber suggests that the significance of the ECSC regime for competition was mainly as a model.[33] But there were also important lessons from the High Authority's practical experience of enforcement in the coal and steel sector, for instance regarding the complex interplay of national and private interests as a site of resistance to supranational efforts to control

---

[30] William Diebold, *The Schuman Plan* (New York, 1959) 352.
[31] See Gerber, n 6 above, 336 *et seq* for a revealing account of the drafting of the ECSC Treaty provisions (including telling anecdotes of American advisers leaving by back doors).
[32] See the discussion below.
[33] Gerber, n 6 above, 341–2.

cartels. An important example was the High Authority's attempts to deal with the Ruhr Coal Syndicate, a notable revival of cartelization in the post-war German coal industry. This was a joint sales organization which resisted, with broader support within Germany, the High Authority's moves to dissolve it. One argument put forward related to the inequality of treatment as between such a *private* organization in Germany and the French publicly controlled coal monopoly which was not subject to the same rules. The particular resolution of this issue was a compromise according to which the syndicate was split into three selling agencies which would operate independently under the supervision of the High Authority.[34] The experience of the ECSC as a whole provides important lessons in the supra- or international regulation of cartels and concentration in a crucial economic sector.

4. The emergence of national regulation of cartels in Europe

Another crucial legal development relating to business cartels in post-Second World War Europe was the widespread enactment of competition legislation in a number of national legal orders. The point was made in Chapter III above that national legislation in Europe in the first half of the twentieth century was both scarce and tentative. During the 20 years following the end of the war in 1945, competition legislation appeared in most West European countries. Writing in 1967, Edwards reports the existence of 'active'[35] competition legislation in the following European States: Austria, Belgium, Denmark, Finland, France, Germany, Ireland, the Netherlands, Norway, Spain, Sweden, Switzerland, and the United Kingdom.[36] This is an interesting phenomenon in itself, of which there is full and revealing analysis elsewhere,[37] and the point here is to note the

---

[34] See Friedmann (ed), n 29 above, 180–7, 513.

[35] 'Active' in the sense of actually being enforced: thus Portugal, with legislation dating from 1936, is excluded from Edwards' list.

[36] Edwards, n 2 above, 25–6.

[37] In particular, the more recent discussion by Gerber, n 6 above, chs 6, 7, and 8, provides an illuminating account of the forces shaping the new national laws. An earlier, detailed, and useful account is supplied by Edwards, n 2 above; see also Edwards' other work, *Trade Regulations Overseas: The National Laws* (Oceana Publications, 1966).

most important consequences of this national level development for the legal control of cartels.

It has already been noted in the discussion above that there was a significantly different view of the impact of cartel activity in the post-war period, and this naturally contributed in part to the emergence of national legislation. Edwards summarizes a number of elements in this altered perspective on cartel activity: a better level of information, particularly for governments, regarding the behaviour and impact of cartels; a concern in the post-war period about price inflation and the perception that regulation of cartels could be used as a way of dealing with this problem; an interest in removing barriers to international trade; a perception, encouraged by American opinion, that restrictive practices adversely affected productivity; and the attractiveness of competition regulation as a middle course between extremes of collectivization and cartelization.[38] The outcome was presented by Edwards in the following terms:

In the early postwar years, legislation appeared to be largely a reflection of American influence and a response to temporary problems of the postwar transition. By the close of the 1950s, this had ceased to be true. In many countries the law had been not only accepted but repeatedly strengthened. It had become an expression of national concern about enduring problems as to prices, barriers to trade, and relations between restrictions and efficiency. The various national laws had become parts of a general trend, and countries such as Spain, initially uninfluenced, had been drawn in.[39]

The 'general trend' included a common approach to regulation: the characteristically European administrative model of control, quite distinct from the North American method. This preference for a less legalistic and more discretionary system of monitoring is emphasized in particular in Gerber's analysis of these developments and he traces an important continuity in this respect between the debates and emerging regulation of the inter-war period and the widespread appearance of national legislation from the later 1940s.[40] With the exception of Germany, where the influence and strong position of 'ordoliberal' ideas led to a more 'juridical' system of control (discussed just below), and to some extent also the United Kingdom, the post-war national legislation reflected an established tradition of 'outcome oriented' scrutiny of anti-competitive practices. The approach contained in much of the

---

[38] Edwards, n 2 above, 9–13.   [39] Ibid., 13.   [40] Gerber, n 6 above, 176 *et seq.*

European national legislation of this time is explained by Gerber in the following terms:

The norms generally focus on the effects of conduct rather than on its character-istics, typically authorizing government officials to control conduct where it has specified harmful effects. Sanctions are seldom attached to particular forms of conduct or specific 'arrangements' (such as cartels). This means that the norms generally apply only to economically powerful firms, either by their terms or because only powerful firms (or arrangements among firms) can create the effects specified.[41]

It will be argued during the course of this work that this traditional European emphasis on outcome rather than conduct, entailing an analysis of impact on markets rather than an investigation into the state of mind of the actors, has resulted in a significant legal culture at both the national and supranational level in Europe, with important implications for any move towards criminalization of cartels. Legislators and enforcement agencies after 1945 inherited a culture of toleration which had recognized some economic and political advantages in cartelization, and despite an increasing acceptance of some unacceptable characteristics and effects this tolerance was also reinforced during the post-war period by the favour shown by many European governments to processes of corporate concentration and collaboration as a means of increasing the competi-tiveness of European companies in the global market.[42] Thus while legal control made a significant appearance on a number of European national stages, it did so in what would appear in comparative terms to be a 'soft' form: cautious, discretionary, and in the administrative rather than judicial sector.

The German legislation, the Gesetz gegen Wettbewerbeschränkungen (GWB), which was enacted in January 1958, should in some important respects be set apart from this main trend. It had its inspiration in the so-called Freiburg School of 'ordoliberalism',[43] a fusion of economic and legal argument which promoted the idea of a competitive economic sys-tem as a necessary element in a just society, and to be ensured through a clear legal and constitutional framework. A logical consequence of this kind of argument is therefore an emphasis on a more juridical method of

---

[41] Gerber, n 6 above, 174.   [42] See, e.g., Gerber, ibid., 178–9.
[43] Gerber, ibid., ch 7.

control. The outcome in the GWB (via a considerable amount of debate)[44] was, in Gerber's words:

a hybrid that reflected, in addition to ordoliberal ideas, contacts with US antitrust law and residual influences from prior German experience. This hybrid was very different from anything that had preceded it, and in those differences lay its extraordinary importance for the development of competition law in Europe.[45]

(This last point was a reference to the use of this model in the EC context.) The salient features of the system of control set up under the GWB combined administrative and juridical elements. The linchpin of the system is the Federal Cartel Office (Bundeskartellamt), an administrative regulatory body with a large measure of independence from central government and a judicial component, in the form of a decision-making section which has to justify its decisions within a clear legal framework. The Office's decisions may be appealed to the regular courts and the latter also have a distinct role in hearing private claims for damages and injunctive relief regarding some types of restrictive behaviour. More specifically in relation to cartels, the legislation lays down a general prohibition, though with the possibility for exemption of some forms of horizontal restraint, such as those aimed at rationalization or the establishment of standards. The model embodied in this law had a clear novelty (and thus exceptional character) at the time of its introduction, but in the longer term has evolved into the European norm, travelling first to the EC and then in due course back to other national systems from there. But even as the eventually prevalent model of legal control, it is important to note that it is still a hybrid with some 'administrative' characteristic and still different in a number of respects from the American approach. This is particularly true of the criteria employed to determine the more precise reaction to cartel activity.

An overall assessment of the early impact of the new national European competition laws on cartel activity suggests a consensual culture of negotiated compliance, rather than one of contentious enforcement. A widespread use of registration and reporting requirements combined with administrative and discretionary (and sometimes confidential) decision-making led to a definite but nonetheless 'soft' regulation of cartel activity in the national context. Typically, registered arrangements would be assessed and certain types of practice would have to be terminated or modified. During this period generally, processes of legal control had a 'comfortable' character since the illegality of many restrictive practices

---

[44] Ibid., 270 *et seq.*   [45] Ibid., 276–7.

was not yet manifest nor subject to strong legal censure. In the same way, attention was at first focused on formal written agreements which could be appropriately dealt with by a process of registration and often it was not clear whether informal collusion (later to be embodied in the concept of 'concerted practice') was within the scheme of control: thus the Austrian legislation was amended in 1958 to cover informal agreements and the German legislation similarly amended as late as 1973 for the same purpose, following a restrictive interpretation by the Bundesgerichtshof.[46] Broadly speaking, therefore, through to the 1970s cartel regulation in these systems was 'above-ground' and non-confrontational. 'Settlements' could be negotiated, sanctions were reserved for enforcement rather than substantive violation, and the cartels themselves were not yet driven into furtive activity with a conscious sense of delinquency.

5. The national position(s): stocktaking in the mid-1960s

It is difficult to gain an exact sense of the extent to which cartels were actually being controlled and affected by this earlier phase of national regulation, especially when decisions were swathed in confidentiality, as was the case in the Netherlands.[47] Edwards, however, in a survey published later in the 1960s, presented some tentative findings.[48] This research provides some impression, in both a quantitative and a qualitative sense, of what was happening during the early period of national cartel control. Perhaps two important facts emerge. First, across Europe, there was an uneven profile of enforcement. Secondly, where enforcement was stronger, it pushed business collaboration into more informal and less easily controllable forms.

(a) Austria

In relation to Austria, Edwards commented that while 'use of the registration process has apparently limited the number of cartels and modified

---

[46] Gerber, n 6 above, 290.

[47] Edwards commented in relation to the Dutch legislation: 'Secrecy in application of the law is pervasive' (*Control of Cartels and Monopolies*, n 2 above, 356.)

[48] Ibid., Appendix B, 342 *et seq*. *Control of Cartels and Monopolies* published in 1967, is the more analytical part of the research, drawing upon the more detailed national reports collected

their restrictions', by 1960 only 74 cartels had been registered and just five of that number disapproved.[49] The modest outcome is attributed to 'the prevalence of deeply rooted attitudes favorable to cartels'.[50] Most significant, perhaps, was his observation regarding the trend towards informal concertation:

Austria is said to have become a land of informal restrictive understanding...No basis exists for an estimate of the prevalence of such non-coercive restrictions or of their substantive character or of the degree to which flexibility or ineffectiveness in the restrictions may have resulted from the transition to informal understandings. That agreements are observed voluntarily, without resort to the courts or to private enforcement, demonstrates that they serve the interests of those who participate. It does not show that they are ineffective, that they are appropriate to the interests of non-participants, or that they are consistent with the public interest.[51]

This is a prescient comment, and perhaps also it is significant that this kind of analysis was being presented by an 'outside' observer, with a background in American law and policy.

(b) Belgium

In Belgium, legislation was not enacted until 1960, after which the government 'moved slowly'—over two years after enactment, no case had yet been completed under the law; in 1963 a number of cases were settled by agreed changes to cartel practices which had been investigated.[52] The policy underlying the Belgian legislation was explained in a ministerial statement along the following lines: 'to suppress cartels by making them illegal might weaken our competitive position as compared with powerful foreign enterprises and create serious economic disorder.'[53] Moreover, there was a strong preference for administrative control within Belgian legal and political culture, administrative officials being trusted more than judges.[54]

---

together in *Trade Regulations Overseas: The National Laws* (Oceana Publications), published in 1966.

[49] Edwards, n 2 above, 343.   [50] Edwards, *Trade Regulations Overseas*, n 4 above, 407.

[51] Ibid. This is also a prescient comment regarding the activities of the Austrian Banks Cartel ('Lombard Club') dealt with recently by the Commission (see Press Release IP/02/844, 11 June 2002).   [52] Edwards, n 2 above, 344.

[53] Senate Documents, 1959: Sénat de Belgique, Session de 1958–1959, séance de 9 Juin 1959, *Projet de loi sur la protection contre l'abus de la puissance économique*, 5–8. See Edwards, *Trade Regulations Overseas*, n 4 above, 144–5.   [54] Ibid., 145.

(c) Denmark

In contrast, the Danish approach to restrictive practices had been more vigorous and determined. In the period between 1955 and 1959, the authorities dealt with 106 cases (only some of which were cartels), 55 of which were settled by compromise, 18 by final recommendation, and 33 subject to corrective order.[55] However, the concern seemed to lie with effect on business opportunity rather than consumer interests, which then benefited incidentally:

The Danish law has been vigorously used, with substantial success, to protect opportunity to engage in business by curbing agreements and the practices of influential firms that excluded enterprises through collective boycott, individual refusal to sell, and exclusive dealing arrangements... In weakening group discipline and in protecting concerns that were in jeopardy from restrictive practices, it probably has done something to give the consumer the benefit of competition among a larger number of enterprises less tightly regimented.[56]

Overall, however, there was a lively culture of legal control in Denmark, dating back to the pre-war period and evidenced for example by detailed presentation of data by the Monopoly Control Authority. As Edwards implies, by the start of the 1960s, it was a mature system: 'more than in most European countries, the existing pattern of restriction constitutes, not the agenda of unfinished business, but the aggregate of what has been regarded as acceptable or beyond attack.'[57]

(d) Finland

In Finland, between 1958 and 1960, about 140 restrictions were registered and a process of consultation had resulted in a reduction of restrictions in about 20 per cent of the registered agreements; some agreements, relating to electrical products, radios, and television equipment, had been cancelled.[58] In Edwards' view, the approach taken in Finland was close to that of neighbouring Sweden.

(e) France

Differently again, the French approach appeared to smack of complacency. In France, a 'mixed' Commission had been established under a decree of 1953, but:

---

[55] Edwards, n 2 above, 345.   [56] Edwards, *Trade Regulations Overseas*, n 4 above, 265.
[57] Ibid., 268.   [58] Edwards, n 2 above, 346.

delayed and limited publication of facts and actions taken has been an obstacle to public knowledge about the Commission's work. By the end of May, 1963, the Commission had acted upon 38 cases, but public information was available only for the first 20, to the close of 1959. In those 20 cases, the Commission had found 13 violations. In only two cases had it recommended prompt action to correct the violation.[59]

In Edwards' view, the opacity of the Commission's work tended to mask an overriding policy imperative concerned with economic expansion and higher productivity, a preocupation which contrasted 'sharply with static standards of abuse used by most other countries that apply discretionary distinctions between good and bad cartels', so that, as a result:

The published reports indicate that relation between cartels and economic progress has been conceived by the Commission in a distorted way... Nowhere in the decisions is there evidence that the Commission considered the effects of a quiet life in the shelter of a restrictive agreement upon the incentive to experiment with new methods of production, new forms of distribution, or new market opportunities... Such formulation of the issues probably has been encouraged by the fact that parts of the French economy, organized along traditional lines and resistant to change, consist chiefly of units too small for efficiency, too timid to take risks, and excessively concerned with stability and security.[60]

Despite the opinion of other observers that anti-competitive practices were prevalent in France at that time, a member of the Commission had said to Edwards that if France had a Sherman Act there would be no restrictions against which to apply it—not surprisingly the final verdict on French enforcement of competition law was that it was 'lukewarm'.[61] The French context, continuing through to the 1970s, was one of sustained economic development and strong governmental influence on business practice. The unsurprising result, in Gerber's words, was that 'competition law in France operated at the margins of economic and bureaucratic life, little known by the public and generally ignored even within the bureaucracy'.[62]

---

[59] Ibid., 348.   [60] Edwards, *Trade Regulations Overseas*, n 4 above, 62–4.

[61] Ibid., 65–6. See also the discussion in Gerber, n 6 above, 180–90; and more generally, the analysis in David S Landes, *The Unbound Prometheus* (Cambridge University Press, 1969) 245.

[62] Gerber, n 6 above, 190.

(f) Germany

In Germany, on the other hand, as might be expected, enforcement was more vigorous under the legislation of 1957, although there was an emphasis on informal resolution: by the end of 1964 over 1,400 cases of violation had resulted in informal correction, and 166 in administrative fines.[63] Edwards concluded that:

Though administrative correction of violations has been preferred to punishment, the policing of the prohibitions apparently has been sufficient to keep noncompliance within manageable limits and to induce would-be cartelizers to act openly by seeking exemption...Initial experience with the law appears to have brought about an increase of support for it. Opposition is less sharp; some groups that were hostile or indifferent now approve; and younger postwar business leaders are appearing, acclimatized to and generally in sympathy with the competitive policy.[64]

But this appraisal is qualified by some hint of future problems, Edwards commenting that 'officials have been less sensitive than their counterparts in the United States to the possibilities of restricting competition by roundabout means'.[65] Increasingly, however, German regulators appeared to be alert to the issue of informal collusion (*abgestimmte Verhaltensweisen*). A discourse wrangle developed, the Cartel Office and some academic opinion arguing on the one hand that the legislation applied to such concerted practices, and the courts taking on the other hand a more conservative view, culminating in the ruling of the Bundesgerichthof (BGH, Supreme Court) in 1971 that what was covered was no more than formal contracts as understood in private law.[66] This interpretation was effectively appealed to the legislature by the Cartel Office and Economics Ministry, finally leading to legislative amendment in 1973, extending the reach of the law to informal forms of collusion.

(g) The Netherlands

At first sight the Netherlands presented a picture of active regulation of cartels by the early 1960s. However, the Dutch law was embedded in a

---

[63] Edwards, n 2 above, 350.
[64] Edwards, *Trade Regulations Overseas*, n 4 above, 205–6. See also the detailed account of the evolution of German law and policy in Gerber, n 6 above, 266–96. Gerber also stresses the juridical character of the discourse contained within the emerging German system of control.
[65] Ibid., 206.   [66] Ibid., 290.

governmental policy of 'neutrality towards concerted restrictions', and Edwards reported that:

most cases are settled informally—apparently about 650 out of a total of about 700 from the close of the war until the end of 1957. Agreements are usually modified rather than cancelled. Action has focused chiefly on two matters, price fixing and exclusion of enterprises from markets...where substantial independent competition exists and schemes do not involve pressure upon independents to conform, price-fixing has been tolerated as harmless.[67]

He therefore counsels a careful reading of statistics relating to action taken against cartels:

Even where the government has acted, cartels continue to operate and to impose restrictions. Dutch policy is not designed to terminate cartelization, but merely to modify cartel programs by eliminating activities regarded as contrary to the public interest; and there is no presumption that substantial restriction is necessarily objectionable. In many cases the government has done no more than substitute an attenuated version of a restrictive provision for a bolder one. The restrictions are less ambitious, but they continue to exist. Hence a numerical count showing the prevalence of restrictive agreements in the Netherlands cannot show the impact of Dutch policy. It can, however, indicate the extent to which important types of restriction continue to exist.[68]

Indeed, although both price and quota cartels were being regularly scrutinized, a significant number stood the test of that inspection and remained in existence. Other types of restriction appeared to be more numerous by the early 1960s (for instance, the number of market allocation agreements increased by over 22 per cent during the period 1955–61). It was therefore possible to conclude that major types of cartel restriction, such as price control, allocation of markets, limitation of output, joint selling and the pooling of profits continued to be prevalent in the Netherlands.[69]

(b) Norway

During the 1950s most action under Norwegian law was taken against unreasonably high cartel prices (use of price orders) and refusals to deal (between 1954 and 1957, such refusals were prohibited in 18 cases but allowed in another 17 instances).[70] But cartels were still prevalent by the

[67] Edwards, n 2 above, 356–7.   [68] Edwards, *Trade Regulations Overseas*, n 4 above, 118.
[69] Ibid., 123.   [70] Edwards, n 2 above, 359.

end of that decade: there were 720 restrictive arrangements registered in 1958 compared to an estimated number of 644 in the mid-1920s. Following considerable debate during the later 1950s, a new Decree of 1960 brought about a radical change in the system of control, shifting the emphasis from a policy of price control to one of prohibition of restrictive agreements. The new law prohibited collective fixing of prices, discounts, and bidding and explicitly covered oral and non-binding agreements and the terms of trade associations. After the Decree was enacted, 565 associations and cartels were found to be engaged in prohibited practices; of these 356 were required to terminate the arrangements and a further 164 sought but were denied exemptions.[71]

(i) Sweden

Sweden appeared as a classic instance of consensual regulation and compromise: application of the legislation of 1953 revealed an active resort to negotiated settlement, based on a strong determination on the part of Swedish businesses to achieve an accommodating resolution to restrictive practice cases. Thus by 1958, about 150 cases involving registered practices had been investigated and resolved by negotiated corrective action. Edwards analysed the dynamic of control in the following terms:

> After the first burst of decartelization, restrictions were eliminated or weakened lest there be adverse action by the Freedom of Commerce Board; and the Board's recommendations were accepted lest a report to the King result in more severe legislation. The presence of officials of the chief business organizations on the Board tended to limit the scope of the recommendations, but also to increase the willingness of enterprises and groups to acquiesce. Recalcitrant enterprises apparently incurred pressure from these business organizations to accept the Board's suggestions rather than run the risk of efforts to strengthen the law such as might be the result of public reports of failure by the Board to the King.[72]

Such a comfortable and accommodating climate of enforcement appeared to take the edge out of the process. In the late 1950s less cases were being dealt with and official attention was more occupied with the surveillance of price levels; Edwards considered that further action against cartels was likely to be sporadic.[73]

---

[71] Edwards, *Trade Regulations Overseas*, n 4 above, 317–18.   [72] Ibid., 363–4.
[73] Ibid., 364.

(j) Britain

In the United Kingdom, control over cartels was laid down in the Restrictive Trade Practices Act 1956, which provided for a system of registration of restrictive agreements relating to goods, based on a rebuttable presumption that such restrictions were contrary to the public interest. It was then for parties to the agreements to provide a justification for the agreement not to be invalidated. Between 1956 and 1965, out of 32 contested cases the Restrictive Practices Court had decided against all or the majority of the restrictions in 22 instances. Edwards commented further that:

Decisions in contested cases led to abandonment of restrictions in numerous other cases, By June, 1961, the restrictions in more than fifty agreements had been terminated in uncontested judicial proceedings. In the ensuing two years about seventeen more agreements were thus ended. By the end of December, 1964, 1635 agreements had been either revised to eliminate all relevant restrictions or else terminated by the parties. In addition, 75 agreements had expired without renewal.[74]

The British system of regulation of cartels, not based on a prohibition as such but operating a tough presumption of illegality, and incorporating a juridical element[75] as significant as that in the German legislation, would therefore have appeared as one of the most stringent in Europe by the 1960s, on paper at least.

There had been at the same time some attempt to evaluate the economic impact of the rules laid down in the 1956 legislation. One such assessment presents a somewhat uncertain picture:

The change in the status of cartels, however, has not obviously lifted British industry to a new plane of efficiency, nor has it transformed the market conditions under which the majority of firms have operated.

Referring to a study published in 1961 which suggested that, following the termination of cartels in June 1959, competition had increased and prices were lower in about one-third of the cases examined, the assessment continued:[76]

This is a substantial result...In some industries, however, the effect on competition was short-lived and the firms found alternative routes to restriction...The

---

[74] Edwards, n 2 above, 367.   [75] See Gerber, n 6 above, 218–19.

[76] J B Heath, 'Restrictive Practices and After', in *Manchester School*, vol XXIX No. 2 (May 1961).

establishment of price leadership seems to have become a quite usual response to the breakdown of formal cartel arrangements. In addition, firms discovered other means for mitigating the severity of unwelcome competition. The most common of these has been the 'open price agreement' or 'information agreement'... Most types of cartel restrictions have their counterparts in informal arrangements.[77]

Similarly, Edwards refers to the spread of information exchange agreements in the United Kingdom during 1959 and 1960.[78] Thus, as in some other systems, it appeared that an apparent success in removing formal cartels, was encouraging businesses to explore more informal methods of collusion which would not be susceptible to a system of control based upon a process of formal registration and a sanction of legal unenforceability.

By the 1960s there was thus at the national level across Europe a patchwork of legal regulation. In some countries there was little or even no competition law as such (for instance in Italy). Within some systems, there was regulation but still a tolerant attitude towards cartelization (France, Belgium, and the Netherlands, for example). Tougher regimes had emerged elsewhere, as in Germany, Britain, Denmark, and Norway, but there were signs of a new kind of legal battle that lay ahead—the regulation of less formal, less visible, and perhaps more subtle forms of collusion, soon to be encapsulated in the EC vocabulary of 'concerted practice'.

6. The Common Market context

While the European Coal and Steel Community provided the first significant model for supranational regulation of economic competition and the activities of business cartels, this process was extended to a wide range of markets with the setting up of the European Economic Community under the EEC Treaty 1957. Competition policy was an integral and crucial aspect of the project of a European Common Market and the regulation of cartels was to emerge as a central feature of this new corpus of competition policy and law.

The regulatory system established under Article 85(1) of the EEC Treaty (now Article 81(1) of the EC Treaty) conformed in broad terms

---

[77] G C Allen, *Monopoly and Restrictive Practices* (George Allen and Unwin, 1968) 97–8.
[78] Edwards, *Trade Regulations Overseas*, n 4 above, 468.

with the emerging European model of legal control, in that it employed an administrative procedure of evaluation of restrictive business practices, combining a 'strong' legal prohibition with the possibility of registration ('notification') for purposes of approval.[79] But it is important to appreciate that the widely cast prohibition, backed by the sanction of legal nullity in the second paragraph of Article 85, was conceived as much as a net as an instrument of censure. The function of Article 85 was to bring the totality of restrictive business practices affecting inter-member state trade within the scope of administrative surveillance, to enable their economic evaluation.[80] At first sight the language of the provision may appear severe: 'shall be prohibited as incompatible with the common market', 'all agreements', 'shall be automatically void'. Moreover, classic cartel activities are specifically listed 'in particular' as prohibited behaviour: such horizontal restrictions as price fixing, the imposition of quotas, and the sharing of markets. But a more careful reading of the wording of Article 85(1) should reveal the implicit process of economic evaluation: what is prohibited is an arrangement *which has the object or effect of preventing, restricting or distorting competition.* Moreover, the real objection is *incompatibility with the common market*: the relevant wording is 'prohibited as incompatible with the common market', not for instance 'prohibited as anti-competitive'. This identifies the principal victim whose interests are to be protected, not so much the consumer, or the small trader but the more nebulous entity of a kind of market. Admittedly, such parties would ultimately and indirectly gain some benefit, but the immediate object of protection was the operation of the larger European market. There is no trace, then, of the Sherman Act's preoccupation with conspiracy and illicit collusion.

It is important to appreciate how this common market context of competition policy informed and directed its development and enforcement, especially during the earlier years of the Community's operation. This will help to explain what may now appear as a relatively easy-going approach on the part of the Commission to major cartels in the first 10 years, until a 'tougher' policy was signalled by the famous *Quinine* and

---

[79] For a discussion of the influences on the drafting of the EC Treaty and other rules on competition, see D G Goyder, *EC Competition Law* (3rd edn, Clarendon Press, Oxford 1998), chs 3, 4.

[80] For a perceptive account of the early years of EC competition law, see Ian S Forrester and Christopher Norall, 'The Laicisation of Community Law: Self-help and the Rule of Reason: How Competition Law Is and Could Be Applied' (1984) 21 *Common Market Law Review* 11.

Dyestuffs decisions at the close of the 1960s. DG IV of the Commission, entrusted with the task of working out the detail of regulation and then enforcing the rules, required at the beginning some knowledge and appreciation of the way in which the setting up and operation of the new common market was affected by anti-competitive trading practices. A particularly relevant issue was the actual or potential effect on trade flows across member state boundaries. It is not surprising therefore that there was a preoccupation at this stage with vertical restraints in distribution and licensing schemes, and the possibility of export bans and other provisions which might inhibit cross-border trading. Moreover, the wide net cast by Article 85(1) coupled with a degree of legal protection arising as an incentive to notify agreements to the Commission predictably resulted in a flood of notifications relating to thousands of vertical trading agreements. For a mixture of both policy and administrative reasons, the Commission's attention was therefore to a large extent diverted to dealing with the more mundane issue of distribution and licensing arrangements, effectively searching for the best route to approve most of them.[81] This left the 'sharp end' of competition policy—for instance, considering the impact of producer cartels and market dominance—in the background until the 1970s.

Moreover, in so far as the Commission did examine horizontal restrictions and classic cartel arrangements, it also appears to have been very much guided by considerations of market integration: the impact of market sharing, quotas, and pricing practices on intra-member state trade. This is evident, for instance, in the examination of a number of trading structures established by national associations which tended to impede the penetration of national markets, and in the focus on multilateral exclusive dealing arrangements. Much of the action taken at a European level against cartels during the 1960s was concerned with this problem of 'closed circuit', protected national markets, particularly in Belgium and the Netherlands. The scene was set for this emphasis in regulation by the Commission's examination of the *Belgian Tile Cartel* (the Convention

---

[81] As Goyder notes: the Commission in its 9th Annual Report indicated that of the 40,000 notifications received in the first years of the system's operation, as many as 29,500 related to exclusive dealing agreements, and more than 25,000 of these were eventually dealt with on the basis on the first group exemption under Regulation 67/67 (Goyder, n 79 above, 71). Viewed in those terms the great achievement of the first decade was (perhaps inevitably) administrative rather than substantive.

Faience case) in 1963–4.[82] This arrangement, organized through two Belgian associations of tile dealers, regulated the supply of tiles within Belgium, not only from Belgian producers but also from a significant number of producers in France, Britain, Germany, Italy, and the Netherlands. The system adopted limited the supply of tiles to about 900 approved dealers, who were themselves obliged to maintain an agreed mark-up and to buy only from the participating suppliers. The Belgian market was divided into two parts for this purpose. The cartel was maintained through the use of internal sanctions: fines imposed against deviating producers, while dealers would be disciplined by boycotts. The anti-competitive features of this kind of arrangement are manifest,[83] but it was also, and especially, the potential impact on trading opportunities across member state borders which rendered it objectionable from the Commission's perspective.

Between about 1963 and 1968 the Commission examined the activities of a number of cartels of this kind, either following their notification or following complaints. These related to:

- *sanitary ware*: 1965; multilateral exclusive supply and price fixing; Belgian market;[84]
- *detergents*: 1965; market sharing; the Netherlands and Belgium;[85]
- *natural sand*: 1965; quotas, exclusive supply, minimum prices; Germany, the Netherlands, and Belgium;[86]
- *rubber and plastics*: 1966; all manufacturers in an unspecified member state; collective rebates;[87]
- *pesticides*: 1966–7; a 16-member national federation; collective resale prices and disciplinary boycotts;[88]
- *building materials*: 1966; quotas, market sharing;[89]
- *fertilizers*: 1967; quotas, price fixing;[90]
- *steel processing*: 1967; market sharing;[91]
- *nitrogeneous fertilizers*: 1967–8; the Belgian association, *Comptoir Belge de l'Azote* or *COBELAZ* and the French association, *Comptoir Francaise de*

---

[82] JO 1167/64 (13 May); Commission, *Ninth General Report*, para. 58; Edwards, n 2 above, 300–2.

[83] Edwards points to some similarities with American practices (the North Carolina Tile Contractors' Association): Corwin D Edwards, 'Legal Requirements that Building Contractors be Licensed', *Law and Contemporary Problems* (Winter, 1947).

[84] *Bulletin EEC*, 6-65.   [85] Ibid.,6-65.   [86] Ibid., 11-65.
[87] Ibid., 1-66.   [88] Ibid., 1-66.   [89] Ibid., 9/10-66.
[90] Ibid., 5-67.   [91] Ibid., 5-67.

l'Azote or *CFA*; joint selling; approved formally with a negative clearance;[92]

- *plaster*: 1967; *Eurogypsum*, a joint study and exchange of information organization based in Geneva; again formally approved by negative clearance;[93]
- '*equipment*': 1967; a national group of retailers and producers; collective exclusive dealing and price fixing; agreed to disband;[94]
- *timber*: 1968; Belgian Union of Importers of Timber; exclusive dealing;[95]
- *cement*: 1968; producers in Belgium, Germany, and the Netherlands; quotas, price fixing and market sharing; adverse formal decision, successfully appealed to the Court of Justice (discussed further below);[96] Belgian cement cartel (Cement Makers' Association and 13 lime-burning companies), judged to be of little economic significance and given a negative clearance.[97]

Apart from the substantive focus of interest (for the most part, the activities of trade associations) in this early Commission practice relating to cartels, the other main point of significance relates to the manner in which these cases were approached in a procedural sense. To a large extent, the Commission took action through a low profile process of negotiation, entailing minimal publicity, teasing from the traders involved the required termination or revision of their arrangement, and apparently holding the use of fines in reserve as only a possible sanction. In fact, it is for this reason difficult to construct a detailed or accurate picture of what was happening in these cases. As a contemporary observer of the emergent European antitrust scene, the following observation by Edwards, relating to the *Belgian Tile Cartel*, sums up well this feature of the process at the time:

Though the facts of the tile case were widely known in Brussels, the official account of the case was brief and relatively uninformative. Without identifying the product, the countries involved, or the scope of the agreement, the Commission described it as one between 'a number' of manufacturers and 'a considerable number' of customers to trade exclusively with each other, said that admission of further manufacturers was subject to approval by those already parties and that new customers must meet 'a number of conditions', and mentioned the means of enforcement. It did not state the content of its recommendation nor the nature of the changes subsequently made by the parties. Thus

---

[92] JO 1968, L 279; [1968] CMLR D45.   [93] JO 1968, L57/9; [1968] CMLR D1.
[94] *Bulletin EEC*, 11–67.   [95] Ibid., 4–68.
[96] Cases 8-11/66, *Cimenteries and others v Commission* [1967] ECR 75.
[97] JO 1969, L 122/8; [1969] CMLR D15.

its announcement had limited value as a basis for development of public opinion about the Commission's policy towards restrictive practices or as a statement from which business enterprises could ascertain the boundaries of permissible concerted action.[98]

It is therefore difficult to identify this practice as a kind of 'case law' since it did not appear to have an intended or usable precedential value. The Commission's own published accounts in the *Bulletin of the EEC* provide minimal detail and the lack of formality did not allow for either third party reliance or legal review. Partly no doubt this reflected the fact that during this period the Commission was feeling its way as a regulator and so would naturally eschew formal, public, and principled decisions. Also, it would appear to reflect the established European preference at a national level for negotiated 'administrative' resolution.

Following from this character of the procedure, the outcomes were similarly informal: negotiation, usually an agreed termination or modification of the agreement, and sanctions used as a negotiating tactic rather than a concrete measure. It is only from about 1967 to 1968 that a greater formality of process becomes evident, for instance, cases such as *Eurogypsum*, *CFA*, *COBELAZ*, and the *Belgian Cement Makers Cartel* resulting in a formal decision of clearance. Then in the later years of the decade it is possible to detect a greater definition of policy, producing in its turn a more legalistic response from the companies subject to examination. This process can perhaps be seen most clearly in the more formal proceedings and litigation which arose from the Commission's dealings with the cement market in the later 1960s.

7. The European cement market: the hardening of cartel control

Cement is the kind of homogeneous product, the market for which has historically led to the formation of cartels.[99] At the European level the Commission has at different times examined and investigated arrangements relating to the production and sale of cement, many of which date back to the inter-war period (VCH, the Dutch Cement Dealers' Association was established in 1928, for instance). Trading in cement,

[98] Edwards, n 2 above, 302.
[99] See the analysis of the cement market in the Commission's decision in 1994 in relation to the *Cement Cartel ('Cembureau')*: [1994] 4 CMLR 341.

particularly in Belgium and the Netherlands, attracted the Commission's attention in the later 1960s and resulted in some of the earliest, and thus formative litigation before the European Court of Justice.

The first real legal contest arose from the Commission's examination of a significant international cartel, founded on an agreement known as the Noordwijks Cement Accoord, entered into in 1956 by 74 undertakings from Germany, Belgium, and the Netherlands, and involving market sharing and the use of quotas (and a related price-fixing arrangement).[100] The agreement was notified to the Commission in 1962, under the 'truce' provisions of Regulation 17, which encouraged notification of existing agreements by offering provisional validity and an immunity from fines. There were a number of exchanges between the Commission and the parties to the Accoord during 1965 and 1966, and finally a 'notice' from the Commission in January 1966, indicating that the Accoord was in breach of Article 85(1), with no scope for any exemption, and should be terminated forthwith, with no further immunity from fines. Although not now a very well-remembered case, this litigation provided in fact the first legal challenge to the Commission's exercise of its powers as a competition regulator, and its first real setback in litigation.

In substance there could be little doubt as to the anti-competitive nature of the arrangements provided for in the Accoord, nor of their effect on inter-member state trade: it was a classic market-sharing agreement.[101] Since the cartel's provisions had been notified, there was no scope for a fine, but it was an opportunity for the Commission to pronounce authoritatively on the objectionable character of this kind of activity. However, the arguments raised on appeal to the Court of Justice related to procedural questions: a legalistic point of admissibility (whether the Commission's 'notice' to the parties was a challengeable decision for purposes of the action for annulment under Article 173 (now Article 230) of the EC Treaty),[102] and the parties' objection that the Commission's decision was insufficiently reasoned. Thus it was unnecessary for the Court to consider the substantive application of Article 85(1). But neither was that aspect of the case contested by the parties; it appears to have

---

[100] For details see the account in Cases 8-11/66, *Cimenteries and others v Commission* [1967] ECR 75.   [101] See the facts as set out in the Court's judgment: [1967] ECR 79.

[102] Advocate General Roemer considered that the measure was not a decision and could not be challenged under Article 173, but agreed that, if it had been a decision, it would have been insufficiently reasoned: see [1967] ECR 99-109.

been accepted that the cartel was, as the Commission asserted, squarely within the frame of the prohibition. On the other hand, the Court's judgment against the Commission on the sufficiency of reasoning was a warning note for the future.[103] It was the first slap of due process: formal procedure required care, and its repressive nature would trigger rights of defence. Within a few years, major investigations of producer cartels in dyestuffs, quinine, and sugar would lead to more lengthy and complex arguments of this kind before the Court of Justice.

An agreement related to the Accoord but not the subject of the proceedings in *Cimenteries* concerned the pricing policies of cement dealers. However, this aspect of the organization of the cement market was subsequently considered by the Commission in its examination of the arrangements of the Dutch Cement Dealers' Association, Vereeniging van Cementhandelaren (VCH).[104] This national association managed the distribution of cement throughout the Netherlands and in effect constituted a price-fixing cartel, operating a system of 'imposed' and 'target' prices for its members. Although at first sight it appeared to be confined to one member state, it was notified to the Commission in 1962. The latter opened a formal procedure in 1970 and issued a decision in December 1971,[105] holding that the pricing arrangements were in breach of Article 85(1), should be terminated forthwith, and could not be exempted. Again, following notification, there would be no fine, but the VCH appealed against the decision, on both procedural and substantive grounds.

The Association had abolished its system of imposed prices earlier in 1971, but the Court of Justice in its judgment in October 1972 found that the target prices alone were sufficient to fall foul of Article 85(1). It stated that:

The fixing of a price, even one which merely constitutes a target, affects competition because it enables all the participants to predict with a reasonable degree of certainty what the pricing policy pursued by the competitors will be.[106]

More generally, the Court agreed that the VCH was in effect operating a rigorous anti-competitive cartel:

An examination of all the rules to which the contested decision relates shows there to be a coherent and strictly organised system the object of which is to restrict competition between the members of the Association.[107]

---

[103] Ibid., 94.
[104] Case 8/72, *Vereeniging van Cementhandelaren v Commission* [1972] ECR 977.
[105] OJ 1971, L 13/34.   [106] [1972] ECR 990.   [107] Ibid.

Finally, the objection that it was a purely national arrangement—in other words, that inter-member state trade was not affected—was not accepted by the Court:

An agreement extending over the whole of the territory of a Member State by its very nature has the effect of reinforcing the compartmentalization of markets on a national basis, thereby holding up the economic interpenetration which the Treaty is designed to bring about and protecting domestic production.[108]

The two 'cement' cases therefore effectively led to the legal condemnation of the interlinked market sharing and price-fixing arrangements which protected national markets and characterized the European cement market in the 1960s. They are legally significant, not only for confirming the reach of the prohibition in Article 85(1), but also in enabling the major cartels to flex their muscles in exercises of legal defence. The Commission was also learning lessons: interestingly, allegations of insufficient reasoning in the VCH appeal did not succeed on that later occasion.

But there are also important indicators of the future direction of legal strategy and argument. Both cases involved 'old' notified agreements, with no fines in prospect. By the close of the 1960s, the Commission was making it clear that such cartels were illegal, would not be exempted, and if set up now would incur penalties. The time had clearly come for price-fixing and market-sharing cartels to go into hiding. Moreover, as the statements in the *VCH* judgment show, in terms of legal argument it was the element of *concertation*—sophisticated signalling, rather than open and obvious agreement—which had become significant. For the cartels, the future would have to be furtive and ambivalent. For the regulators, the future promised problems of proof.

By the start of the 1970s, the pre-history of European cartel regulation had come to an end.

[108] [1972] ECR 990, 991.

V

A Narrative of Cartel Regulation in Europe, 1970 to the Present Time

1. Reading a history of regulation and enforcement: a 30 years' war

The story of a systematic and focused regulation of business cartels at a European level, as a supranational legal activity, begins at the close of the 1960s and gains momentum, especially during the 1980s and 1990s. The Commission's increasingly vigorous 'prosecution' of major, European-wide cartels has produced a body of policy and legal argument which now amounts to a substantial corpus of regulatory material. As a subject, this may now be explored most usefully by investigating a number of key themes: the relevance and use of economic argument; the legal control of regulatory powers and the due process requirements in relation to the exercise of such powers; problems of investigation and evidence, and techniques of gaining evidence; and the juridical nature of the process of control and sanctions associated with that process. But first of all, in order to navigate the subject matter more effectively, it may be helpful to present the reader with a relatively uncluttered narrative and chronological account of the Commission's enforcement activity over the last 30 years or more.

Although the discussion in this chapter is therefore mainly of a descriptive character it can also serve to bring out a sense of historical development, and provide some insight into the role of the main players in this ongoing drama of investigation and litigation. To use the metaphor of the legal and policy battleground and an ongoing 'war' between powerful but opposed interests ('industry' and the 'public regulators') is not too far-fetched. From the time of its first resort to fines in the case of the

Quinine Cartel in 1969, the Commission engaged a powerful and determined opposition and resistance from well-resourced corporate interests. This resistance is naturally significant as a matter of working out the content of policy and enforcement strategies, but also as a source of both substantive and procedural law. The appeal process, triggered in particular by the imposition of fines and the degree of censure which follows from the use of such sanctions, has provided an important and fertile site for legal development. At the same time, this has involved the Court of Justice and more latterly the Court of First Instance in the ongoing drama, in the role of referee, assessing the competing arguments. An understanding of the process of development of policy and law is undoubtedly aided by some insight into the roles and interrelationship between these key players, and a preliminary narrative history may help to clarify the latter.

This is a story which may to a large extent be traced through a reading of a voluminous official documentation. The decisions of the Commission and the subsequent appeal process through the Community courts are recorded in each instance in the *Official Journal of the European Communities* and the *European Court Reports*. There is naturally, in addition, a substantial secondary literature comprising commentary and analysis of the arguments deployed in these proceedings. The primary source material in itself may appear daunting: over a period of 30 years, now amounting to thousands of pages of detailed factual information, economic analysis, and legal argument. Again, a narrative summary may then serve as a means of access for the study of this material. Most importantly, a reading of cases individually does not easily give an idea of the ongoing history of the subject or its longitudinal direction. The purpose in this chapter, therefore, is to present a relatively straightforward and informative retrospective view of the main action of enforcement and legal control as a basis for the more detailed and thematic analysis in the following chapters.

2. The early years of litigation

As noted in the previous chapter, the Commission had spent much of the 1960s taking stock of its imminent task as a competition regulator and developing an administrative system which would enable it to deal with the vast range of anti-competitive activities caught by the net cast by Article 85(1) (now Article 81(1)) of the EC Treaty. Cartel investigations did not yet figure prominently on this agenda, apart from attending to the visible phenomenon of 'closed circuit' systems of national protection, often organized through national trading associations and aimed at resale price maintenance, and prevalent particularly in Belgium and the Netherlands (see the discussion in Chapter IV above). Occasionally, this sector of enforcement threw up a 'big case', perhaps the most well-known example being the litigation arising from the Commission's decisions against cement manufacturers, relating to the Noordwijks Cement Accoord and the Dutch Cement Dealers' Association, VCH.[1] But for the most part, the approach to these arrangements was aimed at settlement (agreed revision or termination) rather than prosecution and penalties. Many of these arrangements had in any case been notified and so were immune from penalties and it was accepted, certainly in the earlier years, that they had developed in relatively tolerant national contexts.[2] The enforcement strategy in this area was therefore one which could be characterized as administrative and preventive, a kind of 'tidying' operation, whose formal outcome would be a requirement to terminate or, more benignly, an exemption[3] or negative clearance[4] for severed, acceptable portions of national trading arrangements.

This line of enforcement activity continued into the 1970s and 1980s, much of the time still focusing on Low Country nationwide arrangements operating through trading associations. Some of the main associations/ cartels dealt with by the Commission from the middle of the 1960s until the mid-1980s are listed in Table V.1.

The majority of these cases were 'settled' rather than 'prosecuted', with only rare instances in which an order to terminate or very exceptional fine provoked an appeal, and thus more substantially developed legal argument. Appeals resulted, for instance, in the *Belgian Wallpaper* case (*Papiers Peints*), in which fines had been imposed in respect of a blatant boycott of a particular customer, and in the *Belgian Cement* case (*VCH*) and the *Belgian Tobacco* case (*FEDETAB*) (see below), against orders to terminate

---

[1] Cases 8-11/66, *Cimenteries and others v Commission* [1967] ECR 75; Case 8/72, *Vereeniging van Cementhandelaren v Commission* [1972] ECR 977.

[2] See, for instance, the comments by Advocate General Trabucchi in his opinion in Case 73/74, *Groupement des fabricants de papier peints de Belgique v Commission* [1975] ECR 1491, at 1528; he recommended some reduction in the amount of the fines since the parties had been operating within a national framework tolerant of resale price maintenance.

[3] e.g. *Sulphuric Acid* [1980] 3 CMLR 429.

[4] e.g. *Belgian Perfume Syndicate (ASPA)* [1970] CMLR D25.

Table V.1: Cartels dealt with by the Commission, 1964–87

1964	Belgian Tiles (Convention Faience)
1969	Belgian, Dutch, and German Cement (Noordwijks Accoord)*
1970	German Ceramic Tiles
	Belgian Perfumes Syndicate (ASPA)
1972	Belgian Central Heating
	Dutch Sanitary Ware (GISA)
	Dutch Cement (VCH)*
1973	Dutch Gas Heaters
1974	Belgian Wallpapers (Papiers Peints)*
1975	Dutch Stoves and Heaters
	Dutch Toiletry (Bomée Stichting)
	Glass Containers (IFTRA)
	Aluminium (IFTRA)
1976	Dutch and Belgian Paper (Cobelpa/VNP)
1978	Dutch Bicycles (CBR)
	Belgian Tobacco (FEDETAB)*
	Belgian Spices
1979	Dutch Pharmaceuticals
1980	Dutch Plywood (IMA)
	German Natural Stone
	Sulphuric Acid
	Italian Cast Glass
1981	Italian Flat Glass
1982	Dutch and Belgian Publishers (VBVB/VVVB)
1983	Belgian Newspaper Publishers (Binon)
	Tobacco Retailers (SSI)
1987	Luxembourg Motor Vehicle Assessors

* On appeal to Court of Justice.

with no fines. But otherwise these national association cases were not legally fruitful or significant long-term precedents, but rather particular stages in a process of mopping up.

But, on the other hand, there was a handful of cases at the end of the 1960s and in the first half of the 1970s which were legally significant, in that they entailed significant appeals to the Court of Justice, and some of which were clear prosecutions with penal intent, resulting in the imposition of fines. As such, they struck a much more confrontational note and set the scene legally for some of the significant legal debates of the later case law. At the same time, this group of cases was quite diverse and thus served to pose a range of legal questions.

The appeal against the Commission's decision on the Noordwijks Cement Accoord, heard by the Court of Justice in 1967,[5] has already been discussed in the previous chapter. This was a notified arrangement, so that fines were not an issue, but the Commission's decision was adverse and the producers successfully challenged the sufficiency of the Commission's reasoning, an early shot in what would become an increasingly complex battleground of due process argument. But during the later 1960s, two major investigations were underway, representing the Commission's first moves at proactive policing of international cartels: the action taken against the *Quinine* and *Aniline Dyes* or *Dysefuffs Cartels*, resulting in two formal decisions, both imposing fines, adopted in July 1969.

The *Quinine Cartel* was based upon a long-standing history of co-operation, dating back to 1913. Quinine and its derivative quinidine are components used in the production of a number of medicines, particularly for the treatment of malaria. The raw material for quinine and quinidine is cinchoma bark and pharmaceutical companies had for some time co-operated for purposes of stabilizing the supply of the bark and the market in quinine. By the late 1950s there was a surplus of supply,[6] and a number of French, German, and Dutch producers organized a defensive cartel, arranging for agreement on prices, allocation of purchases from an American stockpile, and protection of respective national markets. The cartel was internally policed and a leading role was undertaken by the Dutch member, Nedchem. Significantly, it was decided not to notify any of the arrangements to the Commission when the EC rules came into force. By the mid-1960s the market conditions had changed—in particular, demand had increased on account of the American military involvement in Vietnam—and the cartel was disbanded in 1965. Early in 1967, the American authorities commenced an investigation into the cartel and information arising from this process prompted a Commission investigation, extending from the summer of 1967 until 1969. The Commission opened a formal proceeding early in 1969, culminating in a decision[7] which imposed fines on the participating companies. The fines imposed on Nedchem and the German company Boehringer Mannheim were (for the time) quite substantial (respectively, 210,000 and 190,000 units of account). The German

---

[5] Cases 8-11/66, n 1 above.

[6] See D G Goyder, *EC Competition Law* (3rd edn, Oxford University Press, 1998) 159, for an informative and concise account of the background to the case. More generally on the commercial significance of quinine and cinchona bark in the control of malaria, see Mark Honigsbaum, *The Fever Trail* (Macmillan, 2001).   [7] 16 July 1969 [1969] CMLR D41.

company Buchler was fined 65,000 units of account and the French participants between 12,500 and 10,000 units of account. Nedchem's successor company, ACF Chemiefarma, and the two German companies appealed against the decision. Both the decision by the Commission and the subsequent judgment of the Court of Justice[8] are historically significant. This was the first major 'own initiative' investigation of a cartel by the Commission, its first real 'penal' decision, and the first opportunity for the Court to consider a range of substantial legal arguments. Along with the almost contemporaneous *Dyestuffs* case, it provided a significant precedent and pointer towards future legal activity.

In their appeal, the companies raised a number of substantive and procedural arguments, the latter relating to rights of defence, sufficiency of reasoning in the decision, and, for the German companies, a double jeopardy issue. By then, both Buchler and Boehringer Mannheim had been convicted and fined under American law, in proceedings before the Southern District Court of New York, and argued that these sanctions should be taken into account in deciding on the penalties under EC law. None of these arguments succeeded, although the Court did decide on a small reduction of the fines, but on factual grounds relating to the period during which the market was affected by the cartel. The outcome was seen as a major success for the Commission. But it was also a relatively straightforward case, involving clear evidence of collusion (corroborated in the American proceedings) and anti-competitive intent. Hindsight also indicates a lesson from the case which may not have been so evident at the time. First, it was indicative of the resolve and resources which could be used by major companies to challenge even legally 'strong' Commission cases. Secondly, the apparently minor tweaking of the fines was an early indication of how the Court (and also the Court of First Instance) would later consider carefully the Commission's use of evidence.

At the same time, action was being taken against the *Dyestuffs Cartel*, but this was a different kind of case in a number of respects. Legal action was here being taken against a formidable array of corporate 'usual suspects' in the context of cartel activity: companies such as ICI, Bayer, BASF, and Hoechst had a history of involvement in such practices and would appear again in the future, in an increasingly recidivist role. These companies would soon demonstrate a willingness to flex their muscles in

---

[8] Case 41/69, *ACF Chemiefarma v Commission* [1970] ECR 661; Case 44/69, *Buchler v Commission* [1970] ECR 733; Case 45/69, *Boehringer Mannheim v Commission* [1970] ECR 769.

legal contest. *Dyestuffs* was also a case immediately suggestive of both murky delinquency and tricky economics. The Commission had been alerted to the existence of potentially injurious but covert price fixing by the European manufacturers of aniline dyes through information and representations from customer trade associations. In effect, the allegation was one of orchestrated price increases between 1964 and 1967. But this was something far from the realm of notification and indeed of hard material proof: the charge was worked out from market circumstances, reasoning that there was collusion from essentially circumstantial evidence. Following its inquiries, the Commission delivered its decision[9] against nine companies, within and without the EC, in the United Kingdom, Germany, Switzerland, France, the Netherlands, and Italy, one week after its decision appeared in *Quinine*. The decision asserted that the similarity in the timing and percentages of a series of price increases was evidence of collusive price fixing, and relied upon an expert report to support this finding (equally the companies were able to commission a contradictory expert report). Fines, mostly of 50,000 units of account, were imposed on the producers of aniline dyes. Compared to some of the fines in *Quinine*, these were 'moderate' (the subsequent description by Advocate General Mayras).[10] The companies appealed. Whereas the appeal in *Quinine* was decided almost exactly one year after the Commission's decision, the *Dyestuffs* appeal was inevitably a more protracted business: the arguments were more difficult, the Court commissioned its own expert report, and the judgment was not ready until almost three years after the decision, finally handed down on 14 July 1972.[11] The judgment deals with a number of fundamental legal questions and the opinion of Henri Mayras, as Advocate General, still stands as a full and scholarly evaluation of these questions.[12]

In summary, there were four main categories of question put before the Court: whether the linear price increases could of themselves provide

---

[9] 24 July 1969; JO 1969, L 195; [1969] CMLR D23. On the earlier history of the *Dyestuffs Cartel*, exemplifying its 'recidivist' character, see George W Stocking and Myron W Watkins, *Cartels in Action: Case Studies in International Business Diplomacy* (Twentieth Century Fund, 1946) 505–6.

[10] [1972] ECR 704.

[11] Case 48/69, *ICI v Commission* [1972] ECR 619. The mainly similar judgments in the related cases follow sequentially in [1972] ECR: BASF, Bayer, Geigy, Sandoz, Francolor, Cassella, Hoechst, and ACNA. The single opinion of Advocate General Mayras is appended to the first report of the ICI judgment.

[12] The opinion may be highly recommended to students and may be read with benefit alongside the critical broadside delivered against the Court of Justice by F A Mann: 'The Dyestuffs Case in the Court of Justice of the European Communities' (1973) 22 *ICLQ* 35.

convincing evidence of collusion; whether the Commission and Court
had jurisdiction over the non-EC (i.e. British and Swiss companies); a
number of procedural and due process questions; and the imposition of
the fines, in particular whether these should be subject to a period of
limitation. In the outcome, both Advocate General and Court were
broadly speaking supportive of the Commission's case, rendering the
judgment contentious.[13] The discussion of the need for a limitation
period would lead to legislation on that issue, in the form of Council
Regulation 2988/74. On the face of it, the judgment again appeared as a
success for the Commission, but also presaged arguments which would
recur in the future. Although the Court's definition of the concept of
concerted practice under Article 81 (ex Article 85) has become a well-
established precedent, its affirmation of the Commission's case by bringing the Commission's evidence within that definition set the stage for
important later argument relating to oligopoly and collusion. There is an
intriguing moment of *déjà vu* referred to by Mann in his critique.[14] The
German Bundeskartellamt had already taken action against the German
dyestuffs producers and had sought to rely on evidence of a meeting in
Basle in August 1967. However, both the Berlin Court of Appeal and the
Bundesgerichthof were wary of accepting the circumstantial evidence of
the meeting:

the course of the talks on August 18, 1967 and the subsequent attitude of the
participants fail to establish with the certainty necessary for conviction that on
that day or even on a later date consensus about a uniform increase of prices was
agreed.[15]

This hesitation rehearses the approach which was subsequently to be
taken by the Court of Justice in its *Woodpulp* judgment,[16] stating that circumstantial evidence of collusion was insufficient while there were other
possible and plausible explanations for parallel behaviour.

A few months later in 1972 the Court of Justice once again supported
the Commission's expansive approach to cartel control by confirming

---

[13] The arguments made by Mann, n 12 above, give a good flavour of the contentious nature
of the judgment in its own time. Mann's dismay relating to the evidence of collusion and economic analysis would prove to be an enduring issue. The concerns about jurisdiction had a more
political flavour and would abate: 25 years later, the consensus against cartels would produce a
climate of international co-operation rather than jurisdictional resistance.

[14] Mann, n 12 above, 41.

[15] Bundesgerichthof, Judgment of 17 December 1970, (1971) *NJW* 521.

[16] Cases C-89/85 etc., *Ahlström Oy and others v Commission* [1993] ECR 1-1307.

wide definitions of key concepts in the appeal by the Dutch Cement Dealers' Association, VCH, against the Commission's order to terminate their system of 'target prices'.[17] The appeal was rejected, the Court affirming that a system of target prices was price collusion in the same way as 'imposed prices', and that the scope of the Association's arrangements did have an effect on trade between member states.[18] Moreover, due process and insufficiency of reasoning arguments were also rejected.

At this time the Commission had also been preparing another major case, a literally huge assault against the European sugar producers, finalized in its decision of 2 January 1973 in the *European Sugar Cartel* case.[19] The Commission had been carrying out inquiries into the operation of the sugar market between 1969 and 1972, another significant own initiative investigation. This had been prompted by a number of events and pieces of information: some complaints by consumers of refusals to sell; investigations by the Bundeskartellamt into the activities of German producers; notification of an arrangement by a French association, which had aroused suspicion; the Commission's own investigation of a Dutch arrangement; and the outbreak of a 'sugar price war' in the Netherlands in March 1969. The investigation led the Commission to conclude that there had been a significant allocation of markets and collusive tendering as between the producers across the EC, in violation of both Articles 85(1) and 86 (now Articles 81(1), 82) of the Treaty. The decision was adopted against 22 undertakings and fines totalling nine million units of account imposed on 16 of these companies. This was, therefore, a weighty prosecution, and unsurprisingly it provoked a weighty appeal. It was almost three years before the appeal was decided by the Court of Justice in December 1975[20] and the report of the judgment in the *European Court Reports* runs to almost 500 pages, including another substantial opinion by Advocate General Mayras.

Sugar is a difficult case to read and is, above all, a case of factual complexity and challenging economic argument. Part of the complexity arises from the application of both Article 85(1) and 86, but also from the need to consider sugar as a special market—a kind of agricultural market subject already to national and Community regulation. As Advocate General

[17] Decision of 16 December 1971, JO 1972, L 13/34; [1973] CMLR D16.
[18] Case 8/72, n 1 above.   [19] OJ 1973, L 140/17; [1973] CMLR D65.
[20] Cases 40/73 etc., *Suiker Unie and others v Commission* [1975] ECR 1663. The Advocate General's opinion starts at 2045.

Mayras commented: in addition to the problem of considering the application of the competition rules to the production of and trade in an agricultural product:

another [problem] has been grafted: are the instruments and the mechanisms provided by a regulation relating to the common organizations of markets and by Community implementing regulations, on the one hand, and the systems maintained or created by national authorities in the same sector, on the other hand, such as to guarantee or permit, provided that there is neither a cartel nor an abuse of a dominant position, the free movement of the product under consideration and free competition between producers?[21]

In short, in such a sector, was there scope for competition in the first place? The Court's conclusion was that there was, in the context of the European sugar market, still some opportunity for competition, but that it was residual. In this way, it confirmed the Commission's finding of a number of anti-competitive practices seeking to protect national markets, but used the 'residual competition argument' in reducing the level of the fines:

The common organization of the market in sugar, which moreover is tending to emerge from its initial transitional phase and for the reasons which have just been given only left a residual field available for competition, has therefore helped to ensure that sugar producers continue to behave in an uncompetitive manner.[22]

Like *Dyestuffs*, the *Sugar Cartel* case involved difficult assessments concerning the relationship between market conditions and apparently anti-competitive behaviour, which would resurface significantly in later cases. At the same time, the Court's judgment in *Sugar* once more gave some encouragement to the Commission, so that by the middle of the 1970s it was beginning to demonstrate confidence as a cartel regulator. Goyder summarizes the early 1970s experience in the following terms:

In giving strong support to the majority of the findings of the Commission in these important cases early in the history of the Community's competition policy, the Court made an important contribution to underpinning the confidence of the Commission in preparing and bringing substantial cartel cases. The wide definition which the Court was prepared to give to concerted practices, and the willingness of the Court to take a broad view of the exercise of the Commission's discretion in reaching conclusions from the evidence available to it, encouraged it to bring other cases of similar magnitude in following years.[23]

---

[21] [1975] ECR 2047.   [22] Ibid., 2023.   [23] Goyder, n 6 above, 162–3.

With the benefit of hindsight, an overall assessment of the experience of litigation in the first half of the 1970s suggests a series of mixed messages. As Goyder indicates, the Court of Justice had been supportive of the Commission in a number of respects. But at the same time, these early cases had revealed some tricky problems of argument and evidence, especially in relation to market factors and an absence of clear material proof of collusion. Indeed, this had already been the American experience.[24] Moreover, the Court was also showing itself attentive to due process and rigour of process arguments. Although denying a strict analogy with criminal proceedings, there is in these early cases nonetheless an acknowledgement that the repressive nature of the procedure ought to be taken into account and was a signal to the Commission that its argument and evidence should be rigorous. Shortly before handing down its judgment in *Sugar* the Court had decided another appeal, in the *Papier Peints (Belgian Wallpaper)* case, at the end of November 1975.[25] Although originally a notified arrangement, the Commission had imposed fines in respect of a boycott imposed on a particular trader for violating resale price maintenance requirements.[26] The Association's appeal succeeded on a procedural argument. The Court accepted that in principle that such a practice could violate Article 85(1), but was not satisfied that the Commission had explained sufficiently how trade between member states had been affected:

The decision does not explain how the fact that 10% of Belgian imports, representing 5% of the total Belgian market, sold by the Groupement subject to its prices and conditions, is in the absence of exclusive arrangements between the members of the Groupement and foreign manufacturers, liable to affect trade between Member States.[27]

Again, the case was a victory of principle for the Commission, but lost on its more precise prosecution of the defendants. This kind of mixed outcome pointed the way to the future course of litigation.

---

[24] See e.g. *Monsanto v Sprayrite* 104 S.C.R 1551 (1984); also the discussion of price signalling by Advocate General Darmon, in [1999] ECR 1-1487 *et seq.*   [25] Case 73/74, n 2 above.

[26] OJ 1974, L 237/3; [1974] 2 CMLR D102. The fines were imposed on four companies, and ranged between BF 6,750,000 and 1,800,000.

[27] [1975] ECJ 1514. But Advocate General Trabucchi did not share these doubts and referred to the four companies who were fined as controlling about half of the amount of wallpaper sold in Belgium: ibid., 1524.

3. The lull in litigation, 1975–85

The decade between the middle of the 1970s and that of the 1980s was marked by a continuing (and from the end of the 1970s, vigorous) 'prosecution' by the Commission of a number of major cartels, without much consequent appeal and litigation. Admittedly, many of these cases were not contentious in terms of evidence. This was the time at which the Commission developed the use of 'dawn raids' or unannounced inspections, and while the days of voluntary notification were fast passing, techniques of sophisticated covert collusion were still relatively speaking in their infancy. In many instances, there was sufficiently clear evidence of contact and agreement. The most important arguments related to economic context, particularly the issue of difficult market conditions which rendered the cartels 'defensive', or even allowed them to qualify as 'crisis cartels'.[28] Such arguments were taken on board, sometimes to the extent of awarding an exemption under Article 85(3) (now Article 81(3)) of the EC Treaty, though more frequently by mitigating the quantum of the fines. Occasionally, there were questions about procedure, or the Commission's exercise of its powers, but not to the extent which would become evident from the middle of the 1980s.

For present purposes, a brief chronological survey will suffice for this period. In December 1977, following an own initiative investigation, the Commission required termination of an arrangement protecting the Belgian market in spices and providing for price maintenance, but no fines were imposed.[29] Two days later, a decision imposed fines of between 10,000 and 25,000 units of account on French, German, and Finnish companies for market sharing and price fixing in relation to vegetable parchment.[30] In July 1978 the Belgian Tobacco Manufacturers' Association, FEDETAB, was ordered to terminate a price-fixing arrangement, following complaint to the Commission by retailers and tobacco wholesalers.[31] The Association appealed, unsuccessfully, invoking procedural and infringement of basic rights arguments.[32] Two years later, in July 1980, the Commission responded sympathetically to a notified buying pool for

---

[28] For a discussion of the concept of crisis cartels, see e.g. Goyder, n 6 above, 169–72; Richard Whish, *Competition Law* (4th edn, Butterworths, 2001) 132. See also the discussion in Chapter VI below.

[29] *Belgian Spices*, 21 December 1977, OJ 1978, L 53/20.

[30] *Vegetable Parchment*, 23 December 1977, OJ 1978, L 70/54; [1978] CMLR 534.

[31] *FEDETAB*, 20 July 1978, OJ 1978, L 224/29; [1978] 3 CMLR 524.

[32] Case 209/78, *FEDETAB v Commission* [1980] ECR 3125.

sulphur, involving all the British and Irish producers of sulphuric acid. This qualified as a 'crisis cartel', which could demonstrate convincingly that the arrangement would improve distribution to customers and justify an exemption under Article 85(3).[33] Towards the end of that year, one of a number of significant decisions relating to the glass market was adopted.[34] The Commission had of its own initiative undertaken an investigation into market sharing and the imposition of quotas by a number of Italian producers of cast glass. Despite the use of obstructive tactics by the companies during the investigation, no fines were imposed since the violation was of limited implementation and had already been terminated. A few months later, an investigation into similar practices in the Italian flat glass market, led to a similar outcome: no fines imposed on account of the short period of application of the arrangements in question.[35] On the other hand, the decision in relation to market protection measures and quotas for rolled zinc imposed fines of between 400,000 and 500,000 units of account on producers in France, Germany, Italy, and the Netherlands in December 1982.[36]

From 1983 some major investigations produced more explicitly penal decisions on the part of the Commission. A major cartel relating to cast iron and steel rolls, operating from 1968 until 1980, had been uncovered following investigations by the Bundeskartellamt and the Commission's own inspectors in 1980. Almost 40 companies in EC countries and elsewhere in Europe were fined between 8,000 and 111,000 units of account for price fixing and collusive tendering.[37] However, fines already imposed on some of the defendants by the Bundeskartellamt were taken into account, as was the fact of a market in decline and subsequent co-operative efforts by the company to restructure in the face of market difficulties. Some months after, another glass cartel was dealt with severely: following search and seizure operations by the Commission in 1981, sharing out of the Benelux market by French multinational groups was uncovered. Fines of between 765,000 and 1,450,000 ECUs (the latter on St Gobain) were imposed for serious violations, despite 'difficult trading conditions'.[38]

[33] *Sulphuric Acid*, 9 July 1980, n 3 above.
[34] *Italian Cast Glass*, 17 December 1980, OJ 1980, L 383/19.
[35] *Italian Flat Glass*, 28 September 1981, OJ 1981, L 326/32; [1982] 3 CMLR 366.
[36] *Rolled Zinc*, 14 December 1982, OJ 1982, L 362/40.
[37] *Cast Iron and Steel Rolls*, 17 October 1983, OJ 1983, L 317/1; [1984] CMLR 694.
[38] *Benelux Flat Glass*, 23 July 1984, OJ 1984, L 212/13; [1985] 2 CMLR 350.

St Gobain and BSN had been involved in previous infringements and had secretly revived old links. At this stage a clear 'antitrust awareness' and willingness to engage in covert tactics began to be evident on the part of some companies. At about the same time another notified arrangement by a crisis cartel in the chemical industry received sympathetic treatment. An agreement on production quotas, involving some familiar names such as Bayer, Courtaulds, ICI, Hoechst, and Rhône-Poulenc, was given an exemption.[39] But the decision relating to the *Zinc Producer Group* in August 1984, was of the now increasingly familiar pattern. Inspections carried out in a number of locations during 1978–80 had revealed market sharing, price fixing, and the use of production quotas. Fines of between 350,000 and 950,000 ECUs were imposed on companies in Germany, France, United Kingdom, Belgium, and the Netherlands, though also taking into account adverse market conditions.[40] Interestingly, the investigations prompted a significant legal challenge concerning the use of legally privileged correspondence as evidence, arising from the Commission's visit to AM & S Europe's office in Bristol, and leading to the important ruling by the Court of Justice on that issue.[41] Towards the end of that year, the decision in *Peroxygen* resulted in more fines, in respect of secret market-sharing arrangements of long duration. The Commission's investigation had been prompted by American proceedings and the Commission decided on fines of between half a million and three million ECUs, the latter being imposed on the Belgian company Solvay.[42] Finally in 1984, a decision was issued retrospectively in respect of the long-standing *Aluminium Cartel*, employing market sharing and export controls and involving the entire primary aluminium industry of the EC between 1963 and 1976, though no fines were imposed, apparently on account of the age of the agreement.[43]

4. European cartel litigation: a new legal industry

Any chronological boundary is to some extent arbitrary. But the middle of the 1980s does serve some purpose as a historical boundary in the present

---

[39] *Synthetic Fibres*, 19 November 1984, OJ 1984 L 207/17; [1985] 1 CMLR 787.

[40] 6 August 1984, OJ 1984, L 220/27; [1985] 2 CMLR 108; Goyder, n 6 above, 164–5.

[41] Case 155/79, *AM & S Europe v Commission* [1982] ECR 1575.

[42] *Peroxygen*, 23 November 1984, OJ 1985, L 35/1; [1985] 1 CMLR 481; Goyder, n 6 above, 163.

[43] *Aluminium*, 19 December 1984, OJ 1985, L 92/1; [1987] 3 CMLR 813; Goyder, n 6 above, 163–4.

discussion. During the early 1980s a number of Commission investigations had been under way and these were to result in some major formal decisions later in the decade which would in turn themselves spawn appeals and litigation of huge significance. A number of legal storms were brewing, resulting in an unsettling period for the Commission in its role as a competition regulator. Discussion, however, may be clarified by focusing on a small group of landmark cases which served as vehicles for significant argument regarding both the legal concept of the cartel as a subject of regulation and the nature of the process of legal control in this context. This will be the main thrust of this section.

At the same time it should be pointed out that during this period major drama did not characterize the whole field of enforcement. There were still some cases in which the Commission was able to prosecute cartels without too much ensuing legal trauma. For instance, the *Peroxygen Cartel*,[44] mentioned above and decided late in 1984, was a major investigation, involving significant corporate actors such as the Belgian company Solvay, and imposing large fines, but there was no appeal. Similarly, *Meldoc*, decided in November 1986, concerned an important cartel in the Dutch dairy industry, and again fines were imposed with no consequent appeal.[45] Again, although there was an appeal against the decision taken in respect of the *Belgian Roofing Felt Cartel*, the appellant's arguments were wholly dismissed.[46] But against this background of steady enforcement the Commission's hitherto relatively quiet life in court was disturbed by a determined legal assault, mounted by a number of major international corporate actors. The context for this legal contest was the traditional area of economic activity for producer cartels: that sector concerned with the production of basic commodities for manufacturing industry, such as chemicals, thermoplastics, glass, and wood pulp.

During the early 1980s a number of major cartel investigations were initiated. One of the earliest of these concerned the wood pulp sector, and interestingly all the companies concerned were at that time based outside the Community (in Finland, Sweden, the United States, Canada, Spain, and Portugal). The investigations had started in 1977 and related to suspected price fixing from 1973 onwards. After a hearing in the spring of 1982, more information was requested for the period up to 1982. There

---

[44] See n 42 above.   [45] *Meldoc*, 26 November 1986, OJ 1986, L 348/50.
[46] Decision of 10 July 1986, OJ 1986, L 232/15; appealed as Case 246/86, *Belasco v Commission* [1989] ECR 2117.

were attempts to reach a negotiated settlement between 1982 and 1984 but some of the American companies were unwilling to commit themselves to the Commission's plan. Following some dramatic last-minute negotiation in December 1984, the Commission suddenly moved to a formal decision on 12 December and was then adamant that it would not budge from the position adopted in that decision.[47] Those companies who had signed the Commission's proposed settlement benefited from a 90 per cent reduction in the amount of the fines imposed. The decision led to appeals, giving rise to two important judgments in the Court of Justice: the first, handed down in September 1988, concerned the issue of jurisdiction over this collection of non-EC companies,[48] the second, in March 1993, concerned the substance of the case and largely overturned the Commission's decision.[49]

The first *Woodpulp* judgment was in favour of the Commission, confirming the jurisdiction over non-Community firms and largely settling the general jurisdictional issue for practical purposes.[50] The second judgment, however, would prove to be a major blow against the Commission and came hard on the heels of another big setback in the *PVC* appeal, discussed below. The Court considered that for the most part the Commission had not proven its case sufficiently, and the pleadings and judgment raised complex and lengthy argument relating to the fundamental question of what should be proven in a cartel prosecution of this kind and the nature of the evidence used for this purpose. It was partly a matter of how the Commission should frame the 'charge' and therefore becomes in substance a consideration of the nature and definition of the cartel 'offence'. It was also a matter of different categories of evidence and how they may be used in a case of this kind. Both of these questions will be considered in detail in the next chapter.

In the meantime, another major investigation into alleged anti-competitive activities in the thermoplastics sector had begun to spawn a litigation that would continue until the end of the century. Initially, investigations

---

[47] The decision was formally adopted on 19 December 1984, OJ 1985, L 85/1; [1985] 3 CMLR 474. For an account of the negotiations, see the opinion of Advocate General Darmon in the later appeal: [1993] ECR I-1455.

[48] Cases 89/85 etc., *Ahlström Oy and others v Commission* [1988] ECR 5193.

[49] Cases C-89/85 etc., n 16 above.

[50] For a commentary on the judgment, see Dieter G F Lange and John Byron Sandage, 'The *Wood Pulp* Decision and its Implications for the Scope of EC Competition Law' (1989) 26 *Common Market Law Review* 137.

(surprise inspections) had been carried out in 1983 into the activities of a number of polypropylene manufacturers (including some 'usual suspects': Rhône-Poulenc, Petrofina, Atochem, BASF, ANIC (subsequently Enichem), Hercules, DSM, Hüls, Hoechst, Shell, Solvay, ICI, Montedipe, and Chemie Linz). The decision and fines in relation to established price fixing for polypropylene was adopted in 1986[51] and survived a subsequent appeal largely intact.[52] Information gathered in this investigation led to two further investigations into related cartels, involving similar arrangements for PVC and LdPE, and decisions taken late in 1988, again imposing fines on many of the same companies.[53] The first appeal in the *PVC* case was decided by the Court of First Instance early in 1992.[54] This judgment constituted one of the most bizarre episodes in the history of the subject, acceding to a formalistic claim by the companies that there was a defect in the form of the Commission's decision: it had not been properly authenticated and should be overruled for that reason. The Court went so far as to say that this was a vitiating factor so fundamental that it rendered the whole decision, not just void but *inexistent*. This exercise of judicial review is more fully discussed in Chapter VII below. Continuing the bare narrative for the present, not surprisingly the Commission in turn appealed the Court of First Instance judgment to the Court of Justice. The Court of First Instance's argument and conclusions received severe treatment at the hands of Advocate General Darmon, although the Court of Justice was kinder, rejecting the arguments and finding of inexistence, but nonetheless still annulling the decision on account of its lack of authentication.[55] Following that judgment, the Commission readopted the same decision in a properly authenticated form,[56] which in turn was again appealed on a number of procedural grounds, but this time the Court of First Instance largely upheld the decision.[57] Some of the companies appealed against this last judgment on a number of points of procedure and the Court of Justice finally dismissed the great majority of

---

[51] OJ 1986, L 230/1.

[52] Cases T-1/89 etc., *Rhône-Poulenc v Commission* [1991] ECR II-867 (CFI); further appeals to the Court of Justice against the judgment on procedural grounds were unsuccessful: Case C-51/92P, *Hercules Chemicals v Commission* [1999] ECR I-4235.

[53] *PVC Cartel*, OJ 1989 L 74/1 (fines totalling 25 million ECUs); *LdPE cartel*, OJ 1989, L 74/21 (fines totalling 35 million ECUs).

[54] Cases T-79/89 etc., *BASF and others v Commission* [1992] ECR II-315

[55] Cases C-137/92P etc., *Commission v BASF and others* [1994] ECR I-2555. See the commentary by A G Toth (1995) 32 *CMLRev* 271.   [56] OJ 1994, L 239/14.

[57] Cases T-305/94 etc., *LVM and others v Commission* [1999] ECR II-931.

these arguments in October 2002, Advocate General Mischo having already handed down an opinion in October 2001 arguing that the companies complaints should be dismissed.[58] The *PVC* saga of investigation and litigation has thus endured almost 20 years. In the meantime, the Commission's *LdPE* decision had been impugned on the same grounds (lack of authentication) and when the Court of First Instance dealt with the case in 1995, it followed the Court of Justice's ruling in *PVC* by confidently declaring the decision to be void (though not inexistent).[59] Legally the *LdPE* case was closed at that point; the Commission did not readopt its decision in view of the time that had elapsed since the original decision had been taken. There had by that time been so much industry reorganization that few of the original companies still existed: unravelling the changes in ownership would have stretched the meaning of a 'readopted' decision.

Whereas the contest in *Wood Pulp* had been largely concerned with the legal framing of the case and sufficiency of evidence, the drawn-out arguments concerning the thermoplastic cartels were largely concerned with form and procedure. The litigation in these thermoplastics cases contributed a great deal to the Community system of judicial review and the delineation of rights in defence. Above all, these legal arguments were concerned with the nature of the process being used by the Commission in its regulation of cartels, as an administrative procedure but one that in substance suggested an analogy with a criminal proceeding. The litigation was thus the trigger for a detailed analysis of both Community administrative law and the development of fundamental procedural rights.

Another 'big case' arising at this time involved some of the same companies (for instance, Solvay, ICI, and Rhône-Poulenc), this time acting on the soda ash market, and also raised procedural arguments. There had been an alleged long-standing but in more recent years covert market sharing arrangement in relation to soda ash (an important component in the production of glass). In particular, the United Kingdom had been reserved to ICI, with much of continental Western Europe reserved to Solvay. The Commission had again carried out surprise inspections in 1989 and then adopted a decision in 1990, imposing fines of 7 million ECUs on each of Solvay and ICI.[60] The companies' appeal against this decision invoked both the irregular authentication issue exploited in *PVC* and also denial of rights

---

[58] Cases C-238/99P etc., *LVM and others v Commission* [2002] ECR I-8375.
[59] Cases T-80/89 etc., *BASF and others v Commission* [1995] ECR II-729.
[60] 19 December 1990, OJ 1991, L 152/1.

of defence in relation to disclosure of documents from the Commission's file. These arguments succeeded in the Court of First Instance in 1995,[61] providing another major reversal for the Commission, although the judgment in a related Article 86 proceeding involving solvay was in turn appealed to the Court of Justice.[62] By now, the Commission was feeling strongly frustrated. Most of these cases had produced clear evidence of collusion, while the decisions and fines were being wholly or largely overturned on procedural grounds in a context of developing procedural law. The former head of Commission DG1V commented: 'the goalposts cannot be shifted too often. One could almost be left with the impression that in *Soda Ash* the CFI welcomed the possibility to decide these cases on procedural grounds.'[63]

The final blow against the Commission in this clutch of cases, came in further proceedings against the *Italian Flat Glass Cartel*. The Commission revisited this sector in 1986–7 following legal action in the Italian courts earlier in 1986 and complaints to the Commission later that year by a wholesaler. The Commission's decision in December 1988,[64] which this time imposed fines on companies who had previously been found to be in infringement of Article 85(1) (as discussed above), was appealed successfully to the Court of First Instance.[65] On this occasion, the Court emulated the role of the Court of Justice in *Wood Pulp*, looking closely at the sufficiency of evidence in the Commission's case and finding it wanting. The outcome was that most of the decision was overturned, although some evidence (and hence liability to sanctions) survived the scrutiny, leaving the Commission with a minor score against these usual suspects from the Italian glass industry. As the Court stated, it had considered that the Commission's hypothesis of:

a close cartel among the three applicants, as advanced in the decision, has not been proved to the requisite legal standard. However, the Court has found that some of the documents on which the decision is based can prove a more episodic concertation among two or three producers.[66]

Moreover:

The Court takes into consideration the fact that the infringement of Article 85(1) of the Treaty which it has upheld against against FP and SIV was an infringement

---

[61] Cases T-30/91 etc., *Solvay v Commission* [1995] ECR II-1775.

[62] Case 286/95P, *Commission v Solvay* [2000] ECR I-2341, at 454.

[63] Claus Dieter Ehlermann and Berend Jan Drijber, 'The Legal Protection of Enterprises: Administrative Procedure, in Particular Access to Files and Confidentiality' (1996) 7 *European Competition Law Review* 375.   [64] 7 December 1988, OJ 1989, L 33/44.

[65] Cases T-68/89 etc., *Società Italiana Vetro and others v Commission* [1992] ECR II-1403.

[66] [1992] ECR II-1534.

of the express terms of that provision of the Treaty and that the undertakings concerned had already been addressees of the 1981 decision, which however did not impose penalties on them. Accordingly, even though the infringements which the Court has found to exist are much less serious than all the infringements alleged in the decision, the Court considers that the fines cannot be cancelled entirely.[67]

Two further points may be noted about these appeals which were so adverse in outcome to the Commission.

First, in factual terms there was clear collusion of some kind in these cases. There was no real doubt about the actual involvement of these companies in price fixing, market sharing, and the like; the issue concerned the determination of their legal liability in respect of that behaviour. In turn, the essential question was then one of the more precise nature of the 'offence' being prosecuted, and following on that, the extent of the companies' liability (if any) to be fined. In effect—although this is not very evident from a superficial reading of some of these cases—a debate was under way concerning the nature of cartel delinquency.

Secondly, in procedural terms, it is interesting to note the extent to which both courts were willing to undertake an inquisitorial role, regarding matters of both evidence and of the Commission's conduct of the proceeding. Perhaps the most dramatic example of such inquisitorial initiative was the Court of First Instance's first decision in *PVC* to open the issue of lack of authentication and inexistence. This particular Chamber of the Court decided of its own motion to investigate the circumstances in which the decision had been formally adopted, while the point had not been pleaded by the parties (at that stage—it was taken up with enthusiasm thereafter!) The relevant EC Treaty articles provided no clear basis for the exercise of such jurisdiction, nor this use of the concept of 'inexistence' and 'untouchability of the act'. Such an expansive approach to their jurisdiction on the part of both courts may well have contributed to the longevity of the litigation and the willingness of the defending companies to employ as many defensive strategies as possible.

5. Recovering the initiative in enforcement

The cases discussed in the previous section had challenged the Commission's approach to enforcement in relation to cartel activity: as to

[67] [1992] ECR II-1552.

how the Commission framed its case against cartels, the sufficiency of its evidence, and the due process aspects of its procedure. Even taking on board the view that the Court of First Instance's judgment in *PVC* had something of a rogue character, these cases and judgments did raise some significant questions of legal substance and procedure, and inevitably the Commission had to draw some lessons. For instance (and this will be discussed in greater detail later in Chapter VI below), the Commission developed a fuller and clearer 'theory' of cartel prosecution, by identifying more explicitly and precisely the kind of offending conduct which should be prosecuted under the competition rules and be visited with penal sanctions (a response to *Wood Pulp*). Also, defence rights became more clearly delineated, especially in relation to opportunities for 'access to the (Commission's) file' and 'equality of arms', and the Commission issued a Notice on *Internal Rules of Procedure for Processing Requests for Access to the File*.[68]

Equally, lessons were delivered (though not necessarily drawn) on the other side, in relation to the limits to which arguments on rights of defence and procedural propriety could be taken.[69] Significantly, for instance, the episode concerning the 'inexistence' of Commission decisions was brought to an end by the Court of Justice, although in practical terms it served to knock back a number of Commission prosecutions. Overall, the period from the mid- to later 1990s may be regarded as one of steady progress from the perspective of enforcement at the European level. The Commission continued to uncover evidence of major cartel activity in a number of economic sectors and its fining practice became confidently more severe. The appeals also continued unabated; indeed, a regular pattern emerged of appeal first to the Court of First Instance and then to the Court of Justice, usually on the initiative of the defendant undertakings.[70] The outcome of litigation has on balance favoured the Commission, in that most of the appellate judgments have upheld the majority of the Commission's arguments and findings. To be sure, fines have been reduced, particularly in relation to individual defendants, but often on account of insufficiency of evidence regarding their participation

[68] OJ 1997, C 23/3.

[69] A good recent example is provided by the opinion of Advocate General Mischo in Case C-254/99P, *ICI v Commission*, 25 October 2001 [2002] ECR I-8375, dismissing all of the arguments raised by the applicant company.

[70] For a convenient summary of decisions and appeals to both courts, for the period 1986 to mid-2001, see the table in Whish, n 28 above, 419–24.

or its duration. A typical case, and one which may be regarded in some respects as the Commission's least successful outcome during this period, is that of the *Cement Cartel*, which was finally dealt with by the Court of First Instance in 2000.[71] The Commission had imposed fines totalling 248 million euros on the cartel members. As a matter of legal principle the Court accepted a main thrust of the Commission's case: that the majority of the companies, as 'indirect' members of the cartel (the 'direct' members were their trade associations), were in breach of the competition rules through their awareness of the associations' agreements, coupled with their actions in support of the aims of the agreements (the 'cartel as a whole' argument). On the other hand, the Court considered that the Commission had not sufficiently proven its case against some of the companies. Moreover, there had been some procedural violations, regarding access to the file and the statement of objections. Overall, therefore, the Court reduced the total amount of the fines to 110 million euros. But this was the biggest reduction of fines on appeal in recent years.

On the widest view, the Commission has not lost a major legal battle since *Soda Ash* in 1995. Most importantly, perhaps, the Community courts appear to have accepted the Commission's concept of the offence residing in 'the cartel as a whole', so easing its legal and evidential burden. The working out of the concept of the 'cartel as a whole' will be considered more fully in the next chapter. But it would appear now to have achieved judicial endorsement and to have become a central element of legal doctrine for purposes of establishing liability in relation to participation in cartel activity. In its *PVC 2* judgment, the Court of First Instance stated the law in these terms:

An undertaking may be held responsible for an overall cartel even though it is shown to have participated directly only in one or some of its constituent elements if it is shown that it knew, or must have known, that the collusion in which it participated, especially by means of regular meetings organised over several years, was part of an overall plan intended to distort competition and that the overall plan included all the constituent elements of the cartel.[72]

Thus the ghost of *Wood Pulp* would appear to have been laid.

---

[71] Commission decision: OJ 1994, L 343/1; [1995] 4 CMLR 327; Cases T-25/95 etc., *Cimenteries v Commission* [2000] ECR II-491; appeal to the Court of Justice pending, Case C-204/00P, *Aalborg Portland v Commission*.

[72] Case T-305/94, n 57 above, [1999] ECR II-931, at 1146.

The major 1990s cartel investigations and prosecutions by the Commission, leading to formal decisions and, usually, fines and appeals, are listed in Table V.2.

One feature of the list in Table V.2 is the extent to which enforcement has spread from its main traditional context in relation to the raw materials and manufacturing industries to other economic sectors, such as service industries, freight shipping, and telecommunications. Quantifying

Table V.2: Cartel investigations and prosecutions by the Commission, 1989–2002

1989	Welded Steel Mesh
1992	Eurocheque Helsinki (Banks and Credit Institutions)
	Netherlands Building and Construction
1994	Steel Beams
	Cartonboard
	Cement
	Transatlantic Freight Shipping
	Far East Freight Shipping Conference
1995	Dutch Mobile Cranes (Crane Hire)
1997	Ferry Operators
1998	Alloy Surcharge (an ECSC case) (Stainless Steel)
	TACA (Freight Shipping)
1999	Pre-Insulated Pipes
	Greek Ferries
	British Sugar
2000	Seamless Steel tubes
	Dutch Electrotechnical Equipment
	FETTCSA (Freight Shipping)
	Amino Acids*
	Soda Ash
2001	Graphite Electrodes*
	SAS/Maersk (Airline Operators)
	Vitamins*
	Citric Acid*
	German Banks
	Carbonless Paper
2002	Plasterboard
	Methionine*
	Lombard Club: Austrian Banks

* Also an American prosecution.

the penalties initially imposed by the Commission during this period presents another view: four cartels in the steel sector attracted fines totalling 240 million euros; while five cartels in the shipping sector attracted fines totalling more than 300 million euros. Thus the net of enforcement has become wider and deeper in this respect. More recently, investigations were initiated in the brewing sector in March 2000 and into the supply of cell-phone networks in June 2001.

6. Changing modalities of enforcement

Altogether during the last decade antitrust enforcement in Europe has achieved more focus and sharper relief. Attitudes and policy have acquired greater definition. By the end of the 1990s there was a much more certain sense on all sides that such activities as price fixing, market sharing, and the like were delinquent and rarely justifiable. In professional jargon, they had become 'hard core cartels' and 'egregious violations' of the competition rules. In the language of its decisions and its other official statements the Commission was more confidently proclaiming the 'evil' of cartel collusion, such as Competition Commissioner Mario Monti's famous description of such activity as a 'cancer on the open market economy'.[73] Writers had started to use the vocabulary of delinquency and draw stronger analogies with crime and criminal law.[74] This was also happening in a context of a global development of practice and policy (discussed further in Chapters VIII, IX, and X). In 1998 the OECD adopted a strong position on the regulation of 'hard core cartels'.[75] American enforcement action against international cartels became more determined during the 1990s; and a number of European states moved towards criminalization of cartel behaviour.[76]

This shift in official attitude appeared to be reflected in the self-image of the companies engaged in these practices and a growing awareness of their own 'antitrust delinquency'. Commission investigations and the resulting decisions have become more and more revealing of the *behaviour* of individuals within undertakings. There is in these cases sociologically

---

[73] Opening address at the Third Nordic Competition Policy Conference, Stockholm, 11 September 2000.

[74] See, e.g. Christopher Harding, *European Community Investigations and Sanctions: the Supranational Control of Business Delinquency* (Leicester University Press, 1993); Whish, n 28 above, 416.

[75] Organisation for Economic Co-operation and Development, *Ententes Unjustifiables/Hard Core Cartels* (2000).   [76] See Chapter IX below.

fascinating material relating to the internal structure and operation of cartels. Company executives were self-consciously styling themselves as 'Bosses' or 'Heads of State' and 'Experts' (in the *LdPE Cartel*),[77] 'Presidents' (in *Cartonboard*),[78] and 'Popes' and 'Elephants' (in *Pre-Insulated Pipes*),[79] drawing upon a Mafia and governmental vocabulary of power. At a corporate level, the leading participants or 'ringleaders' of the *Polypropylene Cartel* styled themselves 'the Big Four'.[80] There was evidence of the development of defensive strategies: in *Cartonboard* for example, one company engaged external lawyers to stage a 'mock investigation' or 'dummy run'.[81] Moreover, there emerged some orthodox corporate acceptance (for external consumption) of the delinquent nature of anti-competitive collusion, evidenced in an apparent willingness to engage in a dialogue of compliance with regulators. A revealing episode of 'external compliance' and 'internal delinquency' appears in the account of the *Pre-Insulated Pipes Cartel*.[82] The Swedish–Swiss conglomerate ABB (Asea Brown Boveri) claimed that it had a 'mandatory group policy' of compliance with the competition rules, which was nonetheless flouted by senior managers. Nonetheless, there was considerable evidence of a steadfast and more widely disseminated corporate delinquency. Even after investigations had started in June 1995 and a warning from the Commission to desist from any illegal activity, the company continued its cartel arrangements, for instance proposing the establishment of a permanent cartel secretariat in Zurich.[83] The company indicated its willingness to co-operate with the Commission, yet continued to participate in cartel meetings, discussing plans to replace plenary meetings of the cartel with a 'consultant'.[84] The company claimed to have used internal disciplinary measures, in that a number of senior managers were relieved of their duties. The Commission's view was that this action was a highly selective exercise: it was not applied very much to senior executives—one relatively middle-ranking executive left the group, and the former Vice-President of ABB left on the eve of the Commission's decision.

The late 1990s were also marked by significant developments in enforcement policy at the European level. Earlier in the 1990s the US Department of Justice had revitalized antitrust enforcement with its new leniency programme, designed to exploit the inherent instability and

---

[77] OJ 1989, L 74/21, at 23–4.   [78] OJ 1994, L 243/1, at 10.
[79] OJ 1999, L 24/1, at 14.   [80] OJ 1986, L230/1, at 5.   [81] See n 78 above, at 9.
[82] See n 79 above, OJ 1999, L 24/1, at 64 (point 172).   [83] Ibid., point 111.
[84] Ibid., point 172. Confirmed by the Court of First Instance in its judgment of 20 March 2002, in Case T-31/99, *ABB v Commission*, at points 223–4 of the judgment.

internal mutual suspicion within business cartels by an often real and substantial inducement of legal immunity for the first participant to break ranks and supply convincing evidence of a cartel's activity.[85] Setting up this 'race to the courtroom door' enabled the successful prosecution and punishment of a number of major international cartels (*Graphite Electrodes, Citric Acid, Lysine, Vitamins*)[86] and set the example for European jurisdictions. The Commission established its own leniency programme in 1998,[87] and had already supplied a more focused statement on its policy and practice in determining the amount of fines.[88] Also in December 1998, the Commission established a new Anti-Cartel Unit within the Competition DG, dedicated and given resources for the task of dealing only with suspected cartels. Although the Commission's leniency policy has yet to emulate the success of the American programme, the potential fruits of enforcement to be gathered from an effective combination of tough penalties and tempting leniency were suggested by the collapse of the *Pre-Insulated Pipes Cartel* in 1996. Although Commission investigations were well under way at that stage and had garnered a good deal of evidence in dawn raids, a number of companies approached the Commission with offers to co-operate. By that time all were too late to qualify for the maximum discount on fines, some of the companies (including ABB) qualified for a 30 per cent co-operation discount, and two companies gained a 20 per cent discount merely for not contesting the case.[89]

The Commission further refined its leniency programme in 2002, and these new strategies may eventually transform the landscape of enforcement. If leniency does become successful in the same way that it has worked for the US Department of Justice, this should ease the Commission's evidential workload and reduce the scope for some kinds of legal argument on appeal: the cases against cartels could become all too clear. On the other hand, the implementation of leniency may in turn throw up arguments of procedure and due process, simply relocating the context for litigation. Nonetheless, the modalities of the enforcement process could be transformed for the future.

---

[85] See the discussion in Chapter VIII below.

[86] See US Department of Justice, *Status Report: International Cartel Enforcement*, 1 June 2002 (www.usdoj.gov.atr).

[87] *Notice on the Non-Imposition or Reduction of Fines in Cartel Cases*, OJ 1998, C 9/3, 14 January 1998.

[88] *Guidelines on the Method of Setting Fines*, OJ 1996, C 207/4, 18 July 1996.

[89] OJ 1999, L 24 at 61 *et seq.*

VI

Proof of Cartel Delinquency: Fashioning the European Cartel Offence

1. 'Delinquency inflation' and the emergence of the problem of antitrust evidence

As systems of cartel regulation advanced from an earlier phase of consensual notification, compromise, and negotiated settlement to a more prohibitive, confrontational, and repressive mode of control, so issues of evidence came more to the forefront. A system of notified arrangements, in which there is a fair measure of goodwill and co-operation on the part of both companies and regulators may naturally rely on a willingness to reveal most aspects of the trading practices in question (although even in the original EC system, which was heavily reliant on notification, sanctions were laid down in Regulation 17 for the provision of false and incomplete information). But once cartels (or certain types of cartel) had become categorically prohibited, with little prospect of condonation, there was literally everything to hide if the companies wished to maintain their anti-competitive practices. In fact, this represents an interesting aspect of the evolution of 'delinquency': a progression from consensual regulation, to clear prohibition, accompanied by an increasingly covert and self-consciously 'bad attitude' on the part of those engaging in the conduct. This may be described as a process of 'delinquency inflation'. Legitimate agreement is transformed into illegal collusion, and the companies involved in such arrangements are driven more and more into an underground domain of secretive, defiant, and obstructive strategies designed to evade law enforcement. Thus, what was 30 years ago viewed as a mild subject for regulation has evolved into 'brazen' and 'egregious' violations, eventually transformed into fully fledged criminal offences. Inevitably, therefore, there will be problems of proof for enforcement agencies.

In relation to serious antitrust violations, issues of evidence and systems of proof fall into two main categories, which may be broadly described as the economic and the material. Both relate to an understanding of the nature of the offending conduct, and the fact that the 'cartel offence' in the European context[1] has evolved gradually and empirically without a very precise definition. The *economic* issues of evidence arise from a consideration of market context and are essentially concerned with questions of, first, whether the alleged prohibited collusion is real collusion or 'innocent' and natural behaviour on such a market, and secondly, whether market conditions may render collusion justifiable. The problem with such questions of economic evidence resides in their evaluative character as market analysis rather than 'hard' fact. It is in short a species of expert evidence. *Material* issues of evidence are more familiar to lawyers as concerning the conventional modes of using factual evidence to establish prohibited conduct: documentary, verbal, and perhaps some kinds of circumstantial evidence of meetings, agreements, and understandings. From a legal point of view this latter category of evidence is less problematical to handle, but its method of collection, through searches and questioning, may (and does) give rise to arguments relating to procedure and defence rights.

As stated above, whether the subject is market context or factual meetings and communications, both have to be related to defined offensive behaviour. Put very simply: what is any of this evidence being used to prove—what is the offence? In the EC context it has been necessary for the Commission and the Community courts to gradually work out a concept of the business cartel as an offending mode of behaviour. Does the prohibition of Article 85(1) (now Article 81(1)) of the EC Treaty, especially in so far as it requires the application of punitive sanctions, cover any kind of cartel in any kind of market context? Does it apply to a course of conduct over a period of time or to more precise individual acts of collusion? Does it apply to the conduct of specific undertakings in their role as individual participants or to collective actions of all the members of the cartel? These are potentially difficult questions intermeshing legal issues of both

---

[1] Even under American law, with the early definition of a criminal offence under the Sherman Act, working out the more precise parameters of the offence required a considerable amount of litigation and judicial effort.

substantive law and evidence. The starting point in the basic Treaty Article (like the Sherman Act in the United States before it) provides only general guidance in the broad vocabulary of 'agreement' and 'concerted practice'. By the late 1990s the Commission and the Community courts had, through a lengthy and detailed dialogue of appellate litigation, worked out a concept of the cartel offence, although it is not referred to in those precise terms. It is clear that this offence is not 'collective' in the sense of imposing a vicarious liability on every member of the cartel for everything done within the framework of the cartel. But at the same time, it does impose liability on individual participants based on a knowledge or reasonable knowledge of what would follow from their own participation (the so-called 'cartel as a whole' theory).[2] This concept of the cartel 'offence' has important implications for what is required in terms of evidence, as will be seen in the discussion below.

2. Economic evidence: the significance of market context

It is difficult to escape the economic and market context of cartel arrangements in any evaluation of that activity. Cartels exist for economic reasons and this basic fact has to inform any discussion of legal liability. As was clear in the earlier discussion of the emergence of 'modern' business cartels, as an economic phenomenon they represent the desire for stability over the uncertain risks of competition. In turn, that represents a certain economic (i.e. supplier) self-interest, with a cost elsewhere, and the function of legal regulation is to determine how far it is justifiable to allow that interest of the economic supplier to prevail over other interests, either of other market operators or of consumers. Goyder identifies neatly this underlying protective cartel impulse towards certainty and stability in the following terms:

Many agreements are primarily defensive in their objectives and usually introduce what most businessmen regard as welcome certainty and stability into an uncertain world in place of some (even if not all) of the unpredictable elements of competition. In this category we can place price-fixing, between manufacturers and by collective agreement, in order to impose resale price maintenance on distributors

---

[2] See, for instance, the judgment of the Court of First Instance in Case T-305/94, *LVM and others v Commission* [1999] ECR II-931, at 1146.

or retailers, also allocation of markets or customers, collective refusals to supply, collective boycotts, and other collective exclusionary arrangements. Methods may vary considerably...Nonetheless, in nearly every case the objective is similar: to protect an existing position or to prevent a feared deterioration in the relevant market.[3]

In a very wide sense, therefore, cartels are naturally defensive organizations. The problem for economic and regulatory policy is then to determine the limits of what is justifiable as a defensive strategy—where to draw the line between a genuinely difficult market situation on the one hand and on the other, 'the easy life' or too much supracompetitive profit. In relation to the 'market in trouble', policy-makers need to take on board evidence from the market, but this is usually a legislative function, whereby defensive co-operation is substantively defined as an acceptable arrangement, and so outside the scope of prohibition and censure.

In the EC context, this has been the approach taken in principle to deal with the problem of genuine 'crisis cartels'. Some markets may suffer an exceptional and prolonged downturn in trade, in which there is a large and apparently continuing disparity between productive capacity and actual demand for the product in question. In such circumstances, it may be argued that, without some marketwide agreement to limit competition (in particular via the use of production quotas), some businesses may fail altogether, leading to unemployment, social dislocation, and a reduction in the competitive base of the industry. The Commission's reaction to this problem during the prolonged period of recession in the 1970s was to encourage supervised initiatives for restructuring industries in crisis. By means of an informal announcement published in its *Twelfth Annual Report*,[4] the Commission indicated the conditions which would make such restructuring or 'crisis cartels' qualify for exemption under Article 85(3) of the Treaty. At the very least it had to be shown that there was structural overcapacity which had led all the undertakings in the market in question to experience a significant reduced capacity utilization and substantial operating losses, with no prospect of lasting improvement in the medium term. The industry-proposed lower level of capacity would have to be conducive to competition, should enable moves towards specialization of production, and be timed to minimize social dislocation arising from agreed cutbacks. The Commission's decision on the *Synthetic Fibres Cartel*

---

[3] D G Goyder, *EC Competition Law* (3rd edn, Oxford University Press, 1998) 157.
[4] EC Commission, *Twelfth Annual Report on Competition Policy* (1982) 43–5.

(polyester and polyamide) in 1985 illustrates the application of these principles and conditions in a particular market.[5]

In such a way, economic argument can be used to define conduct as legally acceptable, so contributing to the ongoing delineation of the cartel offence. The toleration of crisis cartels, as a response to economic downturn and structural overcapacity, is an especially pertinent example. There are other situations in which cartels may be tolerated for economic or a mix of economic and political reasons. For instance, a number of national competition laws have exempted export cartels from their regulation, since these were not seen as affecting the internal market of those countries and may also have favoured national trading interests.[6] However, export cartels, in so far as they continue to operate from some jurisdictions, do not appear to figure at all prominently in the field of major international cartel activity. The kind of economic argument being considered here is thus principally relevant to competition policy rather than the enforcement of competition rules. What is more relevant to the latter, and especially as a matter of evidential argument, is the view that certain kinds of market conditions may create the appearance of prohibited collusion, whereas the behaviour in question is in fact spontaneous, innocent conduct which naturally arises in such a market.

3. Economic evidence: the problem of parallel behaviour and 'tacit collusion'

It is empirically well attested that cartels frequently appear in concentrated markets, those dominated by a relatively small number of suppliers. This coincidence of concentration and cartelization may be problematic for the legal regulation of cartels, especially for a prohibitory system of regulation which seeks to outlaw cartel arrangements and penalize their planning and implementation. Such a market structure may be brought

---

[5] OJ 1984 L 207/17, [1985] 1 CMLR 787. An earlier example of the Commission's sympathetic approach to this kind of problem, prior to its statement in the *Twelfth Annual Report*, was its decision in *Sulphuric Acid* [1980] 3 CMLR 429.

[6] Perhaps most famously, the Webb–Pomerene Act (1918) in the United States. Exemption and registration of export cartels under British and German legislation has recently been abandoned. American export cartels account for only a small fraction of American trade—see A Dick, 'When are Cartels Stable Contracts?' (1996) 39 *Journal of Law and Economics* 241. The OECD does not consider the issue of export cartels to be a priority: OECD, *Hard Core Cartels* (2000), 28.

into the discussion of cartel regulation in two principal ways. First, in the absence of clear evidence of collusion, regulators may be tempted to point to some of the characteristic features of a concentrated or oligopolistic market, especially parallelism of prices and other marketing strategies, as circumstantial evidence of such collusion. This argument reasons backwards from the apparent market outcome to an intention to achieve that result, similarity of prices then being proof of a fix. As will be seen below, this kind of argument is viewed with suspicion, in both economic and legal terms. Even so, it leaves the possibility that such market evidence could be used *in support* of more direct evidence of collusion. Secondly, features of the market may be used as a defence against an allegation of collusion, arguing that what may appear to be arranged is in fact spontaneous and expected parallel behaviour on that market. In short, it may be seen that economic evidence of *parallel conduct* is inherently ambiguous and may be used to support both directions of legal argument.

The problems and pitfalls involved in drawing upon this kind of evidence and argument are exacerbated by underlying theoretical uncertainties which bedevil such market analysis. Economists could argue endlessly about oligopoly and how it should be understood and interpreted. There is no easy agreement as to how such markets operate, which in turn creates problems for any legal procedure which attempts to employ economic analysis as a form of evidence. The vulnerability of this kind of 'expert' evidence has been summed up by Scherer in the following terms:

The trouble is, economic analysis is an elastic instrument, and I am sorry to report, some economists' consciences are also elastic, so one can find economists who with apparent conviction will explain away any pattern of behaviour, however bizarre, as the consequence of special but highly competitive industry circumstances... Every tacit collusion case... would be a 'big case', drawing big teams of economists to ply the courts with their expert but conflicting opinion... It would not, I fear, be a system highly likely to yield either truth or justice.[7]

The problems of understanding oligopoly[8] are well documented. These need only be briefly rehearsed for present purposes, before turning to the

---

[7] F M Scherer, 'The Posnerian Harvest: Separating Wheat from Chaff' (1977) 86 *Yale Law Journal* 974, at 983.

[8] Oligopoly theory may be traced through earlier models, e.g. from A A Cournot (1838), through to mid-twentieth-century analyses, such as E H Chamberlin, *The Theory of Monopolistic Competition* (1933), more recent critiques such as F M Scherer and David Ross, *Industrial Market Structure and Economic Performance* (3rd edn, Houghton Mifflin, 1990), and application of game theory, e.g., Dennis A Yao and S De Santi, 'Game Theory and the Legal Analysis of Tacit Collusion' (1993) *Antitrust Bulletin* 113.

pertinent question in a discussion of cartel regulation: how, and to what extent, may such market analysis be employed in legal argument concerning alleged anti-competitive collusion?

The main underlying problem in this discussion is that of establishing the extent to which an oligopolistic market is uncompetitive in a deliberated way. In Whish's concise statement:

A problem for competition policy arises in markets in which there are only a few operators who are able, by virtue of the characteristics of the market, to behave in a parallel manner and to derive benefits from their collective market power, without, or without necessarily, entering into an agreement or concerted practice to do so.[9]

The crucial question is whether the participants in such a market achieve their competitive advantage and supracompetitive profits fortuitously, as it were, from the structure of the market, or whether it is something which is necessarily achieved through their conduct and decisions.

In support of the 'structural' view is the conventional theory of oligopoly. This is based on the perception that such concentrated markets are characterized by a non-competitive stability: rival firms are *interdependent* and price competition is minimal or even non-existent. Market interdependence of this kind is supported by game theory analysis which has been employed by economists in analysing this type of market. Such interdependent stability is promoted in particular by a natural process of price 'matching'. If one firm cuts prices, the others naturally and quickly follow suit since they are likely to lose large market shares if they do not do so. On the other hand, there is no incentive for one firm to increase prices unilaterally, since this would also result in a large loss of market share. A small number of suppliers with large market shares[10] will thus naturally have a strong mutual awareness of each others' position, coupled with a realization that, from their lack of competition, there arises a supracompetitive level of profit. All of this is achieved from alignment without actual communication between the rival companies: they have the benefits of

---

[9] Richard Whish, *Competition Law* (4th edn, Butterworths, 2000), 470.

[10] What is a small number? It is often reckoned that with more than 10 or 12 equally matched players, interdependence starts to break down. In terms of game theory, 'a ten or twelve person game may present so many variables as to defy formulation of a rational approach': Joseph F Brodley, 'Oligopoly Power under the Sherman and Clayton Acts' (1967) 19 *Stanford Law Review* 285, at 291. Even so, there have been defence claims of market interdependence (for instance, in the *PVC* and *Polypropylene Cartel* cases) with 12 or 16 players on the market.

price fixing without needing to fix.[11] Economists may refer to this as 'tacit collusion', although lawyers may prefer less self-contradictory formulations, such as 'tacit co-ordination' or 'conscious parallelism'.[12] While this may not be a desirable state of affairs from the perspective of competition policy, it implies that any solutions should be *structural* (for instance, measures of deconcentration) rather than *normative* (for instance, prohibiting and punishing alleged collusion).

But this 'structural' theory of oligopoly is not unchallenged[13] and has some well-known weaknesses.[14] It is argued, for example, that the extent of interdependence may be overplayed (for example, a price cutter may steal a march on rivals if there is a delay before they find out about the reduction); that market structures may not be so simple (rivals may have different cost levels, or command consumer loyalty; transparency may be variable); that competition does exist (especially in relation to quality of product, after sales, or advertising, rather than price) in some concentrated markets. In particular, there is the issue of price increases and supracompetitive profit. Empirically, prices do increase in parallel in some markets—how does this happen without some form of collusion? The usual response to this last objection is to refer to a process of 'price leadership' and 'price signalling', especially in its so-called *barometric* form. This is the situation where one firm 'leads', for instance on account of increasing costs, and the others then follow this 'signal' for the same reasons. Such barometric parallelism may be regarded as reasonable, an 'intelligent adaptation' to competitors' strategies.

All the foregoing is complex and murky. Its use in legal argument has been similarly double-edged. Companies accused of collusion invoke the 'structural' theory, while regulators naturally wish to downplay that

[11] Generally on the theory of oligopoly and its consequences, see Jean Tirole, *Theory of Industrial Organisation* (MIT Press, 1988), ch 6; Dallal Stevens, 'Convert Collusion or Conscious Parellism in Oligopolistic Markets: A Comparison of EC and US Competition Law' (1995) *Yearbook of European Law* 47; Mario Monti, 'Oligopoly: Conspiracy? Joint Monopoly? Or Enforceable Competition?' (1996) 19(3) *World Competition* 59; Simon Bishop and Mike Walker, *The Economics of EC Competition Law* (Sweet & Maxwell, 1999), paras 2.19–2.26. On the application of game theory, see Mario Franzosi, 'Oligopoly and the Prisoners' Dilemma: Concerted Practices and "As If" Behaviour' (1988) 9 *ECLR* 385.   [12] See Whish, n 9 above.

[13] See, e.g. Robert H Bork, *The Antitrust Paradox* (Basic Books, 1978), ch 8. There are good reasons for controversy: in the context of European litigation there has been vigorous resort to oligopoly theory by the defence even in the face of strong evidence of collusion (in the case of the *PVC Cartel*, for instance, when there was factual evidence of a cartel blueprint and monthly meetings).

[14] See Whish, n 9 above, 463–5.

interpretation of parallel behaviour. Thus the oligopoly theory provides an attractive innocent explanation for identical industry pricing, with a variable geometry which will fit a wide range of conduct, and this has given defence advisers opportunities which have been readily exploited.

4. Testing oligopoly argument under European law

(a) The argument in Dyestuffs

The first occasion for testing oligopoly evidence and arguments in the European context arose in the litigation following the Commission's decision against the *Aniline Dyes Cartel*.[15] The Commission's case against the *Dyestuffs Cartel* was based very much on direct and circumstantial evidence of collusion, or what in American antitrust parlance is termed 'plus factors' or 'conduct plus'.[16] Such evidence is 'plus' in the sense of being additional to what may be inferred from an appearance of market collusion and has a probative value in excluding an 'innocent' explanation of the market situation. American case law has categorized such 'plus evidence' into three main categories. First, there is hard evidence: typically meetings and other forms of contact, which may be accepted as collusion, even without direct evidence of what was actually agreed if either the meetings were clandestine, or subsequently the parties behaved in the same way on the market, or the meetings involved an exchange of information from which something like an understanding to fix prices may be reasonably inferred.[17] Secondly, it comprises parallel conduct that by its nature must be regarded as agreed rather than spontaneous: it taxes credulity to imagine that it could have occurred without agreement.[18] Thirdly, there is evidence that the market structure and conditions are conducive to co-ordination.[19] Items of 'plus' evidence may not be individually

---

[15] Cases 48/69 etc., *ICI and others v Commission* [1972] ECR 619.

[16] The term seems to have originated in the trial court judgment in *C-O Two Fire Equipment Co v US*, 197 F 2d 489 (9th Cir 1952). For an engaging discussion of the use of 'plus evidence', see William E Kovacic, 'The Identification and Proof of Horizontal Agreement in the Antitrust Laws' (1993) 38 *Antitrust Bulletin* 5.

[17] See e.g. *Pittsburgh Plate Glass Co v US*, 260 F 2d397 (4th Cir 1958).

[18] *Interstate Circuit v US*, 306 US 208 (1939).

[19] Jonathan B Baker, 'Two Sherman Act Section 1 Dilemmas' (1993) 143 *Antitrust Bulletin* 178: 'economic' evidence that is an elaboration of factual 'plus factors'.

probative, but taken together and in their proper context may admit of no other reasonable explanation than collusion.[20]

So the Commission adduced an array of such 'plus' evidence: meetings in London and Basel to discuss prices, a series of simultaneous price announcements in 1964, 1965, and 1967, and identical language used in price instructions to subsidiary companies. The Court of Justice's judgment, however, tended to focus on a discussion of market analysis and industry structure, since the companies had based their appeal on an argument of conscious parallelism in a concentrated market. Responding to these arguments, the Court emphasized in its judgment that the producers used the system of advance price announcements as a facilitating device that 'eliminated all uncertainty between them as to their future conduct'.[21] This aspect of the judgment was criticized by a number of commentators, who read the statement as basing a finding of collusion on the simultaneous price announcements in themselves.[22] In fact, the Court had been careful to state that by itself parallel conduct would be insufficient evidence of collusion, and read carefully its judgment is following the Commission's approach of taking the range of evidence as a whole—the Court was relying on structural factors to assess whether the price announcements were acting as a 'facilitating device'. The relevant section of the judgment reads:

Although parallel behaviour may not by itself be identified with a concerted practice, it may however amount to strong evidence of such a practice if it leads to conditions of competition which do not correspond to the normal conditions of the market... That is especially the case if the parallel conduct is such as to enable those concerned to stabilise prices at a level different from that to which competition would have led.[23]

If this is put in the context of the Court's 'holistic' or 'overall' approach to the evidence, and in particular its assertion that the price increases were evidence of 'a progressive co-operation', there is no discontinuity with either American jurisprudence or the Court's statements in later cases. On the one hand, for instance, American judges have stated:

'Although ... mere proof of interdependent pricing, standing alone, may not serve as proof of an antitrust violation, we believe that the evidence concerning the

---

[20] *Continental Ore Co v Union Carbide and Carbon Corp*, 370 US 690 (1962).

[21] [1972] ECR 660.

[22] See, e.g., Valentine Korah, 'Concerted Practices' (1973) *Modern Law Review* 220; R Joliet, 'La notion de pratique concertée et l'arrêt ICI dans une perspective comparative' (1974) *Cahiers de Droit Européennes* 251; F A Mann, 'The Dyestuffs Case in the Court of Justice of the European Communities' (1973) *ICLQ* 35.   [23] [1972] ECR 619, paras 65–8.

purpose and effect of price announcements, when considered together with the evidence concerning the parallel pattern of price restorations, is sufficient to support a reasonable and permissible inference of an agreement, whether express or tacit, to raise or stabilise prices.[24]

The Court of Justice refined its formulation of concerted practice in its *European Sugar Cartel* judgment in 1975, when it stated rather more explicitly than in *Dyestuffs* that:

Although it is correct to say that this requirement of independence does not deprive economic operators of the right to adapt themeselves intelligently to the existing and anticipated conduct of their competitors, it does however strictly preclude any direct or indirect contact between such operators, the object or effect whereof is either to influence the conduct on the market of an actual or potential competitor or to disclose to such a competitor the course of conduct which they themselves have decided to adopt or contemplate adopting on the market.[25]

This earlier litigation, therefore, shows that the Court of Justice at least was aware of the risks of basing decisions simply on market evidence of parallel behaviour in price-fixing cases. Perhaps the clearest and most definitive statement of this approach is provided in the Court of Justice's judgment in the *CRAM and Rheinzink* case[26] in 1984 (concerned with an alleged two-company cartel in the steel industry):

The Commission's reasoning is based on the supposition that the facts established cannot be explained other than by concerted action by the two undertakings. Faced with such an argument, it is sufficient for the applicants to prove circumstances which cast the facts established by the Commission in a different legal light and thus allow another explanation of the facts to be substituted for the one adopted by the contested decision.[27]

This is an earlier version of the 'other plausible explanation' argument which would figure so prominently in the Court's *Wood Pulp* judgment, discussed below. If the *Dyestuffs* judgment had sent out any misleading signals, certainly by the mid-1980s the Court's message was clear—parallel behaviour by itself had to be supported by 'plus evidence'.

(b) The argument in Wood Pulp

Most of the cartel cases dealt with by the Commission during the 1980s and which were appealed to the Community courts did not rely strongly

[24] *Re Petroleum Products Litigation*, 906 F 2d 432 (9th Cir 1990).
[25] Cases 40/73 etc., *Suiker Unie and others v Commission* [1975] ECR 1663, at 1942.
[26] Cases 29 and 30/83, *CRAM and Rheinzink v Commission* [1984] ECR 1679.
[27] Ibid., 1702.

on economic evidence or need to become embroiled in price signalling theory, since there was sufficient direct evidence of collusion: documented evidence of price fixing in meetings and related planning documents. Circumstantial evidence was brought into the picture, not to prove collusion, but to show that such collusion was part of a single overall plan. This brings the discussion back again to the interrelated points of offence definition and evidence: what is being prohibited and penalized and what constitutes evidence of the offending conduct? In one sense, Article 81 (ex Article 85) of the EC Treaty prohibits specific acts of collusion, such as an agreement to fix prices. But what was emerging in the Commission's enforcement practice was a policy of identifying and penalizing cartel arrangements which encompassed a number or network of such specific acts of collusion. Although not overtly referred to as such, this was a concept of 'cartel offence', as distinct from a discrete 'price fix' or 'market share' offence. By its nature, the 'cartel offence' (equalling the 'cartel as a whole') would be wider, deeper, and therefore a more significant and serious infringment of the rules. As such it would represent systematic and organized collusion, justifying a greater degree of censure and higher fines.

The Commission's policy of prosecuting and proving these infringements as 'whole cartels' was in due course approved by the Community courts, for example by the Court of First Instance clearly and fully in its judgment relating to the *Polypropylene Cartel*[28] in 1991:

As regards the question whether the Commission was entitled to find that there was a single infringement... in view of their identical purpose, the various concerted practices followed and agreements concluded formed part of schemes of regular meetings, target-price fixing and quota fixing. Those schemes were part of a series of efforts made by the undertakings in question in pursuit of a single economic aim, namely to distort the normal movement of prices on the market in polypropylene. *It would thus be artifical to split up such continuous conduct, characterized by a single purpose, by treating it as consisting of a number of separate infringements.* The fact is that the applicant took part—over a period of years—in an *integrated set of schemes constituting a single infringement, which progressively manifested itself in both unlawful agreements and unlawful concerted practices.* The Commission was also entitled to characterize that single infringement as 'an agreement and a concerted practice', since the infringement involved at one and the same time factual elements to be characterized as 'agreements' and factual elements to be characterized as 'concerted practices'. Given such a complex

---

[28] Cases 1/89 etc., *Rhône-Poulenc v Commission* [1991] ECR II-867.

infringment, the dual characterization by the Commission...must be understood, not as requiring, simultaneously and cumulatively, proof that each of those factual elements presents the constituent elements of both of an agreement and a concerted practice, *but rather as referring to a complex whole comprising a number of factual elements* some of which were characterized as agreements and others as concerted practices.[29] (Emphasis added.)

Such statements confirm the nature of the unspoken 'offence' (the term used carefully in such judgments is 'infringement') and also provide guidance on what therefore should be 'charged' and proven by the Commission. Regarding proof, 'hard' evidence of meetings and briefing documents could be combined with more circumstantial evidence of market behaviour and outcomes to infer a conscious participation in an overall cartel arrrangment—'plus factors'.

In the light of these legal developments, it is not easy at first glance to appreciate how the imbroglio of argument before the Court of Justice in the *Wood Pulp Cartel* appeal[30] arose. Reading the report of the whole case is daunting, on account of the length and complexity of the arguments, but it also has a number of intriguing aspects. The report hints at some real tension between the Commission and the Court, leading both to adopt a dogmatic and obstinate position on some points. Interestingly also, for the history of the subject, the Juge Rapporteur for the case was René Joliet, who had been one of the main critics of the Court of Justice's judgment in *Dyestuffs*.[31]

Advocate General Darmon's opinion is another example from that office of a full and deeply researched analysis of this subject and, although he is ultimately less critical of the Commission than the Court would be, he does give vent to some frustration:

I have been unable, notwithstanding the many hours spent in studying this bulky file, to grasp clearly the precise function played, according to the Commission, by the system of price announcements within the framework of concertation. The defendant's position in this case has the consistency of mercury. Just as one is about to grasp it, it eludes one, only to assume an unexpected shape.[32]

---

[29] [1991] ECR II-1074–5.

[30] Cases 89/85 etc., *Ahlström Oy and others v Commission* [1993] ECR I-1307. For some commentary on the case, see Alison Jones, '*Wood Pulp*: Concerted Practice and/or Conscious Parallelism ?' (1993) 14 *ECLR* 273; Gerwin Van Gerven and Edurne Navarro Varona, 'The *Wood Pulp* Case and the Future of Concerted Practices' (1994) 31 *CMLRev* 575; Femi Alese, 'The Economic Theory of Non-Collusive Oligopoly' (1999) 20 *ECLR* 379.

[31] See n 22 above.   [32] [1993] ECR I-1503.

In terms of both evidence and law, *Wood Pulp* was a hard and gruelling case, but with the benefit of hindsight provides a number of important lessons in antitrust enforcement. In some ways, the case may be seen as a replay of *Dyestuffs*, in that the defending companies again referred to the structure of the market as evidence of non-collusion—the price announcements were no more than innocent transparency. On the other hand, the Commission did possess proof of collusion, but appears to have been intent on framing the case against the companies principally on economic rather than material evidence. In its *Fourteenth Report on Competition Policy* it described the proceedings in *Wood Pulp* as being 'the first time that concertation on prices . . . is proved by an economic analysis showing that under the given circumstances the similarity of prices was inexplicable unless there was concertation beforehand'.[33] Thus the Commission itself was raising the stakes, not content to play safer with the conventional (and clear) evidence of collusive meetings,[34] but wishing to show that collusion could be proven by mainly economic evidence. This strategy set the scene for the legal battle before the Court of Justice.

Unfortunately, the Commission's own presentation of its case lacked clarity, both in the Statement of Objections to the parties (which was criticized by both the Advocate General and the Court for compromising rights of defence)[35] and in the proceedings before the Court. The Advocate General was not clear whether the Commission was prosecuting the price announcements in themselves as an illegal anti-competitive facilitating device, or was using the price announcements as the main evidence of prior collusion,[36] and generally found the Commission's analysis 'shadowy'.[37] Although he agreed that there was clear evidence of specific acts of collusive fixing, at different times involving different parties, he was much less satisfied with the Commission's presentation of its case against the cartel as a whole. While the Commission appeared to be arguing that direct evidence of collusive acts taken together with the system of price announcements was sufficient to implicate all the defendant companies in the cartel, the Advocate General felt that this was too presumptive, since

---

[33] Commission, *Fourteenth Report on Competition Policy* (1985), point 56 (at 57–8).

[34] To provide a single example: one of the Canadian companies' London subsidiaries reported on 9 September 1977: 'We hear that meetings will be held in Stockholm in the next two weeks to determine Swedish/Finnish attitudes on pulp prices and expect that firms will press the point that their 3% devaluation leaves no room for significant reduction.'

[35] [1993] ECR I-1464, 1597. This was one of the grounds on which a major part of the Commission's decision was annulled.   [36] [1993] ECR I-1503 *et seq.*

[37] Ibid., 1547.

their 'cartel responsibility' seemed to derive from their alleged contact via price announcements and not from a substantiated case against each of them individually. In this way, he considered that there was a risk that innocent 'price followers' had been caught in the net.

The Commission fared worse with the Court itself. The Court had asked the Commission to clarify whether it was asserting that the system of price announcements constituted an infringement as such, or was being put forward as evidence of earlier concertation. Neither the Advocate General nor the Court considered that the Commission provided a clear answer to this question, so both went on to consider each of those arguments as alternative hypotheses. On the first hypothesis, the Court was of the view that the announcements could not in themselves constitute a concerted practice under Article 85(1), since they left the parties with a degree of uncertainty as to future market conduct, which undermined a finding of concertation. On the second hypothesis, the Court's reasoning was perplexing in places, but was clearly hostile to the Commission's determination to base its case mainly on economic evidence. First of all, the Court summarily excluded the clear evidence of collusion, based on telex communications, meetings, and documents. It did this because it had asked the Commission to indicate between which producers and for what periods each telex and document was proof of collusion. The Commission replied, maintaining its resolve to prove its case against the whole cartel on mainly economic evidence, that the documents:

merely substantiated the evidence based on parallel conduct and that, accordingly, they were relevant not only as regards the undertakings and the period specifically mentioned therein but also as regards all the undertakings and the entire duration of the parallel conduct.[38]

The Court did not respond to that argument as such (which was partly the 'cartel as a whole' argument) but simply stated in a terse and perplexing *non sequitur* that 'in the light of that reply those documents must be excluded from consideration'.[39] In the Court's view, it was impossible to rely on documents whose probative value in respect of the identity of the companies taking part in the alleged concertation the Commission had been unable to specify.[40] The Court thus left itself to decide the matter

---

[38] Ibid., 1600.   [39] Ibid.

[40] This assertion by the Court is one of the most perplexing. The Commission had in fact supplied further tables containing full details of each individual manifestation of the alleged collusion (Reply to Third Supplementary Question [1993] ECR I-1416–27).

on the evidence of parallel behaviour via the price announcements *alone*. For that purpose, it relied heavily on the experts' report it had commissioned itself (although Advocate General Darmon had urged caution in that respect).[41] Since the experts had concluded that there may be plausible explanations other than collusion for the parallel pricing, the Court followed that argument[42] and dismissed the Commission's reliance on such evidence. In that way the Commission lost most of the case.

Two main comments may be made regarding the use of evidence in this saga of legal argument. First, it appears that the Commission's insistence on pressing its case *primarily* on evidence of parallel conduct provoked both Advocate General and Court into compartmentalizing the case against each defendant rather than treating the cartel as a whole, contrary to the emergent jurisprudence of the Court itself and the Court of First Instance. Secondly, the Court eventually relied very much for its decision on an experts' report which, like other expert reports in the field of economics, was itself contestable,[43] while at the same time peremptorily excluding very clear evidence of a highly collusive market. In the wake of the judgment, there appeared to be some temptation to view the outcome as a victory of 'sensible economics' over 'slippery law', revealing some credulity[44] towards arguments presented by 'experts'. Van Gerven and Navarro Varona commented for example that the judgment was:

a victory for the use of economic theory in EC antitrust cases. After this judgment it will be impossible for the Commission to threaten economic expert reports lightly. The Commission will, itself, have to use economic expert counsel if it wishes to avoid the devastating results of the *Wood Pulp* case, where the experts were able to pinpoint several contradictions and errors in the economic reasoning that the Commission had used.[45]

Such comments appear not to have taken into account the mauling given to the experts' report by Advocate General Darmon in his opinion[46] and to have at least relegated the very clear *legal* evidence of collusion in the wood pulp industry revealed in the Commission's investigation. An

---

[41] [1993] ECR I-1546.

[42] Ibid., 1601–13: several pages of the judgment are given over to the conclusions of the experts' report.

[43] A number of the assertions in the report could be empirically challenged by reference to evidence gained (and judicially accepted) in other cartel cases, such as *PVC*.

[44] Certainly compared to American commentators: see, e.g., the view expressed by Scherer, n 7 above.   [45] See n 30 above: (1994) *CMLRev*, 607.

[46] See n 41 above.

interesting postscript to this discussion of 'expert' evidence is provided by the later investigation of the *Cartonboard Cartel*, in which a pricing study produced for the companies concerned by a firm of economic consultants was hit out of court by a body of convincing documentary evidence: 'the author of the report frankly accepted during the oral hearing that his findings in no way disproved the existence of the cartel.'[47]

There were thus important lessons to be gained all round as to how a case of antitrust collusion should be both charged and proven. The arguments revealed at least the vulnerability of certain forms of evidence. Importantly for the Commission, there were lessons regarding the need for a tighter and clearer framing of the charge against a cartel, both for purposes of showing convincing evidence (in particular, evidence of sophisticated planning and organization), and avoiding due process problems.

5. Forging the cartel offence: marshalling the evidence and framing the charge

What was at least clear following the *Wood Pulp* litigation was that, in cases which might lead to the imposition of sanctions ('offence' cases), competition regulators would need to consider with care the use of certain kinds of evidence and consequently indicate explicitly what the evidence was being employed to prove. Framing the accusation or the charge was thus the nub of the issue. It was clear for instance that simply to charge price announcements or other such 'facilitating devices' as an infringement would be unlikely to survive review in the European courts. Standing by itself, a system of price announcements was economic evidence of an almost certainly ambiguous nature. The *Wood Pulp* arguments had also demonstrated that, while experts' reports might not be convincing in themselves, they could at least be used on either side in litigation to cast sufficient doubt on the probative force of most market-based evidence. The Commission had been tempted to impugn the facilitating device in order to overcome the problems of proving precise involvement of every cartel member at every stage of a continuing and complex web of collusive activity. Quoting again from Van Gerven and Navarro Varona:

If the Commission had hoped to counter the decreased likelihood of finding incriminating evidence because of higher awareness of antitrust laws and higher

---

[47] *Cartonboard Cartel*, OJ 1994, L 243/37 (point 115 of the decision).

sanctions, by focusing more on 'parallel conduct' cases, *Wood Pulp* risks dashing its hopes... The *Wood Pulp* judgment directs the antitrust efforts clearly towards finding documentary evidence of concertation... If there is sufficient evidence of concertation, economic theory will be likely to have to take a back seat.[48]

That may have been a somewhat uncharitable view of enforcement strategy, but the essential prosecutorial problem was to 'wrap up' the whole cartel and its individual participants in a way that satisfied the requisite standard of proof for a legal procedure which was, in substance, not far removed from a criminal proceeding.

With the benefit of hindsight, it may be said that the Commission had been overambitious in the method of its prosecution of the *Wood Pulp Cartel*. On the one hand, it attempted to indict the whole cartel by focusing on the system of price announcements as catch-all evidence of group collusion. On the other hand, it also tried to penalize more specific infringements *within* the cartel network, using very much the same evidence. In this way the Commission fell foul, unsurprisingly, of double jeopardy rules and a suspicion of 'recycling' evidence for multiple charges. A preferable approach would probably have been for the Commission to have alleged one grand overall design to stabilize prices which had been furthered in different ways by the different participants without necessarily having been in actual contact with each other.

In fact, as indicated above, such a strategy already had a large measure of judicial approval. The Court of Justice, as early as its *Dyestuffs* judgment, and the Court of First Instance in its *Polypropylene* judgment in 1991, had broadly approved the 'cartel as a whole' approach. The sensible course was therefore to build upon and refine this strategy, to construct in each case a convincing allegation, supported by a range of 'plus evidence', of involvement in a central collusive plan, implemented over a period of time in perhaps various and varying ways. In such a way, the cartel as a over-arching organization would be caught, but care would have to be taken in determining the extent of responsibility of individual members, particularly for purposes of imposing fines. After all, it was well recognized that in most cartels there were ringleaders and followers, more and less committed adherents, and varying periods of membership and amounts of supporting action. Such is the nature of most conspiracy.

That this enforcement strategy has been largely achieved during the 1990s can be seen, for instance, from an examination of the Commission's

---

[48] See n 30 above: (1994) *CMLRev*, 607–8.

'fresh' or re-adopted 1994 decision against the *PVC Cartel* and its review by the Court of First Instance in 1999.[49] In this *PVC 2* judgment the Court endorsed the Commission's approach of charging the cartel members with participation in the (a) planning and (b) implementation of the cartel as a whole, and using a 'panorama' of evidence to implicate the defending companies in the joint process of planning, although their role in implementation may have been variable. The core of the prosecuting strategy is contained in Article 1 of the Commission's Decision against the cartel, that the parties infringed Article 85 of the EC Treaty by:

participating for the periods identified in this decision in an agreement and/or concerted practice originating in about August 1980 by which the producers supplying PVC in the Community took part in regular meetings in order to fix target prices and target quotas, plan concerted initiatives to raise price levels and monitor the operation of the said collusive agreement.[50]

This charge therefore focuses very much on the conspiracy element of the cartel and is specific regarding the types of collusion on the market in question. The collusion is alleged to have been initiated and then continued by activities which may be described as either agreements or concerted practices in the language of Article 81 (ex Article 85). The framework and language of this part of the decision is approved by the Court of First Instance in the following statement of principle:

In the context of a complex infringement which involves many producers seeking over a number of years to regulate the market between them the Commission cannot be expected to classify the infringement precisely, for each undertaking and for any given moment.[51]

Moreover, the joint classification as an agreement and/or a concerted practice is acceptable in the view of the Court, and must be understood as:

designating a complex whole that includes factual elements of which some have been classified as an agreement and others as a concerted practice.[52]

How this collusion is then proven against the parties in the cartel can then be seen from more detailed points of the Commission's Decision, as approved by the Court in its judgment. Significantly, the Commission indicated in point 21 of the Decision that the proof of concerted action was based not on a mere finding of parallel conduct but on documents which show that the practices were the result of concerted action (in other

---

[49] Cases T-305/94 etc., *LVM and others v Commission* [1999] ECR II-931.
[50] OJ 1994, L 239/14.   [51] [1999] ECR II-1127.   [52] Ibid.

words, clear 'plus' evidence). The Court confirmed that, once the Commission had adduced such evidence, the burden was on the companies, first to submit an alternative explanation for the facts found by the Commission, and secondly to challenge the existence of those facts.[53]

The Commision specified in point 31 of its Decision how the evidence of implementing practices should be related to the basic evidence of planned collusion: the implementing practices were the result of the collusive plan, were continued over a number of years, using the same mechanisms and based on the same common purpose. As such, they should be regarded as constituting a *single permanent collusion, not a series of discrete agreements*. This way of viewing the evidence was confirmed by the Court.[54] The Commission then asserted that the evidence, seen in this way, justified imposing on each participant, not only responsibility for its direct role as an individual member of the cartel, but also a shared responsibility for the operation of the cartel as a whole. Very importantly, the Court again approved this approach and in doing so dealt with the arguments raised in the appeal that this would involve an unjustifiable imposition of collective (or a kind of vicarious) responsibility. The Court stated:

For that purpose, [the Decision] referred to the concept of the cartel considered 'as a whole'. That does not justify the conclusion, however, that the Commission applied the principle of collective responsibility, in the sense that it deemed certain undertakings to have participated in action with which they were not concerned simply because the participation of other undertakings in those actions *was* established... An undertaking may be held responsible for an overall cartel even though it is shown to have participated directly only in one or some of its constituent elements if it is shown that it knew, or must have known, that the collusion in which it participated, especially by means of regular meetings organised over several years, was part of an overall plan intended to distort competition and that the overall plan included all the constituent elements of the cartel.[55]

This confirms that responsibility should be imposed primarily for participation in the planning and organization of the cartel and that the crucial evidence relates to that aspect of the cartel's activity. As the Court affirmed, the Commision had proof of the PVC manufacturers' participation in producer meetings, if not of every undertaking being involved in the implementation of price initiatives.[56]

Following the arguments and uncertainties of *Dyestuffs* and *Wood Pulp*, a ruling such as that of the Court of First Instance in *PVC 2* supplies some

---

[53] [1999] ECR II-1134–5.   [54] Ibid.   [55] [1999] ECR II-1145–6.   [56] Ibid.

welcome clarity to this complex area of law and practice. It confirms, first and most fundamentally, the scope and nature of the 'cartel offence' as a matter of EC law. This may be understood as an offence or infringement of collusive process. The description given by the Commission in its 1999 Decision against the *Pre-Insulated Pipes Cartel* illustrates well the character of such offensive cartel conduct:

These express and explicit agreements were in reality the result of a continuing agreement, understanding and concert of action among the producers. The participants had set up an infrastructure of regular meetings and were involved in a continuing process of business diplomacy aimed at reconciling their respective interests. For the purpose of forming and carrying out their scheme, the participants did things which they had devised and agreed to do, including (but not limited to) participating in meetings to discuss prices, sales quotas and project-sharing; agreeing during those meetings to charge particular prices and to increase and maintain prices; drafting, agreeing and distributing model price-lists to be used for co-ordinating pricing; exchanging information on sales volumes, market size and market shares so as to set up a quota system; and agreeing a sales quota system. The discussions may have involved a shifting constellation of alliances, even threats of reprisal or hostile action, but as part of the developing process of understandings and partial agreements to fix prices, coordinate price increases and allocate markets and market shares that constituted cartel conduct prohibited by Article 85(1).[57]

This is a clear statement of the concept of the cartel 'as a whole', as a process, evidenced 'panoramically' by acts of planning and subsequent implementation.

Following from that, the *PVC 2* judgment confirms what more precisely should be charged by the Commission in alleging the infringment, and then what evidence will suffice to support that charge. It is clear enough (and arguably always was so) that evidence of parallel behaviour on a market in itself will not suffice. But it is now also clear that evidence of collusive planning will implicate those companies involved in the whole operation of the cartel, whatever their proven role in its implementation. Again, a statement in one of the Commission's decisions conveys clearly what may now be seen as the appropriate prosecutorial strategy in cartel cases:

The proper approach in a case such as the present one is to demonstrate the existence, the operation and the salient features of the cartel as a whole and then to determine (a) whether there is credible and persuasive proof to link each

---

[57] *Pre-Insulated Pipes Cartel*, OJ 1999, L 24/1, at 51.

individual producer to the common scheme and (b) for what period each producer participated.[58]

This suggests essentially a two-stage process, of first establishing the
existence of the cartel and its scope, and secondly establishing to the
requisite standard the evidence of participation for each member. In this
context, participation means knowledge of and commitment to the 'common scheme', although the extent of individual participation may then
vary according to evidence of the overall period during which a party was
involved. But, as a matter of standard of proof, the Commission is not
required to establish precise, moment-by-moment collusion once there is
convincing evidence of a 'link' to the 'common scheme':

The Commission as a factfinding authority is not required to compartmentalise
the various constituent elements of the infringement by identifying each separate
occasion during the duration of the cartel on which a consensus was reached on
one or another matter or each individual example of collusive behaviour and then
exonerating from involvemnet on that occasion or in that particular manifestation
of the cartel any producer not implicated on that occasion by direct evidence.[59]

It is clear, therefore, that this approach places a premium on the
collection of convincing 'plus' evidence, in particular documentary proof of
involvement in the planning of and a commitment to the 'common
scheme'.

6. Collecting persuasive proof of cartel participation

There are of course a number of types of 'plus' evidence which may be
used to establish participation in a cartel, even when the behaviour in
question is clandestine. Most importantly, such evidence will relate to
meetings and other communications and will record the working out
and consummation of planned collusion. In the nature of things, such
communications and their outcomes cannot remain wholly unrecorded,
simply kept in the heads of a number of people working in different places
and not wanting to be observed together. Material evidence of some kind,
in hard copy or electronic form, perhaps later further substantiated by
oral evidence, therefore has to be the basis of the case.

---

[58] *Cartonboard Cartel*, n 47 above, OJ 1994 L 243/1, at 38 (points 117–18). This approach
would appear to mirror the American idea of 'foundation evidence' in relation to conspiracy. See
Julian M Joshua, 'Proof in Contested EEC Competition Cases: a Comparison with the Rules of
Evidence in Common Law' (1987) 12 *European Law Review* 315.   [59] Ibid.

As in the analogous domain of criminal investigation, the practical difficulty is one of locating and retrieving such evidence. In its role as a competition regulator, the Commission has called in aid two particular techniques of evidence detection, which have in turn accounted for much of its actual 'cartel-busting' success. The first was a technique of stealth: the surprise inspection of company premises, or so-called 'dawn raid'. The second and later technique was one of cunning, emulating the success of the US Department of Justice: the offer of leniency. The dawn raid relied upon an element of surprise and exploited a certain unavoidable level of human carelessness. The leniency programme relies upon an element of uncertainty and exploits the natural nervousness inherent in cartel conspiracy. Both, in different ways, can trigger a flow of evidence and 'bust' the cartel.

By the end of the 1970s material evidence relating to what would be later referred to as 'hard core' cartel activity was clearly important but in practice difficult to locate. As the Commision pointed out in one of its more recent decisions:

By its very nature, the cartel was a clandestine activity. Considerable efforts were made to conceal its existence and to ensure…that incriminating evidence was not kept…Quite apart however from any concealment of evidence, the extent and availability of relevant routine pricing documentation for the relevant period showing the implementation of different price initiatives by each producer is a largely adventitious circumstance. In some cases documents had simply not been kept.[60]

Investigators therefore face two problems: concealment and destruction of incriminating evidence, coupled with the naturally partial and fortuitous storage of some kinds of detailed documentation, especially after the passage of time. The unannounced visit of inspection ('dawn raid') thus became an important investigative device. Although not much resorted to during the early years of EC competition enforcement, it became a frequently employed strategy from 1979.[61] The necessary powers are laid down in Article 14 of Council Regulation 17/62,[62] and comprise

---

[60] *Cartonboard Cartel*, n 47 above, OJ 1994, L 243/1, at 38 (point 116). The Cartel attempted to cover the traces of its collusion by an absence of official minutes from key meetings, discouraging the taking of notes, and stage-managing the timing and order of announced price increases: ibid., 52 (point 168).

[61] See Julian M Joshua, 'The Element of Surprise: Competition Investigations under Article 14(3) of Regulation 17' (1983) 8 *ELRev* 3.

[62] For a detailed discussion of these powers, and their interpretation by the Community courts, see C K Kerse, *EC Antitrust Procedure* (4th edn, Sweet & Maxwell, 1998). See also the discussion of judicial review in Chapter VII below.

powers of search, interrogation, and verification. Article 14(1) enumerates specific powers: examination of books and business records; the taking of copies of or extracts from these materials; on the spot oral questions; and entry to land, premises, and means of transport. Such powers are of course exercisable only within the geographical jurisdiction of the member states, and the relevant member state authorities have to be informed in good time before an inspection takes place, and be informed of the identity of the Commission officials involved. National officials may be asked to assist in the inspection (under Article 14(5)). In formal terms, there are two types of authority for Article 14 investigations, a written authorization or 'simple mandate' entailing no obligation of compliance (Article 14(2)); and a formal decision, binding on the undertaking to whom it is addressed (Article 14(3)). Surprise inspections for practical purposes need to be made under Article 14(3), but the formality of the process inevitably provides the opportunity for extensive legal argument and has in fact spawned a considerable body of litigation relating to the exercise of these powers and corresponding rights of defence. As drafted, Article 14 awards potentially extensive powers of investigation to the Commission, and these powers have been more closely defined in the case law of the Community courts.

Dawn raids have proven very important in practice in the legal exposure of a number of major cartels, although there has often been an element of luck in these investigations. In some cases, Commission officials have discovered highly incriminating 'smoking gun' evidence in such searches. Perhaps the the most dramatic anecdote relates to the *Polypropylene* investigation. An employee of one of the companies subject to investigation was on holiday at the time of the inspection and had left all the cartel minutes and quota tables on his office window sill (while the offices of colleagues, named in the incriminating documents and 'out of the office' at the time of the inspection, were clear of any evidence). Another major find in the same investigation was the discovery of the 'blueprint' for the *PVC Cartel*, which had been misfiled in a polypropylene folder. However, such carelessness would be increasingly guarded against by companies becoming more alert to the risks of surprise inspections. The *Cartonboard Cartel* case revealed evidence of outside lawyers being engaged to organize mock investigations and dummy runs for company officials (nonetheless, incriminating evidence was still obtained from a search).[63]

---

[63] *Cartonboard Cartel*, n 47 above, OJ 1994 L 243/1, at 9. This was arranged apparently after it was known that a complaint had been made to the Commission. But more generally it may be

Inevitably, the companies subject to these procedures were not slow to test their legality. Judicial review began with the appeal by National Panasonic against one of the earliest dawn raids,[64] arguing that the element of surprise violated basic rights of commercial privacy, and invoking Article 8 of the European Convention on Human Rights. This argument did not prevail before the Court of Justice, which held the the public interest in law enforcement outweighed such rights of privacy. But subsequent case law has defined more exactly the extent of these powers of investigation and in particular has indicated the limits on the power to carry out a forcible search and the kinds of evidence or information which may be legally withheld.

Any inspection will be limited by a statement of its subject matter and purpose as contained in the authorizing decision. This is designed to inhibit open-ended trawling for any evidence whatsover, or 'fishing expeditions'. Advocate General Darmon commented in the *Orkem* case that 'the information requested by the Commission must *appear* to be connected with the infringement at issue'.[65] Commission inspectors cannot roam around offices at will, searching anywhere and everywhere, but they may, in the words of Advocate General Mischo, say: 'Show us the documents relating to such-and-such a meeting', or 'Show us the contents of this filing cabinet', or 'Let us see those files we have just noticed through the window being loaded into that van outside'.[66] Moreover, some evidence may be justifiably withheld, most notably that covered by the criteria of legal privilege (lawyer–client confidentiality), as laid down by the Court of Justice in its *AM & S Europe* judgment.[67] Although there is a general obligation to co-operate during such investigations (Article 14(3) of Regulation 17), this does not extend to giving answers to 'leading' as distinct from 'factual' questions.[68] ('Which companies attended the meeting in Stockholm on 10 January?' is a permissible question; 'What measures have you taken to guarantee market sharing arrangements?' would not have to be answered, since its inevitably self-incriminating nature would

---

argued that such 'training sessions' have a legally ambivalent character—innocent, even commendable, instruction in competition law, or complicit preparation in evidence removal?

[64] Case 136/79, *National Panasonic v Commission* [1980] ECR 2033.

[65] Case 374/87, *Orkem v Commission* [1989] ECR 3283, at 3320. In the same proceedings, the Commission stated that it did not undertake investigations as a means of 'probing'.

[66] In Cases 46/87 and 227/88, *Hoechst v Commission* [1989] ECR 2859, at 2879.

[67] Case 155/79, *AM & S Europe v Commission* [1982] ECR 1575.

[68] Cases 3355 and 27/88, *Solvay v Commission* [1989] ECR 3355. But note that, under American law, the privilege against self-incrimination does not apply to corporations.

compromise rights of defence.) Company executives are entitled to legal advice during the inspection but cannot delay the investigation while awaiting the arrival of a lawyer.[69] Commission officials can only use force to carry out a search with the prior authority to do so under the relevant national law.[70] An idea of the balance of investigating powers and defence rights may be gained from the following statement by the Court of Justice:

> the Commission's officials have, *inter alia*, the power to have shown to them the documents they request, to enter such premises as they choose, and to have shown to them the contents of any piece of furniture which they indicate. On the other hand, they may not obtain access to premises or furniture by force or oblige the staff of the undertaking to give them such access, or carry out searches without the permission of the management of the undertaking.[71]

In summary, a number of points may be made about evidence which is gained from inspections.

First, whatever its probative value, its availability or subsequent utility in legal proceedings may be circumscribed by evidential and due process rules, such as those described imediately above. At the very least, there may be legal challenge of the deployment of such evidence by the Commission in subsequent attempts at judicial review. Some of these issues are discussed further in Chapter VII below.

Secondly, such evidence may be incriminating, but at the same time may only present part of the picture. In most cases, the Commission is likely to want further or more detailed evidence and so will follow the trawl from a dawn raid with requests under Article 11 of Regulation 17 for further information from the companies concerned. Sometimes (and increasingly, in the context of possible leniency deals), these requests may prove very productive for the Commission. A notable example is provided by the willingness of the Swedish company Stora, a member of the

---

[69] Case 136/79, *National Panasonic*, n 64 above. See the comments of Advocate General Warner, [1980] ECR 2069.

[70] Cases 97–99/87, *Dow Chemica Iberica v Commission* [1989] ECR 3165. Article 14(6) of Regulation 17 provides that: 'Where an undertaking opposes an investigation ordered pursuant to this Article, the Member State concerned shall afford the necessary assistance to the officials authorised by the Commission to enable them to make their investigation.' In fact, the Commission can go armed with a national court order or warrant without having first been refused entry by a company.

[71] Cases 46/87 and 227/88, *Hoechst v Commission*, n 66 above, at 2927.

Cartonboard Cartel, to provide substantial incriminating evidence following an Article 11 request. As the Commission stated in its Decision:

Although there was already strong documentary evidence to prove the existence of a cartel, Stora's spontaneous admission of the infringement and the detailed evidence which it provided to the Commission has contributed materially to the establishment of the truth, reduced the need to rely on circumstantial evidence and no doubt influenced other producers who might otherwise have continued to deny all wrongdoing.[72]

There is thus a standard practice of following dawn raids with Article 11 requests, to enable the Commission to flesh out its case. Both measures may exploit the inherent nervousness and mutual suspicion within cartels, especially in the context of leniency programmes.

Finally, and more reassuringly for cartel investigators, there remains some indication that companies do not act quickly to conceal or destroy incriminating evidence, and even some signs of almost reckless behaviour. *Pre-Insulated Pipes*,[73] for example, concerned a well-established, highly collusive, and aggressive cartel which was intent on the destruction of a rival firm outside the cartel. There had been a number of blatant attempts to win over, then threaten, and eventually drive to economic ruin this competing company, Powerpipe. Natural prudence would have suggested that such a determined enemy as this company would itself keep incriminating evidence of contacts and other aggressive activity. After a certain stage, it was predictable that Powerpipe would complain to the Commission. Even after a complaint had been lodged with the Commission, the cartel attempted to impose boycotts on the company. In these circumstances, it is not surprising that the Commission's inspections harvested a large body of documentary material confirming Powerpipe's allegation of market sharing, price fixing, and bid rigging. Equally, it is not then surprising, in view of the strength of the case against the cartel, that Article 11 requests elicited a flood of evidence from the participants themselves, providing information over and above that asked for by the Commission. A reading of the decision in *Pre-Insulated Pipes* is instructive as an account of the activities of a highly anti-competitive and aggressive cartel, of the kind of material evidence which may be used to prove a case against such collusion, and of the combined impact of the elements of surprise in a dawn raid and of temptation under a leniency programme once there has been some spillage of evidence.

---

[72] OJ 1994, L 233/53 (point 171). Stora was rewarded by a large reduction in the amount of its fine. Article 11 requests also triggered a flow of evidence in *Pre-Insulated Pipes*, n 73 below.

[73] OJ 1999, L 24/1, n 57 above.

VII

Judicial Review of Cartel Control: Testing the Evidence and Due Process

1. The role of the Community Courts

Since the 1970s the Court of Justice and, more latterly, the Court of First Instance have played a significant role in monitoring the enforcement of the EC rules against cartels at the European level. Once the Commission had entered a more confrontational and repressive era of enforcement, driving hard-core cartels underground in a legal sense, the whole pattern of enforcement inevitably became more adversarial and legalistic. The stakes became higher for all concerned. For the Commission as a regulatory body, its success in enforcement depended on a perception that it was able to exercise effective control over the most seriously anti-competitive kinds of market behaviour. For the companies who had traditionally engaged in cartel behaviour, not only did they find themselves subject to an increasing level of censure and legal sanction, but also their established business culture was being impugned. It is interesting to pose the question (although difficult to provide a clear answer) whether, in this context, tougher enforcement may have provoked a more determined resistance. At any rate, the major corporate actors who became defendants in cartel proceedings did not submit passively to either the threat or the actual imposition of legal sanctions. In penological terms, it is not evident that many of these companies were deterred by the experience of 'conviction' by the Commission and financial penalties. This topic will be revisited in the discussion in Chapter IX below. But their resistance additionally took another form: a determination to exploit fully the opportunities to challenge legally all possible aspects of the Commission's prosecution. In this way, a significant judicial role was activated, as indeed had happened already in relation to the application of the Sherman Act under American law.

Discussion of the judicial review of cartel control decisions under EC law invites two lines of enquiry in particular. The first concerns the role of the Community courts themselves in this area. One fairly obvious way to view their involvement is to see the judicial role as a kind of refereeing process between the interests of the regulators and the regulated. But in this context the courts did not start to undertake this role with any pre-determined theory of judicial review, apart from a broad sense of testing the 'legality' of the Commission's exercise of powers. It was not explicitly stated in any EC Treaty provisions or secondary legislation what should be regarded as the appropriate grounds or more precise objectives of this process of review. It was thus left to the courts themselves, through their intervention in a continuing dialogue between the Commission and cartel participants, to work out their own role and objectives.

The second line of enquiry concerns more the outcome of this process—the accumulating jurisprudence of the two Community courts, comprising an expanding body of law relating to the enforcement of competition policy. Quantitatively and qualitatively, this case law accounts for a significant part of the total judicial output in the EC system. It is both a major segment of judicial review and has contributed significantly to the emerging European public law of due process and the protection of basic rights. But the origins of this process should also be noted. It may appear as a cynical observation, yet it should be recognized that powerful actors with considerable resources at their disposal are willing and able to engage in litigation, which in turn produces case law, which in turn contributes to the theory and practice of legal protection.

One major outcome of the European regulation of business cartels, which may not have been easily predictable 30 years ago, has thus been the development of a significant system of legal protection. In doctrinal terms this development is of itself of interest on account of its context and analogies. The context should not be forgotten: a system of economic regulation concerned with the activities of large corporate actors. It may be misleading therefore to classify this legal domain as a branch of *human* rights law. Nonetheless, there are some analogies, which the companies themselves have been quick to exploit, especially with reference to the European Convention on Human Rights. There is a further important analogy, which draws a comparison with the concept of criminal offending and criminal procedure. Thus, while the cartel control jurisprudence of the Court of Justice and Court of First Instance may not be either human rights law or criminal law in the proper sense of those terms, both of those domains of law have cast a significant shadow over this area of judicial review. Indeed, it has been necessary to ask in legal argument at a number of points how and to what extent the judicial review of the Commission's exercise of powers should be distinguished from human rights or criminal law argumentation.[1]

There are two formal bases for the jurisdiction of both the Court of Justice and the Court of First Instance over the Commission's cartel control activity. Article 230 (ex Article 173) of the EC Treaty provides for a general jurisdiction to ensure the legality of measures taken by the EC institutions. Although four grounds of legal challenge are listed in this provision (lack of competence, infringement of an essential procedural requirement, violation of the Treaty or other rule of law relating to its application, and misuse of powers), the Court of Justice in particular has construed these grounds widely and adventurously to embrace (especially under the third heading) a wide range of procedural requirements and corresponding defence rights. Secondly and more specifically, Article 229 (ex Article 172) provides for 'unlimited' jurisdiction to be established under secondary legislation with regard to any penalties provided for in such legislation. Council Regulation 17/62, having provided for the use of fines in the competition sector, thus provides for such a jurisdiction in Article 17 of the Regulation. This jurisdiction is 'unlimited' in relation to decisions imposing fines and penalty payments and the court may cancel, reduce, or increase those penalties in the exercise of such jurisdiction. In practice, parties wishing to appeal against Commission competition decisions will invoke both heads of jurisdiction, so as to bring forward arguments concerning the broader legality of the decision and against financial penalties more specifically. The courts themselves have not sought to separate the two heads of jurisdiction in any dogmatic way.

A reading of the text of Articles 229 and 230 does not provide any explicit guidance on the specific role of judicial review in relation to competition proceedings, beyond obviously requiring that the latter should conform to the broad principles of legality of Community action. The

---

[1] See, e.g. Cases 100–103/80, *Musique Diffusion Francaise v Commission* [1983] ECR 1825; Cases T-1/89 etc., *Rhône-Poulenc v Commission* [1991] ECR II-867. On the significance of the classification of competition proceedings for issues of evidence, see Nicholas Green, 'Evidence and Proof in E.C. Competition Cases', in Piet Jan Slot and Alison McDonnell (eds), *Procedure and Enforcement in E.C. and U.S. Competition Law* (Sweet & Maxwell, 1993), ch 17.

precise legal outcomes of successful challenge are set down: annulment of the decision, or its offending part, under Article 230, or cancellation, reduction, or increase of a financial penalty under Article 229. But otherwise matters are left open, as to the character of the procedure before either the Court of Justice or the Court of First Instance, as a process of 'appeal' or 'review'. To some extent the characterization of this 'judicial' process has been determined by the prior characterization of the Commission's decision-making procedure as the subject of review. This has itself been a matter of some debate. The process of investigation and decision laid down for the Commission as a competition regulator under Regulation 17 is very deliberately cast as an 'administrative' procedure.[2] As such the suggested analogy is with the traditional public process of judicial review of administrative action. Yet it has not been possible to escape wholly from the substantive sense that this is not classical 'administrative action', but something which has a strong suggestion of criminal procedure and penal process about it. Undeniably the Commission engages in a process of investigation, hearing, and penalty in a way that brings to mind the institutions of police, trial court, and sentencer. Indeed, the way in which these roles have been awarded to a single authority has itself on a number of occasions provoked separation of powers and due process critique.[3] What then does all this imply for the role of the Community courts under Articles 229 and 230 of the EC Treaty: is it one of classical review of administrative action, or something more and akin to the process of appeal against conviction and sentence in the context of criminal law? The formal answer to this question remains ambiguous. Political considerations and formal legal interpretation incline the Community courts towards a conservative estimate of their own role, and to deny the criminal law analogy and attempts to characterize the Commission in its competition procedure as a kind of 'tribunal'.[4] Yet, in substance, due note has been taken of the standards of legal protection laid down for criminal proceedings under instruments such as the European Convention on Human Rights. As Advocate General Vesterdorf commented in the first *Polypropylene* appeal to the Court of First Instance:

This question touches upon one of the major difficulties which arises in the handling of competition cases...the tension which can clearly be felt...between the procedural

---

[2] See, e.g., the explicit reference in Article 15(4) of Regulation 17 to decisions not being of a criminal law nature.   [3] e.g., *Musique Diffusion Franciaise*, n 1 above.

[4] [1983] ECR 1880.

framework of the cases, consisting of an administrative procedure followed by judicial review of legality, and the substance of the cases, which all broadly exhibit the characteristics of a criminal law case. In many instances the parties' submissions can only be understood with the help of the terminology and the concepts in criminal law and procedure.[5]

In short, there is as yet no clearly articulated 'theory of judicial review' in relation to the process of cartel control at the European level. As just indicated, the courts' own jurisprudence suffers from some inhibition arising from ambiguity in the underlying Treaty provisions. But a reading of the case law does suggest that the courts have evolved for themselves *two* main roles in this area of review. One is perhaps more obvious than the other. The former, more obvious (judicial review) role entails an examination of the Commission's procedure to ensure fair and reasonable treatment of those subject to it: the objective here is to guarantee due process. The perhaps less obvious role, which will be considered first, is that of reviewing sufficiency of evidence. In some respects, this is a more difficult role to evaluate, since it requires some consideration of the courts' jurisdiction and ability to review issues of fact rather than law. But the overall outcome, as will be seen, is an amalgam of judicial review and full factual review, amounting in comparative terms to a generous appellate regime.

2. Testing the evidence: the Court of First Instance rolls up its sleeves

The earlier approach of the Court of Justice to the question of the review of evidence established by the Commission in competition cases was cautious, and as such was broadly consistent with that taken in both English and American law: findings of fact should in general be exempt from review by the courts unless based on no satisfactory evidence. English law had evolved the 'no evidence rule', under which review would only take place if the evidence taken as a whole was not reasonably capable of supporting the finding,[6] or where no such conclusion could reasonably be reached on that evidence.[7] Similarly, American law employed the 'substantial evidence

---

[5] *Rhône-Poulenc v Commission*, n 1 above, [1991] ECR II-867, at 884.

[6] *Allinson v General Medical Council* [1894] 1 QB 750.

[7] *R v Roberts* [1905] 1 KB 407. See generally H W R Wade and C F Forsyth, *Administrative Law* (8th edn, OUP, 2000), 279.

rule', that findings of fact must be supported by substantial evidence on the record as a whole: in relation to findings under the Federal Trade Commission Act, the court 'must accept the Commission's findings of fact if they are supported by such relevant evidence as a reasonable mind might accept as adequate to support a conclusion'.[8] Under this approach, such inadequacy of evidence would in effect constitute an illegality which would justify overturning the decision-making use of such a finding. In a similar vein, Advocate General Slynn had argued as a matter of EC law:

the allegations of facts made by the Commission in a decision must be such as to warrant the conclusion drawn from them. If they do not warrant that conclusion, the decision may be annulled, even in the absence of any evidence adduced by the applicants.[9]

In this way, the role of judicial review was limited to a consideration of the legality of the decision. A decision could be held to be illegal and so annulled for inadequate fact-finding,[10] but it was not the task of the court to 'remake a contested decision'[11] or to 'carry out a comprehensive reassessment of the evidence before it'.[12] However, by the end of the 1980s, a view had developed in the professional legal community in Europe that the Court of Justice had been 'soft' on the Commission in reviewing the latter's handling of competition cases. For instance, van Bael had commented that:

the Court, rather than double checking the findings made by the Commission, will tend to give them full credit, unless, prima facie, there could be something grossly wrong.[13]

Such a statement is both implicitly critical of the approach taken by many legal systems (for instance, under the 'substantial evidence rule') while also advocating a thorough review of evidence on appeal. Green also wrote:

Hitherto, the European Court of Justice had confined its review function to correcting errors of law and manifest factual errors and had embraced the notion

[8] *Universal Camera Corp v National Labour Relations Board* 340 US 474 (1951); Administrative Procedure Act 1946, s. 10(e).

[9] *Musique Diffusion Francaise*, n 1 above, [1983] ECR 1930–1.

[10] See e.g. Cases 29-30/83, *CRAM and Rheinzink v Commission* (1984) ECR 1679.

[11] C K Kerse, *E.C. Antitrust Procedure* (4th edn, Sweet & Maxwell, 1998), 381.

[12] Court of First Instance in Cases T-68/89 etc., *SIV and others v Commission* [1992] ECR II-1403, at 1535.

[13] Ivo van Bael, 'Insufficient Judicial Control of the EC Competition Law Enforcement' (1992) *Fordham Corp. L. Inst.* 733, at 741.

that a review *de novo* of the facts was inappropriate for an overworked Supreme Court. Lawyers and undertakings were often left with the uncomfortable feeling that the Commission's conduct of their competition remit was subject only to the slightest of control and that the hand of judicial supervision was light. As the magnitude of fines on recalcitrant undertakings increased and the importance of the work carried out by the Commission fell more into the public eye so the need for serious control of the Commission became more pressing.[14]

While the Court of Justice may indeed have felt that it was an 'overworked court', it should also be remembered that a review *de novo* of the facts was not usually undertaken by appellate courts at the national level. There is an intriguingly excitable note in some of these comments about the need to 'control the Commission', and significantly the newly established Court of First Instance took up the challenge with relish, invoking the principle of 'unfettered evaluation of the evidence'.[15] While the Court was opening for itself a large new field of jurisdiction, it is interesting to observe that in doing so it was going well beyond judicial practice in the context of American antitrust law. Despite Green's argument that the analogy between the Commission's competition procedure and criminal law proceedings justified stronger judicial review,[16] criminal procedure under the Sherman Act has not provided for an extensive review of the findings of fact. In a criminal trial under the Sherman Act the jury's verdict is essentially final as to the facts and the court of appeals will not review the evidence in a jury case provided that there is some evidence at the trial which supports the verdict.[17] In merger cases, decisions by the District Judge or FTC Commissioners on questions of fact are similarly final. Review of the facts *de novo* was very much an inventive step on the part of the Court of First Instance.

(a) The clamour for stronger review: the cartels strike back

During the 1980s and early 1990s there were strong representations from both industrial interests and the legal profession in parts of Europe for a stronger judicial control over the Commission's activity as a competition regulator, particularly in contentious cases typically involving cartels: 'a climate

---

[14] Green, n 1 above, 127.

[15] Per Advocate General Vesterdorf in Case T-1/89, *Rhône-Poulenc v Commission* [1991] ECR II-867, at 954. Green, n 1 above, described the Court of First Instance as 'a tribunal prepared to roll up its sleeves'.   [16] Ibid., 130.

[17] See Donald I Baker, 'Investigation and Proof of an Antitrust Violation in the United States: A Comparative Look', in Slot and McDonnell, n 1 above, ch 18.

in which the Commission's decision-making process was deemed inadequate and the Court [of Justice]'s review of it perfunctory.'[18] The Commission (and to some extent the Court of Justice) were subject to a growing barrage of critical argument regarding constitutional aspects of the Commission's role, its handling of evidence and a perceived absence of due process in the Commission's procedure.[19] Most of the criticism was articulated by practising lawyers but was deftly targeted at influential official bodies such as the House of Lords Select Committee on the European Communities. A flavour of such critical comment can be gained by dipping into some of the evidence given to the House of Lords Committee for its 1993 Report. The Joint Working Party of the English Bar and Law Society expressed concern about the Commission's procedures in contentious competition cases, citing a 'lack of respect for natural justice and rights of defence'. Sir Jeremy Lever QC referred to a waste of resources arising from defects in enforcement procedures and that matters had not improved in recent years (despite the introduction of the office of Hearing Officer and the jurisdiction of the Court of First Instance). Ivo van Bael (Brussels Bar) urged that there was need for more discipline and greater respect for law and procedure. The Confederation of British Industry (CBI) argued that the Court's judgments had identified procedural irregularities and that it was essential that the Court continue to be adequately resourced so that 'failures by the Commission to follow appropriate procedures are remedied'. Nicholas Forwood QC expressed concern at 'economically dubious reasoning in Commission decisions and apparent lack of respect for economic arguments'.[20]

Much of this was a continuation of earlier argument. In its 1982 Report, the Select Committee had recommended that 'the European Court should, as a matter of urgency, examine its structures and responsibilities with a view to submitting to the Council proposals designed to

[18] Julian M Joshua, 'Attitudes to Antitrust Enforcement in the EU and the United States: Dodging the Traffic Warden or Respecting the Law?' (1995) *Fordham Corp. L. Inst.* 101, at 110.

[19] See, e.g., Ivo van Bael, 'EEC Antitrust Enforcement and Adjudication as seen by Defence Counsel' (1979) 7 *Revue Suisse de Droit International de la Concurrence* 1; Sedemund, 'Due Process in EEC Competition Procedures', *IBA Antitrust Committee Report* (1979); and the evidence submitted to the House of Lords Select Committee on the European Communities, *Report on Competition Practice*, 8th Report, 1981–82 (HL 91) ('the 1982 Report'), and *Report on the Enforcement of Community Competition Rules*, 1st Report, 1993–94 (HL 7-1) ('the 1993 Report'). Significantly, much of the critical commentary and evidence was supplied by members of the (corporate) defence bar.

[20] House of Lords Select Committee, 1993 Report, n 19 above, paras 22, 66, 70.

improve the judicial review of competition cases'.[21] Such arguments led in due course to the proposal for and establishment of the Court of First Instance in 1988, with a particular role in carrying out judicial review of competition decisions. There can be no doubt that the Court of First Instance inherited a certain vision of its role at birth: to be rigorous in its assessment of Commission decisions, in a way that the Court of Justice had not been willing or able to be. There was early evidence of its 'activist' stance, such as its award to itself of jurisdiction to review the facts *de novo* in the first *Polypropylene* judgment (discussed above and below) and its finding of 'inexistence' in the first *PVC* judgment (discussed in Chapter V above). However, after the first few years of 'tougher' review, there appeared to be some mixed reactions concerning the Court's achievement.

Again, there is some telling evidence given to the House of Lords Select Committee for its 1993 Report. On the one hand, there was support for the judicial activism shown so far by the Court. The Joint Working Party of the English Bar and Law Society stated:

All of us who had experience of the work of the CFI have nothing but praise for the way in which they tackle individual cases. The quality of the preparation, the conduct of the hearing (in cases which frequently last for many days) and the quality of the judgments are of the highest order. We consider that this has been a development of great importance in judicial protection of individual rights.[22]

Against such a view should be set the overturning of the Court of First Instance's first *PVC* judgment on the point of inexistence by the Court of Justice, which frankly exposed some flawed legal argument on the part of the fledgling Court (see the discussion in Chapter V above) and the following comment on that case by Toth that:

inherent weaknesses of the judgment are further exacerbated by a judicial style, so characteristic of the CFI, which can only be described as excessively meticulous, repetitious... and occasionally marred by otiose reasoning.[23]

Moreover, there was some indication that not all the hopes of the Commission's critics had been realized. The 1993 Report continued by saying:

There were however areas where the CFI had not yet fulfilled expectations— delays between close of pleadings and oral hearing and between oral hearing and

---

[21] House of Lords Select Committee, 1993 Report, n 19 above, para 69.
[22] Ibid., para 70.   [23] A G Toth, commentary in (1995) 32 *CMLRev* 271, at 292.

judgment and reluctance on the part of the Court to appoint economic experts or to second guess economic assessments of the Commission.[24]

There was some agitation in favour of a right of interlocutory appeal on specific procedural decisions at the time that they were taken. One witness, arguing that this would enable procedural errors to be corrected swiftly (nothing was said about claims of error being rejected) instead of having to wait a long time for a final decision, was led to assert:

Even at the cost of letting guilty people off it may be worth the court striking down decisions where things have been done wrong in order to compel the Commission to do the thing right in the first place.[25]

What is striking about much of this critical commentary is an apparent assumption that alleged defects in the Commission's procedure or unsupportable findings of fact were the norm and regularly established as such. In fact, a survey of much of the Court of First Instance's case law during the 1990s will reveal that a large number of such claims brought under the appeal process are rejected by the Court and indeed sometimes have a spurious character. The Court's first *Polypropylene* judgment illustrates this trend: having given itself the jurisdiction to review the Commission's findings *de novo*, the Court then proceeded to confirm the bulk of those findings as established by the Commission.[26] In that case the great majority of the complaints—all those relating to procedural infringements and most relating to insufficiency of evidence—were rejected. In the case of some of the companies, some of the alleged periods of involvement were found not to have been established from the evidence, and some fines were reduced accordingly. This pattern is repeated in a number of the subsequent appeals involving major cartels: for instance, if those relating to the *Cartonboard Cartel* and *Steel Beams Cartel*, and the Court's judgment in *PVC 2* are taken as a sample.[27] For much of the time during the 1990s, therefore, the Court of First Instance spent its time in cartel cases confirming the Commission's fact finding and approving the manner of its exercise of powers. This of course is reassuring in one sense, but it also

---

[24] 1993 Report, n 19 above, at para 71. Compare the more critical views of expert reports discussed in Chapter VI above.

[25] Jeremy Lever QC, ibid., para 73.

[26] See, e.g., Case T-1/89 etc., *Rhône-Poulenc v Commission*, n 1 above.

[27] See [1998] ECR II-813 *et seq*, [1999] ECR II-289 *et seq*, and [1999] ECR II-931 *et seq*, respectively for the clutch of judgments in each appeal. No procedural irregularities were substantiated in these cases; this point is discussed further below.

raises some questions concerning the claimed necessity for such intensity of judicial review.

(b) Exercising an 'unfettered evaluation of evidence'

In retrospect, the main achievement of the Commission's critics appears to have been not simply the establishment of the Court of First Instance as a new jurisdiction of review, but the emergence of a court which was willing patiently to hear numerous complaints regarding issues of procedure and sufficiency of evidence. A retrospective view also produces a note of irony. Many of the critical comments voiced before the House of Lords Select Committee referred to the length of time taken up by competition proceedings. Yet this was inevitable, given the setting up of a system which enabled and maybe even encouraged the legal challenge of specific points of procedure and evidence.

This was undoubtedly true of the Court's willingness in the first *Polypropylene* judgment to open up completely the review of evidence. This in fact was a remarkable, though largely unremarked legal development, since there was not in the relevant Treaty provisions or any of the instruments setting up the Court of First Instance any clear legal basis for the new jurisdiction. Moreover, the Court of Justice in its earlier case law had demonstrated some wariness in carrying out a probing factual evaluation beyond the point of manifest errors.[28] The basis for such a self-denying approach is summarized by Lasok in the following terms:

the more complex the basic facts, the more likely it is that a number of equally acceptable interpretations can be identified. In such circumstances, the Court cannot always say that a decision-making body was wrong to adopt one rather than another. To do so, is not to review the decision made, a judicial function, but to remake it, an executive or administrative function.[29]

Nonetheless, the Court of First Instance's extensive role in verifying Commission fact finding has been accepted, and even taken up by the Court of Justice, most notably in its second *Wood Pulp* judgment (also its final first instance cartel appeal).[30] This has entailed the development of a notably inquisitorial approach on the part of the Court of First Instance,

---

[28] See, e.g., Cases 56 and 58/64, *Consten and Grundig v Commission* [1966] ECR 299, at 347.

[29] K P E Lasok, *The European Court of Justice: Practice and Procedure* (2nd edn, Butterworths, 1994), 361.

[30] Cases 89/85 etc., *Ahlström Oy and others* [1993] ECR I-1307. See the discussion in Chapter VI above.

although this is carried out in response to very specific rebuttal of the Commission's evidence by the defending companies.

The Court itself in *Polypropylene* glided over the issue of its powers of factual evaluation, holding tersely, in what was to prove a formulaic statement for later judgments, that:

> It is... necessary to verify first of all whether the Commission has established to the required legal standard its findings of fact relating to (A)...(B)...(C)... and (D).[31]

There is more elucidation of what was happening in the opinion of Advocate General Vesterdorf.[32] Even so, the Advocate General assumed rather than explained the necessity for the principle which he invoked:

> It is important to first point out that the activity of the Court of Justice and thus also that of the Court of First Instance is governed by the principle of the unfettered evaluation of evidence, unconstrained by the various rules laid down in the national legal systems.[33]

While there is little discussion of the pedigree of the principle of unfettered evaluation of evidence, there is however in the Advocate General's opinion some very interesting discussion regarding the principle's application, exploring to some extent the relevant standard of proof to be incorporated into such an evaluation. Indeed, for the Advocate General the relevant standard seems to be that usually demanded in criminal proceedings: proof beyond reasonable doubt. He argued that, while the Court of Justice:

> allows only an overall assessment of a document's probative value and simple rules of evidential logic to be decisive in the evaluation of evidence[34] ... However, conclusions drawn from the evidence must never, of course, develop into ill-founded speculation. There must be a sufficient basis for the decision and any reasonable doubt must be for the benefit of the applicants according to the principle *in dubio pro reo*.

But this is reasonable doubt in the context of 'an overall view of the evidence' (so confirming that the Commission was entitled to look at the cartel as a whole in presenting its case). The following statement from the Advocate General's opinion appears to anticipate and inform the

---

[31] [1991] ECR II-1048.

[32] Exceptionally, but appropriately, an Advocate General had been assigned to the case in view of its legal significance and complexity (in this case Judge Vesterdorf, acting as Advocate General).

[33] [1991] ECR II-954.

[34] Cases 40/73 etc., *Suiker Unie and others v Commission* [1975] ECR 1663, at 1939–41.

Court of First Instance's approach to the 'required legal standard', to which it has referred in subsequent judgments:

> Even where it is possible to give a reasonable alternative explanation of a specific document, which may be isolated from a number of documents, the explanation in question might not withstand closer examination in the context of an overall examination of a whole body of evidence. It must accordingly be permissible to apply, as the Commission does, conclusions drawn from periods where the evidence is fairly solid to other periods where the gap between the various pieces of evidence is perhaps larger. After all, there needs to be a particularly good explanation to convince a court of law that in a particular phase of a series of meetings things occurred which were completely different from what had transpired at earlier or subsequent meetings when the meetings were attended by the same people, took place under similar external conditions and indisputably had the same primary purpose, namely to discuss the problems within the industrial sector concerned.[35]

The Advocate General's opinion provides as well some general reflection of how the main types of evidence in competition proceedings should be evaluated.[36] In particular, his discourse at this point emphasizes the probative strength of documentary evidence in such cases. He points out, for instance, that 'under the general rules of evidence, the fact that the documents were drawn up immediately after the meetings and clearly without any thought for the fact that they might fall into the hands of third parties must be regarded as having great significance'. In contrast, he warns of the weaknesses of both oral and expert evidence. Since the Community courts have no power to compel evidence under oath, the persons directly involved in the cases rarely appear before the courts to give evidence, but do send legal representatives and experts to argue on their behalf. Despite the forensic skill of such representatives, any evidence which they present orally in this role should not, in the Advocate General's view, override the intrinsic probative value of documentary evidence. While economic analysis can be of great value, the 'findings of economic experts cannot take the place of legal assessment and adjudication'.

The 'Vesterdorf theory of evidence' in effect provides a useful prolegomenon to the Court of First Instance's subsequent practice in evaluating evidence in cartel cases. As indicated above, to a large extent this process of review has validated the Commission's own use of evidence to establish its findings of fact. One instance when the Court appeared to disapprove strongly of the Commission's fact-finding practice was in one

[35] [1991] ECR II-954.   [36] Ibid., II-956.

of its earlier judgments, relating to the *Italian Flat Glass Cartel* in 1992.[37] This was the infamous case of alleged 'tampering' with evidence by the Commission and raises some interesting issues in its own right. The Court rebuked the Commission near the beginning of its judgment for tampering with some of the handwritten notes that it was using as evidence of agreement on prices:

It emerges from the inquiry carried out by the Court that when the Commission prepared the documentary evidence with a view to communication to the undertakings, certain relevant passages were deliberately deleted or omitted, even though they did not relate to business secrets. In particular nine words were deleted without trace in a hand-written note from SIV... It is self-evident and indisputable that the tenor of the note is changed completely by the omission of the nine words. With those nine words the note could be taken as clear evidence of competitive struggle...At the hearing the Commission tried in vain to supply an objectively justifiable reason for the deletion of those words.[38]

The Court referred to other examples of 'such a procedure', which rendered it incumbent on the Court itself 'to check meticulously the nature and import of the evidence taken into consideration by the Commission'.[39] The issue is not without controversy. In fact, the Commission's defence for excising the words in question was to maintain the confidentiality of one party by not allowing other parties access to the file (although the Court seems to have rejected this justification, but does not discuss the matter further in its judgment). More generally, this incident reveals the difficulties arising from potentially conflicting claims regarding access to the file and claims of confidentiality regarding business secrets as between members of the cartel, and the impact that such an exercise of defence rights may have on the presentation of evidence and construction of the factual case against the cartel. This issue will be revisited later in the chapter.

3. Judicial review and the search for due process: firing the 'big guns of constitutional artillery'

Appeals against cartel decisions of the Commission have, certainly since the advent of the Court of First Instance, followed broadly two main lines of attack. First, as discussed immediately above, cartel participants have

---

[37] Cases T-68/89 etc., *SIV v Commission*, n 12 above.   [38] [1992] ECR II-1442–3.
[39] Ibid., 1444.

challenged the factual basis of decisions against themselves, alleging insufficiency of evidence, though with increasingly limited success. Secondly, more traditional judicial review arguments have been employed, impugning the legality of the process leading to the Commission's decision. This latter area of appellate argument has attracted more attention and has indeed been productive of a substantial case law on defence rights (what has been referred to as 'bringing out the big guns of constitutional artillery').[40] Much of this legal development is well known and fully discussed in the literature[41] and will not be revisited in detail here. Rather, the purpose of the next stage of discussion will be to evaluate this development of due process and probe its significance for the legal control of cartels.

For purposes of the present discussion, judicial review of the legality of the Commission's cartel control activity may be examined under a number of main headings: the juridical nature of the Commission's procedure; the conduct of inspections; and the effective exercise of defence rights. Such discussion must include the evolution of rules relating to the exclusion of certain categories of evidence, but this relates to both the stage of investigation and the subsequent presentation of defence argument.

4. The nature of the Commission's procedure

This in one sense is a fundamental question, since so much else follows from the prior categorization of the whole process of investigation, hearing, and decision. But in another sense, it is a part of the subject which has been rather lost in the detail of due process argument. At the same time, it may be said that discussion of this aspect of the subject has been characterized by an ambivalence which continues to inform (or perhaps dis-inform) the course of legal development.

One way of presenting this topic is to pose the simple question: is the procedure laid down for the investigation and determination of cartel

---

[40] The phrase used by Judge David Edward: 'Constitutional Rules of Community Law in EEC Competition Cases', (1989) *Fordham Corp. L. Institute* 383.

[41] For a useful overview, see K Lenaerts and J Vanhamme, 'Procedural Rights of Private Parties in the Community Administrative Process' (1997) 34 *CMLRev* 531; and *Reports of the 17th Congress of the FIDE (Fédération internationale de droit européen)*, vol III (Nomos Verlag, 1996). For a more detailed, practice-oriented analysis, see C S Kerse, *E.C. Antitrust Procedure*, n 11 above, chs 3, 4. On the general background to the substantive principles of judicial review, see Takis Tridimas, *The General Principles of EC Law* (OUP, 1999).

conduct a criminal or administrative procedure? The significance of that question resides in the consequent legal implications for the conduct of the procedure and the position of defending parties. Put bluntly: if the procedure is 'criminal' (or substantially equivalent to that), then certain higher standards and expectations, as laid down in national legal orders and systems of review such as that under the European Convention on Human Rights,[42] will follow suit. The 'severity' of criminal law sanctions demands a higher level of defence protection, in relation to such matters as the standard of proof, collection of evidence, conduct of investigations, and opportunities for presenting a defence and securing legal review of formal decisions. If, on the other hand, the procedure is 'administrative', then legally, ethically, and socially less is at stake for defending parties, and there is a lesser imperative of legal protection.[43]

Once the Commission had entered a more confrontational phase of enforcement in relation to competition matters, companies were not slow to raise questions about the legal nature of the procedure being used against them, and move to exploit analogous defence rights laid down in instruments such as the European Convention on Human Rights. These matters were tested before the Court of Justice at a relatively early stage. Three main questions were posed. First, was the procedure laid down in Regulation 17 properly speaking 'administrative' in character? The Court's simple answer to this was affirmative (or, to put the matter more explicitly, it was not a criminal proceeding).[44] Secondly, in deciding on infringements of the competition rules, was the Commission acting as a 'tribunal' in the sense of Article 6 of the European Convention on Human Rights? Again, there was a clear answer from the Court of Justice: the Commission was not a tribunal in that sense.[45] Thirdly, was the Commission legally able to combine the roles of investigator, prosecutor, judge, jury, and sentencer in carrying out its regulatory role in competition matters? This was perhaps the most challenging question, since it did not admit so easily of a simple definitional answer, but required some serious consideration of separation of

---

[42] Significant relevant case law under the European Convention on Human Rights includes in particular: *Ozturk v Germany* (1984) 6 EHRR/409; *Stenuit v France* (1992) 14 EHRR/509 (Commission on Human Rights); *Niemietz v Germany* (1993) 16 EHRR/97; *Funke v France* (1993) 16 EHRR/297; *Saunders v United Kingdom* (1997) 23 EHRR/313.

[43] See Christopher Harding, *European Community Investigations and Sanctions* (Leicester University Press, 1993), ch 1.

[44] See, e.g., Case 45/69, *Boehringer Mannheim v Commission* [1970] ECR 153, at para 23.

[45] Cases 100–103/80, *Musique Diffusion Francaise v Commission*, n 1 above, [1983] ECR 1880.

powers argument. Indeed, the Commission itself, over a period of time, took on board such concerns by developing due process elements in its own procedure, notably by adopting its own procedural instrument, Regulation 99/63, introducing the office of Hearing Officer in 1982,[46] and reorganizing the allocation of responsibilities within DG IV in 1984–5.[47] Advocate General Vesterdorf reviews many of these arguments in his keynote opinion in the *Polypropylene* appeal in 1991 and, while accepting that a lack of functional separation between the 'investigation' and 'prosecution' stages might give rise to concern, nonetheless argued that such separation was not necessary to ensure fair procedure.[48]

The establishment of the Court of First Instance in 1989 and the role actually undertaken by the latter in dealing with competition cases has addressed such arguments up to a point. Once it became clear that there was ample opportunity for judicial review, and that the review would be carried out with a fine-toothed comb, many of the points of principle may have appeared less urgent. For the Court of Justice had also made it clear at an early stage that, even if the procedure was administrative, and the Commission was not acting as a tribunal, nor under an obligation to ensure a strict separation of functions, there was an overall duty to act fairly, which would be guaranteed by the opportunity for judicial review.[49] In one sense, the Court's position was reassuring: a rigorous and meticulous process of judicial review should allay any fears concerning a lack of fair treatment. On the other hand, sweeping the definitional questions under the carpet of judicial review left matters largely still in the air: what would be the more precise content of fair treatment, as worked out by the Community courts, when the precise nature of the Commission's procedure was still unclear? Both the Commission and the companies were left to await the outcome case-by-case, as the courts decided what was fair according to the required 'European standard'.[50] But even on specific questions, the outcome has proven to be somewhat elusive; for instance, in relation to the requisite standard of proof, which in the practice of the

---

[46] For the terms of reference of the Hearing Officer, see OJ 1994, L 330/67.

[47] Although this was later abandoned.

[48] Cases T-1/89 etc., *Rhône-Poulenc v Commission*, n 1 above, [1991] ECR II-884–7.

[49] In particular, in its judgment in *Musique Diffusion Francaise v Commission*, n 1 above.

[50] See Advocate General Vesterdorf's reference to the 'European benchmark': [1991] ECR II-885–6.

Court of First Instance appears to be 'beyond reasonable doubt', but is never actually referred to as such.

There remains therefore some ambivalence regarding these legal structures and there are mixed views on the sufficiency of due process guarantees. As Jones and Sufrin comment:

The Commission's multi-faceted role in the enforcement of the competition rules is subject to constant criticism by commentators, very often practitioners who have acted for the undertakings on the receiving end of the enforcement process. It is defended, equally robustly, by Commission officials. One needs to make allowances for partisanship but, even so, there is obviously a serious issue to be tried.[51]

On the one side, the argument persists that, in its very nature, the accumulation of different functions within the same institution, leads to problems. At its simplest, it is urged that the Commission as regulator has inevitably a strong interest in effective enforcement. Therefore, how can it be expected to act impartially as 'judge' (in taking decisions), having been prosecutor? It has been pointed out, for instance, that rarely does there appear to be much difference between the position adopted by the Commission in its statement of objections and that taken in its subsequent decision—so questioning whether there is an effective exercise of rights of defence.[52] Montag points to the sense of uneasiness in this regard:

undertakings often feel that they are treated unfairly and that their procedural rights are violated...because undertakings are uncomfortable...decisions imposing significant fines lack acceptance.[53]

But that is perception (stemming from its own natural bias). Granting that there might be a *systemic* bias in the process, what, however, is the evidence of *actual* bias in the practice of the Commission? One test might be the actual outcome of appeals. In his survey published in 1996,[54] Montag states that the chances of obtaining annulment in a competition appeal were 'slightly better than three to one'. However, Montag's sample is made

---

[51] Alison Jones and Brenda Sufrin, *EC Competition Law: Text, Cases and Materials* (OUP, 2001), 939. The partisan character of much of the legal commentary in this area is an important feature of the literature which should be borne in mind. See the discussion later in this chapter.

[52] F Montag, 'The Case for Radical Reform of the Infringement Procedure under Regulation 17' (1996) *ECLR* 428. The author points out for instance that in the decision relating to the *Steel Beams Cartel*, 90 per cent of the text of the decision was identical to the statement of objections: ibid., 429.   [53] Ibid., 429.

[54] Ibid., 430 *et seq.*

up of appeals decided only up to the mid-1990s and treats all annulments equally. Thus, inclusion of more recent appeals over the last six years or so (as discussed above) would undoubtedly reduce the number of annulments. But perhaps more significantly, it should be pointed out that a careful reading of the cases over 10 years or more of the Court of First Instance's exercise of jurisdiction would show that the majority of annulments have concerned non- (or, to be exact, insufficiently) proven *episodes* of cartel involvement and consequent *small* reductions in fines. Even in 1996 it may have therefore been misleading to claim that the Commission's decisions 'too often do not stand up to scrutiny';[55] to do so now would be even more misleading. To put the matter another way: a purely quantitative analysis may provide only a partial picture, while a qualitative analysis of the *kind* and *extent* of procedural violations resulting in annulment might provide a very different view.

Nonetheless, even clear evidence of respect for due process in practice does not deal fully with the argument that *in principle* there would be a surer guarantee of fair treatment if the role of prosecutor and judge were institutionally separate. Two main proposals have come to the surface in this regard. First, there is the idea of a completely separate EC competition enforcement agency, the so-called 'European Cartel Office' (ECO),[56] which was advocated in particular by the German Government in the deliberations preceding the 1996 Intergovernmental Conference. Secondly, there is the argument in favour of having a true judicial 'trial' of alleged competition violations by transferring that role to the Court of First Instance, leaving the Commission as investigator and prosecutor.[57] But the Commission appears to be unwilling to concede easily its present role, and neither proposal would appear to have much political momentum in the context of the recent 'modernization' project, which has if anything consolidated the Commission's prominent role in dealing with serious violations of the competition rules.

---

[55] F Montag, 'The Case for Radical Reform of the Infringement Procedure under Regulation 17' (1996) *ECLR* 433.

[56] See C-D Ehlermann, 'Reflections on the ECO' (1995) 32 *CMLRev* 471; Alan Riley, 'The European Cartel Office: A Guardian Without Weapons?' (1997) 18 *ECLR* 3.

[57] Advocated, e.g., by Montag, n 52 above, as 'the only solution which would eliminate all of the shortcomings in the infringement procedure and which is likely at the same time to (re-)establish acceptance of decisions' (at 435).

Thus the discussion remains for the foreseeable future rooted in the guarantee of due process through the appeal procedure to the Court of First Instance. As pointed out by a senior Commission official:

Regulation 17 does not set out any separation of powers. The Commission is investigator, prosecutor and 'judge'. However Regulation 17 also grants full jurisdiction to the courts to review the Commission's decisions on fines. This broad judicial review in a way offsets the lack of separation of powers.[58]

In this respect, there is little doubt that the Court has proven meticulous in its approach and that undertakings have ample opportunity to challenge both the factual basis of Commission decisions and the conduct of its procedure. The crucial question therefore relates to the *standards* of review which have been worked out by the Court of Justice and the Court of First Instance in determining issues of legality, or, more exactly, fair procedure. In one sense, much has been achieved simply in terms of the legal ground covered: a number of rights and principles have been more clearly delineated. On the other hand, there has been some criticism of the Community courts in terms of how far they have been prepared to protect defence rights. In particular, it has been alleged that the standard laid down by the latter has not always matched that of the European Court of Human Rights in comparable cases.[59] So, for instance, it has been argued that the Court of Justice's right of non-self incrimination does not match the standard provided under the European Convention on Human Rights, or that it has been less protective of corporate actors compared to the European Court of Human Rights[60] (see the discussion below). But the evaluation of such arguments depends to some extent, as already indicated, on the characterization of the Commission's competition procedure, and that remains opaque.

One problem in comparing the different European jurisdictions as systems of legal protection is that it is not always a comparison of like with like. Articles 6 and 8 of the European Convention on Human Rights were not conceived with either corporate actors or 'administrative' procedures foremost in mind. Moreover, even if the European Court of Human

---

[58] Luc Gyselen, 'Discussion: Fines in EC and US Competition Law', in Slot and McDonnell (eds), n 1 above, ch 16, at 88.

[59] See, e.g., D Spielman, 'Human Rights Case Law in the Strasbourg and Luxembourg Courts: Conflicts, Inconsistencies and Complementarities', in P Alston (ed), *The EU and Human Rights* (OUP, 1999), ch 23, at 764–70.

[60] The *Orkem* and *Hoechst* judgments of the Court of Justice (discussed below) compared with those of the European Court of Human Rights in *Funke v France* and *Niemietz v Germany*, n 42 above.

Rights has insisted that it is the substance of the procedure rather than its formal description that should determine the level of legal protection for defendants,[61] it is still possible to argue that prosecuting a cartel for infringement of the EC rules is different in some important respects from the usual kind of criminal proceeding at the national level. Perhaps most importantly, there is an issue of *subjectivity* that will increasingly need to be addressed: *who* is being prosecuted—companies, individuals within companies, or both, and under what kind of proceeding? As more national legal systems move towards criminalization of *individual* participation in cartel activities, the phenomenon of different proceedings, in different systems, and *perhaps* entailing different standards of legal protection, will become more dominant. The emerging mosaic of different proceedings, involving different types of legal defendant, and complicated by negotiated leniency deals, as discussed in the following chapters, are likely to complicate rather than clarify these issues of judicial review.

5. Investigations and the collection of evidence

Prior to the development of leniency programmes, the use of investigations, especially in their 'surprise' or unannounced form (the 'dawn raid'), was the single crucial strategy for gaining evidence in relation to sophisticated and covert cartel activity. On its face, Regulation 17 provided the Commission with potentially very wide powers of investigation, regarding both the process of search and the asking of questions. Over time, these powers have been more closely defined through legal challenge before the European courts, and the limits imposed on the exercise of these investigatory powers relate also to the construction of the general right for parties under investigation to present an effective defence. In this way, perhaps the most significant limit on the power of investigation concerns the kind of evidence which may be collected or used in legal proceedings, formulated in some rules of exclusion of evidence.

The Commission's basic powers of investigation[62] as laid down in Regulation 17 may be briefly summarized as follows. There is first a power to request information under Article 11, from governments, competent national authorities, and undertakings. Such requests must indicate clearly both the legal basis for and the purpose of the request, so as to

---

[61] *Ozturk v Germany*, n 42 above.
[62] For a detailed analysis of these powers, see Kerse, n 11 above, ch 3.

clarify the extent of any obligation of compliance. Article 11(5) enables the Commission to use a formal decision to *require* the supply of information, if it has not been provided by a stated time, and financial penalties may be imposed for non-compliance with such decisions; but they are also reviewable by the Court of First Instance. Secondly, there is a distinct power of investigation (sometimes referred to as inspection) laid down in Article 14, which provides for visits, oral questions, and searches. So-called 'voluntary' investigations are covered by Article 14(2): these must be based on written authorization, which must again specify the subject matter and purpose of the investigation and indicate any possible penalties for non-compliance. 'Mandatory' investigations are laid down in Article 14(3) and must be based on a formal decision, again indicating the subject matter, purpose, and possible penalties, and as a decision, again reviewable by the Court of First Instance. Article 14(3) is the legal basis for a 'dawn raid', the surprise element of which has been approved by the Court of Justice.[63] Any resistance by an undertaking to entry or search must be dealt with in compliance with the relevant national law authorizing forcible inspections.[64] Obstructive or unco-operative behaviour has sometimes been penalized, a notable example being the periodic penalty payments imposed on the German company. Hoeschst, as a member of the *PVC Cartel*, in 1987.[65]

So much for the powers as such; their exercise has been extensively challenged by undertakings alleged to have been involved in illegal cartels and this has enabled first the Court of Justice and then the Court of First Instance to define more exactly their scope and any concomitant basic rights of defence. The process of review has also generated a body of evidential rules in so far as the relevant issue has been the right to withhold or have excluded certain categories of information. This is also a field of legal argument in which companies have been keen to invoke any analogous protection laid down under the European Convention on Human Rights, and this in turn has generated difficult argument concerning the relationship between the respective jurisdiction of the Community courts and the European Court of Human Rights.[66] Both the Court of Justice

[63] Case 136/79, *National Panasonic v Commission* [1980] ECR 2033.

[64] Cases 97–99/87, *Dow Chemica Iberica v Commission* [1989] ECR 3165 (as provided in Article 14(6) of Regulation 17/62).

[65] The power is laid down in Article 16 of Regulation 17; in the case of Hoechst it was the maximum penalty of 1,000 ECU per day.

[66] See, e.g., the discussion by Spielman, n 59 above.

and the Court of First Instance have emphasized that the legal protection provided as a matter of Community law, although autonomous and ultimately governed by Community objectives, should nonetheless as far as possible comply with a 'European standard', and so draw upon analogies from the Convention system and from member state public law.[67] However, working out in specific cases an appropriate *Community law* solution on the basis of a comparative reading of *other European legal sources* may prove both problematic and controversial. This was evident for instance in the *AM & S Europe* case[68] when the Court of Justice was attempting to identify the extent of lawyer–client confidentiality, and Advocate General Warner observed in his opinion that:

The French Government bore alone the burden of arguing that there was no principle of Community law restricting the powers of the Commission under Article 14 of Regulation 17 ... that the relevant laws of the Member States were too disparate for there to be derived from them any general principle that might apply. The French Government went so far as to suggest that the present case represented an attempt to foist on the Community what was no more than a domestic rule of English law.[69]

It is not then surprising that the outcome of legal argument before the Community courts has sometimes proven controversial, especially in so far as there is any perceived discrepancy between the position adopted by the latter and the European Court of Human Rights in their respective jurisprudence.[70]

In very broad terms the Court of Justice has confirmed the existence, for corporate actors or businesses,[71] of a basic right of protection against 'arbitrary and disproportionate intervention'.[72] But the Community courts, unlike the European Court of Human Rights, have not gone so far as to declare categorically the 'inviolability of business premises' (a 'privacy' right, derived by analogy from protection of the 'home' under Article 8 of

---

[67] See, e.g., Case 46/87, *Hoechst v Commission* [1989] ECR 2859, at paras 12–19.

[68] Case 155/79, *AM & S Europe v Commission* [1982] ECR 1575.   [69] Ibid., 1631.

[70] On this point of discrepancy, see A G Toth, 'The European Union and Human Rights: the Way Forward' (1997) 34 *CMLRev* 491.

[71] The relative protection of 'private' individuals and business actors is one of the points of discrepancy. But Advocate General Mischo, in his opinion in *Hoechst*, was willing to give the same level of protection to businesses as to private individuals: [1989] ECR 2893.

[72] *Hoechst v Commission*, n 67 above.

the Convention European on Human Rights).[73] In its *Hoechst* judgment, the Court of Justice stated:

Since the applicant has also relied on the requirements stemming from the fundamental right to the inviolability of the home, it should be observed that, although the existence of such a right must be recognized in the Community legal order as a principle common to the laws of the Member States in regard to the private dwellings of natural persons, the same is not true in regard to undertakings, because there are not inconsiderable divergences between the legal systems of the Member States in regard to the nature and degree of protection afforded to business premises against intervention by the public authorities... Nonetheless, in all the legal systems of the Member States, any intervention by the public authorities in the sphere of private activities of any person, whether natural or legal, must have a legal basis and be justified on grounds laid down by law, and, consequently, those systems provide, albeit in different forms, protection against arbitrary or disproportionate intervention. The need for such protection must be recognized as a general principle of Community law.[74]

The phrase 'protection against arbitrary and proportionate intervention' perhaps indicates more explicitly the qualification of the basic right, in favour of justifiable intervention in the interests of effective enforcement of the competition rules and the general interest embodied in competition policy. In practical terms, most argument concerning the extent of this right for undertakings in the context of competition proceedings has related to the kinds of information and evidence that may be collected and used in legal proceedings by the Commission. There have been two main issues: confidentiality and self incrimination.

There had already been some reference in Articles 20 and 21 of Regulation 17 to the need to respect information 'covered by the obligation of professional secrecy' and 'business secrets',[75] although these terms are not further defined, and this issue will be further discussed below in relation to arguments concerning 'access to the file'. Another major aspect of confidentiality arose in relation to the communications between companies and their lawyers and whether these would qualify as evidence which could be withheld from the Commission under the doctrine of 'legal professional privilege'. In *AM & S Europe*[76] the Court of Justice accepted that an

---

[73] *Niemietz v Germany*, n 42 above. In this judgment the European Court of Human Rights impliedly rejected the Court of Justice's assertion in *Hoechst* that the scope of Article 8 of the Convention is 'concerned with the development of man's personal freedom and may not therefore be extended to business premises': [1989] ECR 2859, at para 18.

[74] [1989] ECR 2859, at paras 17–19.

[75] See also Case 85/76, *Hoffmann-la Roche v Commission* [1979] ECR 471; Case 53/85, *AKZO Chemie v Commission* [1986] ECR 1965, on the implications of this protection.

[76] See n 68 above.

effective right of defence entails a full and uninhibited consultation between companies and their lawyers, and this should therefore be regarded as confidential and thus not examinable by the Commission. This privilege would apply to confidential communications between a lawyer and client, relating to the latter's right of defence, when the lawyer was independent in the sense of not being an employee of the client.[77] The delineation of this protection provoked some critical discussion at the time,[78] and there has been increasing concern on the part of lawyers outside the EC, especially in the United States, regarding the exclusion of 'in-house' lawyers from the scope of the privilege.

The right not to incriminate oneself, however, has been another matter, productive of continuing legal argument. Indeed, this is a pivotal subject, since at its broadest this right could be construed as a right to with-hold crucial evidence and thus significantly impede the construction of a prosecution case. The 'right to silence' or 'non-self incrimination' made its first important appearance in the *Orkem* case in 1989.[79] The companies in this appeal had invoked the right not to give evidence against oneself in relation to a Commission decision requiring information adopted under Article 11(5) of Regulation 17. The approach taken by the Court of Justice, adhered to subsequently by the Court of First Instance, rejected the view that there was a right to remain silent as such under Community law and denied that such a right could be derived from Article 6 of the European Convention on Human Rights. On the other hand, the Courts confirmed a more limited right not to be compelled to admit involvement in an infringement.[80] More precisely, the courts stated that the Commission:

> may not, by means of a decision calling for information, undermine the rights of defence of the undertaking concerned … Thus, the Commission may not compel an undertaking to provide it with answers which might involve an admission on its part of the existence of an infringement which it is incumbent on the Commission to prove.[81]

Although not very clear in itself, this principle was clarified later in the Court of Justice's judgment by its application to particular questions put by the Commission. In crude terms, the principle distinguishes between

---

[77] [1982] ECR 3193.

[78] See Jonathan Faull, 'Legal Professional Privilege: the Commission Proposes International Negotiations' (1985) 10 *ELRev* 119; Harding, n 43 above, 28–31.

[79] Cases 375/87 and 27/88, *Orkem, Solvay v Commission* [1989] ECR 3283.

[80] Nobody appears to have formulated a concise description of this right, which is in fact a more restricted version of non-self incrimination; writers generally refer to the '*Orkem* principle'.

[81] [1989] ECR 3283, at paras 34–5.

simple questions of fact and 'leading questions'. So, to illustrate: permissible questions would include those seeking factual information relating to the circumstances and participation in specified meetings, or the subject matter and implementation of identified pricing measures; impermissible questions would include those relating to the purpose of action taken or details of activities or processes clearly identified as illegal (for instance, systems or methods or fixing prices or quotas). Put another way, 'what?' questions would generally have to be answered, but 'why?' and 'how?' questions, the answers to which might well confirm guilt, do not have to be answered. Despite later developments in the jurisprudence of the European Court of Human Rights, the Court of First Instance has maintained the *Orkem* approach, notably in its *PVC 2* judgment,[82] and more recently in *Mannesmannröhren-Werke v Commission* in 2001.[83] In its *PVC 2* judgment the Court pointed out that an absolute right of silence would amount to an unjustified hindrance to the Commission in its task of enforcing the competition rules.[84]

Critical opinion maintains that the refusal to abandon the 'limited' protection of the *Orkem* principle is a kind of legal heresy in view of the more generous position subsequently adopted by the European Court of Human Rights.[85] The latter, in its *Funke* judgment,[86] confirmed that Article 6 of the European Convention did provide for a right of silence, although qualified its position later in *Saunders*[87] by saying that this did not extend to documents seized or required to be produced during an investigation, since these comprised material having 'an existence independent of the will of the accused'. But the Court of First Instance (and perhaps also the Court of Justice) appear to be adamant that competition proceedings under EC law can be distinguished if necessary from criminal proceedings under national law for this purpose. In its *PVC 2* judgment, for instance, the Court of First Instance stated:

The fact that the case-law of the European Court of Human Rights concerning the applicability of Article 8 of the ECHR to legal persons has evolved since the judgments in *Hoechst*, *Dow Benelux* and *Dow Chemica Iberica*...has no direct impact on the merits of the solutions adopted in those cases.[88]

---

[82] Cases T-305/94 etc., *LVM and others v Commission* [1999] ECR II-931.
[83] Case T-112/98 [2001] ECR II-729.   [84] [1999] ECR II-1062.
[85] See, e.g., Walter B J van Overbeek, 'The Right to Remain Silent in Competition Investigations: the *Funke* Decision of the Court of Human Rights Makes Revision of the ECJ's Case Law Necessary' (1994) 15 *ECLR* 127; Peter R Willis, '"You Have the Right to Remain Silent...", or Do You?' (2001) 22 *ECLR* 313; Spielman, n 59 above; A Clapham, 'A Human Rights Policy for the European Community' (1990) 10 *YBEL* 309, at 337–8.
[86] See n 42 above.   [87] Ibid.   [88] [1999] ECR II-1056, para 450.

It has been urged that national authorities acting in support of Commission investigations, or even member states more generally in failing to secure Convention rights in the application of EC legislation, could be impugned under the European Convention.[89] But this would still not affect the actual exercise of the Commission's powers, since the EU is not directly subject to the Convention. It seems unlikely, despite the criticism of divergence from the Convention jurisprudence, that the Community courts will be deflected from their present course. Indeed, one recent critic of the Court of First Instance's stance, virtually concedes the main issue by advising careful consideration of the non-self incrimination argument:

> Excessive use may be counter-productive, by encouraging inspectors to pursue their investigations further or to draw adverse inferences from documents seized or indeed from the absence of documents. Indeed in some situations, the optimum course of action will be to admit the infringement immediately and claim the benefit of one of the leniency programmes offered by the Commission or the OFT.[90]

As van Overbeek has commented: 'It is up to the defence to decide whether or not to "bring out the big guns of constitutional artillery".'[91] In terms of defence strategy, such remarks probably provide an indication of the course of future development. With the advent of leniency programmes, strenuous 'big gun' arguments in favour of a wider right of silence may lose their relevance. Certainly, there is some indication of a pointless use of 'right of silence' arguments. In *PVC 2*,[92] for example, violation of the *Orkem* principle was invoked in relation to questions to which no answers had been given in any case. Admittedly, the questions were not permissible, but since there had been no answers, the defending parties had exercised their right, there was no illegally obtained evidence, and no impact on the Commission's decision. The Court of First Instance pointed out that illegality of the question in such a case would not affect the legality of the decision. This is just one example of what is sometimes referred to as a 'so what?' outcome to an argument for annulment of an administrative measure, when there has been a procedural irregularity but not such as to have a material effect on the quality of the eventual decision (known in American law as the 'harmless error' principle). The judicial review of Commission cartel decisions is peppered with such results.

---

[89] Willis, n 85 above (making use of *Matthews v UK* (1999) 28 EHRR 361).

[90] Willis, n 85 above, 319–20. It should be noted that exercise of the right to silence does not prevent a court from drawing an adverse inference from silence: *Murray v UK* (1996) 22 EHRR 29.

[91] Van Overbeek, n 85 above, 133.   [92] See n 82 above, [1999] ECR II-1063.

6. Effective rights of defence and 'access to the file'

The second main area of due process argument has concerned that later stage in proceedings against cartels which may be roughly described as the prosecution phase, from the point following investigation when the Commission decides to take formal legal action against a cartel, up to the time of its decision. This may also be described as the 'hearing' since it begins with a formal 'initiation' or opening of the procedure and then a statement of objections (as laid down in Article 2 of Commission Regulation 99/63), and comprises largely the response or responses of the members of the cartel—in effect a process of defence. There are a number of basic principles which naturally apply to this procedure, such as the provision of reasonable time within which to present a defence (comparable to the right to 'have adequate time and facilities for the preparation of a defence' under Article 6(3)(b) of the European Convention on Human Rights),[93] and the sufficiency and clarity of the Commission's case against the members of the cartel (comparable to the right to be fully informed of the prosecution's case under Article 6(3)(a) of the Convention),[94] both of which are obvious components of a concept of effective defence. The underlying general right of defence is laid down in the fifth recital to Regulation 99:

In accordance with Article 19(1) of Regulation 17 and with the rights of defence, the undertakings and association of undertakings concerned must have the right on conclusion of the inquiry to submit their comments on the whole of the objections raised against them which the Commission proposes to deal with in its decisions.

The procedure is mainly written, but there is provision for an oral hearing under Article 7 of Regulation 99, if the defending parties can show a sufficient interest or if the Commission proposes to impose a fine (which would now invariably be so in a cartel case).

Perhaps the most contentious aspect of the general right of defence in the context of competition proceedings has been the application of the 'equality of arms' principle and associated defence claims of access to the

---

[93] A minimum period of two weeks is laid down in Article 11(1) of Regulation 99/63. Two or more months may be a more reasonable period; see Cases 6 and 7/73, *Commercial Solvents v Commission* [1974] ECR 223.

[94] This in fact, was the ground on which a Commission cartel decision was first successfully challenged: Cases 8–11/66, *Cimenteries and others v Commission* [1967] ECR 75.

Commission's file. Although not explicitly articulated in Article 6 of the European Convention, equality of arms is a well-established concept in Convention jurisprudence. Broadly it connotes the idea that each party to a proceeding should have an equal opportunity to present argument and that neither party should enjoy a substantial advantage over the other in this respect. An important component of this principle is the right to confront and challenge evidence which is material to the opponent's case (specifically listed in Article 6(3)(d) of the Convention in relation to cross-examination of witnesses). In the context of cartel litigation, most of the argument has centred on the extent of the Commission's obligation to disclose to the defending parties material which it has collected in the case and which they may find useful for their defence.

There is common ground regarding the disclosure of material which is relied upon by the Commission in its decision against the parties: that must be made available to the defending parties. But there is contention regarding the disclosure of *unused* material, which defending parties claim *may* have an exculpatory character, so that they should therefore have an opportunity to examine such evidence. In 1991 the Court of Justice confirmed that there was no obligation of blanket disclosure of unused material on the part of the Commission:

Although regard for the rights of the defence requires that the undertaking concerned shall have been enabled to make known effectively its point of view on the documents relied upon by the Commission in making the findings on which its decision is based, there are no provisions which require the Commission to divulge the contents of its file to the parties concerned.[95]

The justification for this restrictive approach has been explained in the following terms:

There is of course a very good reason for this. The Commission, when it carries out Article 14(3) investigations in multi-handed cases, gathers a vast quantity of internal business information from companies. Most of the material eventually turns out to be irrelevant to the fair disposal of any issue in the case but it would provide inquisitive competitors with an open window as to how their rivals conduct their business affairs. It is probably not a 'business secret' in the sense of a secret formula or the like, but it is sensitive: all commercial information has some value. It particularly behoves a competition authority not to air companies' confidential business before all and sundry. If it did, they might well be reluctant to make any disclosure to the agency. So confidentiality is an aid to effective investigation. It is in the public interest to maintain it.[96]

---

[95] Case 62/86, *AKZO v Commission* [1991] ECR-I-3359.   [96] Joshua, n 18 above, 123.

By the early 1990s the Commission was careful to explain its policy on disclosure. In its *Twenty-third Report on Competition Policy* in 1993, for example, the Commission indicated that its practice was to provide defending parties with material on which it intended to rely and also any evidence which in the Commission's view may be exculpatory ('*Brady* evidence').[97] Undertakings were further entitled to request disclosure of documents relating to specified matters. But at the same time the Commission would always have regard to the need to protect confidentiality. There had already been a confrontation between the Commission and the Court of First Instance in 1992 in the *Italian Flat Glass Cartel* case,[98] during which the Commission was accused of tampering with evidence and the Court was unwilling to accept the Commission's claim that certain material had been excised from a written note in order to protect confidentiality (see the discussion in Chapter V, above). But the real test was provided by the *Soda Ash Cartel* case in 1995,[99] when the Court of First Instance ruled that there should be a more extensive right of access to the Commission's file. This was a case legally complicated by the Commission's attempt to establish violations of Articles 85(1) and 86 (now Articles 81(1) and 82) of the EC Treaty in relation to the same activity, and the Court was unhappy about non-disclosure of material in each party's 'Article 86 file' to the other. At the same time, the Court took the opportunity to lay down a general principle concerning the extent of access to the file:

Having regard to the general principle of equality of arms, which presupposes in a competition case the knowledge which the undertaking concerned has of the file used in the proceedings is the same as that of the Commission, the Commission's view cannot be upheld. The Court considers that it is not acceptable for the Commission alone to have had available to it…the documents [in question] and for it to be able to decide on its own whether or not to use them against the applicant, when the applicant had no access to them and was therefore unable likewise to decide whether or not it would use them in its defence. In such a situation the rights of defence which the applicant enjoys during the administrative procedure would be excessively restricted in relation to the powers of the Commission, which would then act as both the authority notifying the objections and the deciding authority, while having more detailed knowledge of the case-file than the defence.[100]

---

[97] Such exculpatory material in the prosecution file is colloquially referred to as *Brady* material or evidence in the United States.

[98] Cases T-68/89 etc., *Società Italiana Vetro and others v Commission* [1992] ECR II-1403.

[99] Cases T-30/91 etc., *Solvay and others v Commission*, Case T-36/91, *ICI v Commission* [1995] ECR II-1847. Advocate General Vesterdorf had already argued in favour of a more generous access to the file in his opinion in the *Polypropylene* appeal, n 5 above, [1991] ECR II-899.

[100] *ICI v Commission*, n 99 above, [1995] ECR II-1890, para 93.

The Court went on to say that business secrets contained in the file should continue to be protected, either by the Commission deleting sensitive passages from copies sent to the applicants and checking with other parties what information they would consider to be sensitive.

This generous version of the right of access is typically enough supported by legal practitioners from the 'defence bar',[101] while criticized by commentators from the regulatory side of the enforcement divide.[102] But, as Joshua points out (and contrary to some other assertions),[103] the Court of First Instance's principle extends much further on the question of disclosure than either American or English law. In the United States, the principle laid down in *Brady*, while outlawing the suppression of exculpatory material, does not require disclosure of unused evidence which is not material to the guilt of the accused.[104] The approach of English law to this issue is summed up by Simon Brown LJ in the following terms:

It is after all for the prosecution to decide in accordance with clearly established principle what is material. That responsibility rests with them . . . I would express the hope that those representing the defendants would not too readily seek to challenge a responsible prosecutor's assertion that documents are in his considered view not material . . . Courts should in my judgment treat such applications with some scepticism and should certainly decline to examine further documents unless the defendant can make out a clear prima facie case for supposing that despite the prosecution's assertions to the contrary the documents in question are indeed material.[105]

In some respects, the Court of First Instance's position on disclosure of evidence and access to the file is consistent with the role it has evolved as reviewer of the facts. Just as the Court has been very willing to review the facts of the case *de novo* in cartel appeals, so it appears happy to give the defending parties the fullest opportunity to carry out an examination of the evidence in the files relating to themselves. Whether this will have proved to be of much advantage to the undertakings in terms of the final legal outcome may be open to question. On the other hand, there may be

---

[101] See, e.g., David Vaughan, 'Access to the File and Confidentiality', in Slot and McDonnell (eds), n 1 above, ch 20.

[102] See, in particular, Joshua, n 96 above, 122 *et seq*; Claus Dieter Ehlermann and Berend Jan Drijber, 'Legal Protection of Enterprises: Administrative Procedure, in Particular Access to Files and Confidentiality' (1996) 17 *ECLR* 375.

[103] Such as the evidence given by a number of British legal practitioners to the House of Lords Select Committee on the European Communities in 1993, n 19 above.

[104] *Brady v Maryland*, 373 US 83 (1963).

[105] *R v Bromley Magistrates Court, ex parte Smith* [1995] WLR 944, at 950.

some tactical gain in drawing out the proceedings and tying up enforcement resources. If this is the usual result, then, as Ehlermann and Drijber comment, the 'companies have nothing to lose ... the guaranteed winners will be the lawyers, the losers might well be the consumer'.[106]

7. The balance of legal protection

The history of the system of judicial review in this area of EC competition regulation is an interesting and telling narrative of legal development in its own right. This is so first of all in relation to the appearance of the Court of First Instance and the way in which it has fashioned for itself a distinctive role as a court of review (and been allowed to do so). Its assumption of jurisdiction over questions of fact and evidence is unusual for an appellate court. Moreover, its review of virtually every aspect of the Commission's procedure has been painstaking. In effect, this has encouraged appeals by undertakings to such an extent that the Court has an almost automatic role in dealing with the Commission's cartel decisions. It would not be an exaggeration to say that it has for practical purposes almost turned itself into a trial court in this context, especially considering that a large number of its own decisions are in turn appealed to the Court of Justice. To put the matter another way: without formally amending the Commission's procedure under Regulation 17, there has nonetheless been a *de facto* separation of functions and an introduction of a distinct judicial trial authority. If the Court of First Instance were formally to be given the role of a trial court in competition proceedings, little would change regarding its substantive role.

In effect, therefore, the separation of powers complaint discussed above has been addressed. In the majority of cartel cases, the Commission's formal decision has evolved into a summative statement of the case for the prosecution, which is then judicially tested before the Court of First Instance. Since the dust has settled on this development, from the middle of the 1990s, both the Commission and the Court appear to have settled into a comfortable relationship, within which the former prepares its cases carefully, and the latter confirms most of the prosecution case.

---

[106] See n 102 above, 383; and see the discussion below on consumer rights. As an illustration of the specious nature of some 'access to file' arguments, consider the outcome in *PVC 2*: after vigorously asserting the right to examine the whole file, not a single further '*Brady*' document was discovered (*LVM and others v Commission*, n 82 above).

As one commentator has recently argued: the Commission and the Court of First Instance are 'singing, fairly consistently, from the same hymn sheet'.[107] This may explain some of the more muted enthusiasm in recent years for the work of the Court of First Instance among some legal practitioners, but the cartels still have their day in court, with the further prospect of appeal to the Court of Justice if they wish to continue the legal battle. The cost of this subtle legal development lies of course in the length of the whole procedure, and reflection on this aspect may prompt some questions about the level of resources now invested in this examination of evidential and procedural matters.[108]

But in the second place, this history of judicial review also prompts some reflections on the *balance* of rights protection which is ensured through this system. As already noted, in one sense this appears as an impressive development—the emergence of another supranational regime which confirms and delineates rights of defence in relation to legal proceedings. But two more critical points may be made about this development, the first relating to the *outcome* of some of the case law, the second relating to the *kind of rights* being protected and not protected.

(a) The significance of procedure and procedural violations

First, looking at the result of proceedings in particular cases, it may be asked whether the quest for procedural rigour has been pursued at the cost of values of substance and underlying policy. This is essentially a matter of appropriate and proportionate remedies. If procedural defects have been identified, they should be regulated and corrected, but should this entail the wholesale annulment of decisions in cases in which there is considerable evidence of illegal behaviour and delinquency? The episode of 'inexistent decisions' arising out of the Court of First Instance's first *PVC* judgment (admittedly soon 'corrected' by the Court of Justice) provides perhaps the most notorious example of overreaction to the infringement of procedural requirements. But there have been other examples. Thus, in *Soda Ash*, the Commission's decision establishing a market sharing agreement, was overturned for not allowing full access to the file, when that had not been sought by the parties in question and what was denied was access to material which may well have had no value

---

[107] Paul M Spink, 'Recent Guidance on Fining Policy' (1999) 20 *ECLR* 101, at 108.

[108] Not to mention the cost to the reader of the *European Court Reports*, confronted with hundreds of pages of now largely repetitive legal argument!

at all for their defence.[109] That appears to be a disproportionate legal response to the violation of a newly established principle, when the more serious violation of withholding material evidence would have only disentitled the Commission from relying on that evidence. Moreover, the principle of wider access to the file was in fact only established in that ruling, some time after the hearing in question took place, so arguably itself violating the well-established and fundamental principle against retrospective application of law, explicitly laid down for instance in Article 7 of the European Convention on Human Rights. Some of these arguments are neatly summarized by Ehlermann and Drijber, when they comment:

> The retroactive effect of court judgments might however have unfair consequences if 'new' jurisprudential standards are applied to 'old' cases. This is the more so where, paradoxically, the only consequence of the failure to disclose a piece of inculpatory information is that it cannot be used as evidence by the Commission (and if it has been used, that it should be discarded), whereas the non-disclosure of documents not relied upon by the Commission may lead the CFI to overturn the whole of the decision.[110]

The underlying point here is that judicial review in the context of cartel cases has mainly comprised an increasingly meticulous examination of procedural matters. As such, it is a system which has for the most part developed, naturally enough, *in response* to the arguments of parties subject to the Commission's procedure and has not therefore been based on a prior articulated theory or classification of procedural rights. Two principal arguments arise from this observation. First, there could be more explicit and systematic judicial consideration of the problem of procedural violations and a possible ranking of such violations in relation to the key concept of 'infringement of an essential procedural requirement' laid down in Article 230 of the EC Treaty. In particular, some assessment of the relative impact of the range of formal defects in procedure on the parties concerned would be helpful, if only as a message to potential complainants in determining the sense and wisdom of their appellate strategies.[111] Certainly, for instance, annulment of a decision, as happened in the *Soda*

---

[109] Moreover, in that case ICI first of all insisted on the confidential nature of its own documents, which should therefore not be disclosed to Solvay, and later demanded to see the same category of evidence from Solvay's documentation!

[110] Ehlermann and Drijber, n 102 above, 381–2.

[111] Ehlermann and Drijber, n 102 above, argue that it is all too easy to allege procedural defects, and that there may be a point at which profligate use of such arguments could be regarded as an abuse of process: ibid., 383.

Ash judgment discussed above, for failing to disclose unused material to which access had not even been requested would appear to be a disproportionate remedy. (But contrast, on the other hand, the Court of First Instance's treatment of claims to violation of the 'right to silence' when questions had not been answered, in its second *PVC* judgment.)[112] In other words, more could be done to clarify and order the 'So what?' principle and explore the material character of procedural deficiencies. Secondly, there is the concern regarding 'ever-moving goalposts'. Rule making through a process of judicial review is by its nature evolutionary and reactive. For this reason, care must be taken to ensure that, as principles are evolved in this manner, they are not thereby applied in the immediate case in a way which is significantly retroactive. There is a real danger of this happening in EC competition appeals given their often protracted nature, so that the relevant procedure being used by the Commission may have taken place some years before the clear emergence of a more rigorous procedural principle in the case law of the Court of First Instance. Conceivably, the Commission itself could challenge the legality of such a situation, invoking the principle of legal certainty and non-retroactive application of rules by analogy with Article 7 of the European Convention.

(b) Different kinds of rights

A second main point regarding rights protection also touches upon the ranking and comparison of different rights violations. As already noted, the Court of Justice and the Court of First Instance have constructed an impressive edifice of judicial review in relation to rights of defence. But it is relevant, taking a wider perspective, to consider the context and genesis of this particular system of rights protection. More bluntly, in sociological terms, this legal development has its origin in the ability and determination of powerful corporate actors to exploit a legal process which has been rightly put at their disposal. But this exploitation of legal opportunity must be understood, first practically, in the context of ample resources (both economic and in terms of access to legal advice) and, secondly ethically, in the context of often clearly evidenced illegal conduct on the part of the undertakings concerned. The thousands of pages of legal argument now contained in the *European Law Reports* and largely relating to

---

[112] See nn 82, 92 above.

procedural questions tends to play down, in the reader's mind, the original policy giving rise to the litigation in the first place. Ultimately, these are cases about the enforcement of competition policy, which in turn is based upon a clearly stated public interest. The protection of competition is a policy and principle which at the European level has an evident constitutional and political basis as cast in key provisions of the EC Treaty. As a value, protection of competition also gives rise to specific basic rights which deserve legal protection: for instance, the economic rights of competing and smaller traders, and the rights of consumers. While such rights may well be espoused in policy statements and legislation, there is not so much opportunity for their fuller legal development in a reactive system of judicial review. Put another way, these are economic rights requiring positive implementation rather than civil and political rights which are naturally invoked in judicial process against the action of public authorities. Factors of legal process and the relative power and situation of the interested parties thus coincide to give companies engaging in cartel activity greater opportunity to have their 'day in court', compared to the injured competitor or consumer.

Thus the Community courts have been asked to pronounce much more extensively on the defence rights of companies than on the economic rights of those allegedly injured by anti-competitive practices. Such a perceived imbalance in rights protection may provoke both jurisprudential questions concerning the ranking and relative claims of different kinds of rights, and political questions concerning possible democratic deficit within the EU system. In a political context, such arguments relate to the problem of 'substantive European imbalance' identified by some writers,[113] especially between 'capital' and 'labour', and more relevantly for the present argument, as between 'corporate' and 'individual consumer' interests. As noted above, it may be that more recently cartels do not so often win the legal battle in judicial review; nonetheless, it may be difficult to avoid the impression that judicial review is largely there to serve their interests.

In short, the underlying dilemma of principle is how to compare and balance, on the one hand, the *procedural* claims of *corporate persons* subject to an *administrative procedure*, with on the other hand, the *economic* claims of *individuals* to a publicly protected material well-being.

---

[113] See, e.g., Paul Craig, 'The Nature of the Community: Integration Theory and Democratic Theory, Two Discourses Passing in the Night', in P Craig and G de Búrca, *EU Law: An Evolutionary Perspective* (OUP, 1999), ch 1.

8. Postscript: the epistemology of the debates on judicial review

It is in the context of the judicial review of the Commission's cartel decisions that legal debate has been particularly contentious. The Commission, and to some extent the Community courts, have been subject to a fair measure of critical commentary and in turn individuals working in a regulatory role have sometimes responded robustly on paper (although doubtless restrained in some ways by the protocol relating to their position as 'officials').[114] It is important, however, to have some awareness of the provenance of much of this critical contemporary writing on the subject. It is a field very much dominated by practitioners on both sides of the regulatory divide, and this gives some of the writing a notably 'partisan' character (to use Jones and Sufrin's description).[115] This is something for the reader to bear in mind when evaluating the arguments which are being deployed in critical commentary.

It may be instructive to take a small sample of literature to indicate the tone and position of authors, as well as the content of their argument. It is perhaps most noticeable in writing which is critical in its stance towards the enforcement process. The following is a sample of argument presented by legal practitioners as authors:

As the magnitude of fines imposed on recalcitrant undertakings increased... so the need for serious control of the Commission became more pressing. (Green, 1993)[116]

There seems to be a feeling in the Court [of First Instance] that the Commission is protecting a worthy cause, market competition, against private interest, and the Court weighs evidence on the basis of who presents it, whereas it should be so that facts are facts. (van Bael, 1993)[117]

---

[114] For an interesting example of 'reprimand' for supposedly derogatory remarks on the part of an official (made at a competition law conference), see the incident referred to in the judgment of the Court of First Instance in Case T-31/99, *ABB v Commission* (20 March 2002), at point 94 of the judgment.

[115] See n 51 above. See also the point made by Heinrich Kronstein and Gertrude Leighton, 'Cartel Control: A Record of Failure' (1945–6) 55 *Yale Law Journal* 297, referred to in Chapter III above (at n 24).

[116] Nicholas Green, 'Evidence and Proof in E.C. Competition Cases', in Slot and McDonnell (eds), n 1 above, ch 17, at 127.

[117] Ivo van Bael, 'Discussion: Information and Procedures', in Slot and McDonnell, n 1 above, ch 26, at 216.

After the recent *Wood Pulp* decision nobody could accuse the CFI of being sloppy, it is a devastating indictment of the Commission's procedures. (Vaughan, 1993)[118]

The only consistency one readily finds in the Community's case law is that the Commission has always fought to keep its discretion as wide as possible and the courts have been quick to endorse the Commission's views on the subject. (van Bael, 1995)[119]

Even if an improvement in the infringement procedure could be achieved to a limited extent... this would not put an immediate end to the crisis in which the cartel infringement procedure finds itself today. (Montag, 1996)[120]

The relative weakness of safeguards in Commission investigations is alarming... It is therefore hard to escape the conclusion that the CFI has moved the goal-posts. (Willis, 2001)[121]

The tone of this kind of critique is evident in the language of 'crisis', 'devastating indictment' and 'alarm'. Responding argument in the literature tends to be less dramatic (as is required of officials by their protocol), with a few exceptions such as Commissioner for Competition Monti's description of cartels as 'cancers' on the open market economy.[122] Nonetheless, the writing of both European and national regulators conveys a very different view of the same subject:

The Commission does indeed have discretionary power to determine whether, and if so how substantial, a fine must be imposed on companies who have committed such infringements... Discretion does not mean arbitrariness. The Commission must exercise its discretionary power in a manner that allows companies to challenge it and courts to review it... Transparency does not mean tarification. The Court has recognised this (Gyselen, 1993)[123]

Business delinquency on a truly massive scale has been revealed... The very success of the Commission in uncovering these violations in three of Europe's biggest 'blue chip' industries is itself disquieting. It is a strong indication that the message that cartels are harmful, damaging and illegal may not have got through. (Joshua, 1995)[124]

---

[118] David Vaughan, in Slot and McDonnell, n 1 above, ch 26, at 216. The statement is a *non sequitur*, since the *Wood Pulp* judgment was, of course, handed down by the Court of Justice!

[119] Ivo van Bael, 'Fining à la Carte: the Lottery of EU Competition Law' (1995) 16 *ECLR* 237, at 237.   [120] Frank Montag, n 52 above, 436.

[121] Willis, n 85 above, 313 and 319.

[122] Opening speech at the Third Nordic Competition Policy Conference, Stockholm, September 2000.

[123] Luc Gyselen, 'The Commission's Fining Policy in Competition Cases', in Slot and McDonnell, n 1 above, ch 10, at 63 (Commission official).

[124] Joshua, n 18 above, 101–2 (Commission official).

One could almost be left with the impression that in *Soda Ash* the CFI welcomed the possibility to decide these cases on procedural grounds. There is clearly nothing wrong in imposing procedural obligations on the Commission; with the level of fines going up, the procedural standards will inevitably become more refined. The point is that procedural rights are not an end in themselves; they are designed to achieve a proper result on the substance. Likewise, annulment on procedural grounds is justified only if the procedural defect really mattered. (Ehlermann and Drijber, 1996)[125]

[the Commission's new Leniency Notice] represents a significant step forward in the ongoing fight against the seemingly endemic level of cartels at large within the Union…[the 1996 Notice] was not as successful as hoped at eradicating cartels, the most egregious form of anti-competitive behaviour. (Jephcott, 2002)[126]

Again, it is possible to pick up key words which reveal the tone of argument: 'delinquency', 'fight', 'eradication'. None of this is, of course, surprising, since defence advocates and competition regulators naturally each have their own orientation on the subject. But it is well to remember that such 'partisan' tone does characterize a good proportion of the literature (especially journal literature), somewhat in contrast to the more measured contributions of the rather rarer academic commentators, as indicated in this final example:

The recent Commission notice on fining policy must be regarded as a defensive measure, prompted by external criticism of the lack of transparency of its procedures in this field. However, if the comprehensive judicial review undertaken in *Cartonboard* tells us anything, it is at least that the Commission and the CFI are singing, fairly consistently, from the same hymn sheet. (Spink, 1999)[127]

---

[125] Ehlermann and Van Drijber, n 102 above, 383 (Commission officials).

[126] Mark Jephcott, 'The European Commission's New Leniency Notice: Whistling the Right Tune?' (2002) 23 *ELCR* 378, at 378 (official, UK Competition Commission).

[127] Spink, n 107 above, 108 (University of Stirling).

VIII

Negotiating Guilt: Leniency and Breaking the Code of Silence

1. The psychology of business truce: 'your cheating heart'

During the 1990s there occurred a transformation in the enforcement of rules against business cartels in the United States. As discussed in Chapter VI above, one of the main problems of enforcement in this context has been that of securing sufficient evidence of collusion on the part of sophisticated undertakings acting in a determined and covert fashion and maintaining an impressive 'code of silence'. While American regulators had the possibility of using probing powers of criminal investigation and surveillance, they did not avail themselves of these powers until the middle of the 1990s (previously tending to view cartel conspiracy as a kind of civil offence).[1] But the real breakthrough for American enforcement came with the decision of the Department of Justice (DOJ) to employ a sharply focused carrot-and-stick strategy. With an armoury of substantial sanctions ready to be applied—including imprisonment for individual business executives—the DOJ exploited a natural nervousness within the ranks of cartels by holding out a tempting offer of immunity or leniency for the first, but only the first, to provide evidence. In a single move, this tactic first, through the temptation it provided, increased the likelihood of detection, and then secured the evidence through the 'race to the courtroom door'. The success of the DOJ leniency programme naturally

---

[1] In more recent years, the Department of Justice has exploited its criminal law powers to develop increasingly sophisticated techniques of gathering evidence, drawing upon the surveillance methods used in relation to organized crime and racketeering. The classic example is provided by the investigation of the *Lysine Cartel*, when the DOJ obtained covert video recordings of cartel meetings. See K Eichenwald, *The Informer* (Broadway Books, 2000).

led to the adoption of this strategy in other legal systems, including that of the EC, so that by the end of the 1990s leniency had become a prominent element of antitrust enforcement across a number of systems. To understand the effectiveness and growing significance of this method of enforcement, it is necessary first of all to say something more about the internal dynamic of business cartels, so as to appreciate their inherent vulnerability to such a strategy.

The point has been made in Chapter I above that in economic and sociological terms a business cartel, though powerful in its external appearance and behaviour, is internally a nervous and potentially unstable form of organization.[2] It is perhaps most useful to view the cartel as a product of *truce* rather than as a genuine alliance. It must be remembered that, for all of their efforts of collusion, the members of the cartels remain independent rivals. Their collusion is born of self-interest and also dependent on a continuing belief in that self-interest. Once a reading of their own economic situation suggests that co-operation is no longer an advantage, then the will to co-operate rapidly disappears. Membership of a cartel is a continual process of calculating the advantages and disadvantages of participation in the scheme of collusion. Cartel 'loyalty' is usually so contingent that it may be inappropriate to use that term in the first place. This ever-present and powerful possibility of cheating is a significant distinguishing feature of the business cartel, and renders it, as an organization, a fascinating site for exploring the dynamic of conspiracy as a complex interaction of co-operation and potential betrayal.

Such calculations concerning the benefits of membership have attracted the attention of economists and sociologists employing game theory and 'Prisoners' Dilemma' exercises to probe both the formation and the dissolution of cartels. At the beginning of a cartel's life, it is a matter of working out the dynamics of competition: what are the consequences of one competitor lowering prices, the other following suit, and the two agreeing not to alter their prices? But once the cartel is in existence, the self-interest of each member will continually prompt private questions concerning the advantages to each of maintaining collusion. The game theory is applied by Bishop and Walker, for example, in the following terms:

[the Prisoners' Dilemma game] shows that even though a high price outcome benefited both firms, competition resulted in low price outcome. However, this

---

[2] See Chapter I above.

description of competition assumed that firms could not co-ordinate their behaviour. If both firms could in some manner agree to charge a high price then the high price outcome might be sustainable... However, as this game also illustrates, while there is an incentive for firms to collude, there is also an incentive for one firm to 'cheat' on the agreement. The best course of action for each firm where the other firm pursues a high price strategy is to choose a low price. But if both firms attempt to do this, this will lead back to the competitive outcome—both firms pursuing a low price strategy. This illustrates that while firms may have an incentive to collude, achieving and then sustaining a collusive outcome can be extremely difficult.[3]

This kind of analysis therefore suggests that, while the rewards of collusion may be considerable, they are unstable and uncertain and the collusion may not operate by itself but have to be orchestrated and enforced. There is much empirical support for this view of cartel behaviour from the evidence of cartel investigations. It is quite clear that many apparently successful and significant cartels have not been plain sailing, but have required unremitting internal diplomacy and policing. The *Zinc Producers' Group* case, dealt with by the Commission in 1984,[4] provides an example of a an arrangement which had already fallen apart by itself by the time it became subject to legal control. The Commission noted in its decision that:

The firms concerned did not decide to end the infringements on a given date. Instead, the ZPG gradually fell apart because one by one the firms stopped observing all the agreements and eventually the cohesion between them broke down.[5]

The history of the *PVC Cartel* also illustrates the strenuous efforts which may be required to maintain the cartel in working order. As the Commission observed in its decision:

The suggestion that some of the producers may have cheated does not detract from the clear evidence that the compensation scheme [in relation to quotas] was put into operation, albeit for a limited time.[6]

Later in the decision the Commission stated that it was aware:

that in spite of the efforts of the producers to ensure common price discipline the concerted price initiatives in PVC often met with only mixed success or in some cases were considered a complete failure... It is also true that some of the producers who took part in the meetings were named as aggressive or disruptive in

---

[3] Simon Bishop and Mike Walker, *Economics of E.C. Competition Law: Concepts, Application and Measurement* (Sweet & Maxwell, 1999), 79–80.   [4] OJ 1984, L 220/27.
[5] OJ 1984, L 220/42.   [6] OJ 1989, L 74/1.

certain markets by other producers who considered themselves as strong supporters of price initiatives and were prepared to lose volume in order to force through the increase.[7]

As a final illustration, the internal dissension, suspicion, and policing of 'cheating' and 'lack of discipline' within cartels is well conveyed in the following extracts from the Commission's description of the operation of the *Pre-Insulated Pipes Cartel* in 1998:[8]

There were, however, still complaints about indiscipline and low prices...During regular meetings of the contact group, individual projects were monitored and the progress of the bidding procedure and the offers of each producer scrutinised so as to ensure compliance...clearly the producers were required to explain themselves if any deviation from the agreement was suspected.[9]...

When Tarco had in Henss' view undercut the 'Euro price' and thereby been promised a project which Henss had claimed, the managing director of Henss Rosenheim 'reacted in an uncontrolled fashion and demanded that I withdraw our offer'...Henss was always able to discover what the true prices and orders were and in telephone calls and at meetings of the directors' club repeatedly accused Tarco of cheating.[10]...

ABB's intelligence network had also identified KWH as a possible source of supply for some of Powerpipe's requirements for the contract...The relevant report asks: 'can this be controlled?' KWH confirmed that it had been warned by ABB to comply with the boycott.[11]

Such accounts provide a vivid picture of intra-cartel tension, a reluctance to commitment, and a natural readiness to break ranks. Typically, individual participants will have different levels of commitment to the collusion; some will be 'core', others peripheral; there will be natural 'ringleaders', who also then undertake a policing role, which may range from diplomacy to crude bullying, and may include the enforcement of formal compensatory or penal measures within the cartel. In short, these undertakings find themselves in the role of conspirators who cannot afford to trust each other, but also cannot easily, nor necessarily wish, to dissociate themselves from the conspiracy. What should be emphasized in this account is perhaps not so much the fissile quality of cartels, as the continuing element of *dilemma* regarding membership. This is because often the material benefits of participation are considerable and for that reason some cartels prove to be very durable, enduring for years or even

---

[7] OJ 1989, L 74/8.   [8] OJ 1999, L 24/1.   [9] OJ 1999, L 24/29–30.
[10] OJ 1999, L 24/29.   [11] OJ 1999, L 24/39.

decades, or reviving after earlier dissolution. All things considered, it is therefore a situation which is ripe for assault by a deft deployment of a carrot and stick, testing such a climate of mutual suspicion in order to crack the code of silence.

The offer of immunity (especially DOJ style: *complete* immunity to *only* the first to confess) to cartel members places them in classic 'Prisoners' Dilemma' territory. Each cartel member is then very much in occupation of a closed-off cell, left to speculate on whether and when any of the occupants of the other cells will be tempted to confess and win the sole prize. But for the dilemma to be real, two factors must be present: a belief in the likelihood of detection, and fear of the consequences of detection. Again, as Bishop and Walker argue, the maintenance of a cartel and its 'code of silence' depend upon the expected gains of collusion outweighing the expected losses from detection. They state:

Cartel behaviour is more likely both where the possibility of detection is low and where the punishment of operating a cartel is merely an order to desist than if detection carries with it the possibility of large fines. Hence the toughness of the stance of competition law towards detecting and punishing cartel behaviour can have a significant effect on its existence.[12]

The first essential factor, likelihood of detection, may result from the known availability of an irresistible offer of reward (complete immunity if you confess as soon as possible). The second essential factor would reside in genuinely feared sanctions in the event of detection and conviction. As will be seen in the discussion below, the strategy fashioned by the DOJ embodied both these components.

2. Leniency: the American model—designing the irresistible offer

The successful version of the American Corporate Leniency Policy was introduced by the DOJ in 1993. An earlier leniency programme had been in operation since 1978, but was of a discretionary character; it had attracted a minimal number of applications and did not lead to the detection of any international cartels.[13] The success of the revised programme is clearly

---

[12] Bishop and Walker, n 3 above, 82.
[13] Mark Jephcott, 'The European Commission's New Leniency Notice. Whistling the Right Tune?' (2002) 23 *ELCR* 378.

attributable to a number of key features. The amnesty is automatic for the first company to come forward with evidence before an investigation into the cartel in question has started. The immunity offered extends to all directors, officers, and employees of the company in relation to criminal prosecution and removes the risk of corporate fines. There is also an alternative amnesty in relation to co-operation which is provided subsequent to the start of an investigation ('post-investigation leniency'). The essential 'carrot' in American leniency is provided by the element of certain immunity from criminal prosecution and therefore from prison terms for individuals, and its automatic availability to the winner of the race to the courtroom door, even after the start of an investigation. There are a certain number of conditions: full and ongoing co-operation with the investigation as it proceeds; prompt termination of involvement with the cartel; restitution to injured parties, so far as possible; and a 'ringleader' exclusion—to qualify the company must not have 'coerced another party to participate in the illegal activity and clearly was not the leader in, or originator of, the illegal activity'.[14] 'Alternative amnesty' is subject to a number of specific conditions, some of which require an element of evaluation: the DOJ must not yet have evidence 'likely to result in a sustainable conviction'; the grant of amnesty must not be unfair to others; consideration will be given to the timing of the co-operation; and the approach to the DOJ must be a 'truly corporate act', not an isolated individual confession.

The 1993 programme led to a significant increase in the number of applications, to something more than one per month.[15] Automatic immunity for the first to come forward clearly proved a very tempting carrot. The DOJ itself stated in 2002:

In the last five years, cooperation from amnesty applications has resulted in scores of convictions and well over $1.5 billion in fines. In fact, the majority of the Division's major international investigations have been advanced through the cooperation of an amnesty applicant.[16]

The material gains for the informant can be easily illustrated, for instance, by comparing the fate of Christie's and Sotheby's in relation to price fixing in fine art auctions. Christie's was the first to apply for amnesty, and gained immunity from fines and any sanctions in relation to

[14] For the full text, see (www.usdoj.gov/atr/public/guidelines/lencorp.htm).
[15] Department of Justice, Antitrust Division, *Status Report: Corporate Leniency Program* (February 2002).   [16] Ibid.

its then-current executives (the leniency programme does not extend, however, to former directors and employees, and Christie's former chairman was indicted). Sotheby's were behind in the race to the courtroom door and paid the cost in a $45 million fine (after co-operating by pleading guilty) and criminal prosecution of its CEO and Chairman.[17] In 1999 the DOJ extended its leniency programme by introducing an 'Amnesty Plus' provision. If a company loses 'the race to the courtroom door' in relation to a cartel in one market, but is the first to produce evidence of an illegal activity in a second market, it will of course receive full immunity in relation to the latter (the 'amnesty' part), and will then also be treated more favourably in any plea bargain in relation to the first prosecution (the 'plus' part).[18] Amnesty plus is therefore a combination of leniency and an extra and consequential reward in the plea bargaining arena.

The DOJ therefore offers three variations on leniency, each comprising full immunity for the first company to the courtroom door: for the first whistleblower pre-investigation, 'alternative post-investigation' leniency, and 'amnesty plus' for related markets. One complicating factor, but a further important element in the inducement to companies, is a concession to confidentiality. The DOJ has accepted that it should not disclose the identity of, or information received from amnesty applicants to, authorities in other legal systems without prior agreement from the applicant. This recognizes the weight of an important calculation on the part of would-be whistleblowers: to be able to reduce the risk of punishment by confessing with immunity in one sytem, but then thereby to expose themselves to legal sanctions under the competition laws of other states. But this also has implications for the transnational enforcement of anti-cartel laws across a number of jurisdictions.

The success of the DOJ's leniency strategy appears to be based on three essential elements. First, there is a genuinely good offer: be the first to blow the whistle and there will be complete immunity from a big penalty—a big fine and prison sentences for sure when (and not just if) the cartel is found out. Secondly, it generates and exploits a nervousness that other cartel members may well be tempted by the same offer and win the 'race to the courtroom door'. Thirdly, the ploy is reinforced by the general knowledge that only the first whistleblower gets the big prize.

---

[17] See *Cartel Regulation 2002* (published by *Global Competition Review*), 135.

[18] Gary R Spratling, 'Making Companies an Offer They Shouldn't Refuse', address at the Bar Association of the District of Columbia's 35th Annual Symposium on Associations and Antitrust, February 1999.

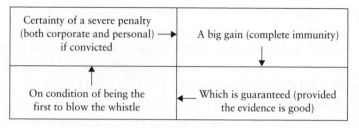

Figure VIII.1: The race to the courtroom door

It is thus reminiscent of the classical 'Prisoner's Dilemma'—whether to play ball now, and quickly, or risk losing altogether. The strategy thus promotes within the cartel the sense of a higher risk, first, that somebody will blow the whistle, and secondly and consequently of the other members being convicted. This serves to outweigh the previous benefits of solidarity, i.e. of big profit from the offence plus a low risk of detection and conviction.

In summary the strategy is based on a combination of unacceptably high risk of detection and certainty of severe punishment, as prerequisites for successful exploitation of the natural nervousness within cartels. The essence of the strategy is to encourage immediately the race to the courtroom door, sending out the message: 'co-operate, or else—remember, it hurts to come in second.' The temptation to confess may be represented in a diagram of strategic cycle (see Figure VIII.1).

Successful deployment of the offer of leniency therefore combines the carrot with the stick: the carrot must be juicy and the stick must be big. The gain from whistleblowing is so tempting since it avoids a *highly probable* and *severe* penalty *both* for the company and for individuals. But the advantage for the DOJ was that it was working in a legal environment within which criminal penalties were well established and realistic, so that what it could offer was clearly very worthwhile to potential whistleblowers. This, then, was the model which was ready for export elsewhere when the global campaign against cartels was mobilized in the later 1990s.

3. Leniency: the EC model—a 'prisoner's dilemma' playground

Other jurisdictions have followed the American example, although not always employing the strategy in exactly the same way, so leading to what has been described as a 'patchwork' of leniency programmes.[19] The European Commission, although the first to jump on the leniency band-wagon, faced an immediate dilemma in its position compared to the DOJ: it had no criminal sanctions (and in particular, no prison terms) with which to back up its offer of immunity. It is in this context that the complexities of the European legal environment become evident. For many purposes, European legal activity is now two-tiered, involving the making and implementation of law at both an EU and at national levels. It is true enough that in the field of competition policy the EC rules have priority and have of course so far to a large extent been directly applied and enforced by the Commission itself. But there has always been some reliance (which is likely to increase in the future) on member state enforcement and this is particularly the case if there is any wish to make use of criminal law and its sanctions for enforcement purposes. Mainly for reasons of political sensitivity, EU member states have been and remain unlikely to transfer a criminal law competence to the EU institutions. It may seem, therefore, at first sight that the emergence of cartel offences at the EU member state level (see the discussion in Chapter IX below) would be a welcome development for the Commission in its role as a competition enforcement agency. However, matters are more complicated.

It should in any case be noted that the Commission's first attempt at a leniency strategy, introduced in 1996,[20] did not emulate the DOJ's success in a number of respects. Although it provided an incentive for the first cartel member to confess, and so set up a race to the courtroom door (or, rather that of the office in Brussels), it fell short of the prerequisites of a successful leniency programme mentioned above. It should also be noted that 'leniency' in the EC context is less specific than its American counterpart, since the European term is used also to include fine reduction on a number of grounds, what in the United States would be part of criminal law plea bargaining.

[19] Lidwyn Brokx, 'A Patchwork of Leniency Programmes' (2001) 22 *European Competition Law Review* 35.

[20] Commission Notice, 18 July 1996, on the non-imposition or reduction of fines in cartel cases, OJ 1996, C 207/4. For an overview and critical discussion of the Commission's leniency programmes, see in particular Stephen Hornsby and Joan Hunter, 'New Incentives for "Whistle Blowing": Will the EC Commission's Notice Bear Fruit?' (1997) 18 *ECLR* 38; Brokx, n 19 above; Johan Carle, Stefan Pervan Lindeborg, and Emma Segenmark, 'The New Leniency Notice' (2002) 23 *ECLR* 265; Jephcott, n 13 above; Julian Joshua and Nils Von Hinten-Reed, 'Rethinking Leniency at the European Commission' (2002) *Global Competition Review* 16.

There was in the first place a low score on certainty of severe sanctions: the criminal law sanctions, particularly the provision of personal criminal liability and the prospect of prison sentences, were largely absent. Moreover, although the Commission itself was in a position to impose large corporate fines, there was still a perception in the European context that the possibility of detection and thus the reality of such sanctions was small.[21]

Secondly, there was a low score on the guarantee of immunity: the Commission offered for the most part reductions on a possible fine rather than complete immunity. Perhaps more significantly, this was conditional on the Commission's (possibly lengthy) assessment of the value of the evidence (the 'wait and see' policy). Furthermore, the process was complicated by 'degrees' of leniency which might materialize at different stages and for different degrees of co-operation. 'First degree leniency' (75 per cent or more fine reduction) was offered in return for being the first company to come forward with 'decisive evidence' before an investigation had formally begun. 'Second degree leniency' comprised a 50 to 75 per cent reduction in fine, after an investigation had begun, but before it had produced evidence sufficient to 'initiate a procedure leading to a final decision'. Then, 'third degree leniency'—a 10 to 50 per cent reduction in fine—was available for later co-operation: providing evidence, prior to the statement of objections, which materially contributed to the Commission's case, or, after the statement of objections, not substantially contesting the facts alleged by the Commission (this last being in effect a kind of plea bargain). All of this was fraught with uncertainty for the would-be whistle-blower, who would be unlikely to have a clear idea of how much evidence the Commission might have from other sources or how the Commission might assess the value of the evidence provided. At the same time, 'third degree leniency' provided rewards for mere co-operation rather than provision of evidence which might be not far short of the gains from giving substantial evidence, so reducing the incentive to provide the latter.[22] Finally, the Commission officials negotiating with a company were not in a position to indicate firmly the Commission's eventual position on the value of the evidence or the amount of the fine which may be reduced.

---

[21] To be more exact, a perception that cartels might well avoid detection since there was a low risk of an investigation being opened. Once started, Commission investigations have had a good strike rate. But relatively few cases have been started, thus the perceived low risk of detection for that reason.   [22] Carle, Lindeborg, and Segenmark, n 20 above, 267.

From the point of view of potential whistleblowers, therefore, the benefits were uncertain: there *might* be *some* relief in relation to a *potential* fine
from the Commission. Also the Commission could not legally guarantee
immunity from any subsequent legal action (which was beginning to
include the possibility of criminal prosecution) at the member state level,
nor (perhaps more importantly) in the United States if the company in
question had not won the race to the courtroom door under the DOJ's
programme. In such circumstances, would it be worthwhile blowing the
whistle in Brussels? It would seem not, judging by the experience of the
Commission's 1996 leniency programme. As Jephcott has commented:

it is unremarkable that relatively few undertakings chose to confess. To forego the
near certainty of inflated profits which flow from collusion . . . in exchange for the
possible, but by no means guaranteed, reduction in fines under the 1996 policy
clearly did not appeal.[23]

In a Press Release of July 2001, Competition Commissioner Mario
Monti admitted that the 1996 Leniency Notice had not provided sufficient incentives for companies to denounce cartels.[24] Carle, Lindeborg,
and Segenmark sum up the five-year tally of the leniency programme in
the following terms:

since its entry into force in July 1996, the 1996 Notice has, as far as we are aware,
merely been applied in approximately 16 cartel cases. In the majority of these
cases the co-operating entity was only granted a reduction of 10–50 per cent. A
very substantial reduction of 75 per cent has, as far as we have been aware, been
granted in a handful of cases under the 1996 Notice.[25]

In fact, the Commission confirmed that between 1996 and 2001, full
immunity was granted on only three occasions: for cartel recidivist
Rhône-Poulenc (a member of two vitamins cartels), for a subsidiary of
Interbrew (a member of the Luxembourg brewers' cartel), and the South
African company Sappi (a member of the carbonless paper cartel).[26]

(a) The St Valentine's Day Notice

The Commission has more recently in 2001 issued a revised Leniency
Notice, amending the original leniency programme; this came into effect

---

[23] Jephcott, n 13 above, 380.
[24] Press Release of 18 July 2001, 'Commission launches debate on draft new leniency rules in
cartel probes', IP/01/1011.   [25] Carle, Lindeborg, and Segenmark, n 20 above.
[26] See respectively Press Releases IP/01/1625, 21 November 2001; IP/01/1740, 5 December
2001; and IP/01/1892, 20 December 2001.

in February 2002.[27] Most importantly, the new Notice provides for full immunity from Commission fines for the first company to disclose the existence of a cartel of which the Commission was previously unaware, and an abandonment of the 'wait and see' policy. The immunity is conditional primarily on the Commission's confirmation that it had received sufficient evidence to carry out dawn raids on the other suspects ('point 8(a) leniency'), or evidence sufficient to enable the Commission to find a cartel infringement ('point 8(b) leniency'). These changes go some way towards making the carrot more appetising, by employing more of the 'certainty principle' considered to underlie the success of the DOJ's leniency programme. But there remain some doubts about its operation.

The 'dawn raid sufficiency' test has been criticized for some unpredictability. There is no defined legal standard for ordering a dawn raid—the decision is very much a matter of discretion—whereas it is claimed that in practice the earlier 'decisive evidence' test under the 1996 Notice was clear, amounting invariably to documentary evidence of the existence of the cartel.[28] There is also uncertainty for the Commission; as Joshua and Von Hinten-Reed argue:

Besides the uncertainty for the applicant, the test does not optimise the Commission's chances of obtaining convincing evidence and is open to manipulation by the unscrupulous. What is there to stop the grantee of amnesty on the basis of an oral story relenting and warning the others to clean up in advance of the Commission's investigation? It also places the Commission in an interesting quandary if a second firm comes in hoping for leniency before the dawn raid triggered by the first has been executed.[29]

The alternative 'point 8(b)' test for leniency, that the evidence enables an infringment to be established, has a contingent character: the immunity cannot be offered once point 8(a) (dawn raid) immunity has been granted. So, although point 8(b) immunity is available later (after an investigation has started) and would provide the Commission with more substantial evidence (sufficient to prove an infringement), there is a risk for the would-be whistleblower, who cannot be sure whether another company has already won the race under point 8(a).

The new leniency programme would therefore appear to be as much of a playground for 'Prisoner's Dilemma' calculations as its predecessor.

---

[27] OJ 2001, C 205/18. The Notice has been colloquially referred to as the 'St Valentine's Day Notice' since it became operational on 14 February 2002.
[28] Joshua and Von Hinten Reed, n 20 above.   [29] Ibid., 17.

There are other features of the programme which might also have to be taken into account. There is a further inducement for companies to approach the Commission, since the Notice allows a tentative approach, offering evidence in hypothetical and abstract terms and finding out if the evidence is likely to meet the conditions for full immunity. In this way, both sides reveal their hand to a limited extent. There is also further scope for leniency in the form of lesser fine reductions if a company comes forward at a later stage of the case with evidence of 'significant added value' to the Commission, enabling it to strengthen its case against the cartel. Once again, there is a gamble for the company, not knowing how much evidence the Commission may have at that particular moment, and therefore how the 'added value', if any, will be reflected in an eventual reduction of fine. Finally, there are a number of general conditions for either immunity or fine reduction: maintaining full co-operation, ending involvement in the cartel, and the exclusion of cartel members who have coerced the participation of others (points 11(a)–(c)).

There would appear to be two main points of comparison between the American and European approaches to leniency in this context. First, the European model remains more complicated and less predictable in its operation. Secondly, the American approach benefits from its location in a context of criminal justice. These points are succinctly captured by Joshua and Von Hinten-Reed:

All it takes in the US to get convictions against all the conspirators is for one member of the cartel to come in and talk. The rest then scramble to get the best plea bargain they can. Rarely does anyone risk a higher sentence by going to trial. By contrast, without the full weight of the criminal justice system behind it, the Commission has no power to keep co-operating companies on track. Oral declarations or proffers have no evidential value for the Commission. Its procedure relies primarily on contemporaneous documentary evidence. There is no machinery in Regulation 17 to compel the co-operating company officers to testify before a grand jury or later in court if the others insisted on going to trial. Nor is there any way of persuading the other parties to plead guilty and shorten the proceedings.[30]

In short, the Commission is still labouring under the disadvantage of lamer procedures and less predictable sanctions in the background compared to the situation of the DOJ, with its immediate leverage of federal criminal law jurisdiction over individuals. Yet, bearing in mind these

---

[30] Ibid., 16.

important differences, the American and European systems are now *in principle* more closely aligned, as can be seen from a relatively simplified hypothetical example:

Take the case of a cartel comprising three companies: A, B, and C. Each can provide sufficient evidence to establish the existence of the cartel and the involvement of each company in the cartel, but not evidence of the total involvement of each other. C was the instigator and enforcer within the cartel.

Under the DOJ leniency programme: A comes forward to co-operate. A will receive full immunity; B and C can then gain no immunity; C would have been disentitled in any case. But B and C may consider the possibility of Amnesty Plus in relation to other markets, though C would not be entitled to leniency in relation to the first market. Both may plead guilty to secure sentencing discounts.

Under the Commission's leniency programme: If A comes forward to co-operate, it will secure immunity *from any EC fine*. B and C will then not be able to obtain immunity, and C would have been excluded anyway in so far as it had used any coercion. However, B may be able to offer 'value-added' evidence to secure *an EC fine reduction* (30 to 50 per cent reduction if it is the first to do so).

Under both systems, therefore, A may gain full immunity (although the American full immunity is wider since it embraces all criminal sanctions for both corporate and individual offenders) and B may gain some reduction in the sanctions.

4. A European 'patchwork' of leniency: 'amnesty international'?

By its nature, the activity of major international cartels is likely to relate to the territories and markets of a number of countries, and hence a number of jurisdictions with separate systems for the enforcement of competition law. Within Europe, there is the possibility also of overlapping jurisdictions: those of the EC, and its respective member states. In the past, for cartels facing investigation and possible sanctions, this has given rise to questions of 'double jeopardy', and indeed the principle *non bis in idem* was invoked at an early date by members of the *Quinine* and *Dystuffs Cartels* before the Court of Justice.[31] However, the more recent preoccupation of cartels facing multi-jurisdictional enforcement, has been the problem of navigating the benefits and risks arising from leniency

---

[31] Case 14/68, *Wilhelm v Bundeskartellamt* [1969] ECR 1 (*Dyestuffs Cartel*); Case 45/69, *Boehringer Mannheim v Commission* [1970] ECR 769 (*Quinine Cartel*). (Wilhelm was the then director of the German company, Bayer.)

programmes now being simultaneously offered in a number of jurisdictions. For a company involved in a 'European' cartel, there is now a complex European patchwork of leniency programmes to negotiate (the EC, France, Germany, United Kingdom), all potentially available in parallel though operating somewhat differently. Again, this is a nice playground for the game theorist. For it is rarely a matter of calculating the consequences of leniency in just one legal system. Even if company A has won the race to the courtroom door in jurisdiction X, another member of the cartel, B, may have just done so in another jurisdiction, Y, so exposing A to the risk of sanctions there. In other words, leniency is likely, in the case of international cartels, to be a transnational game.

With the proliferation of leniency programmes and the associated higher risk of detection, cartel participants would thus appear to be exposed to a possible range of sanctions (including individual criminal liability) in multiple jurisdictions. The risk arises in two ways: from a company's own confession, or from another company's confession elsewhere. The first situation may be dealt with to some extent by confidentiality requirements. For, example, the DOJ has a clear policy on confidential handling of an informant's evidence and identity. Moreover, the DOJ has recognized that, to maintain 'the force and integrity of its leniency policy', it should agree not to disclose the identity of or information obtained from amnesty applicants to foreign authorities without the prior consent of the applicant.[32] Canadian practice is similar. Across Europe, however, there is a less predictable assurance of confidentiality. The Commission's practice is not to reveal the identity of a whistleblower while an investigation is under way, but there are no specific rules on the subject. However, for individual informants, as distinct from corporate actors, some obligations of confidential treatment may be derived from the case law of the Court of Justice.[33] Under German law, again practice is to treat information supplied in the context of a leniency programme as confidential, but there is no absolute legal guarantee and there may be practical risks of exposure, for instance via other companies' defence access to the competition authority's file, or intelligent guesswork from evidently low fines.[34] The position is similar under UK law.[35] Similarly, French law provides for confidentiality provided that it does not conflict with other parties' rights of defence.[36] It would seem that in

---

[32] *Status Report* (2002), n 15 above.
[33] Case 145/83, *Adams v Commission* [1985] ECR 3539.
[34] *Cartel Regulation 2002*, n 38 below, 64.   [35] Ibid., 127.   [36] Ibid., 59.

general terms, and for practical rather than legal reasons, the anonymity of a whistleblower, and consequently knowledge of its involvement in a cartel, cannot be withheld indefinitely.

But in any case, the real risk would seem to come via the second route: the revelation by another member of the cartel in order to gain immunity in another jurisdiction. Once a company has lost the race for any immunity in another relevant jurisdiction, it is immediately exposed there to investigation and possible liability to sanctions, and by their nature leniency programmes will not take into account immunity gained elsewhere: each race for immunity is run separately.[37] It would seem, therefore, that the safest tactic for a company interested in immunity would be to identify those legal systems to which the cartel's activity may be subject and apply for leniency as soon as possible in all of them. Even then, there remains some risk from any relevant jurisdiction not yet operating a leniency programme (for instance, at present some EU states, such as Austria, Finland, Ireland, Italy, Portugal, Spain, and Sweden). Estimation of multi-jurisdictional risks in a context of a higher possibility of exposure and detection therefore entails not only a calculation of possible immunities, but also of the the kind and level of sanctions when immunity is not forthcoming. Companies facing these risks, and their personnel, ought therefore to have some awareness[38] of the nature of sanctions in different jurisdictions (adminstrative or criminal law); whether they apply to companies or individuals, or both; the level of fines; and the possibility of prison sentences (see also the discussion in Chapter IX below).

At the present time, European companies and their executives would have most to fear from detection and an absence of immunity if their activities fall within American jurisdiction. The United States has the best record now in detecting and proving the case against cartels and is also likely to impose the toughest sanctions on both companies and individuals.[39] For instance, in 1999, following the successful prosecution by the DOJ of the *Vitamins Cartel*, Swiss pharmaceutical company Hoffman-la Roche was fined and two of its executives agreed to plead guilty to personal criminal

---

[37] The Canadian Competition Bureau specifically warns companies that leniency granted elsewhere should not lead to any expectation of 'special consideration' in Canada; see Brokx, n 19 above, 43.

[38] This should give some indication of the most likely readership of a publication such as *Cartel Regulation 2002* (produced by *Global Competition Review*) and revealingly sub-titled 'Getting the Fine Down in 25 Jurisdictions Worldwide').

[39] See DOJ, *Status Report: Criminal Fines* and *International Cartel Enforcement* (2002).

offences and serve prison terms as well as pay substantial fines.[40] Some
other jurisdictions are now indicating (as did the United Kingdom) that
they will follow the American approach, so the risks appear to be becoming wider. (The *Vitamins Cartel* case also indicates how an investigation in
one jurisdiction can then trigger further investigation elsewhere, since the
Commission followed suit with its prosecution of the cartel for its operation in the European market.)

Apart from the possibility of exploiting whatever leniency progammes
may be available, the only other way of possibly avoiding multi-jurisdictional
sanctions may be a reliance on double jeopardy arguments. The EC rules
on double jeopardy appear to draw something of a distinction beween
sanctions applied in EC member states and in third countries. A competition infringement relating to the EC market and a member state market
has an identity of territorial impact such as to qualify as the 'same'
offence, for which it would be unfair to impose more than one penalty. In
its *Wilhelm* ruling the Court of Justice stated:

> If...the possibility of two procedures being conducted separately were to lead
> to the imposition of consecutive sanctions, a general requirement of natural
> justice...demands that any previous punitive decision must be taken into account
> in determining any sanction which is to be imposed.[41]

On the other hand, the Court of Justice, in its judgment in *Boehringer
Mannheim v Commission*, indicated that cartel activities relating to both
the United States and Europe had an impact on different markets and so
constituted separate offences.[42] The Commission and member state competition authorities are therefore likely to take into account each others'
penalties: the British Director General of Fair Trading's guidelines on
fines, for instance, include a reference to avoiding double jeopardy.[43]
But an increasing resort to double jeopardy arguments may still perhaps
be anticipated, especially in the context of different types of sanction
(criminal law, administrative) being applied to different persons (corporate, individual) in relation to the same cartel activity (as, for instance,
recently in the case of the *Graphite Electrodes Cartel*, dealt with under both

---

[40] Ibid.

[41] *Wilhelm v Bundeskartellamt*, n 31 above, [1969] ECR 15. The French Government, on the
other hand, had argued that there was no double jeopardy in relation to any French competition
sanctions, since they were of a criminal law nature, whereas the EC fines were administrative.
See also the detailed discussion by Advocate General Roemer [1969] ECR 24–6.

[42] See n 31 above. But there is no real discussion of the point by either the Court or the
Advocate General.   [43] DGFT, *Guidance as to the Appropriate Amount of Penalty*, para 2.15.

American and EC law, and resulting in both corporate and individual penalties).

In many respects, therefore, the leniency strategy in Europe is unlikely to achieve the sharper simplicity of the American model. Using the metaphor of the Monopoly Board, it may not be certain what may be gained from the Community Chest and in the meantime Go To Jail (in the United States).

5. The lessons of leniency

These are still early days for purposes of taking stock of these developments. In general terms the use of leniency programmes, against a background of stronger and more criminal law, has transformed the enforcement of cartel regulation. But, more specifically, the experience so far has varied from one side of the Atlantic to the other, resulting in a major success story for the DOJ and, on the other hand, a rather uncertain and potentially legally complicated outcome for the European jurisdictions. As a result, the overall global pattern of regulation and enforcement is as yet difficult to assess. However, there are also some more general theoretical observations arising from the emergence of leniency as a significant strategy of enforcement.

First, these developments signal some important shifts in legal categorization and method: a shift from *competition law* to *criminal law*, and what some may perceive as an Americanization of the subject and/or a globalization of enforcement. Whatever the interpretation, this is a matter of interest for both competition lawyers (who will need to become criminal lawyers as well) and criminal lawyers and criminologists, who have (in Europe at least) acquired a new domain of activity and study. Following on from this last point, there should be some important lessons from this experience in the near future in relation to the legal control of business delinquency. As a subject, the regulation of cartels thus provides a laboratory for testing strategies of legal control in a particular environment of delinquent conduct.

The strategies being employed in this context also raise theoretical concerns in their own right. In the European context, criminalization appears to be an important (or at least potentially important) component of the new strategies, but is in itself a controversial policy, giving rise to both ethical and political questions (as discussed in Chapter IX below).

Moreover, the complexity of the emerging European legal infrastructure (non-criminal EC law, which needs to be co-ordinated with criminal, administrative, and civil processes at the member state level) is beginning to supply a new field for legal study and evaluation.

Having moved the subject more into the realm of criminal law, the use of leniency programmes then present questions for criminal jurisprudence and penal theory. The problem lies in the fact that, while there is criminal law on paper, criminal law may be difficult to carry through as a process, on account of the problems of evidence and prosecution already discussed. The leniency programme is a strategy which enables criminal law to happen as a process, but at a cost to its theoretical basis. The whole practical thrust of a leniency strategy compromises some core values of criminal and penal jurisprudence, by excusing (and rewarding) a major offender, in the pursuit of utilitarian objectives. The evidence is secured, the number of convictions maximized, and the case is closed, yet at a certain retributive cost in the immunity of the whistleblower offender. In ethical terms, a serious offender against legal rules who also (under a different code) betrays an earlier cause, emerges as a clear 'winner' in the legal arena. This is not, of course, a new dilemma of law and morality and is a classic example of competing retributive and utilitarian values, but it presents the contest in a graphic form.

However, it should be noted that in the practice of leniency programmes there is usually some concession to retributive concerns, in the form of the principle of 'ringleader' or 'bully exclusion': a provision that the immunity should not be available to a cartel member who was an instigator ('ringleader' or 'gang boss') or coerced other members of the cartel. Thus, the DOJ's programme excludes leniency for corporations or individuals who either coerced others into participating in the cartel or were 'leaders' or 'originators' of the cartel. The Commission's earlier leniency programme similarly excluded companies who had used coercion or were 'instigators' or had 'played a determining role'. The UK leniency programme follows this first EC approach, and the German programme excludes those who played a decisive role in the cartel. There is therefore in this practice an adherence to a general retributive principle that serious delinquency within the cartel will be recognized, not only in the quantum of any penalty but also in exclusion from the benefits of leniency.

But, interestingly, the new EC leniency programme has restricted this exclusion to coercers. The Commission has explained that both the concept of 'instigator' and that of 'playing a determining role' left room for interpretation and uncertainty.[44] This is a puzzling argument. First, it may be argued that there is no less scope for interpretation and uncertainty in the concept and proof of coercion, which remains as a ground for exclusion. Secondly, the 'ringleader' role is still very relevant for purposes of deciding on the amount of penalty and there would seem to be ample experience in that context of clarifying the nature of instigating activity and playing a determining role. To take just one recent example, reference could be made again to the Commission's assessment of the *Pre-Insulated Pipes Cartel*.[45] In that case there was clear evidence of the role of the Swiss–Swedish multinational company ABB (Asea Brown Boveri) as both ring-leader and cartel bully, which was confidently taken into account by the Commission in its determination of the fine. Thus the Commission stated:

It is abundantly clear that ABB systematically used its economic power and resources as a major multinational company to reinforce the effectiveness of the cartel and to ensure that the other undertakings complied with its wishes.[46]

The Commission listed as aggravating factors, first, ABB's role as ring-leader and instigator of the cartel, bringing pressure on the other under-takings to persuade them to enter the cartel, and secondly, its 'systematic organization of retaliatory measures' against the competitor Powerpipe, aimed at the latter's elimination from the market. In this context, then, it would seem no less problematical to establish an instigating role than a coercive role. But more generally, this serves to illustrate the nature of the retributive and penal debate that has occupied a prominent ground in the subject, both in relation to the determination of sanctions and the operation of a strategy such as leniency.

As a concluding reflection, it is tempting to say that, if this is criminal justice, then it is clearly criminal justice of a particular kind. Despite the move towards personal criminal liability, many of the main offenders remain corporate persons. The process is largely one of negotiation, in the sense of striking a deal, rather than retributive logic. There is 'diversion' from punishment, in fact there is a reward for good evidence and a gamble on the optimum moment at which to supply that commodity. Criminal law may have colonized competition law, but the methods of business appear to be influencing this newly colonized domain.

---

[44] Press Release, 13 February 2002, IP/02/247.   [45] OJ 1999, L 24/1.
[46] OJ 1999, L 24/1, 63–5.

IX

Sanctions: Dealing with Business Delinquency

1. Sanctions, censure, and effectiveness

The discussion in the preceding chapters has traced the development of law and policy relating to business cartels in Europe over a period of more than a hundred years. The unfolding story has been one of increasing regulation and, at least in the last 30 years, more explicit condemnation. From being viewed as a condonable, if in some respects problematic, phenomenon, the classic price fixing, market sharing cartel has in the legal context been driven underground and become strongly prohibited and, more recently still in some systems, criminalized. Thus, it may appear, Europe has caught up with the United States and the spirit of the Sherman Act presides in Brussels, London, Berlin, and other centres of European competition regulation. The reality and consequences of this transformation will be examined further in the final chapter. In the meantime, one major aspect of this story of legal developments remains for further discussion: the legal response to the cartel as a prohibited and delinquent form of business organization. Once cartels have become subject to prohibition, what are the appropriate sanctions for dealing with infringements of those prohibitive rules?

The answer to this question depends partly on a legal categorization based upon the purpose of the measures which may be adopted to deal with cartel 'infringements' (to employ a neutral term for the moment). Broadly speaking, for the sake of exposition, three main purposes may be listed. The first main objective, and in some ways the most straightforward, is *injunctive*: simply to bring the infringement to an end. In its simplest form, this comprises an order to stop, and is presented in its classical form by the American 'cease and desist' order. However, in practice, 'ending' the infringement may also require the ordering of something specific in relation to future behaviour, so as to ensure that the infringement will not continue or be allowed to recur (see the discussion below). The second objective is *restorative* and seeks to address the injury caused by anti-competitive behaviour. Here, the remedy is backward-looking, in the sense of addressing past damage. The classic form of the sanction for this purpose would be an award of compensation to injured parties on the basis of civil liability (and is also classically represented in American tort law). The third main objective, which will comprise the subject of most of the discussion in this chapter, is also backward-looking in seeking to redress the sense of wrongdoing and violation of legal ordering. This is the realm of the *penal* sanction, entailing resort to measures having a retributive and deterrent character. The classic version in Europe of the penal measure in the context of competition violations is the corporate fine. But, as criminalization gains ground, personal liability to imprisonment has come into the picture. Moreover, there is also the possibility of more constructive penal measures, such as the American measure of corporate probation.

The subject of sanctions is significant for two main reasons. First, sanctions provide the signals for the process of legal control, acting as signifiers of the nature of the prohibition. It is through the choice of sanctions that a society conveys the quality of its censure, and in this respect the choice between administrative, civil, and criminal sanctions is a central element of the subject. Secondly, sanctions act as indicators of legal effectiveness in that perceptions and measurement of their impact is one of the principal means of assessing the health and vigour of the system of legal control. The two main hinges of discussion are thus, first, the choice of sanctions and, secondly, their impact.

2. The repertoire of sanctions

It is perhaps useful to begin an examination of the choice of antitrust sanctions by presenting a kind of menu (see Table IX.1), but to remember as well that the availability of items on this menu may be contingent upon historical, cultural, and administrative factors. Approaching the subject in this way may help in an understanding of why, for instance, prison terms are a real possibility under American law but a remote prospect for the EC system of legal control.

Table IX.1: Choice of antitrust sanctions

Type of measure	Function	Examples
Order of prohibition	Injunctive	American 'cease and desist' order EC Decision requiring termination under Article 3 of Regulation 17
Award of damages in civil proceedings	Compensatory	Tort claims under national law American triple damages Class actions
Administrative fine (a) corporate (b) individual	Penal	EC fines (Regulation 17) Administrative fines under national law
Criminal law fine (a) corporate (b) individual	Penal	Fines under national criminal law
Imprisonment	Penal	Prison terms under national criminal law (e.g. American, now some European systems)
Corporate probation	Penal/ reformative	Corporate probation under American criminal law

Within such a scheme, the preponderance of discussion within the present European context would relate to the use of penal measures, and especially the administrative fine imposed on companies. In other words, civil claims for compensation and 'positive' measures such as corporate probation do not as yet figure very prominently on the European legal stage. Criminal proceedings, and the possible use of imprisonment as a sanction, however, have recently become a seriously considered strategy at the national level across Europe, and this is a significant development requiring further discussion.

(a) Orders to desist

The 'cease and desist order' or 'order to terminate' does not in itself generate very much legal argument, partly no doubt since it is both a necessary but relatively straightforward legal device. It is a measure which follows naturally from a finding of infringement: this must be formally and authoritatively confirmed by an order to bring the infringement to an end (and implicitly, not to repeat the violation). In the EC context, the Commission's decision identifies the prohibited conduct in the case in question and then simply requires the parties to desist from that conduct. Even if the parties have already by that time brought their infringement to an end, there is still some legal point in the Commission handing down its decision and ordering them to desist. The authoritative finding of a violation will be of legal value for purposes of any related legal proceedings,[1] such as civil claims for compensation. Moreover, the order to stop will be legally useful in dealing with any continuation or repetition of the offending conduct.

The Commission's power to make such orders is formally laid down in Article 3 of Regulation 17/62, which provides simply that the Commission 'may by decision require the undertakings or associations of undertakings concerned to bring such infringement to an end'. There has been some discussion of what may more specifically be incorporated into such a requirement, in relation to any future behaviour or positive action on the part of the undertakings concerned, over and above a simple negative order to desist. The Court of Justice and Court of First Instance have applied a test of necessity in this regard: that the Commission may require specific conduct in so far as it is necessary to give effect to the prohibition of the behaviour in question. In this respect, a distinction has been drawn between Article 81(1) of the EC Treaty (the prohibition of offending agreements and the like) and Article 82 (prohibition of abuse of a dominant position). Prohibition of abusive conduct under Article 82 may reasonably and necessarily require some positive action on the part of the 'abusive' company, such as recommencing supplies to a customer.[2] However, under Article 81, the prohibition relates to agreements and comparable instruments. Therefore, the Commission may order that an unlawful agreement be terminated but not that anything further be done as a consequence of that termination: thus, it is possible to order an agreement not to supply to be brought to an end, but not possible to order the supplies to take place. Failure to give effect to the consequences of termination would be a matter for civil proceedings.[3]

---

[1] As confirmed, for instance, by the Court of Justice in Case 7/82, *GVL v Commission* [1983] ECR 483.

[2] See, e.g., Cases 6 and 7/73, *Commercial Solvents v Commission* [1974] ECR 223.

[3] See the ruling of the Court of First Instance in Case T-24/90, *Automec v Commission (No 2)* [1992] ECR II-2223.

However, specific action may be required in so far as it relates to the possible continuation or repetition of the agreement *in itself*. Any necessary constituent elements of the prohibited agreement may be specifically prohibited by means of a requirement as to future action or behaviour (and this is likely to be of a negative nature). There was discussion of the legality of such a requirement in one of the appeals arising from the Commission's decision concerning the *Cartonboard Cartel*.[4] The Commission had required that certain exchanges of information should not take place between the companies in the future. The Court of First Instance ruled, as a matter of general principle, that:

It is settled case law that Article 3(1) of Regulation 17 may be applied so as to include an order directed at bringing to an end certain acts, practices or situations which have been found to be unlawful, and also at prohibiting the adoption of similar conduct in the future. Moreover, since Article 3(1) of Regulation 17 is to be applied according to the nature of the infringement found, the Commission has the power to specify the extent of the obligations on the undertakings concerned in order to bring an infringement to an end. Such obligations on the part of the undertakings may not, however, exceed what is appropriate and necessary to attain the objectives sought, namely to restore compliance with the rules infringed.[5]

Applying that test in the immediate case, the Court found that a prohibition of any future exchange of information was within the Commission's power under Article 3(1), in so far as it related to information concerning deliveries, prices, plant standstills, order backlogs, and machine utilization rates, which had been exchanged before in order to underpin the cartel. But the Commission's requirement that there be no future exchange of purely statistical information exceeded what was necessary for the order to desist:

Such a prohibition exceeds what is necessary in order to bring the conduct in question into line with what is lawful because it seeks to prevent the exchange of purely statistical information which is not in, or capable of being put into, the form of individual information on the ground that the information exchanged might be used for anti-competitive purposes.[6]

Thus it would appear in general terms that Article 3(1) orders may impose negative requirements as to future conduct, which are necessary

---

[4] Case T-334/94, *Sarrió v Commission* [1998] ECR II-1446.   [5] [1998] ECR II-1524.
[6] [1998] ECR II-1527.

to ensure that the prohibited arrangement comes to an end and may not be revived.

(b) Compliance programmes

It is clear then that anything in the nature of an 'antitrust compliance programme' could not be required as an element of such an order under Article 3(1). In effect this would exclude a European equivalent to the American sentence of 'corporate probation', by which companies convicted under the Sherman Act may be sentenced to a term of probation of between one and five years.[7] It should be noted, however, that such compliance programmes are used in a European context, but depend on the initiative of companies themselves and occur very much in a plea bargaining context (discussed below), as an attempt to mitigate fines. In this way, the Commission has at least encouraged the adoption of compliance programmes by looking favourably upon such measures, in so far as they appear to be genuine and effective responses to earlier corporate delinquency. This is distinct from probation, in that the measure is neither formally imposed, nor formally monitored; nonetheless in substance there are similar objectives and possible outcomes.

In some earlier cases, the voluntary institution of compliance programmes earned points from the Commission when deciding on the quantum of fines. For instance, in the *National Panasonic* case,[8] the Commission accepted that the Japanese company Matsushita had taken 'urgent steps to regulate the overall marketing policies of its subsidiaries' and 'conducted an audit of its legal practices in the Community and issued codes of conduct to all its subsidiaries', resulting in a comprehensive, detailed, and carefully considered antitrust programme, with appropriate legal advice. This enabled senior management within the company to be in a position 'to control the behaviour of the whole group in the market place and thereby establish effective internal rules for competition'.[9] Similarly, in dealing with the *Wood Pulp Cartel* and assessing the amount of the fines, the Commission took into account undertakings on the part of a number of the firms:

---

[7] See United States Sentencing Commission, *Sentencing Guidelines*, paras 8D1.1, 1.2 (November 1998).   [8] OJ 1982, L 354/28.
[9] Ibid., para 68.

as to further behaviour which is likely to reduce the artificial transparency of the market and thus to improve the competitive conditions of the relevant market and to lessen the risk of further infringements.[10]

Therefore, to some extent, this kind of 'negotiated' settlement (compliance programme earning a reduced fine) enables the Commission to overcome the limits on its powers under Article 3 of Regulation 17, noted above.

However, to earn mitigation, such compliance programmes must appear both genuine and effective. Indeed, adoption of a 'compliance' strategy may be ambivalent, representing either real contrition and a genuine attempt to confront a culture of collusion within corporate structures, or on the other hand a cynical exploitation of the penalty discount system. As one Commission official commented:

If a company has a compliance programme and is nevertheless found guilty of an antitrust infringement, the existence of such a programme can hardly be considered to be a mitigating factor. Perhaps the Commission should be entitled to *assume* that the infringement has been committed intentionally.[11]

In other words, the coincidence of a compliance programme and a serious infringement would suggest at the worst a cynical and manipulative strategy, or at best ineffective management, and either way a high level of antitrust awareness at a senior level. It would seem ingenuous then for Van Bael to argue[12] that the above statement is the 'wrong message to send to the business community', since it would encourage company executives not to seek legal advice or to consider compliance programmes. That would be to assume a level of innocence on the part of companies which is contradicted by much of the evidence from the cases. After all, using the analogy of the probation order, to adopt a compliance programme

---

[10] OJ 1985, L 85/26, 50–1. The text of the undertaking entered into is appended to the Commission's decision.

[11] Luc Gyselen, 'The Commission's Fining Policy in Competition Cases', in Piet Jan Slot and Alison McDonnell (eds), *Procedure and Enforcement in E.C. and U.S Competition Law* (Sweet & Maxwell, 1993), ch 10, at 74.

[12] Ivo Van Bael, 'Fining à la Carte: The Lottery of EU Competition Law' (1995) 16 *European Competition Law Review* 237, at 239. Van Bael argues that there may be an 'absurd' result in that a compliance programme prior to an infringement being established may be seen as an aggravating factor, whereas one adopted subsequently may be viewed as mitigation. But such an outcome is not absurd in so far as it takes into account either the ineffectiveness or cynical manipulation of the compliance programme.

and then to engage in a serious infringement of the rules would be similar to a breach of a probation order.

The use of compliance programmes also takes the discussion into the realm of corporate and individual responsibility, and indeed the underlying question of the nature and more precise location of cartel delinquency. Ultimately, who should be regarded as the responsible delinquent actor—the company, particular executives, or both? This is a crucial question in relation to the application of sanctions and is assuming a greater significance with the advent of individual criminal liability in a European context. In relation to compliance programmes, one possible scenario is that of the law-abiding company struggling to control law-breaking employees. In a factual sense, the analysis of responsibility is likely to be complicated and variable, and what needs to be considered in particular is the possibility of a complex culture of interaction between corporate and individual conduct. This issue is discussed more fully below.

(c) Claims for compensation

Theoretically, there is the possibility of injured third parties—other traders, or consumers—invoking rules of civil liability (under the relevant member state law in the European context) in order to claim compensation for the anti-competitive damage they have suffered. This has been a significant element in the enforcement of American antitrust law, but much less so in a European national context.[13] Moreover, there appears to be little prospect of significant change in that position. Nonetheless, such civil claims for damages require some discussion in order to appreciate the overall structure and theory of the system of antitrust sanctions.

Parallel private enforcement of the antitrust rules was a feature of American enforcement from the beginning, provided for first in the Sherman Act and then in the Clayton Act of 1914. Section 4 of that statute allows for a private right of action for any person injured by a violation of the antitrust rules, to be taken before a district court, and enabling recovery of 'threefold the damages by him sustained, and the cost of the suit, including a reasonable attorney's fee'. This was based

---

[13] See generally Clifford Jones, *Private Enforcement of Antitrust Law in the EU, UK and USA* (Oxford University Press, 1999); F Jacobs, 'Civil Enforcement of EEC Antitrust Law' (1984) 82 *Michigan Law Rev* 1364; Richard Whish, 'The Enforcement of EC Competition Law in the Domestic Courts of Member States' (1994) 15 *European Competition Law Rev* 81.

upon a recognition that public enforcement resources would be limited and the possible award of treble damages was thus clearly an encouragement of the private initiative in enforcement. Although this system of enforcement has been subject to criticism on a number of grounds,[14] it is a well-established and integral component of the American system of enforcement. From an international and comparative perspective, it should be perceived as both a first and an additional route of enforcement. There are approximately 10 private antitrust cases[15] in the United States for every one government case, and for those companies dealt with via public enforcement under the Sherman Act, both civil claims and the possibility of prison terms for individual employees represent additional sanctions[16] that are at present still largely unknown in a European context. It should also be noted that the American treble damages principle is a consciously thought-out aspect of deterrence theory. This is explained by Collins and Sunshine in the following terms:

First, deterrence is improved because treble damages alter a potential antitrust violator's decisional calculus. Any firm contemplating behaviour violative of the antitrust laws—assuming good information—will weigh the potential gains of the conduct against the risk of detection and prosecution multiplied by the total exposure. Where the total exposure is single damages, the potential gain is usually the same as the exposure, and since the risk of detection and successful prosecution is always less than 100 per cent., the deterrent effect is eviscerated. Multiple damages remedies this deficiency by causing the exposure to far exceed the gain ... Second, actual injury in antitrust actions is typically measured by the amount of price increase resulting from the anti-competitive activity. Actual or single damages awarded on this basis do no more than compensate the injured party for the wealth transfer from plaintiff to defendant caused by the defendant's conduct. Yet most anti-competitive practices also cause a reduction in total output. Thus the deadweight loss resulting from the foregone production, that is the lost surplus value of that production, is not accounted for by single damages. Multiple damages address this deficiency ... the use of a standard multiple, three

---

[14] For a convenient overview of such critical discussion, see Wayne D Collins and Steven C Sunshine, 'Is Private Enforcement Effective Antitrust Policy?', in Slot and McDonnell (eds), n 11 above, ch 8.

[15] Several hundred cases annually. Claims by affected customers are usually brought as class actions. For a discussion of the civil claims brought in relation to the *Lysine, Citric Acid*, and *Vitamins Cartels*, see John M Connor, *Global Price Fixing: Our Customers Are The Enemy* (Kluwer, 2001), ch 16.

[16] The processes of enforcement impact upon each other: civil claims may be activated or expedited by criminal proceedings, since a plea agreement or conviction will provide prima facie evidence of civil liability.

times the actual damage, allows courts to avoid the difficult task of measuring the deadweight loss while at the same time 'remedying' the injury to commerce.[17]

In comparative terms, the American triple damages perform a role comparable to that of EC administrative fines, which naturally embody an attempt to calculate anti-competitive gain and loss for deterrent purposes. But, as noted above, private claims in respect of anti-competitive damage have been and remain rare in the context of member state legal systems. Writing in the early 1990s, Hall reported on a survey carried out by the Research and Documentation Division of the Court of Justice of national legal proceedings involving either Article 85 or Article 86 (now Article 81 or Article 82) of the EC Treaty. His tally amounted to 43 proceedings for the period 1960–9; 96 during 1970–9; 311 during 1980–9 (but including 104 cases dealing just with state or local monopolies in France); and 79 for the period 1990–3.[18] There are a number of possible explanations for the different pattern of resort to private litigation which characterizes the European context of enforcement: in summary, reference can be made to the uncertainty of outcome (which is not mitigated by a prospect of treble damages), practical and financial disincentives (such as the general unavailability of class actions, and the possibility of having to pay costs), and different cultures of litigation.[19] There may also be considerable problems of proof, and even waiting for a long time for Commission proceedings in Brussels to finally establish an infringement still might not provide sufficient evidence of infringement for purposes of national law. The Commission attempted in the earlier 1990s to encourage greater use of national legal proceedings[20] in a move towards decentralization of the enforcement of the competition rules before switching the focus of this policy to the role of NCAs, rather than that of member state courts. In more recent years, the shift in policy towards a more robust protection of consumer interests against the damage caused by 'hard core' anti-competitive

---

[17] See n 14 above, at 52.

[18] D F Hall, 'Enforcement of E.C. Competition Law by National Courts', in Slot and McDonnell, n 11 above, ch 7. See also the data in Behrens (ed), *EEC Competition Rules in National Courts* (Nomos Verlgsgesellschaft, 1992).

[19] See in particular Karen Yeung, 'Privatizing Competition Regulation' (1998) 18 *Oxford Journal of Legal Studies* 581; also Hall, n 18 above; Christopher Harding, *European Community Investigations and Sanctions: The Supranational Control of Business Delinquency* (Leicester University Press, 1993), 115 *et seq*.

[20] Notice on Co-operation between National Courts and the Commission in Applying Articles 85 and 86, OJ 1993, C 39/6.

behaviour has encouraged some governments to contemplate not only criminalization but also procedural change which may encourage civil claims. Thus in the United Kingdom, the remit of the Competition Appeal Tribunal (CAT) has recently been widened to enable faster and less expensive claims by both businesses and consumers in respect of anti-competitive damage, and also to allow representative bodies to bring actions for damages before the CAT on behalf of groups of named and identifiable consumers.[21] Sweden is another state in which the possibility of class actions is being actively considered. (Outside of Europe, the Canadian provinces of Ontario, British Columbia, and Quebec have recently introduced class action legislation.) But the fact remains that in Europe generally there is an insignificant tradition of private litigation in relation to anti-competitive damage, and that is likely to provide the main hurdle to substantial change.

Whether or not 'private' enforcement of cartel prohibitions via civil proceedings develops further in a European context in the coming years, it constitutes a significant element of both the theoretical structure of sanctions and also of the global legal picture. It is an important aspect of the latter on account of its significance within the American legal system. International cartels subject to American antitrust law have to engage in a calculus which takes into account the possibility of both having to pay 'penal' compensation and also of individual criminal liability and possible prison terms. In turn, this brings into sharper relief the theoretical dimension, by posing questions about the range of sanctions. If a clear distinction is maintained between compensatory and penal functions, the overall system of sanctions is likely to remain coherent and morally defensible. Injury to competitors and consumers is dealt with via civil claims for damages, while the injury to the competition norms is dealt with via penal sanctions, whether of an administrative or criminal category. But if the award of damages takes on a penal aspect, over and above the compensatory role, and moreover is additional to the imposition of corporate or individual fines, and perhaps also again individual prison sentences, a question of multiple punishment arises. This is an issue which may give rise to double jeopardy objections and may also affect the overall coherence of the system of sanctions. It is an issue, moreover, which is likely to gain in significance as the enforcement of rules against cartels becomes more globalized.

---

[21] Enterprise Act 2002, ss 17–19.

3. The penal option: financial penalties

(a) The legal character of EC fines

By far the most significant legal response to prohibited cartel activity at the EC level, at least from the 1970s by which time it had become prohibited in strong and clear terms, has been the imposition of administrative but nonetheless undoubtedly penal fines, under Article 15 of Regulation 17/62. Paragraph 2 of Article 15 enables the Commission to impose fines of between 1,000 and 1 million units of accounts (now euros), or up to a maximum figure representing 10 per cent of an undertaking's business turnover, for negligent or intentional infringements of Articles 81(1) or 82 of the EC Treaty, Article 15(4) of Regulation 17 stating that decisions to impose such fines 'shall not be of a criminal law nature'. The first fines were imposed on members of the *Quinine* and *Dyestuffs Cartels* at the end of the 1960s. Since the later 1970s, fines have been regularly applied to cartel violations and have involved ever-increasing amounts.[22] There is now a considerable body of case law arising from appeals against such fines,[23] and it would not be an exaggeration to talk in terms of the Commission as a 'sentencing authority' in respect of this particular role.

Despite their formal designation as 'non-criminal' or 'administrative' measures, the Article 15(2) fines were designed and have been used as punitive and deterrent sanctions. Advocate General Mayras remarked in a relatively early case before the Court of Justice that:

Although in the strict sense of the term the fines prescribed by Article 15 are not in the nature of criminal-law sanctions, I do not consider it possible, in interpreting the term 'intentionally', to disregard the concepts which are commonly accepted in the penal legislation of the Member States.[24]

The Court of Justice itself confirmed the punitive and deterrent role of these fines, stating that the Commission's task 'certainly includes the duty to investigate and punish individual infringements' and that, in deciding on the amount of a fine, the Commission should 'ensure that its action

---

[22] For a very convenient summary of fining decisions in relation to cartels from 1986 to 2000, see the table in Richard Whish, *Competition Law* (4th edn, Butterworths, 2001), 419 *et seq.*

[23] For a detailed account and analysis of the Commission's fining practice and appellate decisions on fines, see C S Kerse, *Competition Law: Enforcement and Procedure* (4th edn, Sweet & Maxwell, 1998), ch 7.

[24] Case 26/75, *General Motors v Commission* [1975] ECR 1367, at 1388.

has the necessary deterrent effect, especially as regards those types of infringement which are particularly harmful to the attainment of the objectives of the Community'.[25] This approach to the use of the fines is also implicit in the wording of Article 15(2), which stipulates that 'in fixing the amount of the fine, regard shall be had to both the gravity and to the duration of the infringement'. Reference to these criteria of 'offence seriousness' suggests a retributive basis for the sanction, embodying a quest for a legal response which is proportionate to both the degree of wrongfulness in the infringement and the extent of harm resulting from it. Indeed, it should be noted that the 'penal' calculations of both the Commission and the Courts of Justice and First Instance have contributed to the legal construction of a 'cartel offence' in the EC context. In working backwards from the need to determine an appropriate quantum of punishment, the Commission and the appellate courts have delineated different degrees of offending anti-competitive behaviour and also indicated an important legal line of division between wholly unacceptable (and so punishable) violations of the competition rules and those infringements which may be condonable (and thus not 'offences'). In this way, fining law and practice has been used to help identify the crucial sense of delinquency in cartel and other seriously anti-competitive conduct and so fashion the substantive law of 'competition offences'.[26]

In general terms, therefore, these fines are intended, in both a retributive and deterrent fashion, to take into account and reflect the seriousness of the anti-competitive 'offence'. In most systems of criminal law, offence seriousness may be seen as comprising two main elements: what may be summarized as the moral blameworthiness of the conduct on the one hand, and the harm resulting from the behaviour in question on the other hand. The penal calculus usually relates these two aspects of the conduct in an attempt to judge the degree of seriousness of the violation. In carrying out such a calculation, different emphases and weighting may be given to these two elements. More obvious illustrations would include, for instance, the greater stress placed upon moral culpability rather than actual injury in the case of inchoate offences of attempt and planning (conspiracy being a classic example), or on the other hand the greater emphasis placed on harmful outcome in the case of 'danger' offences

---

[25] Case 100/80, *Musique Diffusion Francaise v Commission* [1983] ECR 1825, at 1906. See also the opinion of Advocate General Slynn in that case, in which he stresses the deterrent function of the fines [1983] ECR 1947.   [26] See the argument in Harding, n 19 above, 82–3.

based upon strict liability. It has been noted in the discussion in Chapter II above how American antitrust law has tended to emphasize the element of conduct or moral blameworthiness in criminalizing anti-competitive behaviour under the Sherman Act as conspiracies, while the approach under EC law, as demonstrated by fining practice, has tended to emphasize the market impact of offensive anti-competitive behaviour. Thus it was suggested that American law has adopted a 'conduct-oriented' approach, while that of EC law is 'outcome-oriented'. This observation should be borne in mind in the analysis of the Commission's fining practice presented below.

(b) The Commission as a sentencing authority

As noted already, there is now a large body of 'sentencing practice' arising from the imposition of fines in response to serious violations of the EC competition rules (primarily cartel activities and abuses of market dominance) over the last 20 or more years.[27] In most cases, appeals have been lodged against these fines to the Court of Justice and the Court of First Instance, so that it has been possible to extrapolate a number of principles from this case law. More recently, the case law has been supplemented by the Commission's own guidelines[28] on its fining practice, which now provides a kind of codified basis for it own decisions. The Guidelines thus now provide the starting point for any critical discussion of the fining practice, which can then be developed further by reference to case law.[29]

The 1998 Guidelines indicate that the Commission first of all works out a 'base gravity figure'[30] or a kind of cardinal point on a tariff (bearing

---

[27] For detailed discussion, see Kerse, n 23 above, ch 7, for an overall and full account; Gyselen, n 11 above; Wouter P J Wils, 'E.C. Competition Fines: To Deter or Not To Deter?' (1995) 15 *Yearbook of European Law* 17; Van Bael, n 12 above; Wouter P J Wils, 'The Commission's New Method for Calculating Fines in Antitrust Cases' (1998) 23 *European Law Review* 252; Paul M Spink, 'Recent Guidance on Fining Policy' (1999) 20 *European Competition Law Review* 101; Russell Richardson, 'Guidance Without Guidance: A European Revolution in Fining Policy?' (1999) 20 *European Competition Law Review* 360.

[28] See OJ 1998, C 9/3, *Guidelines on the method of setting fines pursuant to Article 15(2) of Regulation 17*, discussed already in Chapter II above. These guidelines should be read alongside the Notices on Leniency, which also of course have an impact on the application of sanctions, discussed in Chapter VIII above.

[29] It is not the intention here (nor is there sufficient space) to enter into a detailed analysis of this now considerable body of law. For such purposes, reference should be made to the sources listed in n 27 above.   [30] Guidelines, s 1(a).

in mind that the latter comprises a minimum point of 1,000 euros, and alternative maxima of 1 million euros or 10 per cent of annual turnover). This calculation takes into account, as required by Article 15, the gravity and duration of the offending conduct. As a concept, 'duration' is relatively straightforward (although its proof may be factually difficult). 'Gravity' is in itself less well-defined and immediately gives rise to some discretionary evaluation. But from the Commission's practice, it may be said that gravity is interpreted to refer to the nature of the anti-competitive infringement, its market impact, and economic significance or 'size'[31]—all three of these factors are in fact closely interrelated and may be seen as emphasizing 'outcome'. This approach is evident in the Commission's threefold classification of infringements laid down in the Guidelines. Infringements of the competition rules which may be fined are classified as 'minor', 'serious', and 'very serious':

- 'minor infringements': trade restrictions with a limited market impact, typically vertical restraints, affecting a limited area of the EC—likely fines of up to 1 million euros;
- 'serious infringements': more rigorously applied restrictions, comprising horizontal or vertical restraints, or abuse of dominance, with a wider market impact and affecting extensive areas of the EC—likely fines of between 1 million and 20 million euros (thus within the 10 per cent of turnover threshold);
- 'very serious infringements': usually horizontal infringements typified by price fixing and market sharing cartels, or clear abuse of dominance by companies commanding a virtual monopoly, as practices which jeopardize the proper functioning of the single market and involving partitioning of national markets—likely fines in excess of 20 million euros.

Clearly, therefore, the emphasis is very much upon the impact upon competition in the EC market, and this is reinforced by the application of the other main criterion, the duration of the anti-competitive conduct,

---

[31] For an example of the kind of factors taken into account in determining base gravity, reference may be made to the list given by the Commission in fixing the base gravity for the members of the *Cartonboard Cartel* (OJ 1994, L 243): very serious nature of the infringement (price fixing and market sharing); cartel covered the whole territory of the EC; importance of the cartonboard market (2,500 million ECU per annum); cartel accounted for virtually the whole of the market; systematic, institutionalized, and detailed regulation within the cartel; elaborate measures to cover up the cartel; and the cartel was largely sucessful in its objectives.

which is also concerned very much with market impact. Duration is also categorized on a threefold scale for purposes of tariff calculation:[32]

- 'short-term duration': less than one year—usually no increase in the amount indicated by the gravity criteria;
- 'medium-term duration': one to five years—usually an increase of up to 50 per cent of the gravity figure;
- 'long-term duration': more than five years—usually an increase of up to 10 per cent per annum over the period of the infringement.

In this way the duration figure acts as a multiplier (x zero, x > 50%, x >10% p.a.) of the base gravity figure, so arriving at a 'cardinal' point on the tariff, in respect of each company found to have committed an infringement. However, the duration weighting may not just serve as a simple multiplier but could depend on the *intensity* of the anti-competitive conduct during different periods within the total duration—for instance, the enforcement of measures in support of a cartel may be stronger in some years than others, so that the multiplier may be raised and lowered to reflect this through the whole duration of the cartel. To this extent, it could be said that 'conduct' factors are also being taken into account at this stage.

The formula 'x gravity + y duration = basic amount of fine'[33] may therefore appear to be misleadingly simple, since both gravity and duration may involve complex calculations based on the evidence of the infringement. Moreover, the Commission indicates in the Guidelines that there are certain 'cardinal' criteria which may be used to refine the determination of base gravity. It refers at this point[34] to: 'effective economic capacity to cause damage to other market operators and consumers'; large companies' 'legal and economic knowledge and infrastructures' (what might be termed antitrust awareness, again more of an attitudinal or 'conduct-oriented' element); and each party's relative position within a cartel regarding these last issues. The result is a mix of quantitative and qualitative criteria, or of mathematical calculation and discretionary evaluation. On the one hand, periods of time and market position may be subject to some fairly precise quantification; on the other hand, effects on competition and legal awareness are more matters of assessment which may be open to argument. All of this leads the Commission to conclude:

---

[32] Guidelines, s 1(b).
[33] Referred to at the end of s 1 of the Guidelines.   [34] Guidelines, s 1(a).

The principle of equal punishment for the same conduct may, if the circumstances so warrant, lead to different fines being imposed on the undertakings concerned without this differentiation being governed by arithmetical calculation.[35]

Having established the base gravity amount or cardinal point on the tariff, this may then be moved upwards or downwards between the maximum and minimum points by reference to more specific aggravating or mitigating 'ordinal' factors. The most likely aggravating and mitigating elements are listed in the Guidelines. Important aggravating features thus comprise: recidivism; lack of co-operation, or obstruction during the investigation; a role as 'ringleader' or instigator; employment of retaliatory measures in enforcing the infringement; and a significant amount of illegal gain from the infringement.[36] Mitigating or 'attenuating' circumstances are listed as: a passive or 'follow-my-leader' role within a cartel; practical non-implementation of anti-competitive measures; prompt termination upon inspection; reasonable doubt on the part of a company as to the unlawful nature of the activity; negligent or unintentional participation; and effective co-operation under the leniency provisions.[37] Some of these aggravating and mitigating features are of course the reverse of each other, such as obstructive or co-operative behaviour. But what is evident is the emphasis on conduct as distinct from market impact in this identification of elements which will move the offence to more precise ordinal points on the tariff.

Finally, the Guidelines refer to a set of 'tailpiece criteria', described as 'objective' factors.[38] This is a reference to particular features arising from the context of the infringement or the circumstances of individual companies, and the following factors are mentioned: specific economic context;[39] the economic or financial benefit derived by the offending companies;[40] specific characteristics of the undertakings in question; and the real ability to pay the fine in a social context.[41] It should also be noted that the working out of the alternative maximum (the 10 per cent of turnover figure) has caused argument on a number of occasions. The Court of Justice has confirmed that both the total turnover of a company

---

[35] Ibid., last paragraph of s 1(a). [36] Ibid., s 3. [37] Ibid., s 4. [38] Ibid., s 5(b).

[39] For instance, the 'regulated' market context in the case of the *European Sugar Cartel* in the early 1970s. See the discussion by the Court of Justice in its judgment: Cases 40/73 etc., *Suiker Unie and others v Commission* [1975] ECR 1663, at 2022–3.

[40] See the Commission's *Twenty-first Report on Competition Policy*, point 139.

[41] See, e.g., the discussion of this issue in the case of the *Iron and Steel Rolls Cartel*, OJ 1983, L 317/1.

and turnover in the relevant market affected by the infringement may be taken into account. As the Court explained:

> it is permissible... to have regard both to the total turnover of the undertaking, which gives an indication, albeit approximate and imperfect, of the size of the undertaking and its economic power, and to the proportion of that turnover accounted for by the goods in respect of which the infringement was committed, which gives an indication of the scale of the infringement.[42]

More recently SCA Holding, a member of the *Cartonboard Cartel*, argued that insufficient account had been taken by the Commission of total turnover (which was relatively small in this instance).[43] Some commentators have argued that the Court of First Instance in that case then implied that the key figure was the turnover on the relevant market, implying that the size and power of the company in markets unconnected with the infringement was of peripheral significance.[44]

In summary, the Guidelines indicate a considerable range of factors which are taken into account in determining the amount of the fine, and the relation of these to each other in the whole process of calculation. This is a sophisticated and potentially complex process which fuses a certain amount of transparent mathematical calculation with discretionary evaluation of the circumstances of individual cases and offenders. Combining the abstract formulation of the Guidelines and the discussion of the application of these criteria in the case law, there is now ample evidence of how this process operates in practice. But this fining practice has provoked not only a large number of appeals (predictably enough), but also a good deal of critical debate. Much of the latter has centred upon the balance between 'transparent' mathematical calculation and discretionary evaluation in the fixing of the amount of fines.

A review of recent debate on the EC fining case law reveals yet again the partisan character of some of the critical argument. Typically, the Commission (and also the Court of Justice and the Court of First Instance, to the extent that the latter confirm the Commission's decisions) are criticized for a lack of clarity, consistency, and coherence in their guidelines,

---

[42] Case 100/80, *Musique Diffusion Francaise v Commission* [1983] ECR 1825, at 1909. See the discussion by Harding, n 19 above, 88 *et seq.*

[43] Case T-327/94, *SCA Holding Ltd v Commission* [1998] ECR 1426 *et seq.*

[44] See Spink, n 27 above, at 107.

decisions, and rulings.[45] But more often than not, the basis for such comment lies in the fact that fines have been appealed and that companies subject to fines wish to question their legality, so apparently equating the companies' interest in challenging fines with actual legal deficiency. Richardson argues, for instance:

The fact that several of the Decisions are already under appeal indicates that undertakings are far from satisfied that the Commission has fairly and correctly calculated the fine. It will be interesting to see how the European courts approach the interpretation of the Guidelines.[46]

In fact, there was ample evidence of the Court of First Instance's review of the Commission's fining practice which could have been referred to by the author, including the significant judgments arising from the *Cartonboard Cartel* appeals, which largely approved the Commission's approach.[47] The argument about transparency is largely an argument against discretion, suggesting sometimes that discretion should be taken out of the process as productive of unacceptable variation of treatment. Richardson at the same point argues that:

It is true that, by looking at a Commission decision taken using the Guidelines, an undertaking can follow the steps in the Commission's calculations. However, such an approach does pose a 'transparency' problem, in that it is very dependent on the Commission's legal and economic appraisal.[48]

But, as Spink has pointed out, a purely mechanistic (and so transparent) system of calculating the amount of fines would doubtless undermine the deterrent effect of the measure:

full transparency would tend to reduce the flexibility of [Commission] decision-making processes, and create an environment in which it is easier to manipulate and abuse the enforcement regime...That said, however...it is possible to extract much specific guidance from Commission decisions and Court judgments. When this is overlaid on the basic framework provided by the 1998 notice, a good overall picture of current fining policy can be obtained.[49]

---

[45] See, e.g., Van Bael, n 12 above; Richardson, n 27 above.   [46] Ibid., 365.

[47] Discussed in detail by Spink in an earlier article in the same journal: see n 27 above.

[48] Richardson, n 27 above, 365. Van Bael's earlier article (n 12 above) is a classic broadside attack on the use of discretion.

[49] Spink, n 27 above, 108. The same author notes succinctly, regarding the need for a deterrent impact: 'A little uncertainty in this respect is a healthy thing': ibid., 103.

Moreover, as the Commission itself indicated in its Guidelines, absolute equality of treatment, based upon a uniformly applied mechanistic formula, would not lead to *fair* outcome in retributive terms. For both retributive and deterrent purposes, much depends upon the position and circumstances of each offender, and taking the latter into account is inevitably a matter of appraisal rather than exact quantification. The Court of First Instance has clearly endorsed this line of argument, stating for instance in an appeal from the *Welded Steel Mesh Cartel* decision, in which it had been argued that there had been a violation of the principle of equality of treatment, that:

Fines constitute an instrument of the Commission's competition policy. That is why it must be allowed a margin of discretion when fixing their amount, in order that it may channel the conduct of undertakings towards observance of the competition rules.[50]

A clear and coherent framework for decision-making, as may be provided by sentencing guidelines, is a *desideratum* of penal decision-making. But that should not be confused with what is required for a fair decision in individual cases. That much may be evident to the criminal lawyer and penal theorist. But this may again be an indication of the epistemological problems encountered by competition lawyers beginning to explore new territory.

(c) Sentencing discounts and 'plea-bargaining'

Some care should be taken in using the term 'plea-bargaining' in the context of EC competition fines. Strictly speaking, there is a well-established practice of mitigation, taking into account co-operative conduct on the part of undertakings which has clearly aided the enforcement process. This is therefore not plea-bargaining in the sense of trading a guilty plea for a lesser charge and consequently lighter penalty. But the Commission's judicially approved practice is to offer a 'reward', either in the form of a reduced fine, or, more significantly and as discussed in Chapter VIII above, immunity or a reduced fine as part of the leniency programme, in return for help in successfully prosecuting competition infringements. The Community courts have confirmed the legality of such procedures, stating in general terms that the Commission is entitled to mitigate the level of fines in recognition of conduct which has enabled it to prove an

---

[50] Case T-150/89, *Martinelli v Commission* [1995] ECR II-1165, at II-1186.

infringement more easily.[51] The main categories of 'good conduct' in this sense comprise: the provision of crucial evidence (which may lead to immunity or a fine discount under the leniency programme); not contesting the case and co-operating during an investigation; and demonstrating the existence of a genuine and effective compliance programme (see the discussion below).

Concern has been expressed about the use of such fining discounts. First, it has been argued that such an approach compromises retributive justice. Van Bael, for instance, has put the view that:

It is submitted that the purpose of imposing different fines should be to reflect the differing degrees of culpability of each party. However, when substantial rebates are granted such as in the *Cartonboard* case, a party with a high degree of culpability (who chooses not to defend itself) may end up with a fine considerably lower than a party who is showed to have played a very minor role (if any) in the conduct complained of, simply because the latter party has decided to use its fundamental right to defend itself. There is no principle of law to justify such discrimination.[52]

In terms of retributive argument, there is no denying the logic of this point. In so far as there can be said to be a principle of law which justifies the discrimination, it is a pragmatic and utilititarian principle, widely employed in a number of legal systems, and concerned with the effective enforcement of prohibitive rules of law. Such enforcement, and a fair use of resources for that purpose, may be seen as being in the wider general interest. When questioned about its use of 'plea-bargaining' in the European Parliament, the Commission had replied to that effect, pointing out that 'similar transactions' are allowed in the legal systems of member states.[53] Indeed, the practice of using prosecutorial discretion for 'out of court settlement' (for instance, 'compounding' in the United Kingdom, or the Dutch *transactie*) and the award of sentencing discounts for co-operative behaviour is widespread at the national level of criminal law.[54] General legal practice thus balances utilitarian considerations against the retributive imperative.

[51] For instance, see the ruling of the Court of First Instance in Case T-354/94, *Stora Kopparbergs Bergslag v Commission* [1998] ECR II-2111, at II-2164 (an appeal by a member of the *Cartonboard Cartel*).

[52] Van Bael, n 12 above, at 242. The same argument in relation to the use of leniency programmes has been considered in Chapter VIII above.   [53] Van Bael, n 12 above, at 242.

[54] See the discussion in Christopher Harding and Gavin Dingwall, *Diversion in the Criminal Process* (Sweet & Maxwell, 1998), chs 5, 8, and 9.

If this is then an inevitable fact of legal life, then the second point of concern becomes particularly relevant: that there should be procedural safeguards to ensure that defence rights are respected and that undue pressure is not used to persuade defending parties to co-operate. Earlier research into the way in which guilty pleas were being made in the United Kingdom suggested that some criminal defendants were being pressurized against their own best interests[55] and such concerns need to be taken seriously. In the context of EC competition fines, the safeguard at present lies with the extensive powers of review available to the Court of First Instance, as discussed in Chapter VII above. Since the Court of First Instance has acquired for itself a wide jurisdiction for purposes of factual review, the circumstances of defendant co-operation and resulting discounts in the amounts of fines can be fully considered by the Court on appeal (and are fully considered, given the present practice of almost automatic appeal against fines). The role of the Court of First Instance is then to ensure that fining discounts are used by the Commission in a consistent and proportionate manner for purposes of aiding the enforcement of the competition rules.

The treatment of these issues by the Court of First Instance may be gauged from a reading of some of the appeals from the Commission's *Cartonboard Cartel* decision, in which a number of aspects of fining practice had been raised.[56] One of the main areas of discussion centred upon the role of one of the companies, the Swedish forest products group Stora, a 'ringleader' within the cartel who came forward with a large amount of crucial evidence. The Commission had been first alerted to the possible existence of the cartel through complaints from customers in the United Kingdom and France and carried out dawn raids in April 1991. It gained in this way a certain amount of incriminating documentation, following which it sent out requests for further information. The latter elicited 'vague and anodyne' responses from most of the companies concerned, but in August 1991 Stora came forward with a large amount of detailed evidence which enabled the Commission to put together a much fuller case against the cartel. As a result, Stora secured a two-thirds reduction of the otherwise substantial fine it would have been required to pay as a leading party within the cartel. Some of the other parties challenged the

---

[55] See the classic study by J Baldwin and M McConville, *Negotiated Justice: Pressures to Plead Guilty* (Martin Robertson, 1977).   [56] See also the commentary by Spinks, n 27 above.

Commission's decision to mitigate Stora's fine in this way, but the Commission's approach was upheld by the Court of First Instance, which indicated the extent of the help provided by the company:

the Court points out that Stora provided the Commission with statements containing a highly detailed description of the nature and object of the infringement, the operation of the various bodies of the PG Paperboard, and the participation of the various producers in the infringement. Through these statements, Stora provided information well in excess of that which the Commission may require to be supplied under Article 11 of Regulation 17. Although the Commission states in the Decision that it obtained evidence corroborating the information contained in Stora's statement... it is clear that Stora's statements constituted the principal evidence of the existence of the infringement. Without these statements, it would therefore have been, at the very least, much more difficult for the Commission to establish or to put an end to the infringement.[57]

The underlying principle being applied here is therefore one of mitigation based upon evidential value of the co-operation. There was also some discussion of the reliability of Stora's evidence: some of the other companies suggested that the financial inducement of a large discount in the fine would tempt a whistleblowing party to embroider or exaggerate evidence. The Court of First Instance rejected this argument, since no specific assertions of unreliable evidence had been made, while Stora's statements were in fact corroborated by other evidence.[58] Moreover, as the Commission had stated in its decision: 'Stora's own statements make it abundantly clear that the companies in its group...were among the ringleaders. Its statements are against its own interests and as such are wholly credible.'[59]

Stora's role in these proceedings is that of the classic 'whistleblower'. It appears as a parent company making efforts to 'clean up' delinquent trading practices on the part of a number of companies within the group.[60] Indeed, Stora had also set up a compliance programme at the time when it came forward with the evidence and later argued that this should be taken into account in mitigation. Both the Commission and Court of

---

[57] Case T-352/94, *Mo Och Domsjo v Commission* [1998] ECR II-1989, at II-2098. In fact, Stora later secured a further reduction in the fine, on the basis of arguments relating to undertaking identity and succession. [58] [1998] ECR II-2099.

[59] OJ 1994, L 243/1.

[60] Kopparfors had been a wholly owned subsidiary since 1986, but had determined its business policy on the cartonboard market largely on its own (the Stora group operated a decentralized structure). Feldmühle had been acquired by Stora only in 1990 and so the latter had no control over its activities during most of the period of the cartel's operations. Nonetheless, the Court of First Instance confirmed that the Commission was entitled to impute the behaviour of these companies to the parent company: Case T-354/94, *Stora*, n 51 above [1998] ECR II-2140–1.

First Instance rejected this argument, apparently on the ground that this did not materially assist in proving the case against the cartel.[61] This point would, however, seem to be open to argument. On the one hand, it may be claimed that 'it is somewhat cheeky... to expect credit for a promise to obey the law in the future'.[62] On the other hand, this may have been a situation in which the adoption of a compliance programme was genuine evidence of contrition, at least in the sense of one part of a corporate structure making efforts to change attitudes elsewhere in the group.[63]

Finally, the *Cartonboard* appeals serve to confirm the principle that 'guilty pleas' may be rewarded, though not to the same extent as the provision of significant evidence. The companies who did not contest the Commission's allegations (so, in effect, 'pleading guilty') were viewed by both the Commission and the Court as assisting the task of finding and terminating the infringement.[64] On the other hand, mere passivity, such as a response to the effect that a company is not expressing a view on allegations, will not earn any discount since it would be of no active assistance.[65]

From this, it would appear that there is a kind of hierarchy of co-operative conduct for purposes of fine mitigation:

- provision of evidence ('whistleblowing') ranks most highly (and indeed, supplied at the right moment may also now qualify for leniency and hence full immunity); supplying evidence may in itself also be ranked according to the degree of material assistance arising from the evidential value of the information;
- not contesting the charge (effectively 'pleading guilty') has a second ranking (it helps, though not as much);
- adopting a compliance programme has the lowest and least certain ranking, since it is more difficult to demonstrate that this clearly assists the successful prosecution of infringements, in view of its mainly prospective impact; the alternative justification for rewarding compliance programmes would be as evidence of improved attitude, but the apparently manipulative use made by some companies of compliance programmes in this context has undermined this ground of mitigation in practice.[66]

---

[61] [1998] ECR II-2164.   [62] Spinks, n 27 above, 104.

[63] On the other hand, the company had earned a large reduction in the amount of its fine for its overall co-operation.   [64] Case 352/94, *Mo Och Domsjo*, n 57 above [1998] ECR II-2096.

[65] Ibid., II-2096-7.

[66] See, e.g., the Commission's decision in *Volkswagen*, OJ 1998, L 124/60. The use of a compliance programme was seen as a sham (para 219 of the decision), and as such could be regarded as an aggravating rather than mitigating factor.

4. The penal option: criminalization and imprisonment

Discussion of the choice of sanctions in response to prohibited cartel behaviour is necessarily related to the issue of responsibility for such conduct, and the nature of such behaviour as delinquent and legally proscribed conduct. The issue of such responsibility has only recently engaged much attention outside of the American context, but is now coming more to the forefront as part of the debate about criminalization, and the associated question of the possible use of imprisonment as a penalty. In terms of the development of the subject, this represents a shift from a predominant resort to financial penalties (whether in the form of criminal or administrative fines, or even 'punitive' treble damages) to the use of other sanctions which are based upon individual rather than corporate responsibility.

In a more theoretical context, discussion of legal responses to cartel offending is part of the issue of corporate behaviour and raises the question of how the law should respond to such 'non-human' and organizational conduct. There is a burgeoning literature on the subject of corporate liability,[67] and more particularly corporate criminal liability.[68] In recent years, for example, the issue of corporate and individual responsibility for acts resulting in serious and large-scale harm to others ('disaster' cases) has provoked a good deal of debate, centred on the concept of corporate manslaughter.[69] The activities of cartels raise similar questions, although the discussion has occurred in reverse order compared to the corporate manslaughter debate: the question, in relation to cartels, is now whether individuals should be held liable in addition to or in the place of corporations, whereas for homicide and personal injury the question has become one of corporate in place of individual actors.

On some reflection, this is a self-evident question in relation to the activities of cartels. This is especially so in the case of cartel arrangements,

---

[67] See Mark Bovens, *The Quest for Responsibility: Accountability and Citizenship in Complex Organisations* (Cambridge University Press, 1998), and the bibliography therein.

[68] See, in particular, Celia Wells, *Corporations and Criminal Responsibility* (Clarendon Press, 1993); P French, *Collective and Corporate Responsibility* (Columbia University Press, 1984).

[69] See, e.g., Celia Wells, 'The Decline and Rise of Murder: Corporate Crime and Individual Responsibility' (1988) *Criminal Law Review* 788; Stewart Field and Nico Jorg, 'Corporate Liability and Manslaughter: Should We Be Going Dutch?' (1991) *Criminal Law Review* 695; UK Law Commission, *Legislating the Criminal Code: Involuntary Manslaughter*, Law Com No 237 (1996).

since they are by their nature deliberate and specific and any particular cartel activity can be causally traced back to definite discussion on the part of individuals. At the same time, there is a distinctive behavioural and organizational aspect of cartel activity, comprising a necessary *combination* of individual and corporate action. That is to say, cartels are planned and organized by individuals within a corporate structure but materialize as corporate conduct. In the vocabulary of criminal law, it might be said that the *mens rea* of the cartel offence is located in individual behaviour, while the ultimate *actus reus* is a corporate action. Cartel delinquency is in this view an intriguing amalgam of individual and corporate conduct and it may therefore be argued that this perspective should inform discussion of legal liability and the choice and application of sanctions. Moreover, on this analysis, the historical preference for the use of corporate financial penalties reveals a preoccupation with the *outcome* of the conduct in question, which of course has manifested itself as corporate market behaviour.

Yet, as has been said of war crimes,[70] the reality of the business delinquency underlying prohibited cartel behaviour is that it is committed by men (still men rather than women) as much as by abstract entities. Thus, from both a retributive and a deterrent viewpoint, it would seem sensible to ask whether liability and sanctions should be applied to individual businesspersons in addition to or instead of companies. As Wils has recently argued:

In order to design an effective enforcement system, it is however important to gain some understanding as to who really commits, initiates, executes, or contributes to, the act or acts which are deemed to form the undertaking's violation. Indeed, companies or undertakings cannot 'personally' commit prohibited acts, such as participating in a price fixing meeting with competitors: such acts are necessarily taken by individuals within the firm. This is not to say that the firm is a mere fiction, however. Rather to the contrary, it constitutes an economic and sociological reality which substantially determines the incentive structure and the cultural climate in which individuals act.[71]

In penal terms, such a perception implies a justifiable joint liability, since the cartel delinquency and resulting harm to competition may be

---

[70] In the words of the International Military Tribunal at Nuremberg: 'Crimes against international law are committed by men, not by abstract entities' (Tribunal Judgment, 1946) (1947) 41 *American Journal of International Law* 172.

[71] Wouter P J Wils, 'Does the Effective Enforcement of Articles 81 and 82 EC Require not only Fines on Undertakings but also Individual Penalties, in Particular Imprisonment?', in C D Ehlermann (ed), *European Competition Law Annuals* (Hart Publishing, 2002), 4. See also his earlier discussion, 'To Deter or Not to Deter', n 27 above.

a product of, first and most immediately, individual action but also, and less directly, a culture and supporting infrastructure which is corporate. There is an interesting body of American research which has attempted to penetrate the causal dynamic of antitrust and other business delinquency (a kind of anthropology and criminology of unlawful business behaviour) which underpins the kind of argument made above.[72] Conley and O'Barr, for instance, consider the leading involvement of the American firm Archer Daniels Midland in the *Lysine Cartel*, uncovered and prosecuted by the DOJ in the 1990s, and postulate a link between the structure, history, and culture of a corporate entity and the individual conduct of its executives and employees which could result in activities such as price fixing. In their view:

Organizing a price-fixing conspiracy seems to have been an almost natural development in an autocratic, top-down corporate culture that prized influence and control above all else. In the business world, price-fixing is the ultimate form of control—control over the vicissitudes of the market. It is the economic equivalent of a sailor being able to control the wind. Regardless of where in the company the scheme originated, it may have seemed like a reasonable idea. If it came from the very top, it probably struck those below as just an incremental step along the continuum of power and influence. If it originated closer to the middle, this was the kind of cultural environment in which it would have been propagated quickly, indeed enthusiastically. It was the sort of thing this company did.[73]

The argument in favour of both individual and corporate liability for cartel conduct is reinforced by a consideration of the efficacy of the financial sanctions which are at present imposed regularly on companies found to be in breach of the competition rules. The very fact of widespread recidivism on the part of a number of large companies, even following detection and the imposition of fines, casts doubt on the deterrent effect of such sanctions. It has also been argued that fines as such are unlikely to

---

[72] See, e.g., J Sonnenfeld and P R Lawrence, 'Why Do Companies Succumb to Price Fixing?' (1978) *Harvard Business Law Review* 145; C D Stone, 'Sentencing the Corporation' (1991) 71 *Boston University Law Review* 383; J M Conley and W M O'Barr, 'Crime and Custom in Corporate Society: A Cultural Perspective on Corporate Misconduct' (1997) 60 *Law and Contemporary Problems* 5; N K Katyal, 'Deterrence's Difficulty' (1997) 95 *Michigan Law Rev* 2385; G E Lynch, 'The Role of Criminal Law in Policing Corporate Misconduct' (1997) 60 *Law and Contemporary Problems* 23. For a rarer instance of European writing on the subject, see R M Feinberg, 'The Enforcement and Effects of European Competition Policy: Results of a Survey of Legal Opinion' (1985) 23 *Journal of Common Market Studies* 373. For a detailed study of American criminal law enforcement during the 1990s, dealing in particular with the *Lysine, Citric Acid*, and *Vitamins Cartels*, see Connor, n 15 above.   [73] Conley and O'Barr, n 72 above, 13.

have deterrent impact as a matter of rational calculation on the part of offenders. Quite simply, it is urged that fines need to be set at an extremely high level to be deterrent. The rational price fixer may calculate the likely gain from an anti-competitive practice and set against that what would be lost through detection and punishment. American literature on the deterrent impact of such financial penalties suggests that, taking into account the estimated gain from an activity such as price fixing, and the average duration of such an arrangement, and then considering the historically low probability of detection, the threshold for a deterrent impact of a fine would be 300 per cent of the annual turnover in the products covered by the violation. (This formula assumes a 10 per cent mark up from a price fix, an average five-year duration and 16 per cent probability of detection.)[74] As Wils argues, such a minimum threshold for deterrent impact would be impossibly high for a number of reasons.[75] Most importantly, the majority of companies simply would not be in a position to pay such high fines,[76] since even huge profits from anti-competitive conduct would not be retained in liquid form, nor would they have sufficient assets, since annual turnover often exceeds assets. Imposition of such severe fines would drive many companies to bankrupcty,[77] with significantly wider economic and social consequences, drawing third parties into the fall-out from the sanction. The collection of such mega-fines would be administratively complex and expensive. Moreover, there may be retributive objections arising from arguments of proportionality (bringing into play the familiar tension between retributive and deterrent philosophies). There is evidence that already the DOJ has encountered offending companies' ability to pay fines as a serious problem.[78]

In summary, all this suggests that corporate fines have limited deterrent impact and cannot realistically be made more severe. In the context of such a conclusion, the argument in favour of alternative sanctions and imposing liability on individuals become more compelling. From the point of view of deterrence, individuals may be more susceptible, not so

[74] Much of this argument is conveniently summarized by Wils, n 71 above. See also G J Werden and M J Simon, 'Why Price Fixers Should Go to Prison' (1987) *Antitrust Bulletin* 917; L M Froeb, R A Koyak, and G J Werden, 'What is the Effect of Bid-Rigging on Prices?' (1993) 42 *Economic Letters* 419; P G Bryant and E W Eckhard, 'Price Fixing: The Probability of Getting Caught' (1991) *Review of Economic and Statistics* 531. The estimated 10 per cent mark up from price fixing has been used by the US Sentencing Commission in its Guidelines.

[75] Wils, n 71 above.   [76] Werden and Simon, n 74 above.

[77] C Craycraft, J L Craycraft, and J C Gallo, 'Antitrust Sanctions and a Firm's Ability to Pay' (1997) 12 *Review of Industrial Organisation* 171.   [78] Werden and Simon, n 74 above.

much to financial sanctions (which could be absorbed or taken over in some way by the company), but certainly to the prospect of a prison term. Werder and Simon have argued:

Prison sentences send a special message not conveyed by fines, and they send it much better, because prison sentences for white-collar crimes are much more newsworthy than fines and, thus, will be given more coverage in the media and will be more noted by other businessmen.[79]

American experience of imposing prison terms for antitrust violations (actually a relatively recent development) has encouraged some optimism regarding the possibilities of deterrence, with assertions of the kind: 'to the businessman ... prison is the inferno, and conventional risk-reward analysis breaks down when the risk is jail.'[80] Wils also argues that alternative sanctions imposed on individuals, such as adverse publicity or disqualification may be circumvented or indemnified, whereas imprisonment is much more unavoidable and has a clear expressive force.[81]

However, any significant move towards the use of imprisonment as a sanction directed at individuals needs retributive as well as deterrent justification. In particular, it may be necessary to convince both courts and juries, and public opinion more generally, that planning and operating a cartel is conduct so morally offensive as to justify both criminal liability and punishment by imprisonment. Thus, any deterrent gain depends upon a willingness to adopt *and apply* such sanctions in the first place. As noted in Chapter II above, this is an especially relevant consideration in the historically more cartel-tolerant European context. The basis for a persuasive criminalization of cartels and the use of imprisonment in this context would depend upon a convincing argument that cartel behaviour is serious delinquency. This in turn would require evidence of both moral offensiveness and real harm.

The moral condemnation has been achieved under American law through the concept of a conspiracy—the sense of deliberate, exploitative, furtive, knowingly unlawful plotting for purposes of illicit gain. European legal ordering needs to import something of this nature into its projects of criminalization. The potential difficulty of doing so will be discussed further below in relation to the present criminalization of cartels under UK law. Demonstrating harm may be less problematic, since evidence of

---

[79] Ibid., 933–4.
[80] A L Lipman, 'The Paper Label Sentences: Critique' (1977) 86 *Yale Law Journal* 619, at 631.
[81] Wils, n 71 above.

the unfair gain which may be achieved through operating cartels may be drawn from American sources. A recent example of this approach is provided by the Irish Competition Authority's *Guideline on Cartels*,[82] quoted in Chapter I above. This kind of statement is clearly intended to have an educative function and draws upon conventional American assessments of anti-competitive loss, embodying the two main elements of 'transfer of wealth' (gain from consumers) and 'deadweight-loss'.[83]

For European policy-makers, lawyers, and public opinion, both criminalization of participation in cartel activity and the possible use of prison sentences constitute a legal quantum jump. It may prove problematical for a number of reasons, but interestingly for purposes of the present discussion, it now appears to be taking place.

5. The European criminalization of cartels

(a) *The global campaign against cartels*

Even as recently as the earlier 1990s, to talk of business cartels as criminal organizations or of the possible imprisonment of business persons for planning anti-competitive activities would have sounded a strange note beyond North America. Yet at the turn of the century cartel criminalization had become a significant legal project in a number of European systems. Taking a global view, by 2000, a number of states, in addition to the United States, had provision for criminal liability for both companies and individuals in respect of participation in 'hard core' cartels (Austria, Canada, Ireland, Israel, Japan, Norway, and South Korea), while France, Greece, and Switzerland provide for just individual criminal liability.[84] In 2001 the British Government indicated that it would move energetically

---

[82] Irish Competition Authority, *Guideline on Cartels: Detection and Remedies* (www.irlgov.ie/compauth/CARTEL).

[83] See, e.g., Werder and Simon, n 74 above. A typical resulting formula would be: price increase resulting from a price fix of 10% + dead-weight loss at 10% of volume of trade + interest × duration of cartel.

[84] See OECD, *Hard Core Cartels/Ententes Unjustifiables* (OECD, 2000), Annex A. Interestingly, in addition, German courts have upheld the application of the general offence of fraud under German law to deal with a case of anti-competitive bid-rigging: Thomas Lampert and Susanne Götting, 'Opening Shot for Criminalisation of German Competition Law?' (2003) 24 *European Competition Law Rev* 30.

to criminalize cartels in its drive to establish a 'world class competition regime' in the United Kingdom[85] (see the discussion below).

Such activity should be put in the context of what appears to be an international campaign, concerned with a more vigorous prosecution and effective legal control of transnational business cartels. This international movement is typified by the robust position adopted by the OECD, an international organization with a highly relevant membership in terms of competition policy which has emerged as a significant forum for the development of policy on cartels. In the spring of 1998 the OECD Council adopted a Recommendation on Effective Action Against Hard Core Cartels.[86] There are two significant features of this instrument. First, it provides a definition of 'hard core' cartel activity,[87] which effectively serves as a template for national legislation, and supplies some real legal content to the concept of a prohibited cartel as such. Secondly, it exhorts OECD member states to 'ensure that their competition laws effectively halt and deter firms and individuals from participating in such cartels' and in particular provide for effective sanctions and enforcement procedures. The Recommendation serves therefore as a kind of 'soft law' instrument for purposes of legal development and harmonization at the national level, not requiring but implicitly encouraging criminalization. Moreover, the OECD's Competition Law and Policy Committee (CLP) called for an expanded three-year second phase of the Organisation's anti-cartel programme.[88] All of this provides a clear international message, portraying cartels as a phenomenon very much contrary to the public interest and requiring a more determined and effective legal control—a 'green light' for criminalization.

This trend is evident, although its impulses may be more obscure. It may be interpreted as either an 'Americanization' or as a 'globalization' of cartel control. Undoubtedly, it relates in some ways to increased American concern in the early 1990s regarding the operation of international cartels and their impact upon the American economy. But the outcome is emerging

---

[85] White Paper, *Productivity and Enterprise: A World Class Competition Regime*, Cm 5233 (2001), ch 7.   [86] OECD, Paris, 27–28 April 1998 (C(98)35/Final).

[87] 'An anti-competitive agreement, anti-competitive concerted practice, or anti-competitive arrangement by competitors to fix prices, make rigged bids (collusive tenders), establish output restrictions or quotas, or share or divide markets by allocating customers, suppliers, territories, or lines of commerce': ibid., para 2.   [88] OECD, n 84 above, 5.

clearly enough, at least at the national legislative level: more criminal law, and the possibility of prison terms for convicted cartel planners.

(b) Criminalization at the national level: the British model

It may be instructive to consider the recent move to criminalization of cartel activity by the United Kingdom, both as an example of how this process operates at the national level and to give an indication of some likely complications in the wider European context. From having a traditionally 'mild' policy towards and legal regulation of business cartels, the United Kingdom has moved swiftly in recent years to a more 'mid-Atlantic' position, by adopting tough rhetoric and demonstrating an apparent determination to deploy severe criminal law sanctions. The first major changes were introduced in the Competition Act 1998, which aligned the UK regulation of anti-competitive practices with that laid down in Articles 81 and 82 of the EC Treaty, thereby enabling the Director General of Fair Trading to impose administrative fines in relation to serious violations such as price fixing and market sharing.[89] Following its re-election in 2001, the British Labour Government quickly outlined further proposed changes in its White Paper, *Productivity and Enterprise: A World Class Competition Regime*.[90] Most relevantly for the present discussion, there was a proposal, subsequently incorporated into sections 188 *et seq.* of the Enterprise Act 2002, to introduce criminal liability for individuals engaging in the discussion and planning of certain listed cartel activities. This list follows that provided in the OECD Council Recommendation (the 'hard core' list) and the move towards criminalization may be seen as a positive response to the urgings of the Recommendation. The new legislation therefore introduces—quite suddenly—a new criminal offence, and one that is ranked as serious in terms of the possible sanctions (quite substantial prison terms) for convicted cartel organizers. The outcome is also a dual system of regulation: administrative regulation and fines, directed at companies as cartel participants, alongside criminal proceedings and sanctions which target the individuals within companies in respect of their role in organizing cartels. Another

---

[89] See Richard Whish, *Competition Law* (4th edn, Butterworths, 2001), 348 *et seq*. Fines may be imposed under s 36 of the Act in respect of infringements of Chapter 1 or Chapter 2 of the Act, up to a maximum of 10 per cent of a company's UK turnover. See also *The Director General of Fair Trading's Guidance as to the Appropriate Level of a Penalty* (OFT 423, March 2000).

[90] See n 85 above.

way of viewing the result is to see the new UK system as penalizing in parallel the *corporate administrative offence of outcome* and the *individual or personal criminal offence of planning*, which is more an offence of *conduct*.

Definition of the new offence[91] was a matter of some difficulty, partly because there were few appropriate precedents to draw upon. Existing English criminal law rendered problematical the adoption of the Sherman Act model of an offence of conspiracy. There is a logical reluctance under English law to cast as a criminal conspiracy a plot to do something which is not necessarily in itself illegal conduct. The problem lies in the fact that hard core cartel activities, though strongly condemned, are not illegal per se under EC law (and ought not then to be illegal per se under UK law). It is therefore difficult in this context to criminalize either the cartel conduct *in itself* or a conspiracy *itself* to engage in such conduct.[92] For this reason, another possible option was rejected for the new UK law—that of coupling participation in listed cartel activity with a characterization of such activity as a breach of Article 81 or its Competition Act 1998 equivalent. If the breach is not necessarily a per se violation, this raised the spectre of complex economic evaluation as to whether there is a breach of the competition rules bedevilling the legal argument in criminal proceedings.[93]

What emerged eventually was a definition supported by a specially commissioned report[94] and which sought a criminal element in the activity via the existing criminal law concept of dishonesty. The offence is based on a 'dishonest participation in an agreement which has as a purpose one or more of the specified hard core cartel activities.'[95] The element of dishonesty has clearly been introduced in order to signal a sense of serious delinquency, but is not a wholly appropriate concept for purposes of conveying an idea of offensive behaviour involving a deliberately illegal, furtive, and contumacious attitude—what, indeed, might be best encapsulated in the idea of 'conspiracy'. Moreover, the normal test of dishonesty under English criminal law,[96] embodying both an objective and

---

[91] For a detailed analysis of the definition of the new offence, see Christopher Harding and Julian Joshua, 'Breaking Up the Hard Core: the Prospects for the Proposed Cartel Offence' (2002) *Criminal Law Review* 931.

[92] Although recent Irish legislation has virtually criminalized the cartel in itself. See Philip Andrews, '"Modernisation"—Irish Style' (2002) 23 *European Competition Law Review* 469.

[93] As has happened for instance in Canada, and may happen in Ireland. See the discussion in Harding and Joshua, n 91 above.

[94] Sir Anthony Hammond and Roy Penrose, *Proposed Criminalisation of Cartels in the UK* (Report prepared for the Office of Fair Trading, November 2001).

[95] Enterprise Act 2002, s 188.   [96] As laid down in *R v Ghosh* [1982] QB 1053.

subjective element, may well be deftly exploited by defence counsel (that, for instance, the defendant honestly believed that the conduct was acceptable under Article 81 or the Competition Act 1998). Nor is the concept of 'agreement' free of potential problems, since the reality of dealing with hard core cartels is one of searching for elusive and sophisticated 'concertation', rather than open and clear agreement in the usual sense of the word. On the other hand, there is some indication that the OFT anticipates a very selective policy of prosecution of the new offence.[97] On either reading of the prospect—it may be difficult to prove or convince juries of liability, or it will be reserved for a few very serious cases—there is some sense that the British criminalization may be more significant in rhetorical terms than actual application of law.

There may be a general lesson here in relation to the current trend towards criminalization. A reading of developments at the legislative level may give an impression of vigorous new activity. But, as is true of any legal change, there may be a gap between prescriptive action and enforcement. Given the requisite political will in the appropriate place, legislation may be easily achieved, as the British example has demonstrated. But its application and enforcement may be another matter, especially if wider legal culture lags behind the pace of legislative change.

(c) *Problems at the interface with European law*

Moreover, there may be further legal complications arising from national criminalization of cartel activity in a European context, regarding its relation to EC level 'administrative' regulation of major cartels. In short, introduction of criminal liability for cartel participation in the United Kingdom will lead to a number of jurisdictional and regime-interface issues. The emerging structure of enforcement within the United Kingdom can be summarized as shown in Figure IX.1.

Thus the OFT will find itself acting as a prosecuting authority under the criminal law provisions of the Enterprise Act 2002, and as 'regulatory' authority applying the 'administrative' provisions of the Competition Act 1998 while also helping the Commission to some extent in its Article 81 investigations (under Article 13 of Regulation 17), and eventually

---

[97] This is implied for instance in the OFT's Consultation Note on its proposed 'no action' letter (i.e. to gain leniency): see the OFT website (www.oft.gov.uk).

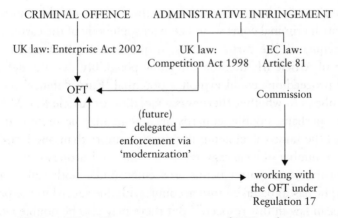

Figure IX.1: Emerging structure of UK enforcement

(following the 'modernization' of the EC competition law regime)[98] applying Article 81 by delegation from the EC level. The result brings together within one legal framework both criminal law and administrative regimes, and both national and European jurisdictions. This is likely to give rise to a number of issues at these respective interfaces.

First, there is an issue of prescriptive jurisdiction. A single transEuropean cartel could be subject at the same time to the following jurisdictions:

- English criminal law (Enterprise Act 2002): criminal liability of individuals;
- Competition Act 1998: non-criminal law liability of companies;
- EC law (Article 81), as applied by the Commission;
- EC law (Article 81), as applied by the OFT.

This raises in principle the issue of ensuring consistency, in terms of both implementation and outcome, as between these 'parallel' processes, each of which should be seen as serving the same underlying objectives, though by different methods. In relation to hard core cartels, embodying what are generally regarded as serious violations of competition rules, there are unlikely in practice to be conflicting final decisions. The problem may be rather to ensure that parallel proceedings do not undermine

[98] Commission White Paper on *Modernisation of the Rules Implementing Articles 85 and 86 of the EC Treaty*, OJ 1999, C 132/1. These proposals are now embodied in Council Regulation 1/2003, but will not come into force until May 2004.

each other's effectiveness. For example, although it is highly improbable that a British criminal court would convict somebody of the cartel offence and subsequently the cartel activity in question not be found to be in violation of Article 81, there is still some possibility that the defence in criminal proceedings could exploit a potential 'Euro-defence' (i.e. raise some doubt as to whether there was a violation of Article 81). More significantly, perhaps, double jeopardy arguments may be presented in the context of the same cartel being dealt with in more than one jurisdiction or under a number of legal regimes. As a matter of European law, the possibility of the same matter being prosecuted under both European and national law has to be taken into account, with due regard to the primacy of European law in this respect.[99] But there may also be double jeopardy objections to the 'same' offending conduct being the subject of both administrative sanctions (imposed on the company) and criminal law sanctions (imposed on individuals). This aspect of the subject raises intriguing conceptual questions and awaits further legal testing: do the breaches committed by the company and by individuals constitute the same or different[100] offences? On the one hand, it may be argued that the anti-competitive practice is the (corporate) breach of the competition rules, while the planning of the latter is a separate (individual) breach of criminal law.[101] On the other hand, it could be maintained that the two activities are inseparable, in that the anti-competitive practice cannot exist without its planning, and that to divorce the two would constitute a kind of double counting or 'recycling' of conduct, in itself a violation of the principle *non bis in idem*. Indeed, such questions probe the justification for parallel 'administrative' and 'criminal' sanctions.

There are in addition a number of issues of enforcement jurisdiction, relating to investigations, exchange of information, dealing with offenders abroad, and the operation of leniency programmes. As part of 'modernization', the Commission will be giving to national authorities such as the OFT some of its existing monopoly in relation to the application of Article 81. Thus the OFT (although acting under the direction of a case

---

[99] Case 14/68, *Walt Wilhelm v Bundeskartellamt* [1969] ECR 1. See Julian M Joshua, 'A Sherman Act Bridgehead in Europe, or a Ghost Ship in Mid-Atlantic?' (2002) 23 *European Competition Law Review* 231, at 232–3. The OFT will take account of EC sanctions, as indicated in the *DGFT's Guidance as to the Appropriate Amount of Penalty*, n 89 above.

[100] In the *Wilhelm* proceedings, n 99 above, the French Government argued that criminal and administrative fines were different in nature, hence no double jeopardy.

[101] This appears to be the assumption of the British Government and the OFT: see Joshua, n 99 above, 234.

controller from the Serious Fraud Office) may find itself carrying out criminal investigations under the Enterprise Act 2002 while also investigating the same cartel activity under Article 81. How easy will it prove in practice for the same authority to carry out these two roles? For instance, would the OFT be able to use information gained in an EC investigation in national criminal proceedings? The relative chronology of national and EC investigations may prove problematical. For example, should the OFT await the conclusion of an EC investigation, and so risk the loss in the meantime of local evidence? Or, if the EC investigation has been completed, would an adverse finding in Brussels constitute prejudicial pre-trial publicity in relation to the later prosecution of individuals in the United Kingdom?[102] Moreover, the report on cartel criminalization prepared for the OFT[103] recommended that any investigation likely to lead to criminal prosecution be conducted to criminal standards from the outset, but, as Joshua has commented:

The mechanics of how OFT officials could simultaneously assist the Commission while observing criminal law investigative standards under the Police and Criminal Evidence Act 1984 are not explored. The prospect of company employees being 'Mirandised' by the OFT before a simple request for oral explanations could be made by the Commission officials under Article 14(1)(c) [of Regulation 17] is intriguing.[104]

A number of legal complications may arise, therefore, at the interface of investigations.

If the use of criminal law in the United Kingdom is intended to focus on serious cartel violations, many of these are likely to have an international or European dimension, for instance involving crucial meetings, and so evidence located, outside the United Kingdom. The availability of evidence from abroad for purposes of a British prosecution may be problematical. Present practice in relation to mutual legal assistance is often limited by requirements of confidentiality and double criminality. For instance the existing mutual legal assistance treaty (MLAT) between the United States and the EU does not provide for the exchange of confidential information or enable one party to exercise investigative powers to obtain evidence to be handed over to and used by the other.[105] If the other

---

[102] See also the provisions in the Enterprise Act 2002, ss 102–3.

[103] Hammond–Penrose Report, n 94 above.   [104] Joshua, n 99 above, 235.

[105] US–EC Agreement on the Application of Competition Laws, 23 September 1991, as supplemented by the US–EU Agreement on the Application of Positive Comity Principles in the Enforcement of their Competition Laws, 4 June 1998.

jurisdiction in which evidence may be located is less enthusiastic about cartel criminalization, mutual legal assistance may not be very forthcoming in practice. Moreover, compelling the appearance in British criminal proceedings of suspects from other states is also subject to any existing dual criminality conditions between most European jurisdictions.[106]

Finally, criminalization at the national level may have an impact on the operation of leniency programmes. As discussed in Chapter IX above, it seems clear that the probable application of criminal sanctions is an important element in the success of the DOJ's leniency programme in the United States. But that is in the context of a single legal order. From the perspective of the EC leniency programme, or that of any other national system, the possibility of criminal sanctions elsewhere is a complicating factor—in effect, constituting an additional risk in coming forward in the first place, since any one system cannot guarantee leniency in another jurisdiction. Even if a whistleblower applies simultaneously for leniency in every relevant system, there is a multiple risk of not qualifying elsewhere, especially if other systems are less predictable in their decision-making. This would appear to be a likely assessment of the proposed UK procedure for granting leniency in relation to individual prosecutions. The OFT's Consultation Document of July 2002, suggests that 'no action' letters (i.e. leniency) will only be available to the 'most guilty' individuals. Even if this implies that only the 'most guilty' will face prosecution in the first place, it renders the whistleblower's overall calculation very uncertain. Moreover, American prosecutors (and the American criminal justice system) historically have demonstrated a more robust and pragmatic attitude towards leniency 'deals' than has been the case in the United Kingdom. Therefore, unpredictability regarding possibly severe criminal sanctions in Britain may undermine the working of leniency programmes elsewhere. As Joshua envisages:

Can it seriously be expected that those at the helm of a company who risk criminal prosecution and jail in Britain will come forward to denounce a cartel to the Commission when they cannot secure a bankable guarantee as to their personal position as part of a single deal?[107]

In a number of respects, therefore, criminalization at the national level may serve to complicate the European context of enforcement.

---

[106] See Joshua, n 99 above, 241.   [107] Ibid., 236.

6. The outlook: an escalation of sanctions?

As may be judged from the discussion above, there have in recent years been significant and fast-moving developments in relation to the enforcement of the rules against cartels and the sanctions that may be employed for that purpose. Driven partly by a more determined enforcement of the American law by the DOJ, international and national enforcement generally has become more robust, more focused, and more severe. The deft resort to leniency strategies has enhanced the level of detection and conviction, but part of this strategy has been to present companies with a convincing prospect of both being apprehended and then being dealt with severely. One outcome therefore has been an *escalation* of sanctions. This is so in a number of senses. First, more cases are being successfully prosecuted and so more penalties are being imposed. Secondly, the penalties are becoming more severe, both in kind and in quantum. Thirdly—a related point—the range of sanctions has expanded to embrace both criminal and administrative penalties, and both fines and custodial measures, applied to both corporate actors and individuals. Fourthly, the application of sanctions against international cartels across a range of jurisdictions has given the subject a transnational (some might say 'globalized') dimension, multiplying the risks for cartel offenders.

One significant conclusion is therefore that enforcement has become tougher. This is most evidently so within the American jurisdiction, which serves as a kind of enforcement leader. At the corporate level during 2002, 26 companies were fined a total of US$303 million, an average of US$11.8 million for each defendant. Individual fines can exceed US$100 million, such as that imposed on Mitsubishi for its involvement in the *Graphite Electrodes Cartel* (US$134 million).[108] At the level of individual criminal liability, prison terms have increased in severity. MacAvoy and Donnelly report that:

Individuals convicted of criminal antitrust violations face an increasing risk of being sentenced to significant time in jail. Forty-eight individuals were imprisoned for antitrust offences in 1999 and 2000—more than the number of individuals imprisoned for antitrust offences in the previous five years combined. Moreover, 15 of the 48 individuals received sentences of 12 months or more...

[108] Christopher J MacAvoy and Kenneth W Donnelly, 'Trends in US Government Antitrust Enforcement', *The Antitrust Review of the Americas 2002* (*Global Competition Review* Special Report 10), 13.

a food company executive recently was sentenced to four years' incarceration, with a US$1 million fine, for his role in a bid-rigging conspiracy involving New York City schools. Finally reflecting the priority placed on attacking international cartels, six foreign nationals were sentenced to imprisonment in the past two years.[109]

American criminal enforcement (supplemented by civil class actions) represents the sharp end of global or transnational enforcement. EC fines are significant too and have also gained in severity in recent years,[110] but it should be remembered that EC sanctions are not criminal, nor do they apply to individuals. Nor do claims for compensation figure significantly in Europe. As noted above, there has emerged recently a strong rhetoric of criminalization in the European national context, but the enthusiasm for this strategy is still uneven and its actual application remains uncertain. While government ministers and legislators may be won over to the cause, a vigorous resort to such sanctions by prosecutors, courts, and juries awaits demonstration. Relatively severe sanctions have been available in Ireland since 1996, giving the appearance of one of the toughest regimes outside the United States, yet a 'landmark' victory for the Irish Competition Authority in October 2000 resulted in a corporate fine of just IRL£1,000.[111]

Moreover, the cocktail of enforcement strategies now appearing across European jurisdictions can lead to procedural complications. Whereas the availability of criminal proceedings may be seen as a *sine qua non* of successful enforcement in the American context, their appearance within the very different legal structures in Europe may be more of a mixed blessing. Part of the difficulty arises from the fact that the *overall* European pattern of enforcement and sanctions has not been planned as such and could not fairly be described as a 'system'. Although now developing speedily, this is happening in a reactive and haphazard fashion. The EC jurisdiction is the 'master' regime in the European context, but is hobbled by its formal and practical limitations: an absence of criminal law,

---

[109] Christopher J MacAvoy and Kenneth W Donnelly, 'Trends in US Government Antitrust Enforcement', *The Antitrust Review of the Americas 2002* (*Global Competition Review* Special Report 10), 13.

[110] Recent examples include the fines imposed on the *Vitamins Cartel* (a total of 855 million euros), the *Graphite Electrodes Cartel* (a total of almost 219 million euros), the *Citric Acid Cartel* (a total of 135 million euros), and the *Lysine Cartel* (a total of 110 million euros).

[111] Philip Andrews, ' "Modernisation"—Irish Style' (2002) 23 *European Competition Law Review* 469. The fine (imposed on Estuary Fuel Ltd) was low partly on account of the company's plea of guilty.

some reliance on national enforcement resources and a complex and uneven national-level culture and history of regulation and enforcement in relation to anti-competitive conduct. While there is now a flurry of legal activity across Europe, it is not evident that recidivist price fixers and their like are overawed by the escalating fines (although their executives may be increasingly concerned by the prospect of *American* prison terms). Predictions of future trends in enforcement thus remain difficult in the European context—a topic which inevitably requires consideration in the final chapter, in assessing any globalizing tendencies in the subject.

X

Cartel Law in the Twenty-First Century: Globalized and Criminal?

1. Conversion, convergence, or global mosaic?

The foregoing discussion has presented an account of the evolving regulation of business cartels in Europe, at the same time seeking to present this discussion in the broader international context and comparing European and American approaches to the subject. The result is an instructive narrative of legal development, also indicating a process of legal change in Europe which has accelerated in the closing years of the twentieth century. In short, in a European context, the subject of cartel regulation appears very different at the beginning and at the end of the last century. European law—both in the sense of EC law and law at the national level—has moved from an earlier stance of tolerance coupled with some ambivalence to a position of strong condemnation. In this way, it may be said that European law has over that period of a hundred years caught up with American law, which had the categorical censure embodied in the Sherman Act in place by the last decade of the nineteenth century. The discussion in this concluding chapter will seek to read and interpret this story of legal development in Europe (and beyond). At the outset it would seem clear that a number of readings are possible and at the same time it must be recognized that at the present point in time the story is continuing rather than complete, and predictions for the future are not wholly certain. But a number of main questions naturally pose themselves. Is this a tale of conversion to, or at least a successful exportation of, the American model—*tales of Yankee power*? Or is it a tale of late-twentieth-century globalization, involving an internationalization and harmonization of legal policy and regulatory method? Or is it a tale of apparent convergence masking enduring and resilient differences of legal culture and legal policy, so that important elements of the European system of regulation are likely to remain distinctive and present a significant alternative model for the coming century?

These underlying questions will be addressed in three main sections of discussion. First, a retrospective overview will take stock of the evolving European legal position on cartels over the last hundred years or more and probe the nature of this legal change. In particular, it will be asked whether this reflects a change in the nature and operation of business cartels, or a shift in the perspective of policy-makers, regulators, and wider public opinion. Is this a phenomenon of *parallax*—has the subject matter changed position, or have those observing and dealing with the subject altered their stance? Secondly, in an attempt to assess the present legal position in Europe, a summary account will be given of 'European cartel law' at the turn of the century, drawing out its salient characteristics as a legal regime. This hopefully will aid comparisons with the approach which has been taken to the subject elsewhere, and particularly in North America. In the third place, and with more of an eye to the future, something will be said about the emerging international and transnational picture of cartel regulation. How should the present mosaic or patchwork of national and supranational regulation be understood for purposes of twenty-first century legal development? What are the prospects for a globalized[1] and harmonized system of regulation emerging from the present complex and interlocking series of regimes?

2. Retrospective: a parallax view?

A summary of the preceding discussion in this book would indicate a major and intriguing divergence in the underlying approach to the legal regulation of business cartels in North America and Europe during the course of the twentieth century. But the European position has shifted significantly in the last half of the twentieth century, prompted in particular

---

[1] 'Globalization' is a term which can bear different meanings according to context. Writers refer for instance to 'global cartels', usually meaning 'widely spread around the world', or more than European or American in their geographical scope. 'Globalization' as a process is a complex and widely used but not always specifically defined concept. In the context of the discussion in this chapter, the term will be used to indicate a shift towards an international as distinct from national or European legal infrastructure and method.

by the establishment of the European Community and its preoccupation with the injury which may be caused by certain kinds of anti-competitive activity to the single market project. By the 1970s there was a vigorous prosecution of cartels with a European dimension by the EC Commission. Although this has in formal terms not matched the criminal prosecution of antitrust violations under the Sherman Act in the United States, it may be nonetheless fair to say that the result of the increasingly rigorous EC legal action against cartels has been to implant a definite sense of delinquency regarding cartel behaviour in European legal culture and at the same time drive the cartels themselves underground, so that they have become self-consciously covert and unlawful operations. While questions may still be posed as to the effectiveness of these efforts at legal control, there can be little doubt as to the transformation in legal policy and prescriptive law. More recently, this transformation has been further manifested in the move towards tougher efforts of legal control at the national level, and in particular the adoption of criminalization as a legal strategy in a number of jurisdictions. It has been noted that the resulting overall landscape of legal control across Europe, and indeed globally, is complex and may prove problematical. Nonetheless the main conclusion should be one of impressive legal change. Broad toleration has evolved by way of an increasingly uncomfortable ambivalence to outright censure by the close of the last century. Cartel law has come of age in Europe and the regulation of business cartels is now a significant legal business.

In seeking to understand and account for this transformation it may be important to ask whether this reflects a change in the subject matter itself or in the perspective on the subject. May it be said that the behaviour of cartels and the impact of the behaviour is different in any significant ways as between the earlier and later twentieth century? Or have European views altered, coming, for whatever reasons, into line with the American outlook on the subject which gave rise to the Sherman Act a century earlier? In short, it may be asked whether this is a phenomenon of legal parallax: to what extent the subject may have remained constant, but the position of those observing that subject has altered.

Evidence of the operation of business cartels, whether possessing a national or international dimension, over the course of the last hundred years or so would suggest a largely constant form of behaviour. In very broad terms modern business cartels have served private producer interests in their wish to control markets and have consistently employed certain basic strategies for this purpose—price fixing, market sharing, limitation of production, and bid rigging, these often being interrelated. In this way it is possible to refer to 'classic' forms of cartel, and this typology has in recent years provided the basis for the definition of offences, as can be seen for instance in the OECD Council Recommendation in 1998 and the recent UK legislation criminalizing participation in cartels.[2] Regulatory practice and now widely accepted economic analysis would therefore seem to agree on the identification of a consistently practised and (from the companies' point of view) tried and tested mode of anti-competitive behaviour put into effect via the arrangement now commonly referred to as a 'cartel'. In that sense, cartels in the earlier part of the twentieth century would appear to have been similar in their purposes and market operation to those which have been organized in more recent periods. The evidence to be gained from earlier studies, such as those of Hexner[3] or Stocking and Watkins,[4] reveals a similar pattern of conduct and activity as that which may be derived from recent legal investigations in a number of jurisdictions.

On the other hand, there may be different interpretations of the prevalence and longer-term patterns of cartel activity. The recently published American study by Connor,[5] for example, identifies a cyclical pattern of cartel activity during the modern period from the later nineteenth century through to the end of the twentieth century, in a series of three main 'epidemic' waves of global cartel activity—the late 1800s through to the outbreak of the First World War, the period preceding the Second World War, and then the late 1980s and the 1990s. Moreover, this account of the subject tends to see cartel activity as having a kind of contagious quality. Connor argues for instance:

The outbreak of global cartelization after nearly fifty years of dormancy may be compared to biological contagion. Price fixing behaviour on a global scale had erupted in the decades just before World War I and again just prior to World War II. U.S. prosecutions in the late 1940s (and in one famous case in 1960) helped douse the fires of conspiracy for two decades or more, but in the remarkably short period of 1989–1991 several new cartels sprung into action. The conspiracies also resemble contagion in the sense that within some firms with multiple lines of business, once one product line was proving the profitability of price fixing, it

---

[2] See the discussion in Chapter IX, this volume.

[3] Ervin Hexner, *International Cartels* (Pitman, 1946).

[4] George W Stocking and Myron W Watkins, *Cartels in Action: Case Studies in International Business Diplomacy* (Twentieth Century Fund, 1946).

[5] John M Connor, *Global Price Fixing: Our Customers Are the Enemy* (Kluwer, 2001).

infected another line of business. There is evidence that a conspiracy in the global market for vitamins that began in 1990 spread within and across multinational companies to citric acid in 1991 and lysine in 1992.[6]

Such interpretative metaphors of epidemics of contagious disease or outbreaks of fire are interesting for their suggestion of discontinuity, but it may be questioned whether such a reading is really one of legal reaction, rather than of the phenomenon of cartelization itself. Certainly, it does not accord so much with the European evidence, which suggests a remarkably resilient and continuous cartel activity, interrupted sure enough, but quickly recovering from the two major Wars and their political and economic aftermath. European cartel history also indicates a continuity of business actors. Consider, for instance, the prominent role in the later twentieth century of successor firms to some of the cartel leaders of the earlier parts of the century.[7] Such evidence points rather to a deeply ingrained pathology rather than a body prone to invasion by epidemics of contagious disease. To be sure, cartelization is encouraged by certain economic conditions, especially recession and its consequence of low profitability, which are temporary and cyclical features of the economy. But the point being made here is that the underlying tendency towards and motivation for cartelization appears to be a constant in the modern business environment. To view it mainly as a response to shifting economic conditions—indeed, to see the matter in predominantly economic terms[8]—leaves aside an important human element in the subject. For cartels, even though economic devices, are organized by human actors who are intent on achieving power and control. Seeking to control

---

[6] John M Connor, *Global Price Fixing: Our Customers Are the Enemy* (Kluwer, 2001), 11.

[7] Although there is no single complete 'history of European business cartels' for the whole of the twentieth century, it is possible to trace such continuity of participation in cartel activity from such sources as Hexner (n 3 above), Stocking and Watkin (n 4 above), the Leiden University Historical Institute's *Interwar Cartel Database* (www.let.leidenuniv.nl/history/rtg/cartels), and data from the EC cartel investigations contained in the *Official Journal* (for Commission decisions) and the *European Court Reports*. For instance, in the Commission's decision on the *Soda Ash Cartel (Solvay/ICI)* in 1991, there is reference to the 'Page 1000' document, discovered at ICI, which refers to a new agreement between Solvay and ICI in 1945. This places on record the belief of the two companies that 'the pre-war co-operation between them (which had gone on for nearly seventy years) in the technical and commercial development of the alkali business has been of benefit to both of them' (OJ 1991, L 152/1, at 5).

[8] The traditional stance of course in 'competition' law, and of many economists, especially the Chicago School (the view that economic analysis should prevail in the competition law decision-making process in order to maximize consumer welfare through economic efficiency, and that socio-political considerations would be harmful to that goal).

a market is not an abstract economic process and springs from an essentially human ambition. It is this human and personal dimension of the subject which appears to have been intuitively captured in the American initiative which bore fruit in the Sherman Act, with its emphasis on the element of conspiracy. On this view of the matter, cartels may almost be seen as a natural feature of modern (both industrial and post-industrial) economies. As Conley and O'Barr have suggested, controlling the vicissitudes of the market is the equivalent of the sailor controlling the wind.[9] It is, in its context, a highly significant power and thus for people working in a naturally thrusting and ambitious environment a natural and compelling temptation. On such a view, the impulse to cartelize in order to control markets through strategies such as price fixing and market sharing arises from within the business community and is not visited on it from the outside, and is thus, in so far as it is seen as constituting unacceptable harm to others, a form of delinquency ranking alongside fraud and other predatory economic practice.

It is by charting the emergence and more definite articulation of this interpretation of cartel behaviour that it becomes possible to understand the transition in European attitude and policy. For particular historical reasons, explored in Chapter II above, it was possible to defend private endeavours to control markets in the European context in the earlier twentieth century in a way that was not possible in the United States. A study of the earlier twentieth-century history of the policy debates on cartels in the most significant site of activity in Europe during that period—in Germany—is very instructive.[10] It reveals a developing dialogue between government and industry, but one that was not especially confrontational. There was for some considerable time a willingness on the part of public officials, academic opinion, and even wider public opinion in Europe to accept the argued advantages of privately administered market control, as a strategy of desirable economic stability. As Stocking and Watkins commented, as late as 1946:

Such producer planning became a marked, if not the outstanding, characteristic of business between the two world wars. In certain countries, notably Germany and Japan, scarcely a major product came to market free from cartel controls. Even in those countries where economic liberalism had taken firm hold, notably

[9] J M Conley and W M O'Barr, 'Crime and Custom in Corporate Society: A Cultural Perspective on Corporate Misconduct' (1997) 60 *Law and Contemporary Problems* 5, at 13.

[10] See, in particular, David J Gerber, *Law and Competition Law in Twentieth Century Europe* (Oxford University Press, 1998), chs 4 and 5.

England and the United States, businessmen were regulating competition as a regulator of economic activity and turning with increasing frequency to cartels to temper competitive forces and diminish business risks.[11]

What was to change in later years was the appreciation of what might underlie these private policies of market regulation, and in particular the developing perception of both private gain and public injury which could arise from such strategies. But it is still far from clear how widely spread this shift in perception may be at the present time. As argued already, the cogency of cartel criminalization depends in large measure on the conviction that cartels are not only matters for regulation but are in addition delinquent features of economic life.

But a retrospective survey needs to enquire further into this shift in the view of the subject, in order to determine whether what is under discussion is both a transformation in external perception and in internal attitude. In other words, do the businesses engaging in cartels see their own behaviour differently now compared to how their business predecessors may have reflected on their own roles in the earlier twentieth century? In one sense, the answer to such a question must almost necessarily be affirmative. External censure will certainly affect internal self-awareness. For so long as the law did not prohibit or strongly condemn price fixing or like behaviour, those engaging in such practices could justifiably see themselves as carrying out an acceptable and even laudable role. This is evident in a number of the contemporary statements recorded from that earlier period and referred to in Chapter II. But as legal prohibition hardened, and tolerance evolved into censure, so too the self image of the cartel participant would alter. Moreover, associated with this process of regulatory change is an important historical fact: the altered external perception did not remove the impulse to continue the activities in question. Instead, as the law hardened, the private market regulators moved 'underground', became increasingly covert, and more self-consciously unlawful in their operations. In effect, the process was one of spiralling delinquency, as the outlook of both regulators and cartel organizers became firmer and more definitely oppositional to each other. Thus, to some extent, changing habits of legal regulation produced increasingly entrenched attitudes on the part of the main actors. It is unlikely that German or British businessmen in the 1920s would have

---

[11] Stocking and Watkins, n 4 above, 4.

said, in furtive celebration of their economic role: 'the customer is our enemy.'[12] But equally, public officials of that time would not have described cartels as equivalent to 'cancers on the open market economy.'[13]

The conclusion therefore is that business cartels have remained constant in terms of their economic role and methods, and appear to be a resilient feature of modern trading systems. On the other hand, in the European context, the view of this activity has changed significantly and, in most recent years, also dramatically. But at the same time, the shift in external perception has inevitably transformed the internal *human attitude* of those business persons engaged in the organization and operation of cartels. It is no longer feasible to present a convincing justification for such behaviour in terms of a wider public good, in the form of economic stability. As a result, the honest justification or, rather, explanation, from both an external and internal viewpoint, is that of private gain and public loss, and so the cartel participant has evolved into a 'conspirator', a 'fixer' of prices and a 'rigger' of bids, an 'egregious' violator of rules, and probably, for the twenty-first century, a 'criminal'. Up to a point, therefore, it has been a phenomenon of parallax—the position of the observer has shifted rather than the subject of observation. But at the same time the changing position of observation has had an impact on that of the subject, moving it after all into a domain of more definite delinquency and criminality.

3. The character of contemporary European cartel law

It is perhaps justifiable to talk now in terms of a distinctive body of law and legal activity which may be termed 'cartel law', in a range of jurisdictional contexts: national, supranational, European, and even perhaps, in a globalized form as a new area of international law. If so, it would be illuminating to enquire further into the epistemological features of this legal phenomenon: what are the salient juridical features of such law, and *whose* law may it be considered?

---

[12] The infamous quotation from the transcript of a meeting of the *Lysine Cartel*. Indeed, in certain areas of business culture, cartel involvement may have provided good credentials for ambitious executives.

[13] The equally well-known statement by EC Commissioner for Competition, Mario Monti, in the opening speech at the Third Nordic Competition Policy Conference, Stockholm, September 2000.

(a) The economist's tale: cartel law as competition law

In terms of subject matter the conventional location for discussion of cartels—certainly in the European context—is the subject domain now well established as 'competition law'. This, after all, is where policy on business cartels has its origins, for instance in Title VI, Chapter I of the EC Treaty, headed 'rules on competition'. Cartels represent an extreme and classic form of anti-competitive business practice and the objection to them is rooted in economic argument relating to consumer damage (customer overcharge) and socio-economic harm ('deadweight loss'). Inevitably therefore, much of the discussion of cartels and their regulation has been the business of economists and competition lawyers. Inclusion within the regulatory structure of Article 81 of the EC Treaty (now the dominant European model for the regulation of competition), with its emphasis on the methodology of registration, economic evaluation, and exemption, and reluctance to adopt formally per se prohibition, has served to lock the cartel in a market-outcome oriented process of evaluation. In psychological terms, there may be a great deal of difference between the concepts of 'competition' and 'antitrust' (as explored in Chapter II) and what is implied in these concepts for processes of legal control. This dichotomy has also affected the epistemology of the subject: for while American antitrust law became partly but significantly the domain of criminal lawyers, the same is only now beginning to happen in respect of the European legal control of cartels.

In short, competition lawyers in the European sense do not naturally or comfortably think in terms of a delinquent and reprehensible subject matter, set in a context of moral censure and penal sanctioning. Competition law is very much concerned with the balance between pro- and anti-competitive aspects of business, as judged by essentially economic criteria. In epistemological terms, this is not a fertile ground for the development of rules relating to the prosecution of deliberate and self-consciously illegal activities. Competition lawyers have sometimes expressed impatience with the 'legalistic' aspect of the Commission's regulatory practice, as being too insensitive to 'relevant' market considerations and too swift to condemn corporate behaviour.[14] So it can be argued that

---

[14] For instance, Valentine Korah, *An Introductory Guide to EC Competition Law and Practice* (6th edn, Hart Publishing, 1997), 5, 11, 66.

the contemporary regulation of cartels is unhappily located in that section of the library shelf.

It may indeed be said that the way in which the law deals with cartels is no longer competition law in this sense of the term. Despite the absence of a European per se prohibition, there is now a categorical condemnation of the regular and predictable strategies engaged in by cartels. Economic argument, in so far as it may be used to justify the core elements of cartel behaviour, has now disappeared from view. At one stage it appeared that cartel prosecutions had become bedevilled by arguments concerning oligopoly, as demonstrated in particular in the unravelling of the *Wood Pulp Cartel* litigation, discussed in some detail in Chapter VI. But once the Commission had retreated from its attempts to establish collusion on the basis of circumstantial market evidence, the 'expert' testimony of economists on this point also lost its relevance. More recently, economic analysis has entered into argument concerning the quantification of penalties, for instance in relation to the appropriate use of 'global' or 'relevant market' turnover calculations. But this is an example of economic argument being used in the service of penal law, just as it may be more frequently found in American litigation in the assessment of damages.

The pertinent question would therefore seem to concern the continuing location of the topic of cartels and their regulation in works and courses on competition law.

(b) The prosecutor's tale: cartel law as the law of evidence

A glance at the subject matter of cartel litigation before the Court of Justice and Court of First Instance over the last 20 years would reveal that much of the legal argument is concerned with issues of proof. Once the major European cartels had gone underground in a legal sense, the centre of gravity of legal argument shifted from market analysis to matters of evidence and in one way or another evidential issues have dominated the legal process since then, especially from the point of view of the Commission: for instance, the use of dawn raids, arguments about oligopoly in relation to attempts to draw conclusions from circumstantial market evidence, the construction of the prosecution case around the 'cartel as a whole', numerous appeals based on the sufficiency of evidence of participation on the part of individual cartel members, and more recently the exploitation of whistleblowers' evidence via leniency deals (as detailed in Chapters VI and VIII). The result has been the fashioning of a new supranational European law of evidence. Viewing this body of law, it is naturally possible to detect some important analogies with rules of criminal evidence in the national context. But it is also possible to identify some distinctive features, arising from its own procedural context: a predominantly written procedure, and evidence being assessed in two successive phases, first by the Commission as prosecutor-jury, then (since the start of the 1990s) by the Court of First Instance, exercising a full jurisdiction to review the facts.

What is striking is the way in which the significant resources of both the regulatory agency and the companies as defending parties have been channelled into a now very large body of legal argument, in turn generating a new body of principle. Put another way, as the stakes have risen in European cartel litigation, both sides have been motivated to develop and test evidential argument in a way that has broadened the frontiers of the subject. Theory and practice in relation to a number of categories of evidence have been tested in new ground—'expert' economic testimony in relation to the operation of market forces; the cumulative and corroborative potential of various types of material evidence; the exploitative potential of whistleblowing evidence. In some respects, this has been a different experience from that in American antitrust litigation which has operated within the existing framework of criminal procedure and evidence.

Two important points arise from these observations: first, the conclusion that cartel law, as a distinct corpus of legal activity, is significantly a law of evidence; secondly and consequently, there may be some instructive lessons for evidence lawyers, many of whom have yet to have their attention engaged by these European cases.

(c) *The defence lawyer's tale: cartel law as corporate rights law*

A central point to emerge from this discussion is that cartel law is very much about legal process and litigation. One part of that is proving the case, and naturally the reverse side of the coin, the defence perspective, is also important. In the context of European cartel litigation that has been not just a matter of contesting the evidence used by the prosecution, but also of exploiting the conduct of the process by asserting respect for defence rights. At one and the same time, cartel litigation has provided good business for corporate defence lawyers, while fostering the development of a body of 'corporate' (as distinct from 'human') rights law.

The impact of the development of competition and cartel law on the legal profession as such is an interesting subject in its own right. This is a topic which has for some time attracted discussion in the American context, in which there has been a long-standing engagement of legal services for both plaintiffs pursuing civil claims against anti-competitive companies and the defendants in both civil and criminal proceedings. Generally, this is an expanding area of legal business. Connor, for instance, has recently commented that:

The proliferation of cartels in the 1990s has generated large fees for law firms with expertise in antitrust law...Price fixing conspiracies probably rank second [to merger cases] in antitrust revenues. The global scope of cartels has stimulated U.S. law firms to expand abroad. Several U.S. firms now derive more than one-quarter of their revenues from work outside the United States.[15]

The interest of the legal profession in this burgeoning sector of legal process is itself an important element of legal development. Clearly, there has been and may continue to be a difference in scale as between the United States and Europe, since there is a much lower level of civil litigation in the European context. Another difference lies in the fact that the engagement of the private legal profession (as distinct from public service lawyers) in Europe has been largely on the defence side of litigation. Nonetheless the nature of the process at the EC level, comprising both lengthy proceedings before the Commission and frequent, almost automatic, appeals to the Court of First Instance, requires considerable legal support. Also of significance is the fact that the parties concerned— invariably large corporations—have both an interest in pursuing legal action and the financial ability to do so. All of this has led to the development of a significant expert and elite sector of the legal profession in Europe, specializing in this area of corporate defence. Incidentally, therefore, there is a distinct professional dynamic contributing to cartel litigation as a profitable business and seeking to develop that business. One fruitful area of development in that regard has been the exploitation of defence rights argument into a new sub-category of public law: not precisely an area of human rights, but the analogous topic of corporate rights. The activity of this sector of the legal profession is also evident in a more doctrinal context, through publication in specialist journals and participation in meetings of experts (as has been noted in places in the earlier discussion in this book).

[15] Connor, n 5 above, 503.

Defence claims in European cartel litigation have been bold in the sense of readily resorting to the 'big guns of constitutional artillery',[16] so elevating the subject to the level of a kind of human rights discourse. There has been a frequent reference to national constitutional precedents and to the other main European template for such debate, the European Convention on Human Rights, so steering first the Court of Justice and then the Court of First Instance into a rights discourse which is, as a subject matter, quite distant from the traditional argument and method of competition law. At the same time, the resulting discussion of defence rights as basic rights has (like the discussion of evidential matters referred to above) broken some new ground. The context for these arguments has in a number of respects been novel. In the first place, these are rights which in the great majority of cases are excercisable by corporate rather than human actors. Secondly, these are actors operating in an essentially economic and commercial environment. Thirdly, the legal process to which the rights relate is distinctive, being supranational and involving an institutional actor and public agency, in the form of the Commission, which does not have easy analogies at the national level. Thus, while the vocabulary of rights may be similar to that employed in national constitutional law or under international instruments such as the European Convention, its application has taken place in a different context. This is not an issue which is commonly addressed in an explicit way in discussion of the subject, but is relevant in a number of ways, for instance in relation to possible divergence between the jurisprudence of the Community courts and the European Court of Human Rights. To pose the underlying question bluntly: is there, or should there be, a difference between 'human' and 'corporate' rights?

Some 40 years ago, cartel law as basic rights law may not have been easily predicted as an outcome of the application of Article 81 (ex Article 85) of the EC Treaty. In one sense, this legal development is also a *cost* of law enforcement, or at least of law enforcement of a particular kind. To view the matter in those terms may imply some judgement regarding the deployment of resources and raise questions as to the arguably wasteful character of some of the underlying litigation. On the other hand, it may not be justifiable to view legal opportunity in simply economic terms. As Connor, again, has noted in relation to American antitrust litigation:

However, in the end most of the legal expenses were simply a necessary outgrowth of constitutionally guaranteed rights to due legal process. And high as

---

[16] Judge David Edward, 'Constitutional Rules of Community Law in EEC Competition Cases' (1989) *Fordham Corporate L. Institute* 383.

they were, these legal transactions costs may be low when compared to the economic costs of the alternatives [such as monopolistic distortions in affected markets].[17]

(d) The penologist's tale: cartel law as criminology

The final main characteristic of cartel law as a legal category is its significant element of penality. The kind of business conduct being dealt with as 'cartels' is now of a clearly prohibited nature, and the legal prohibition is reinforced by penal sanctions, implying a clear element of delinquency in this form of anti-competitive conduct. As has often been noted, this area of EC 'competition law', despite its formal description, has analogies with criminal law in national jurisdictions. More recently, some national legal systems have moved towards criminalization of certain aspects of cartel activity, thus further emphasizing the epistemological shift towards criminal law and criminal justice. A good deal of the argument in appeals in cartel cases to the Court of First Instance is now concerned with the fines which have been imposed by the Commission, so leading the Court to a consideration of 'sentencing' questions. Therefore, in so far as cartel law is very much based on an idea of a 'cartel offence' and the imposition of penal sanctions in relation to such offending, it has become part of the province of criminal lawyers and penologists. Moreover, any enquiry into the causes of such business delinquency brings the subject within the scope of criminology.

Even more than in case of evidence and rights argument, this observation about epistemological shift towards the criminal and the penal has implications for the future direction of legal activity in this area. In a real sense, European cartel regulation has evolved into a system of quasi-criminal law and in a wider context its interaction with national systems of regulation (especially in the United States, but also increasingly in Europe as well) is increasingly an engagement with criminal law and procedure (as demonstrated clearly, for instance, by a consideration of the international patchwork of leniency programmes). As such, the assumptions and methods of cartel regulation are now some way removed from those of competition law of the kind that deals with such matters as mergers, joint ventures, and distribution and licensing arrangements. The practical aspect of this development comprises both an uneasiness on the part of competition lawyers in confronting the more adversarial and penal features of

---

[17] Connor, n 5 above, 507.

cartel regulation, and the lack of familiarity of criminal lawyers with the business context of cartels. In professional terms, what may be envisaged is some transfer of work from competition lawyers to criminal lawyers, but at the same time the need for the latter to learn more about the subject.

In a more theoretical sense, a new field of criminological research should be opening. American criminologists have already engaged with the subject matter, since it has long been a category of business delinquency. But there has been little criminological investigation in Europe, simply because the issue has not until recently been defined as criminal. It is symptomatic perhaps that the recent study of three major international cartels of the 1990s carried out by Connor, which could be categorized as a criminological enquiry, has an American focus and only deals incidentally with European cartel activity. But research of the criminological kind will become increasingly important. Indeed, it may be asked whether the criminalization 'project', which has gained ground in recent years, has been sufficiently informed by a relevant knowledge and understanding of the *behaviour* of business cartels. The effectiveness of criminal procedure and criminal sanctions naturally depends upon their appropriate use, and that in turn depends upon an understanding of how and why cartels come into being, not so much in an economic sense, but as a form of prohibited conduct. As noted in Chapter IX, the whole debate about the choice of sanctions, their effectiveness, and the issue of personal and corporate liability presents a challenging subject, and one that cries out for more information of a rigorously researched kind.

4. Prospective: the globalization of cartel regulation?

The third main question to be considered in this final chapter is one relating to the future direction and form of the legal control of cartels. Taking stock of the way in which the European system of regulation has evolved over the last century or more, and of the significant recent changes discussed above, what may be foreseen regarding both the European and the wider context of the subject in the coming years? Bearing in mind that during the last decade there has been a more determined effort of legal control at the international level, does this imply the emergence of an international system of legal control: a globalization of law and its enforcement? 'Globalization' in itself may of course signify different things and, as already pointed out, care has to be taken in using such terminology, but an attempt will be made here to consider two particular aspects of the regulation of cartels. First, it may be enquired whether there are *globalizing forces* which may be seen as driving and forming the process of legal control. Then, it may be asked whether the *outcome* of these developments may be said to have a global character.

(a) Globalizing forces: the global economy

What has been generally evident since the later 1990s has been a more determined effort at enforcement of the legal rules, whatever their form, against business cartels across a number of jurisdictions. This has manifested itself in the adoption of new strategies of enforcement, such as the use of leniency programmes, the application of more severe sanctions, and moves towards criminalization beyond its historical base in North America. But what may be considered to be the reasons for this upsurge in legal activity?

Undoubtedly a major factor in this development was the energization of American enforcement policy and a clear shift in the focus of attention of the latter to international cartels. Thus Connor has observed that 'commentators of all stripes have noted that attention to global cartels was a hallmark of the late Clinton administration'[18] and Klawiter has commented that 'the most significant and enduring antitrust enforcement initiative of this era will be the aggressive criminal enforcement of international cartels by the antitrust division'.[19] Statements by DOJ officials confirmed this policy initiative which had international cartels as its principal target. As a result the profile of American antitrust enforcement has changed remarkably in recent years, so that the proportion of foreign-based individual or corporate defendants indicted for price-fixing violations rose from less than 1 per cent prior to 1995 to 50 per cent in 1998–9. In addition, between 1996 and 1999, 76 per cent of the total of US$10 million-plus corporate fines were imposed on companies based outside the United States.[20]

---

[18] Connor, n 5 above, 5.
[19] Donald C Klawiter, 'Criminal Antitrust Comes to the Global Market' (1998) 13 *St John's Journal of Legal Commentary* 201.   [20] Connor, n 5 above, 5–7.

It seems clear that much of this enforcement activity has been triggered by the perception that the American economy is now more prey to the predations of large international cartels. Joshua has argued:

As the US economy has become increasingly globalized, the exposure of its undiluted capitalist model to price-fixers abroad as well as at home posed a challenge which the government took up with conspicuous zeal. The Antitrust Division [of the DOJ] proclaims the detection and prosecution of international cartels under the Sherman Act as its highest enforcement priority and its top officials unceasingly repeat the belligerent message that attacks on American business and consumers will not be tolerated.[21]

In short, the globalization of markets, particularly as the result of large-scale mergers producing complex multinational corporations with a significantly international commercial reach, has affected more evidently the American market itself, indicating the vulnerability of the latter to corporate decisions (or networks of decisions) being taken outside the United States.

This policy, its objectives, and its outcomes are clear enough from the DOJ's own documentation. Its 1999 *Status Report on International Cartel Enforcement* opens with the statement that:

The Division's strategy of concentrating its resources on international cartels that victimize American businesses and consumers has continued to lead to remarkable success in terms of cracking international cartels, securing the conviction of the major conspirators, and obtaining record-breaking fines.[22]

The Report then goes on to exemplify the international character of this enforcement activity: over 30 grand juries looking into suspected international cartels; the subject matter of investigations spread over five continents and over 20 different countries and meetings in nearly 80 cities in 30 countries, including most of the Far East and Western Europe. It was estimated that since the beginning of the financial year 1997, the DOJ had prosecuted international cartels affecting over US$10 billion in American commerce, costing American businesses and consumers many hundreds of million of dollars annually.

(b) A globalized regulation?

The economic interest of the United States in achieving more effective legal control of transnational cartels has given rise to some important

---

[21] Julian M Joshua, 'Cartels International Inc.: The New Global Business', unpublished paper, ILC Dublin Conference, Spring 2001.   [22] (www.usdoj.gov/atr/public/speeches/2275.htm).

legal strategies, which themselves have contributed to an upward spiral of transnational legal activity. A number of American initiatives may be briefly noted: an extension of American territorial jurisdiction (the *Nippon Paper* ruling in 1997);[23] the provision of incentives to foreign witnesses and defendants to submit to American jurisdiction;[24] promotion of mutual legal assistance treaties (MLATs) with other states;[25] development of the DOJ Leniency Programme as a highly effective incentive to voluntary co-operation from foreign targets;[26] and more dedicated resort to substantial fines and prison sentences to demonstrate the resolve to use tough enforcement.[27]

Has this then resulted in either an internationalization or harmonization of cartel regulation? Up to a point it is possible to detect some shift towards both. There has in recent years been a great deal of convergence in the context of national systems of competition law, especially of course in Europe, where the EC legislative model has been extensively adopted at the national level.[28] Such convergence also extends to the policy on enforcement: for instance, a number of systems now proclaim the control of cartels to be a priority.[29]

But, on the other hand, it would appear that, so far, more effective regulation of international cartels has come about through *developing the reach of national jurisdictions* (especially that of the United States) rather than via international co-operation as such. International co-operation in this field has had to overcome a traditional attitude of suspicion or even

---

[23] *US v Nippon Paper Industries*, 109 F 3d 1 (1st Cir. 1997).

[24] In particular, a 1996 Memorandum of Understanding (MOU) between the Antitrust and Immigration and Nationality Divisions of the DOJ that convicted felon status would not lead to permanent exclusion from the United States (Memorandum of Understanding between the Antitrust Division, the Department of Justice and the Immigration and Naturalization Service, 15 March 1996).

[25] The United States has now concluded about 30 such treaties, many applying to antitrust offences: Report of the International Competition Policy Advisory Committee (ICPAC), February 2000, 181.

[26] See Gary R Spatling, *The Corporate Leniency Policy: Answers to Recurring Questions* (Department of Justice, 1998); and the discussion in Chapter VIII above.

[27] Donald C Klawiter, 'After the Deluge: The Powerful Effect of Substantial Criminal Fines, Imprisonment and Other Penalties in the Age of International Cartels' *George Washington Law Review Symposium*, March 2001.

[28] During the 1990s there was an impressive programme of legislative recasting of national competition laws in many European countries, based on the model laid down in Articles 81 and 82 of the EC Treaty, e.g. the UK Competition Act 1998.

[29] OECD, *Hard Core Cartels* (OECD, 2000), 25–7.

hostility in a number of jurisdictions. It was stated, for instance, in a report of the American Bar Association in 1991:

International disputes often arise when the cartel prohibitions of one nation are invoked to challenge conduct that is engaged in by foreign nationals or that occurs in foreign territory... Some jurisdictions have enacted 'blocking' and 'clawback' statutes, seeking to protect their nationals from what they perceive as overly aggressive antitrust enforcement or improper extensions of national jurisdiction. In other cases efforts to enforce cartel prohibitions have been frustrated altogether. It seems likely that at least some efforts to invoke legal rules prohibiting cartels are rarely attempted because of the obstacles to the eventual success of international enforcement efforts.[30]

Admittedly, there are now a number of assistance agreements in force, but it is important to note some of the practical limitations affecting their operation. Although the United States has entered into bilateral antitrust agreements with a number of other jurisdictions (Brazil, Canada, the EU, Germany, Israel, and Japan), much crucial evidential material cannot be transferred under these agreements,[31] most importantly confidential data, or for instance, in the case of the EC authorities, information obtained by dawn raids which may not be used for any purpose other than its own investigations. Again, although a number of MLATs now cover antitrust offences, only a limited number of jurisdictions have the legal authority to use coercive measures for purposes of searching for or producing evidence to be used in another jurisdiction. Formal co-operation therefore remains limited and for practical purposes rudimentary. However, as in many contexts of international collaboration, more may be achieved informally by administrative action than might be suggested by a reading of formal legal measures. Joshua has noted:

At the day-to-day level individual contacts and a shared sense of camaraderie between enforcement officials can ensure that without exchanging any confidential information they can by-pass protocol and hierarchy and at least arrange not to tread on each other's toes.[32]

This practice is often referred to as 'pick up the phone co-operation' and is indicative of the change in attitude and culture, which would seem to be advancing ahead of formal legal arrangements.

In contrast, the recent determination and energy demonstrated by the American authorities in using the tools and strategies of *domestic* law

---

[30] *Report of the Special Committee on International Antitrust*, ABA Section of Antitrust Law, 1 September 1991.

[31] See generally, Report of the International Competition Policy Advisory Committee (ICPAC), February 2000, 181–4.   [32] Joshua, n 21 above, 13–14.

have revealed how much can be achieved without formal international co-operation. The most dramatic change has come about through the revision of the DOJ's leniency policy so as to exploit successfully the perceived inherent instability and mutual suspicion within the ranks of cartels, as discussed in Chapter VIII above.

The lesson of this leniency strategy has now been exported to other jurisdictions. The emerging picture is therefore one of increasingly effective national (including EC) enforcement measures against international cartels. This complicates the response of the cartels themselves, regarding their own strategies of how to react to leniency prospects in a number of relevant jurisdictions, especially while these leniency programmes may still differ in some respects from each other.[33] But for the present there would appear to be little incentive for the various jurisdictions to align their policies exactly. However, for the cartels, the risks have become *multinational*,[34] resulting from some international convergence though not necessarily co-ordination of action.

In conclusion, it may be said that so far, the most impressive enforcement gains have been in terms of an extended and more effective exercise of national jurisdiction, especially on the part of the US Department of Justice. In particular, the DOJ has pioneered the use of leniency strategies which have succeeded in penetrating cartel solidarity and gaining crucial evidence. In this way one of the major obstacles to legal control of cartels—insufficiency of evidence of collusive behaviour—has been successfully tackled. This approach now provides a model for other key national jurisdictions and is transforming the overall profile of global enforcement action. This last development has been underpinned by a significant transformation in legal culture, in the sense of changing official attitudes to the whole issue of business cartels. In other words, there has been a successful *villification* of cartels, so that the more ambivalent (mainly European) view is being supplanted by a clear perception of delinquency inherent in cartel behaviour, which has historically informed American efforts of legal control.

This does not, however, imply an *internationalization* of anti-cartel law, in the sense of either harmonized *international* rules of substantive law or international agencies, procedures of enforcement, or tribunals.

---

[33] See generally the survey presented by Lidwyn Brokx, 'A Patchwork of Leniency Programmes' (2001) 22 *European Competition Law Review* 35.

[34] As Brokx, n 33 above, notes: it is the companies who need to take a co-ordinated approach to co-operation with competition authorities (at 46).

Enforcement interests are probably satisfied by a delegated form of enforcement or what may be described as the 'directive' model (following the example of the EU directive), even in the present OECD form of a 'soft law' recommendation. Provided that there is a consensus among national legal systems regarding enforcement objectives, the definition of targeted conduct (i.e. cartel behaviour), the energy and commitment of enforcement, enforcement strategies, and the types of and quantum of sanctions, then it may well be sufficient to leave to national systems the responsibility for enforcement and the more precise choice of means. Admittedly, this implies a certain degree of *enforcement integration* but of such a kind comparable to that which is fostered by a measure such as an EU directive.[35]

This argument is based on a sense that the underlying impulse for the regulation of cartels may remain predominantly national rather than international. After all, the injury arising from cartel activity is to economic interests which are still primarily identified and defined in national terms. One main exception to this is the EC (within which damage to the single market objectives has been a significant motive for the regulation of cartels), but then again, in this respect, the EC would rank alongside states as a single jurisdiction. For the foreseeable future, the United States, the EC, and other significant national jurisdictions are likely to wish to retain their own initiative in controlling cartels,[36] whether national or international in scope. In so far as different jurisdictions collide in their enforcement it may be necessary to have a measure of international co-ordination. But otherwise the vision for the near future may be an interrelated mosaic or patchwork of jurisdictions, singing the same chorus, largely the same tune, but still with some occasional different notes.

---

[35] See also Christopher Harding, 'The Globalisation of Anti-Cartel Law and Enforcement', in Peter Nahamowitz and Rüdiger Voigt, *Globalisierung des Rechts II: Internationale Organisationen unde Regelungsbereiche* (Nomos Verlgasgesellschaft, 2002), 319.

[36] For instance, the United States has not demonstrated enthusiasm for assigning an antitrust or cartel enforcement role to the WTO. See Connor, n 5 above, 93.

BIBLIOGRAPHY

1. Legal literature on cartels in Europe

Although there are no major works which provide a systematic study of business cartels in the European context over the last half century, as a subject in its own right and from a legal perspective, there are, however, a number of significant sources, both earlier and more recent, which deserve special consideration. Some of these have been drawn upon extensively in the present work.

As noted in Chapter III above, the subject of business cartels gave rise to particular interest and debate in Germany during the first half of the twentieth century and there was therefore a large body of critical and analytical literature produced there, and of course predominantly written in German, in that period. In particular, the journal *Kartell-Rundschau*, established in 1903, provided a continuous source of commentary on the subject. Much of the literature of this period is conveniently digested and catalogued in David Gerber's *Law and Competition in Twentieth Century Europe* (1998). The English translation of Robert Liefmann's overview of the topic, *International Cartels, Combines and Trusts* (1927, out of print) provides an accessible contemporary introduction to the main European debates on cartels during the 1920s. There are then two major mid-century accounts of the operation of international business cartels during this period which supply valuable insights and detailed material: Ervin Hexner's *International Cartels* and George W Stocking and Myron W Watkins' *Cartels in Action* (both published in 1946, and both out of print). These two works are immensely valuable for their picture of the phenomenon during the first half of the twentieth century and illuminating as works of contemporary analysis. The University of Leiden Historical Institute's *Interwar Cartel Database* is a significant source of factual information on the pre-war operation of cartels.

Since then, the main sources have not taken cartels as the main focus of discussion but have instead considered the subject more incidentally as part of the emerging landscape of European competition regulation. Corwin D Edwards' two major works of the middle 1960s, *Trade Regulation Overseas* (1966) and *Control of Cartels and Monopolies: An International Comparison* (1967) (both also out of print), consititute a major report on the evolving European legal regulation of competition matters in the two decades after 1945, and interestingly also from the perspective of an American writer. Gerber's *Law and Competition in Twentieth Century Europe*, already referred to and first published in 1998, is essential reading, comprising a magisterial historical and legal analysis of the twentieth-century development of European competition regulation. Gerber's account contains much information on cartel control, although of course does not focus on that topic as such. For those who wish to gain a sure insight into the underlying philosophy and mindset of European competition and cartel regulation, it is necessary and engaging reading.

By way of comparison, John M Connor's recently published *Global Price Fixing: Our Customers are the Enemy* (2001) is a very informative and revealing turn-of-the-century study of American antitrust enforcement relating to international business cartels, but is scant in its view of the European dimension, and its analysis arguably misses some lessons which may be drawn from the recent European evidence.

In terms of primary material relating to the activity of cartels and the legal control of such activity in post-Second World War Europe, a major source from the 1960s onwards is provided in the published reports of the European Commission (*Official Journal of the European Communities*), as a cartel regulator, and of the judgments of the European Courts of Justice and First Instance (*European Court Reports*), in dealing with appeals against Commission decisions. Cumulatively, these official EC sources now provide thousands of pages of detail relating to the operation of the relatively small number of cartels which have been investigated, and of legal argument relating to both cartel activity itself and the way in which the EC system has sought to regulate cartels. Some of this material is repetitive and not always easily accessible to readers without a training in European law, but by its nature it remains a core source for research and discussion. Some of the opinions of the Advocates General in these cases may be especially recommended for their sure and informative presentation of the main legal argument, and are often more readable accounts for those coming from a non-legal background. On American antitrust enforcement, the US Department of Justice provides a large body of official documentation.

Finally, turning to non-legal scholarship, the Select Bibliography below will show that, naturally enough, the subject of cartels in Europe has to date attracted more attention on the part of economists than that of sociologists and criminologists. Hopefully, that will now change in the near future.

2. Select Bibliography

ALESE, Femi, 'The Economic Theory of Non-Collusive Oligopoly' (1999) 20 *European Competition Law Review* 379

ALLEN, G C, *Monopoly and Restrictive Practices* (George Allen & Unwin, London, 1968), chs 3, 4, and 10

ANDREWS, Philip, '"Modernisation"—Irish Style' (2002) 23 *European Competition Law Review* 469

BAKER, Donald I, 'Investigation and Proof of an Antitrust Violation in the United States: A Comparative Look', in Piet Jan Slot and Alison McDonnell (eds), *Procedure and Enforcement in E.C. and U.S. Competition Law* (1993), ch 18

BAKER, Jonathan B, 'Two Sherman Act Section 1 Dilemmas' (1993) 143 *The Antitrust Bulletin* 178

BISHOP, Simon and WALKER, Mike, *The Economics of EC Competition Law: Concepts, Application and Measurement* (Sweet & Maxwell, 1999)

BORK, Robert H, *The Antitrust Paradox* (Basic Books, 1978)

BORKIN, Joseph, *The Crime and Punishment of I. G. Farben* (Andre Deutsch, 1979)

BRITISH INSTITUTE OF INTERNATIONAL AND COMPARATIVE LAW (BIICL), *Comparative Aspects of Anti-Trust Law in the US, the UK and the EEC* (BIICL, 1963)

BRODLEY, Joseph E, 'Oligopoly Power under the Sherman and Clayton Acts' (1967) 19 *Stanford Law Review* 285

BROKX, Lidwyn, 'A Patchwork of Leniency Programmes' (2001) 22 *European Competition Law Review* 35

BRYANT, P G and ECKHARD, E W, 'Price Fixing: The Probability of Getting Caught' (1991) *Review of Economics and Statistics* 531

CARLE, Johan, PERVAN LINDEBORG, Stefan, and SEGENMARK, Emma, 'The New Leniency Notice' (2002) 23 *European Competition Law Review* 265

COLLINS, Wayne D and SUNSHINE, Steven C, 'Is Private Enforcement Effective Antitrust Policy?', ch. 8 in Piet Jan Slot and Alison McDonnell (eds), *Procedure and Enforcement in E.C. and U.S. Competition Law* (1993), ch 8

COMMISSION OF THE EC, Notice on co-operation between national courts and the Commission in applying Articles 85 and 86, OJ 1993, C 39/6

—— Notice on the non-imposition or reduction of fines in cartel cases, OJ 1996, C 207/4

—— Guidelines on the method of setting fines imposed pursuant to Article 15(2) of Regulation 17, OJ 1998, C 9/3

—— White Paper on Modernisation of the Rules Implementing Articles 85 and 86 of the EC Treaty, OJ 1999, C 132/1

CONLEY, J M and O'BARR, W M, 'Crime and Custom in Corporate Society: A Cultural Perspective on Corporate Misconduct' (1997) 60 *Law and Contemporary Problems* 5

CONNOR, John M, *Global Price Fixing: Our Customers are the Enemy* (Kluwer, 2001)

CRAYCRAFT, C, CRAYCRAFT, J L, and GALLO, J C, 'Antitrust Sanctions and a Firm's Ability to Pay' (1997) 12 *Review of Industrial Organisation* 171

CROUZET, F *et al* (eds), *Essays in European Economic History 1789–1914* (London, 1969)

DICK, A, 'When Are Cartels Stable Contracts?' (1996) 39 *Journal of Law and Economics* 241

EDWARD, Judge David, 'Constitutional Rules of Community Law in EEC Competition Cases' (1989) *Fordham Corporate Law Institute* 383

EDWARDS, Corwin D, 'Regulation of Monopolistic Cartelization' (1953–4) 14 *Ohio State Law Journal* 252

—— *Trade Regulation Overseas: The National Laws* (Oceana Publications, 1966)

—— *Control of Cartels and Monopolies: An International Comparison* (Oceana, New York, 1967)

EHLERMANN Claus-Dieter, 'Reflections on the ECO' (1995) 32 *Common Market Law Review* 471

—— and VAN DRIJBER, Berend, 'The Legal Protection of Enterprises: Administrative Procedure, in particular Access to Files and Confidentiality' (1996) 7 *European Competition Law Review* 375

EICHENWALD, K, *The Informer* (Broadway Books, 2000)

FIDE (Fédération internationale de droit européen), *Reports of the 17th Congress of the FIDE*, vol III (Nomos Verlag, 1996)

FEINBERG, R M, 'The Enforcement and Effects of European Competition Policy: Results of a Survey of Legal Opinion' (1985) 23 *Journal of Common Market Studies* 373

FRANZOSI, Mario, 'Oligopoly and the Prisoner's Dilemma: Concerted Practices and "As If" Behaviour' (1998) 9 *European Competition Law Review* 385

FRIEDMANN W (ed), *Anti-Trust Laws: A Comparative Symposium* (Stevens, London, 1956)

——*Law in a Changing Society* (2nd edn, Penguin, Harmondsworth, 1972), ch 8

GERBER, David, *Law and Competition in Twentieth Century Europe: Protecting Prometheus* (Clarendon Press, Oxford, 1998, reprint 2001)

GOYDER, D G, *EC Competition Law* (3rd edn, Clarendon Press, Oxford, 1998)

GREEN, Nicholas, 'Evidence and Proof in E.C. Competition Cases', in Piet Jan Slot and Alison McDonnell (eds), *Procedure and Enforcement in E.C. and U.S. Competition Law* (1993), ch 17

GYSELEN, Luc, 'The Commission's Fining Policy in Competition Cases', in Piet Jan Slot and Alison McDonnell (eds), *Procedure and Enforcement in E.C. and U.S. Competition Law* (1993), ch 10

HALL, D F, 'Enforcement of E.C. Competition Law by National Courts', ch 7 in Piet Jan Slot and Alison McDonnell (eds), *Procedure and Enforcement in E.C. and U.S. Competition Law* (1993), ch 7

HAMMOND, Sir Anthony and PENROSE, Roy, *Proposed Criminalisation of Cartels in the UK* (Report prepared for the Office of Fair Trading, 2001)

HARDING, Christopher, *European Community Investigations and Sanctions: The Supranational Control of Business Delinquency* (Leicester University Press, 1993)

——'The Globalisation of Anti-Cartel Law and Enforcement', in Peter Nahamowitz and Rüdiger Voigt, *Globalisierung des Rechts II: Internationale Organisationen unde Regelungsbereiche* (Nomos Verlagsgesellschaft, 2002)

——'Business Cartels as a Criminal Activity: Reconciling North American and European Models of Regulation' (2002) 9 *Maastricht Journal of European and Comparative Law* 393

—— and JOSHUA, Julian, 'Breaking Up the Hard Core: the Prospects for the Proposed Cartel Offence' (2002) *Criminal Law Review* 933

HENDERSON, W O, *The Industrial Revolution on the Continent 1800–1914* (Frank Cass, 1967)

——*The Rise of German Industrial Power 1843–1914* (Temple Smith, London, 1975)

HEXNER, Ervin, *The International Steel Cartel* (University of North Carolina Press, 1943)

—— *International Cartels* (Pitman, London, 1946)

HORNSBY, Stephen and HUNTER, Joan, 'New Incentives for "Whistle Blowing": Will the EC Commission's Notice bear Fruit?' (1997) 18 *European Competition Law Review* 38

HOUSE OF LORDS SELECT COMMITTEE ON THE EUROPEAN COMMUNITIES, *Report on Competition Practice*, 8th Report, 1981–2 (HL 91)

—— *Report on the Enforcement of Community Competition Rules*, 1st Report, 1993–4 (HL 7-1)

IRISH COMPETITION AUTHORITY, *Guideline on Cartels* (www.irlgov.ie/compauth/CARTEL.htm)

JACOBS, F, 'Civil Enforcement of EEC Antitrust Law' (1984) 82 *Michigan Law Review* 1364

JEPHCOTT, Mark, 'The European Commission's New Leniency Notice—Whistling the Right Tune?' (2002) 23 *European Competition Law Review* 378

JOLIET, R, 'La notion de pratique concertée et l'arrêt ICI dans une perspective comparative' (1974) *Cahiers de Droit Européennes* 251

JONES, Alison, '*Wood Pulp*: Concerted Practice and/or Conscious Parallelism?' (1993) 14 *European Competition Law Review* 273

—— and SUFRIN, Brenda, *EC Competition Law: Text, Cases and Materials* (Oxford University Press, 2001)

JONES, Clifford, *Private Enforcement of Antitrust Law in the EU, UK and USA* (Oxford University Press, 1999)

JOSHUA, Julian M, 'The Element of Surprise: Competition Investigations under Article 14(3) of Regulation 17' (1983) 8 *European Law Review* 3

—— 'Proof in Contested EEC Competition Cases: a Comparison with the Rules of Evidence in Common Law' (1987) 12 *European Law Review* 315

—— 'The Right to be Heard in EEC Competition Procedures' (1991–2) 15 *Fordham International Law Journal* 15

—— 'Attitudes to Antitrust Enforcement in the EU and the United States: Dodging the Traffic Warden or Respecting the Law?' (1995) *Fordham Corporate Law Institute* 101

—— 'The Criminalisation of Cartels: a Clash of Cultures', in *Cartel Regulation 2002: Getting the Fine Down in 25 Jurisdictions Worldwide* (Global Competition Review* Special Report, 2002)

—— 'A Sherman Act Bridgehead in Europe, or a Ghost Ship in Mid-Atlantic? A Close Look at United Kingdom Proposals to Criminalise Hard-Core Cartel Conduct' (2002) 23 *European Competition Law Review* 231

—— and VON HINTEN-REED, Nils, 'Rethinking Leniency at the European Commission' (2002) *Global Competition Review* 16

—— 'Will the Enterprise Bill's Bracing New Regime be Effective?' (2002) *Global Competition Review* 37

KATYAL, N K, 'Deterrence's Difficulty' (1997) 95 *Michigan Law Review* 2385

KERSE, C K, *E. C. Antitrust Procedure* (4th edn, Sweet & Maxwell, 1998)

KLAWITER, Donald C, 'Criminal Antitrust Comes to the Global Market' (1998) 13 *St John's Journal of Legal Commentary* 201

KORAH, Valentine, 'Concerted Practices' (1973) *Modern Law Review* 220

KOVACIC, William E, 'The Identification and Proof of Horizontal Agreements in the Antitrust Laws' (1993) 38 *Antitrust Bulletin* 5

KRONSTEIN, Heinrich and LEIGHTON, Gertrude, 'Cartel Control: A Record of Failure' (1945–46) 55 *Yale Law Journal* 297

LANDES, David S, *The Unbound Prometheus: Technological Change and Industrial Development in Western Europe from 1750 to the Present* (University of Cambridge Press, 1969)

LANGE, Dieter G F and BYRON SANDAGE, John, 'The *Wood Pulp* Decision and its Implications for the Scope of EC Competition Law' (1989) 26 *Common Market Law Review* 137

LASOK, K P E, *The European Court of Justice: Practice and Procedure* (2nd edn, Butterworths, 1994)

LEIDEN UNIVERSITY HISTORICAL INSTITUTE, *Interwar Cartel Database* (www.let.leidenuniv.nl/history)

LENAERTS, K and VANHAMME, J, 'Procedural Rights of Private Parties in the Community Administrative Process' (1997) 34 *Common Market Law Review* 531

LETWIN, William L, 'Congress and the Sherman Act: 1887–1890' (1956) 23 *University of Chicago Law Review* 221

LIEFMANN, Robert, *International Cartels, Combines and Trusts* (Europa Handbooks, Europa Publishing and George Routledge, London, 1927) ('Introduction' by Charles T Hallinan)

LYNCH, G E, 'The Role of Criminal Law in Policing Corporate Misconduct' (1997) 60 *Law and Contemporary Problems* 23

MACAVOY, Christopher J and DONNELLY, Kenneth W, 'Trends in US Government Antitrust Enforcement', *The Antitrust Review of the Americas* 2002 (*Global Competition Review* Special Report 10)

MACHLUP, Fritz, *The Political Economy of Monopoly: Business, Labor and Government Policies* (John Hopkins Press, Baltimore, 1952)

MANN, F A, 'The Dyestuffs Case in the Court of Justice of the European Communities' (1973) 22 *International and Comparative Law Quarterly* 35

MASON, Edward S, 'International Commodity Controls: Cartels and Commodity Agreements', in Seymour E Harris (ed), *Economic Reconstruction* (McGraw-Hill, 1945)

—— *Economic Concentration and the Monopoly Problem* (Harvard University Press, Cambridge, 1957)

MONTAG, F, 'The Case for Radical Reform of the Infringement Procedure under Regulation 17' (1996) 17 *European Competition Law Review* 428

NEALE, A D, *The Antitrust Laws of the U.S.A.: A Study of Competition Enforced by Law* (2nd edn, Cambridge University Press, 1970)

OECD (Organisation for Economic Co-operation and Development), *Hard Core Cartels/Ententes Unjustifiables* (OECD, 2000)

PERITZ, Rudolph J R, *Competition Policy in America 1888–1992: History, Rhetoric, Law* (Oxford University Press, 1992)

POSNER, Richard A, *Antitrust Law: An Economic Perspective* (University of Chicago Press, 1976)

RICHARDSON, Russell, 'Guidance Without Guidance—A European Revolution in Fining Policy?' (1999) 20 *European Competition Law Review* 360

RILEY, Alan, 'The European Cartel Office: A Guardian Without Weapons?' (1997) 18 *European Competition Law Review* 3

SCHACHTER, Oscar and HELLAWELL, Robert (eds), *Competition in International Business: Law and Policy on Restrictive Practices* (Columbia University Press, 1981)

SCHERER, F M, 'The Posnerian Harvest: Separating Wheat from Chaff' (1977) 86 *Yale Law Journal* 974

—— and ROSS, David, *Industrial Market Structure and Economic Performance* (3rd edn, Houghton Mifflin, 1990)

SCHWEITZER, Arthur, *Big Business in the Third Reich* (Eyre & Spottiswoode, London, 1964)

SLOT, Piet Jan and MCDONNELL, Alison (eds), *Procedure and Enforcement in E.C. and U.S. Competition Law* (Sweet & Maxwell, 1993)

SONNENFELD, J and LAWRENCE, P R, 'Why Do Companies Succumb to Price Fixing?' (1978) *Harvard Business Law Review* 145

SPAR, Deborah L, *The Cooperative Edge: The Internal Politics of International Cartels* (Cornell University Press, Ithaca, 1994)

SPINK, Paul M, 'Recent Guidance on Fining Policy' (1999) 20 *European Competition Law Review* 101

STEVENS, Dallal, 'Covert Collusion or Conscious Parallelism in Oligopolistic Markets: A Comparison of EC and US Competition Law' (1995) *Yearbook of European Law* 47

STOCKING, George W and WATKINS, Myron W, *Cartels in Action: Case Studies in International Business Diplomacy* (Twentieth Century Fund, 1946)

STONE, C D, 'Sentencing the Corporation' (1991) 71 *Boston University Law Review* 383

SULLIVAN, Thomas E (ed), *The Political Economy of the Sherman Act: The First One Hundred Years* (Oxford University Press, New York, 1991)

THORELLI, Hans B, *The Federal Antitrust Policy: Origination of an American Tradition* (John Hopkins Press, 1955)

—— 'Antitrust in Europe: National Policies after 1945' (1959) 26 *University of Chicago Law Review* 222

TIROLE, Jean, *Theory of Industrial Organisation* (MIT Press, 1988)

TUGHENDAT, Christopher, *The Multinationals* (Penguin, Harmondsworth, 1973)

UK GOVERNMENT, White Paper, *Productivity and Enterprise: A World Class Competition Regime*, Cm 5233 (July 2001)

UNITED STATES DEPARTMENT OF JUSTICE, Antitrust Website (www.usdoj.gov/atr)

—— *Status Report: Corporate Leniency Program* (2000)

UNITED STATES DEPARTMENT OF JUSTICE, *Status Report: Criminal Fines and International Cartel Enforcement* (2002)

VAN BAEL, Ivo, 'EEC Antitrust Enforcement and Adjudication as Seen by Defence Counsel' (1979) 7 *Revue Suisse de Droit International de la Concurrence* 1

—— 'Insufficient Judicial Control of the EC Competition Law Enforcement' (1992) *Fordham Corporate Law Institute* 733

—— 'Fining à la Carte: The Lottery of EU Competition Law' (1995) 16 *European Competition Law Review* 237

VAN GERVEN, Gerwin and NAVARRO VARONA, Edurne, 'The *Wood Pulp* Case and the Future of Concerted Practices' (1994) 31 *Common Market Law Review* 575

VAN OVERBEEK, Walter B J, 'The Right to Remain Silent in Competition Investigations' (1994) 15 *European Competition Law Review* 127

VAUGHAN, David, 'Access to the File and Confidentiality', in Piet Jan Slot and Alison McDonnell (eds), *Procedure and Enforcement in E.C. and U.S. Competition Law* (1993), ch 20

WERDEN, Gregory J and SIMON, Mailyn J, 'Why Price Fixers Should Go to Prison' (1988) *The Antitrust Bulletin* 924

WHISH, Richard, 'The Enforcement of Competition Law in the Domestic Courts of the Member States' (1994) 15 *European Competition Law Review* 81

—— *Competition Law* (4th edn, Butterworths, 2001)

WILLIS, Peter R, ' "You Have the Right to Remain Silent . . .", or Do You?' (2001) 22 *European Competition Law Review* 313

WILS, Wouter P J, 'E.C. Competition Fines: To Deter or Not To Deter?' (1995) 15 *Yearbook of European Law* 17

—— 'The Commission's New Method for Calculating Fines in Antitrust Cases' (1998) 23 *European Law Review* 101

—— 'Does the Effective Enforcement of Articles 81 and 82 EC Require not only Fines on Undertakings but also Individual Penalties, in Particular Imprisonment?' in C D Ehlermann (ed), *European Competition Law Annuals* (Hart Publishing, 2000)

YAO, Dennis A and DE SANTI, S, 'Game Theory and the Legal Analysis of Tacit Collusion' (1993) *The Antitrust Bulletin* 113

YEUNG, Karen, 'Privatizing Competition Regulation' (1998) 19 *Oxford Journal of Legal Studies* 581

INDEX